RESEARCH METHODS »IN SPECIAL EDUCATION

Series Editor
Dee Berlinghoff, PhD

RESEARCH METHODS »IN SPECIAL EDUCATION

Brittany L. Hott, PhD, BCBA-D
University of Oklahoma
Norman, Oklahoma

Frederick J. Brigham, PhD
George Mason University
Fairfax, Virginia

Corey Peltier, PhD
University of Oklahoma
Norman, Oklahoma

SLACK
INCORPORATED

SLACK Incorporated
6900 Grove Road
Thorofare, NJ 08086 USA
856-848-1000   Fax: 856-848-6091
www.slackbooks.com/books
© 2021 by SLACK Incorporated

Senior Vice President: Stephanie Arasim Portnoy
Vice President, Editorial: Jennifer Kilpatrick
Vice President, Marketing: Mary Sasso
Acquisitions Editor: Tony Schiavo
Director of Editorial Operations: Jennifer Cahill
Vice President/Creative Director: Thomas Cavallaro
Cover Artist: Stacy Marek

Instructors: *Research Methods in Special Education* includes ancillary materials specifically available for faculty use. Included are an *Instructor's Manual* and PowerPoint Slides. Please visit www.efacultylounge.com to obtain access.

The procedures and practices described in this publication should be implemented in a manner consistent with the professional standards set for the circumstances that apply in each specific situation. Every effort has been made to confirm the accuracy of the information presented and to correctly relate generally accepted practices. The authors, editors, and publisher cannot accept responsibility for errors or exclusions or for the outcome of the material presented herein. There is no expressed or implied warranty of this book or information imparted by it. Care has been taken to ensure that drug selection and dosages are in accordance with currently accepted/recommended practice. Off-label uses of drugs may be discussed. Due to continuing research, changes in government policy and regulations, and various effects of drug reactions and interactions, it is recommended that the reader carefully review all materials and literature provided for each drug, especially those that are new or not frequently used. Some drugs or devices in this publication have clearance for use in a restricted research setting by the Food and Drug and Administration or FDA. Each professional should determine the FDA status of any drug or device prior to use in their practice.

Any review or mention of specific companies or products is not intended as an endorsement by the author or publisher.

SLACK Incorporated uses a review process to evaluate submitted material. Prior to publication, educators or clinicians provide important feedback on the content that we publish. We welcome feedback on this work.

Library of Congress Cataloging-in-Publication Data

Names: Hott, Brittany L., author. | Brigham, Frederick J., author. | Peltier, Corey, author.
Title: Research methods in special education / Brittany L. Hott, Frederick J. Brigham, Corey Peltier.
Description: Thorofare, NJ : Slack Incorporated, 2021. | Series:
   Evidence-based instruction in special education | Includes bibliographical references and index.
Identifiers: LCCN 2021001008 (print) | LCCN 2021001009 (ebook) | ISBN
   9781630917562 (paperback) | ISBN 9781630917579 (epub) | ISBN
   9781630917586 (pdf)
Subjects: LCSH: Special education--Research--Methodology. | People with
   disabilities--Education--Research--Methodology.
Classification: LCC LC3969 .H65 2021 (print) | LCC LC3969 (ebook) | DDC 371.9--dc23
LC record available at https://lccn.loc.gov/2021001008
LC ebook record available at https://lccn.loc.gov/2021001009

Printed in the United States of America.

Last digit is print number: 10   9   8   7   6   5   4   3   2   1

DEDICATION

In memory of Brian R. Bryant, PhD, a model for all who aspire to teach and conduct special education research.

CONTENTS

Instructors: *Research Methods in Special Education* includes ancillary materials specifically available for faculty use. Included are an *Instructor's Manual* and PowerPoint Slides. Please visit www.efacultylounge.com to obtain access.

ACKNOWLEDGMENTS

This book would not have been possible without an amazing team who supported us each step of the way. We received nothing short of excellent advice and feedback from Series Editor Dr. Dee Berlinghoff and the entire team at SLACK Incorporated. We are convinced that Tony Schiavo is the most patient and kind acquisitions editor imaginable. Jennifer Cahill, Director of Editorial Operations, ensured a smooth copyediting process. Both Dee and Tony gave generously of their time and went above and beyond to ensure that we met deadlines and had all of the resources needed. This book would not have been possible without Dee, Tony, and Jennifer's support.

We also appreciate the valuable work of our colleagues who served as contributors and experts in their respective method and to Sarah Heiniger, doctoral student and graduate research assistant at University of Oklahoma, who assisted with editing and creating supplementary materials.

We are appreciative of our families who supported us in doing this work, especially our partners, Jaffar, Tiffany, and Michele, and our children, Asher, Harper, Henry, Luke, and Rye.

Finally, we are most thankful for the educators who choose to teach students with exceptionalities and those who pursue graduate education to contribute to science and improve practice. Your work makes a difference, and we are hopeful that our text serves as a useful resource.

About the Authors

Brittany L. Hott, PhD, BCBA-D is an associate professor in the Department of Educational Psychology at the University of Oklahoma in Norman, Oklahoma. Prior to joining the faculty at the University of Oklahoma, Dr. Hott served as an associate professor in the special education program and STRIDE lab director at Texas A&M University–Commerce. She has more than a decade of public school experience, serving in numerous capacities, including as a classroom teacher, special education coordinator, and district instructional specialist. Dr. Hott currently teaches graduate assessment and measurement, introductory research methods, and single case research design courses. Her interests include assessment and measurement, evidence-based practice, and the effective translation of special education research to practice. The majority of her work is completed in collaboration with rural and remote districts. She is an associate editor for *Rural Special Education Quarterly* and is a member of the *Learning Disability Quarterly, Remedial and Special Education,* and *Teacher Education and Special Education* review boards. Dr. Hott's work has been recognized by the Texas Council for Exceptional Children, the International Council for Learning Disabilities, and the Teacher Education Division of the Council for Exceptional Children.

Frederick J. Brigham, PhD is a professor of special education at George Mason University in Fairfax, Virginia. Prior to a career in higher education, Dr. Brigham served as a classroom teacher in special and general education and as a school administrator (program coordinator, director of special education). His tenure includes serving on the faculties of Valparaiso University, Bowling Green State University, The University of Virginia, and George Mason University. Dr. Brigham was editor of *Behavioral Disorders* for two terms and served as an associate editor for *Exceptional Children.* Dr. Brigham is past president of the Council for Exceptional Children–Division for Research. His interests include response to intervention, educational assessment, secondary content instruction, and research methods.

Corey Peltier, PhD is an assistant professor in the Department of Educational Psychology at the University of Oklahoma in Norman, Oklahoma. He leads the Achievement in Mathematics Lab, whose aim is to improve mathematical outcomes for all students by conducting rigorous, high-quality research and disseminating new knowledge to preservice and practicing teachers. Two secondary interests of Dr. Peltier are the use of meta-analysis to inform policy and practice and improving single case research design methodology to increase its use in determining evidence-based practices in the field of special education. Dr. Peltier teaches courses related to single case research design, assessment, and meta-analysis. Dr. Peltier serves on numerous editorial review boards including *Assessment for Effective Intervention, Remedial and Special Education,* and *School Psychology Review.*

CONTRIBUTING AUTHORS

Reesha Adamson, PhD (Chapter 3) is an associate professor at Missouri State University in Springfield, Missouri. Her research interests include translating best practice into applied and practical approaches for teachers, specifically around reading instruction, accommodations, and paraeducator training. Before becoming a professor, she was a district behavior consultant and learning specialist for students with emotional and behavioral disorders.

R. Nicolle Carr, PhD, BCBA-D (Chapter 4) is a lecturer and applied behavior analysis program coordinator in the Department of Educational Psychology at the University of Oklahoma. Her research interests include ethics in clinical practice and research.

Jason C. Chow, PhD (Chapter 9) is an assistant professor in the College of Education at the University of Maryland at College Park. His research focuses on language, behavioral, and social development, as well as supporting teachers and related service providers in promoting positive outcomes for children with or at risk for language, learning, and behavioral difficulty. He teaches courses in special education, research methods, meta-analysis, and grant writing.

Art Dowdy, PhD, BCBA-D (Chapter 10) is an assistant professor in the College of Education and Human Development at Temple University. Dr. Dowdy's research centers on using Applied Behavior Analysis to increase the quality of life of learners with and without disabilities in natural contexts. Dr. Dowdy primarily uses quantitative methods to conduct research that often includes single case research design. He teaches courses in applied behavior analysis, special education, single case research design, and experimental analysis of behavior.

Kimberly Floyd, PhD (Chapter 15) is an associate professor at West Virginia University. Her research interests include assistive and instructional technology, rural teacher preparation, inclusive early childhood special education, early literacy, and trauma-informed supports and practices. Kim serves as the vice president of ISET, has been named an Honors Faculty Fellow and received the Big 12 Fellow from her university, as well as the Outstanding Teaching Award for her college in 2011 and 2013.

Rachel N. Freedman, MA, MS, BCBA, LABA (Chapter 2) is a Board Certified Behavior Analyst and licensed special education administrator. Her current professional practice and research interests center on supporting families of children and adults with autism spectrum disorder and leveraging telehealth models to support individuals with autism and related developmental disabilities across the lifespan. She is currently enrolled in the doctoral program in Special Education with an emphasis in Autism Spectrum Disorder and Related Disabilities at the University of Idaho.

Lynn E. Gates, MLIS (Chapter 5) is an associate professor and librarian at the University of Colorado Colorado Springs Kraemer Family Library, where she is the director of Cataloging & Metadata Services. She holds a Master in Library and Information Science from Rutgers University and a Bachelor of Arts in International Studies from Aquinas College.

Maeghan N. Hennessey, PhD (Chapter 14) serves as chair of the Department of Educational Psychology at the University of Oklahoma. She teaches classes in assessment methodology and design, research methods, and program evaluation. Dr. Hennessey's research focuses on validity theory, assessment design, transition assessment, and epistemic cognition. Her work has appeared in numerous educational psychology and special education journals, such as *Journal of Educational Psychology, Instructional Science, Remedial and Special Education,* and *Career Development and Transition for Exceptional Individuals,* and she is a co-author of the Transition Assessment and Goal Generator.

Jason P. Herron, PhD (Chapter 14) is the Chair of the Educational Psychology program and Director for the Center for Educational Research and Evaluation Services (CRES) at Wichita State University. He teaches classes in statistics, assessment methodology and design, research methods, and program evaluation. His research interests are in teacher/and teaching efficacy, pupil control ideology, and problem solving and decision making.

Aleksandra Hollingshead, EdD (Chapter 2) is an associate dean for inclusion and an associate professor of special education at the University of Idaho (Moscow). Dr. Hollingshead serves as an associate editor for the *FOCUS on Autism and Other Developmental Disabilities* journal. Dr. Hollingshead's research agenda focuses on student engagement in learning and Universal Design for Learning (UDL). She teaches courses related to special education curriculum, collaboration, culturally responsive pedagogy, and UDL.

Melissa C. Jenkins, PhD (Chapter 13) is an assistant professor of special education at the University of Mary Washington in Fredericksburg, Virginia. Prior to transitioning to higher education, she served students with disabilities in Virginia public schools for 15 years as a teacher and administrator. Dr. Jenkins' research interests include early mathematics intervention and professional development models for special education teachers and paraprofessionals.

Joshua Jessel, PhD, BCBA-D, LBA (Chapter 10) is an assistant professor at Queens College in New York City where he is teaching master's level courses in Applied Behavior Analysis. Dr. Jessel's research interests include (a) developing safe and efficient methods for assessing problem behavior of those diagnosed with autism and other related developmental disorders and (b) evaluating different function-based treatments informed by those assessments. Dr. Jessel promotes a practitioner-scientist model and is currently serving on the editorial board of the *Journal of Applied Behavior Analysis*.

Beth A. Jones, PhD (Chapter 5) is an associate professor and graduate program coordinator at Texas A&M University–Commerce. Her research interests and service focuses on visual impairments, assistive technology, and collaboration with families.

Randa Keeley, PhD (Chapter 15) is an assistant professor of special education at Texas Woman's University with a research concentration in classroom interventions that promote inclusive learning environments for students with special educational needs and disabilities. Her research interests include the application of quantitative and qualitative measures to analyze the effects of inclusive practices, culturally responsive teaching, and co-teaching as they relate to the teacher and student. Randa currently works with preservice teachers and graduate students in the area of special education teaching courses in collaboration, instructional, and behavioral interventions.

John William McKenna, PhD (Chapter 6) is an associate professor of moderate disabilities and an affiliate of the Center for Autism Research & Education at the University of Massachusetts Lowell. His research interests are evidence-based academic and behavioral interventions for students with and at risk for emotional and behavioral disorders. Additional areas of interest include responsible inclusion and effective methods for preparing and supporting teachers in urban settings. His service efforts focus on improving student access to research-based instruction, interventions, and supports in dedicated and inclusive settings

Jessica Nelson, EdD, BCBA, LBA (Chapter 3) is an assistant professor at Missouri State University in Springfield, Missouri. Her research interests include creating antecedent interventions, use of teacher praise, mentoring and training of preservice and beginning career teachers, as well as academic interventions for students with the most significant cognitive disabilities.

Maria B. Peterson-Ahmad, PhD (Chapter 15) is a visiting associate professor at Texas Woman's University. Her research interests include teacher preparation, technology in education, and high leverage practices. She was awarded the T. H. Gentle Professorship Award in 2019 and serves in leadership capacities in professional teaching organizations including the Council for Exceptional Children, American Association of Colleges for Teacher Education, and Council for Learning Disabilities.

Felicity Post, EdD (Chapter 3) is an assistant professor at Peru State College in Peru, Nebraska. Her research interests include training of preservice and beginning career teachers, the use of aversive interventions, positive behavioral supports, trauma, and social emotional learning. Before becoming a professor, she was an elementary resource teacher for 11 years in the Manhattan-Ogden School District.

Delia E. Racines, PhD (Chapter 12) is the owner and lead consultant of From Insight to Equity consulting firm supporting administrators, teachers, and instructional coaches. She is also an adjunct professor with the USC Rossier School of Education and previous lecturer with the Gould School of Law. She serves as an ETK-8 principal with the Azusa Unified School District, where she supports educators to ensure equitable opportunities and outcomes for English learners.

Kathleen M. Randolph, EdD, BCBA-D (Chapter 5) is an assistant professor at the University of Colorado–Colorado Springs. Her research interests focus on supporting teacher implementation of evidence-based practices using iCoaching. She also serves as treasurer of the Teacher Education Division of the Council for Exceptional Children.

Andrew R. Scheef, PhD (Chapter 2) is an assistant professor of special education at the University of Idaho (Moscow). Prior to this appointment, he worked as a public school teacher for 14 years and has a strong interest in connecting research with practice. Dr. Scheef was awarded a Fulbright Distinguished Award in Teaching, which allowed him to study special education in Singapore. His research interests are focused on supporting youth with disabilities through post-school transition.

Tracy E. Sinclair, PhD, BCBA, LBA (Chapter 1) is an assistant professor in the Neag School of Education at the University of Connecticut. Dr. Sinclair teaches preservice teachers in the special education undergraduate and graduate programs. Her research interests are couched in applied behavior analysis and self-management strategies, transition and postsecondary outcomes, assessment development, and teacher preparation. Dr. Sinclair was both a public school general and special educator, and was awarded teacher of the year on multiple occasions.

Reginald B. Snoddy, MS (Chapter 14) serves as a full-time professor of Spanish in the Humanities Division at Rose State College in Midwest City, Oklahoma. He teaches beginner through intermediate level Spanish, including in grammar-based, medical, conversational, and introductory literature courses. Professor Snoddy is currently a PhD student in Instructional Leadership and Academic Curriculum at the University of Oklahoma, with an emphasis in World Languages Education.

Nathan A. Stevenson, PhD (Chapter 11) is an assistant professor of special education at Kent State University. His research interests include the development of academic and behavioral supports to improve the quality of inclusive education and school-wide systems of support. He is currently associate editor for *Assessment for Effective Intervention* and serves on the editorial board for numerous professional journals. In 2016, Dr. Stevenson was co-recipient of the Early Career Research Award from the Society for the Study of School Psychology.

Sharon Sullivan, PhD (Chapter 7) is an associate professor of education and special education at Brescia University. Her research interests include learning strategies and strategic instructional approaches. Her university teaching focuses on special education teacher preparation and includes, among others, both introductory and advanced classes in diagnostics, methods, and legal issues. Sister Sharon is also an Ursuline Sister of Mount Saint Joseph in Maple Mount, Kentucky.

Wilhelmina van Dijk, PhD (Chapter 8) is an assistant professor of special education at Utah State University. Her research focuses on preventing reading failure in young children through examining reading development for typical and struggling readers, effective components of reading interventions, and how to best prepare future teachers of reading.

Andrew L. Wiley, PhD (Chapter 11) is an associate professor of special education at Kent State University. His research and teaching focus on critical issues in special education, such as evidence-based practices, specially designed instruction, inclusive education, disproportionate representation in special education, and the under-identification and under-service of students with emotional and behavioral disorders. Dr. Wiley serves on the board of the national Badar-Kauffman Conference on Contemporary Issues in Special Education Research held annually in Kent, Ohio.

PREFACE

Practitioners, researchers, and policymakers all play essential roles in ensuring that students with disabilities receive quality instruction that aligns with the best evidence available. Although it is widely understood that research addressing the needs of the special education field is important, less attention has focused on the translation of special education research to practice and supporting educators in the implementation of evidence-based practices. To make strides in each of these areas, it is important for educators to have an understanding of why research is conducted and how to evaluate evidence presented. We developed this textbook to provide a comprehensive resource for advanced undergraduate and graduate students embarking on this journey.

This book grew out of our own experiences in special education—the successes, the challenges, and the failures. Our work, including leading special education research and evaluation teams, obtaining external funding, and teaching special education research courses, shaped the ideas for teaching not only methodology but also the skills needed to successfully conduct special education research. Our experiences, prior to entering higher education, as general education teachers, special education teachers, interventionists, Board Certified Behavior Analysts, and school administrators also provided valuable insight. We worked alongside contributors who are experts in their respective methodologies and hold a variety of positions in special education. The team included school administrators, postdoctoral fellows, early career faculty, and seasoned academics working in a variety of localities, including non-profit research firms, teaching colleges, research intensive universities, and PreK-12 public schools. Each author and contributor has supported students, teachers, administrators, paraprofessionals, and families of children from birth to age 21 years and beyond, which provides not only the formal training but also the practical experience to develop, disseminate, and implement special education research.

Research Methods in Special Education begins with an introduction to evidence-based practice and the role of special education research followed by chapters focusing on how to locate, read, and evaluate a research article; maintain compliance with ethical standards; and form effective partnerships. Dedicated chapters address common methodologies frequently used in special education research but that are often excluded from traditional research methods texts. For example, chapters address single case research design and research synthesis including meta-analysis. We also include chapters on program evaluation; survey research; and qualitative, experimental, and mixed-methods research.

On SLACK's efacultylounge.com, you will find additional resources to accompany each chapter, along with additional supporting materials. The main goal of this textbook is to provide educators with a resource that can be referred to beyond the university classroom. Thank you for pursuing research training. These skills will provide the foundation to enhance special education practice.

Evidence-Based Practice in Special Education

Constructing an Operational Definition

With contributions from Tracy E. Sinclair, PhD, BCBA, LBA

INTRODUCTION

In the field of special education, there is a continuous debate about the research-to-practice gap. Central to this debate is the concept of evidence-based practice (EBP). Further complicating this is the lack of consistency in nomenclature, identification, and implementation of EBPs. This chapter outlines the historical origin of EBPs in the medical field, and the adaptation of this approach in special education. The ultimate goal of dissemination of EBPs to teachers is to dispel application of pseudoscience to our most vulnerable learners—students with disabilities. Prominent organizations in the field—Council for Exceptional Children (CEC), What Works Clearinghouse (WWC), and National Technical Assistance Center on Transition (NTACT)—describe various levels of evidence as it pertains to special education teaching practices. Frameworks from each institution, as well as comparisons between them, are described within this chapter to provide guidance on language and indicators of methodological rigor and quality. Implementation of EBPs in the field of education is a priority in federal legislation in both general education—Every Student Succeeds Act (ESSA)—and special education—Individuals with Disabilities Education Act (IDEA), and this chapter provides guidance on selection of a practiced based on available scientific evidence. The CEC's High-Leverage Practices (HLPs) are included as an exemplar of using EBPs as an educational approach for promoting best practices for students with disabilities.

Hott, B. L., Brigham, F. J., & Peltier, C.
Research Methods in Special Education (pp. 1-15).
© 2021 SLACK Incorporated.

CHAPTER OBJECTIVES

→ Describe the differences between promising practices, research-based practices, and evidence-based practices.

→ Compare and contrast the approaches that organizations take in evaluating the research to determine evidence-based practices.

→ Examine strategies to enhance the sustainability of evidence-based practices and combat pseudoscience.

→ Discuss the impact that individual, system, and policy decisions have on special education.

KEY TERMS

- **Council for Exceptional Children (CEC)**: An international professional organization dedicated to promoting the success of individuals with disabilities. CEC is composed of special educators, paraprofessionals, higher education faculty, and related service providers.

- **Every Student Succeeds Act (ESSA)**: Passed in 2015, ESSA replaces the No Child Left Behind Act (NCLB) and serves as the main public education law. Central to ESSA is the use of scientific evidence applied to practices to improve education for all students.

- **Evidence-Based Practice (EBP)**: A practice with substantial quantity and quality of experimental research demonstrating meaningful, positive effects on student outcomes. Determination of quality varies by organization; however, in general, it involves an evaluation using a quality appraisal rubric. The specific number of quality experiments required varies depending on the type of design used and the organization.

- **External Validity**: Refers to the design and implementation of an experiment; particularly, the ability to decipher whether effects from the study would transfer to other settings, participants, or implementers.

- **High-Leverage Practice (HLP)**: HLPs were developed in partnership between CEC and the Collaboration for Effective Educator Development, Accountability, and Reform (CEEDAR) Center at the University of Florida. Twenty-two practices in four domains are identified as most critical for all special educators to master. Successful implementation of HLPs has demonstrated improvements in outcomes for students.

- **Institute of Education Sciences (IES)**: The U.S. Department of Education's source of educational statistics, research, and evaluation. IES provides guidance on scientifically based practices in education through various forms, including the What Works Clearinghouse.

- **Internal Validity**: Refers to the design and implementation of an experiment; particularly, the ability to decipher whether changes in the dependent variable can be attributed solely to the independent variable by experimentally controlling for confounding variables.

- **National Technical Assistance Center on Transition (NTACT)**: NTACT identifies and promotes practices rooted in scientific evidence in the field of transition. This organization is funded through the U.S. Department of Education to focus on improving postsecondary outcomes for all students with disabilities.

- **Neuromyths**: A subcomponent of pseudoscience, practice, or theory about how the brain works that is promoted without evidence from rigorous experimental research.

- **Promising Practice**: A practice with limited quantity and quality of experimental research demonstrating meaningful, positive effects on student outcomes. Determination of quality varies by organization; however, in general, it involves an evaluation using a quality appraisal rubric. The specific number of quality experiments required varies depending on the type of design used and the organization.

Figure 1-1. Language used to classify practices based on scientific evidence.

- **Pseudoscience**: A practice or theory that is promoted without evidence from rigorous experimental research.
- **Research-Based Practice (RBP)**: A practice with sufficient quantity and quality of experimental research demonstrating meaningful, positive effects on student outcomes. Determination of quality varies by organization; however, in general, it involves an evaluation using a quality appraisal rubric. The specific number of quality experiments required varies depending on the type of design used and the organization.
- **What Works Clearinghouse (WWC)**: The WWC reviews and evaluates research on practices, programs, products, and policies in education. Determination of level of scientific rigor is used to promote evidence-based decision making in selection of resources used in schools and classrooms.

EVIDENCE-BASED PRACTICE

When comparing special education to other disciplines, we are a relatively young field. Our literature base and research methodology has rapidly evolved over the years, and likely will continue as the field becomes more established. The bedrock, and likely catalyst for the future of special education research is to promote practices with evidence obtained from rigorously designed experiments. Although varying definitions are available in the field, the term *evidence-based practice* (EBP) has been promoted to denote a practice with sufficient quantity and quality of research demonstrating meaningful, positive effects on student outcomes (Figure 1-1).

However, jargon in the educational sector has blurred the lines of which practices to adopt or drop. Prominent organizations in the field (e.g., CEC, NTACT, WWC) use a similar framework to categorize practices based on the quality and quantity of experimental research. Although rubrics across organizations are not identical, there are similarities. The rubrics identify critical aspects of the research design and prompt evaluators to determine if the design has addressed the threat to internal validity. The WWC, funded through the Institute of Education Sciences (IES) and the Department of Education, is the largest organization, although not the only organization, engaged in systematic evaluation and dissemination of quality appraisals of practices and programs. As the list of practices with evidence grows, the field has struggled to address "the last mile problem"—getting these practices into the hands of teachers. Identifying strategic ways to replace pseudoscience and neuromyths with EBPs is an essential last step of the research process. One hypothesized method for bridging research and practice is via teacher-researcher partnerships. To effectively engage in the identification and dissemination of EBPs, researchers must understand how individual, system, and policy decisions impact special education. See Table 1-1 for an overview of guidance on the identification and quality of research rigor as it pertains to EBPs.

As a practitioner who may not be familiar with identification of EBPs, place yourself in the shoes of Ms. Perez.

CASE STUDY

Ms. Perez is planning an icebreaker activity to get to know her students and use this information to plan for instruction throughout the year. She logs onto TeachersPayTeachers.com and searches for icebreaker activities. She finds a really cool template for a foldable students can create along with a brief formative assessment allowing students to identify: (a) whether they are right- or left-brain dominant (see Geake, 2008 for description), (b) their predominant learning style (e.g., kinesthetic, auditory, visual; see Willingham, 2018 for description), and (c) identify strengths across the multiple intelligences (see Willingham, 2004 for description). Ms. Perez shares her project with her team lead, Ms. Jimerson. Ms. Jimerson said she had heard of learning styles, but was unaware of the other two theories or how they would inform instruction. She also had not come across these theories or ideas through the reputable resources she typically uses to plan instruction (i.e., Center on Response to Intervention, National Center on Intensive Intervention, WWC Practice Guides). She told Ms. Perez she would reach out to their university partner for additional information on these theories and whether they have sufficient research supporting their use.

Although Ms. Perez may have the best intentions and spent a considerable amount of her time researching icebreaker activities online, is she making sound scientifically based instructional decisions? What are teachers to do when selecting materials for classroom instruction?

The Evidence-Based Practice Movement

The EBP movement originated in the medical field during the 1990s (Sackett et al., 1996). At its inception, the EBP movement was backed by proponents with the intention of increasing the quality of clinical decision-making by providing the best available evidence for specific practices, thus improving the likelihood of patients receiving desirable outcomes. Furthermore, the EBP movement aimed to prevent clients from receiving fad treatments that not only may not improve outcomes, but in some cases might increase the likelihood of negative outcomes. However, the EBP movement was met with criticism for several reasons: (a) some viewed proponents of EBPs as arrogant, (b) fear that the EBP movement was more focused on saving money and less on client well-being, and (c) fear that the movement was meant to suppress clinical freedom (Graham-Smith, 1995). The medical field has continued to adapt frameworks that prioritize reliance on scientifically grounded treatments while also acknowledging the benefit of doctors leveraging their expertise to individualize treatments based on client preference and needs. See Figure 1-2 for a framework adopted in the medical field to demonstrate how EBPs are comprised of three underlying factors: (a) clinician (or teacher) expertise; (b) patient (or student) preference, belief, and needs; and (c) selection of treatments (i.e., practices) with evidence from rigorous research methodologies to provide meaningful benefit to patients (i.e., students). Furthermore, practice guidelines are based on research; physicians and other medical providers are bound by ethical standards to follow such guidelines.

TABLE 1-1. QUALITY INDICATORS AND GUIDANCE STANDARDS IN SPECIAL EDUCATION RESEARCH EXEMPLARS

DOCUMENT DESCRIPTION	REFERENCE
Quality Indicators for Qualitative Research	Brantlinger, E., Jimenez, R., Klingner, J., Pugach, M., & Richardson, V. (2005). Qualitative studies in special education. *Exceptional Children, 71*(2), 195-207. https://doi.org/10.1177/001440290507100205
Quality Indicators for SCRDs	Horner, R. H., Carr, E. G., Halle, J., McGee, G., Odom, S., & Wolery, M. (2005). The use of single-subject research to identify evidence-based practice in special education. *Exceptional Children, 71*(2), 165-179. https://doi.org/10.1177/001440290507100203
Quality Indicators for Group and QEDs	Gersten, R., Fuchs, L. S., Compton, D., Coyne, M., Greenwood, C., & Innocenti, M. S. (2005). Quality indicators for group experimental and quasi-experimental research in special education. *Exceptional Children, 71*(2), 149-164. https://doi.org/10.1177/001440290507100202
Quality Indicators for Correlational Research	Thompson, B., Diamond, K. E., McWilliam, R., Snyder, P., & Snyder, S. W. (2005). Evaluating the quality of evidence from correlational research for evidence-based practice. *Exceptional Children, 71*(2), 181-194. https://doi.org/10.1177/001440290507100204
CEC Guidance for Evidence-Based Practices	Cook, B., Buysse, V., Klingner, J., Landrum, T., McWilliam, R., Tankersley, M., & Test, D. (2014). Council for Exceptional Children: Standards for evidence-based practices in special education. *Teaching Exceptional Children, 46*(6), 206. https://doi.org/10.1177/0040059914531389
WWC Design Standards	What Works Clearinghouse (2020). Standards handbook (Version 4.1). What Works Clearinghouse. https://ies.ed.gov/ncee/wwc/Handbooks
NTACT Effective Practices Matrix	https://transitionta.org/effectivepractices
CEC = Council for Exceptional Children; NTACT = National Technical Assistance Center on Transition; QED = quasi-experimental design; SCRD = single case research design; WWC = What Works Clearinghouse.	

Much like the medical field, the EBP movement in the field of special education is a major area of focus. A driving force for this movement was the special issue published in *Exceptional Children* in 2005. The special issue aimed to unpack the rationale for identifying EBPs in the field of special education and the role of scientific research in making these determinations. In addition, the issue provides guidelines for evaluating the methodological rigor of prominent research methodologies (i.e., group design [see Chapters 8, 9], single case design [see Chapter 10], correlational research [see Chapter 7], and qualitative research [see Chapter 12]). The special issue served three major foci: (a) a response to the WWC's exclusive focus on the evaluation of group design studies to identify effective practices; (b) to highlight how the four identified research methodologies provide unique information to inform practice; and (c) to contextualize the conversation of methodological rigor and EBP in the field of special education. These quality indicators are discussed in more depth in the above-mentioned chapters in respect to the research design.

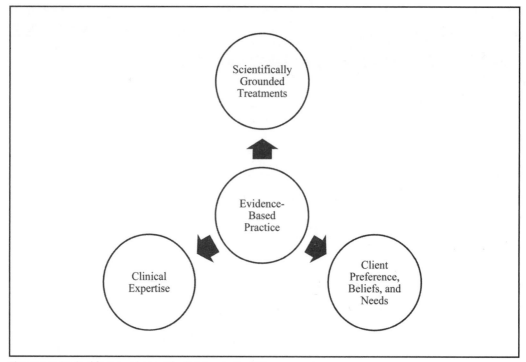

Figure 1-2. Medical framework to guide clinicians in the EBP movement.

Evidence-Based Practices and Federal Legislation

Language in federal legislation also mandates teachers to implement practices with evidence in promoting meaningful, positive effects for students. First, the passage of the No Child Left Behind (NCLB) Act of 2001 used the phrase "scientifically based research" throughout the document to refer to the types of professional development and academic instruction that should be implemented across the nation. In 2004, the Individuals with Disabilities Education Improvement Act (IDEA) was updated and added the language, "scientifically based research" and "peer-reviewed research" when specifying the responsibilities of state educational agencies (SEAs) in their provision of technical assistance and local educational agencies (LEAs) in their provision of direct services to students with disabilities (Zirkel & Tessie, 2009). Although this language and the mandate from federal law does not explicitly require the use of EBPs, the spirit of the law suggests SEAs and LEAs should select practice and programs with substantial evidence obtained from rigorous methodology demonstrating their effect on student outcomes. In 2015, NCLB was reauthorized and renamed the Every Student Succeeds Act (ESSA). Due to the ambiguity surrounding the term "scientifically based research," ESSA used the term "evidence-based intervention" to identify the types of professional development and practices schools should be implementing. Furthermore, ESSA provided a hierarchy to describe the different tiers a practice could be classified under based on the quantity and quality of scientific evidence supporting its use and a process for selecting interventions, practices, and programs (Figure 1-3). The four tiers, in descending order of evidence, are strong evidence, moderate evidence, promising evidence, and demonstrates a rationale.

Impact of Evidence-Based Practices

The impact of the EBP movement on the field is visible in many ways. Although it is not an exhaustive list, we highlight four major contributions to the field. First, researchers consulted guidelines for evaluating the methodology of the four major research designs when designing experiments

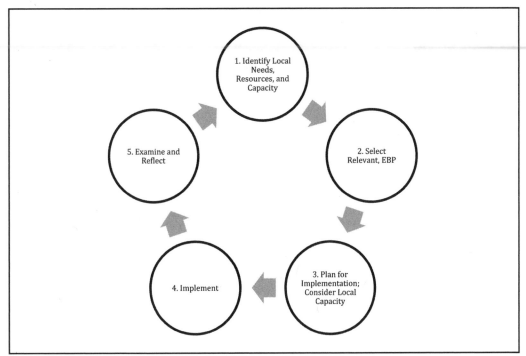

Figure 1-3. Framework for selecting interventions under ESSA guidance.

to increase the rigor in their design and reduce threats to internal and external validity. Second, a large uptick was observed in the frequency of systematic reviews focused on appraising the quality of a literature base to determine if a specific practice meets the criteria to be labeled an EBP (e.g., Gage et al., 2017). Third, a push was made by professional organizations and academic journals to disseminate information to practitioners on the research evidence of various instructional practices. Fourth, institutions of higher education who prepare preservice teachers realigned curriculum to emphasize the use of EBPs (see the Council for Exceptional Children's [CEC] Special Educator Preparation Standards). An exemplar in special education of attempts at dissemination of EBPs to preservice and in-service teachers in CEC's High Leverage Practice (HLPs). Table 1-2 lists all 22 HLPs. Despite advances in the field, issues with jargon and approaches to identifying EBPs have inhibited a smooth translation of research-to-practice.

FRAMEWORKS FOR EVIDENCE-BASED PRACTICES

Due to the various terms (e.g., evidence-based, research-based, scientifically based, evidence-aligned, research-aligned, peer-reviewed) used to describe practices and ambiguous definitions of this language, the special education field needed to respond. Prominent organizations created task forces to create frameworks to clarify terminology and classify practices in order to improve the dissemination efforts to practitioners.

Council for Exceptional Children

The CEC is the largest organization in the field of special education and serves as one of the leading avenues for translating research to practice. In 2005, a special issue of *Exceptional Children* (the flagship journal of CEC) outlined quality indicators for research guidance in special education

TABLE 1-2. COUNCIL FOR EXCEPTIONAL CHILDREN'S HIGH-LEVERAGE PRACTICES

DOMAIN	PRACTICES
Collaboration	• HLP 1: Collaborate with professionals to increase student success. • HLP 2: Organize and facilitate effective meetings with professionals and families. • HLP 3: Collaborate with families to support student learning and secure needed services.
Assessment	• HLP 4: Use multiple sources of information to develop a comprehensive understanding of student's strengths and needs. • HLP 5: Interpret and communicate assessment information with stakeholders to collaboratively design and implement educational programs. • HLP 6: After special education teachers develop instructional goals, they evaluate and make ongoing adjustments to students' instructional programs.
Social/Emotional/ Behavioral	• HLP 7: Establish a consistent, organized, and respectful learning environment. • HLP 8: Provide positive and constructive feedback to guide students' learning and behavior.* • HLP 9: Teach social behaviors. • HLP 10: Conduct functional behavioral assessments to develop individual student behavior support plans.
Instruction	• HLP 11: Identify and prioritize long- and short-term learning goals. • HLP 12: Systematically design instruction toward a specific learning goal. • HLP 13: Adapt curriculum tasks and materials for specific learning goals. • HLP 14: Teach cognitive and metacognitive strategies to support learning and independence. • HLP 15: Provide scaffolded supports. • HLP 16: Use explicit instruction. • HLP 17: Use flexible grouping. • HLP 18: Use strategies to promote active student engagement. • HLP 19: Use assistive and instructional technologies. • HLP 20: Provide intensive instruction. • HLP 21: Teach students to maintain and generalize new learning across time and settings. • HLP 22: Provide positive and constructive feedback to guide students' learning and behavior.*

*Duplicated intentionally. This HLP spans two domains.

(Odom et al., 2005). Quality indicators were set forth by experts in the field regarding methodologies of: (a) single case designs (see Horner et al., 2005), (b) group designs (see Gersten et al., 2005), (c) correlational research (see Thompson et al., 2005), and (d) qualitative designs (see Brantlinger et al., 2005). In the field of special education, this was a formal call for researchers to adhere to rigorous research designs meeting specific quality indicators. Creating a framework for the standardization and methodological rigor of special education research laid the foundational groundwork for a systematic way to evaluate practices and their supporting evidence. Following this special issue, CEC created a task force to synthesize comments from the field and put forth standards for determining EBPs in the field of special education. This led to the publication of Council for Exceptional Children: Standards for Evidence-Based Practices in Special Education (Cook et al., 2014). In this document, the collaborative used a Delphi procedure to develop a tiered approach in classifying practices depending on the quantity and quality of evidence currently available. This explicit framework also clarified terminology to improve the communication of practices and their research credibility to a broader audience. The framework proposed by CEC used the following terms in a hierarchical fashion to define the evidence supporting their use: *evidence-based practice* used to define a practice with the highest level of evidence supporting its use; *potentially evidence-based practice* used to define a practice with some evidence supporting its use; *mixed evidence* used to define a practice with some evidence supporting its use with additional evidence not supporting its use; *insufficient evidence* for a practice with limited evidence either for or against its use; and *negative effects* for a practice with evidence demonstrating negative outcomes for participants.

National Technical Assistance Center on Transition

In 2018, the NTACT published its own indicators and criteria for determining the quality of evidence for practices and predictors in the context of transition. The task force used the CEC Standards for Evidence-Based Practices in Special Education (Cook et al., 2014) to establish its criteria; thus, there are many similarities across the procedures used to determine the level of evidence for individual practices. However, it is worth noting that NTACT used different language to define the levels of evidence: *evidence-based practice* used to define a practice with the highest level of evidence supporting its use; *research-based practice* used to define a practice with some evidence supporting its use; *promising practice* used to define practices with some evidence supporting its use but to a lesser extent than research-based criteria; and *unestablished practice* used to describe practices without evidence supporting its use.

What Works Clearinghouse

Although not unique to the field of special education, the WWC has been a leading agency in the evaluation and dissemination of evidence on practices. The WWC published their initial handbook (Version 1.0; May 2008) that included procedures and standards for determining the effectiveness of a practice. The WWC has subsequently published versions that included additions, revisions, and clarifications on the process: Version 2.0 (December 2008), Version 2.1 (September 2011), Version 3.0 (March 2014), Version 4.0 (October 2017), and Version 4.1 (January 2020). Across all of these iterations, the WWC has remained consistent in the language used to describe a practice: *strong evidence* used to define a practice with sufficient quantity and quality of evidence, ruling out other causes for improvement, that produces improvement on student outcomes; *moderate evidence* used to define a practice with limited quantity and quality of evidence, which raises concerns of other factors that could be attributed to cause the improvement observed; and *minimal evidence* used to define a practice with no causal evidence. Table 1-3 includes language used across organizations to classify level of evidence supporting a practice.

TABLE 1-3. HIERARCHIES USED TO CLASSIFY PRACTICES BASED ON LEVEL OF EVIDENCE

	WWC	CEC	NTACT	ESSA
LEVEL OF EFFECTIVENESS FROM HIGHEST TO LOWEST	Strong evidence	Evidence-based practice	Evidence-based practice	Strong evidence
	Moderate evidence	Potentially evidence-based practice	Research-based practice	Moderate evidence
	Minimal evidence	Mixed evidence	Promising practice	Promising evidence
		Insufficient evidence	Unestablished practice	Demonstrates a rationale
		Negative effects		

CEC = Council for Exceptional Children; ESSA = Every Student Succeeds Act; NTACT = National Technical Assistance Center on Transition; WWC = What Works Clearinghouse.

IMPLICATIONS FOR TRANSLATING RESEARCH TO PRACTICE

The language used to define a practice led to several issues translating research findings to practice. First, differences in language used across organizations (i.e., CEC, NTACT, WWC) can cloud interpretations. Second, determining what constitutes a "practice" also can lead to confusion. For example, one approach to teaching mathematical problem solving to students at risk of or identified with a specific learning disability is to prime students to identify the underlying structure of the word problem (see Jitendra et al., 2015). The authors conducted a systematic review and evaluated studies using the quality indicators listed in the CEC Standards for Evidence-Based Practices in Special Education (Cook et al., 2014). The authors concluded this approach should be deemed an EBP based on the quantity and quality of evidence demonstrating its effectiveness. However, this approach is defined broadly—there are specific interventions that are classified under this umbrella approach. One specific example is schema-based instruction. As a teacher, is schema-based instruction an EBP because it falls under the umbrella approach of priming students to identify the underlying problem structure? Would this approach be evidence-based for a different population of students (e.g., students identified with emotional or behavior disorders), or would a systematic replication of empirical research be needed before making this claim? Organizations have classified schema-based instruction based on its quantity and quality of scientific evidence and the results would be confusing for teachers to interpret. When defining the evidence for schema-based instruction for students with a specific learning disability, three different terms can be used to describe the evidence for this practice: (a) research-based practice (NTACT; see NTACT, 2017), (b) promising evidence-based practice (CEC; see Cook et al., 2020), or (c) strong evidence (WWC; see Woodward et al., 2012).

The clarification of what constitutes a practice and the target population can lead to immense confusion for teachers and school district leaders who aim to select practices with the highest evidence of effect. Also, the various language used by the organization can lead to confusion if teachers and school district leaders are not versed in the different classification schemes used across the organizations. Finally, the standards used by each organization to operationally define the components of each experiment evaluated differ, which can lead to a different rating for practice (i.e., highest, middle, low; see Maggin et al., 2014). Figure 1-4 offers example questions to ask when examining a potential program, strategy, practice, or intervention.

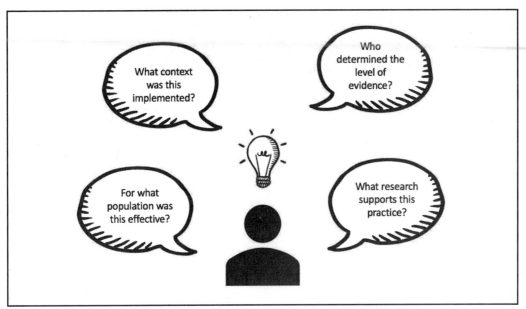

Figure 1-4. Questions to ask yourself about an intervention, practice, strategy, or curricular program.

IMPLEMENTATION OF EVIDENCE-BASED PRACTICES IN THE FIELD

The field has made efforts to increase the implementation of EBPs at the state, district, school, and classroom levels. Fixsen and colleagues (2009) eloquently stated the challenge of this endeavor: "an evidence-based practice is one thing, implementation of that practice is another thing altogether" (p. 5). Scholars have identified that the implementation at the system level (i.e., state, district, school) is a "wicked" problem (Fixsen et al., 2009) because of the pushback from staff (Rittel & Webber, 1973) and the system's desire to maintain the status quo by all means necessary (Fixsen et al., 2013). Implementation science literature has generated important knowledge to continue tackling this issue. First, the "train and hope" (Stokes & Baer, 1977) model to professional development is ineffective despite its long-term use by educational entities (Joyce & Showers, 2002). Fixsen and colleagues (2005) identified several critical factors to enhance implementation:

1. The implementation team must understand that the needs and unique contexts of the community are essential for implementation to be successful.

2. There are core components to the implementation process: (a) staff selection, (b) staff training, (c) staff coaching, and (d) evaluation and fidelity.

3. The core implementation components are not implemented within a bubble; there are organizational and social, economic, and political factors influencing the process.

At its core, special education is an individualized process designed to best support each particular student's needs. Circling back to the clinical framework for medical professionals—the individual client's needs must be considered and at the forefront of decision making. The same holds true for students with disabilities. Practices chosen at the individual level may be more heavily weighted based on student/family preference versus high levels of scientific evidence. This complicates implementation of EBPs in classroom settings.

Further muddying the waters of EBP implementation at the systems level is the question of local capacity. How well might a school district implement an EBP that has strong evidence, but comes at the significant cost of draining limited funding? Potentially, a promising practice can be more effectively implemented across the entire district. ESSA (2016) provides non-regulatory guidelines

TABLE 1-4. COMMON MISCONCEPTIONS AND CLARIFICATIONS ABOUT EVIDENCE-BASED PRACTICES

MISCONCEPTION	BETTER UNDERSTANDING
A practice labeled evidence-based means it works for *everyone*.	A practice identified as an EBP is based on application to specific populations of students, and what may have evidence with one group of students may not translate into positive outcomes for another group. Furthermore, an EBP may not be effective even for an individual who qualifies as a member of the intervention group. It is important to consider individual learner needs, teacher expertise, and scientific evidence, not just one aspect of EBP identification.
A 1-day professional development session in a specific EBP means all participants will be able to: (a) return to their respective classrooms an expert in the intervention, (b) be able to implement the intervention with high fidelity, and (c) be fluent in all components of the intervention.	Research shows "train and hope" models do not work (see Stokes & Baer, 1977). To become fluent in an EBP requires training, coaching, tracking, and monitoring of implementation.
A practice labeled as promising should never be used because it isn't "good" enough.	Much like misconception one, teachers need to account for scientific evidence, their own expertise, and learner needs and attributes. Although a promising practice might be approached with caution regarding implementation, teachers should not shy away from new practices. However, teachers should track implementation fidelity and student outcome progress.

suggesting a framework for implementation of EBPs to include questions of local needs (see Figure 1-3). Local needs are defined as those by both SEAs and LEAs and vary widely across states depending on appropriation of special education funding. These sweeping policy changes to federal law, such as that of IDEA (2004) or ESSA (2016), must then be translated at the state and local level for implementation in the special education classroom. This process varies in timelines, resource supports, and translating policy into practice. Table 1-4 includes a list of common misconceptions associated with the evidence-based practice movement, and Table 1-5 provides additional resources to consult. Chapter 15 discusses EBPs and the translation of research to practice in more detail.

TABLE 1-5. ADDITIONAL RESOURCES

RESOURCE	DESCRIPTION
Center on Response to Intervention at American Institutes for Research https://buildingrti.utexas.org/links-websites/center-response-to-intervention-american-institutes-for-research	This website provides an overview of MTSS/RTI. The Center on RTI provides professional development in implementation and scaling-up of MTSS/RTI and essential components.
Comprehensive Integrated Three-Tiered Model of Prevention https://www.ci3t.org	Comprehensive, Integrated, Three-Tiered Model of Prevention (Ci3T) provides a model for addressing three tiers of intervention in academics, behavior, and social competencies. Ci3T promotes data-informed decision making based on research.
Council for Exceptional Children's Evidence-based Practice Resources https://www.cec.sped.org/Standards/Evidence-Based-Practice-Resources-Original	CEC's downloadable handbook outlines standards for evidence-based practices in special education.
Evidence for ESSA https://www.evidenceforessa.org	Consortium group dedicated to providing guidance on proven programs that meet ESSA evidence standards.
Evidence-Based Intervention Network http://ebi.missouri.edu	University of Missouri's EBIN provides guidance on selection and implementation of EBPs.
High Leverage Practices in Special Education https://highleveragepractices.org	CEC's website dedicated to HLPs. Downloadable documents, guides for professional development, and videos for all 22 HLPs are included.
IES's Procedures and Standards for Determining Evidence-Based Practices https://ies.ed.gov/ncee/wwc/Handbooks	WWC handbooks for download regarding procedures and standards of EBPs.
IRIS Center Evidence-Based Practices Summaries https://iris.peabody.vanderbilt.edu/resources/ebp_summaries/	IRIS Center's research summaries in 11 domains providing guidance on level of effectiveness, applicable age groups, and links to further research.
National Center on Intensive Intervention https://intensiveintervention.org/	NCII at American Institutes for Research provides guidance and resources on implementation of intensive evidence-based interventions.
National Professional Development Center on Autism Spectrum Disorder https://autismpdc.fpg.unc.edu/evidence-based-practices	University consortium to promote EBPs for children and youth with ASD. Downloadable resources for selected EBPs included.

(continued)

TABLE 1-5. ADDITIONAL RESOURCES (CONTINUED)	
RESOURCE	**DESCRIPTION**
National Technical Assistance Center on Transition's Effective Practices and Predictors https://www.transitionta.org/effectivepractices	NTACT's effective practices and predictors matrix, skills taught, and operational definitions of practices are included for download.
What Works Clearinghouse https://ies.ed.gov/ncee/wwc/	WWC's designations of EBPs in 11 domains. Intervention briefs, practice guides, and resources available for download.

SUMMARY

To ensure we are providing recommendations that increase the likelihood of positive student outcomes, we need to rely on findings from rigorous experimental research. In addition, we need to acknowledge that science is always evolving, and we will never have all the answers to every question. This is why the field has pushed to think of EBP as a process-oriented activity (Cook & Cook, 2016), much like the medical model illustrates in Figure 1-1. To improve the EBP decision-making framework, various educational entities have created language to specify the tier of evidence supporting individual practices based on the quality and quantity of experimental studies. Ultimately, large-scale implementation efforts are needed to translate research to practice and should include critical components, an understanding of the community context, and the ability to address organizational as well as social, economic, and political factors.

CHAPTER REVIEW

1. What is the rationale for distinguishing between promising practices, research-based practices, and EBPs?
2. How could a practice be identified as an EBP using the WWC guidelines but not the CEC guidelines? What does this mean?
3. What steps have the field undertaken to solve the "last mile problem"?
4. What impact do policies and systems have on research and practice in special education?
5. How can teachers gather information about whether a practice is a promising, research-based, or evidence-based practice?

REFERENCES

Brantlinger, E., Jimenez, R., Klinger, J., Pugach, M., & Richardson, V. (2005). Qualitative studies in special education. *Exceptional Children, 71*(2), 195-207. https://doi.org/10.1177/001440290507100205

Cook, B., Buyesse, V., Klingner, J., Landrum, T., McWilliam, R., Tankersley, M., & Test, D. (2014). Council for exceptional children: Standards for evidence-based practices in special education. *Teaching Exceptional Children, 46*(6), 206-212. https://doi.org/10.1177/0040059914531389

Cook, B. G., Collins, L. W., Cook, S. C., & Cook, L. (2020). Evidence-based reviews: How evidence-based practices are systematically identified. *Learning Disabilities Research & Practice, 35*(1), 6-13.

Cook, B. G., & Cook, L. (2016). Leveraging evidence-based practice through partnerships based on practice-based evidence. *Learning Disabilities: A Contemporary Journal, 14*(2), 143-157.

Fixsen, D., Blase, K., Metz, A., & Van Dyke, M. (2013). Statewide implementation of evidence-based programs. *Exceptional Children, 79*(2), 213-230.

Fixsen, D. L., Blase, K. A., Naoom, S. F., & Wallace, F. (2009). Core implementation components. *Research on Social Work Practice, 19*(5), 531-540. https://doi.org/10.1177/1049731509335549

Fixsen, D. L., Naoom, S. F., Blase, K. A., Friedman, R. M., Wallace, F., Burns, B., Carter, W., Paulson, R., Schoenwald, S., Barwick, M., Chambers, D., Petrila, J., Rivard, J., & Shern, D. (2005). Implementation research: A synthesis of the literature. Tampa, FL: University of South Florida, Louis de la Parte Florida Mental Health Institute, The National Implementation Research Network (FMHI Publication #231), iii-119.

Gage, N. A., Cook, B. G., & Reichow, B. (2017). Publication bias in special education meta-analyses. *Exceptional Children, 83*(4), 428-445. https://doi.org/10.1177/00144029217691016

Gersten, R., Fuchs, L. S., Compton, D., Coyne, M., Greenwood, C., & Innocenti, M. S. (2005). Quality indicators for group experimental and quasi-experimental research in special education. *Exceptional Children, 71*(2), 149-164. https://doi.org/10.1177/001440290507100202

Graham-Smith, D. (1995). Evidence based medicine: Socratic dissent. *British Medical Journal, 310*, 1126-1127.

Horner, R. H., Carr, E. G., Halle, J., McGee, G., Odom, S., & Worley, M. (2005).The use of single-subject research to identify evidence-based practice in special education. *Exceptional Children, 71*(2), 165-179. https://doi.org/10.1177/001440290507100203

Jitendra, A. K., Petersen-Brown, S., Lein, A. E., Zaslofsky, A. F., Kunkel, A. K., Jung, P., & Egan, A. M. (2015). Teaching mathematical word problem solving: The quality of evidence for strategy instruction priming the problem structure. *Journal of Learning Disabilities, 48*(1), 51-72. https://doi.org/10.1177/0022219413487408

Joyce, B., & Showers, B. (2002). *Student achievement through staff development*. (3rd ed.). Association for Supervision and Curriculum Development.

Maggin, D. M., Briesch, A. M., Chafouleas, S. M., Ferguson, T. D., & Clark, C. (2014). A comparison of rubrics for identifying empirically supported practices with single-case research. *Journal of Behavioral Education, 23*(2), 287-311. https://www.jstor.org/stable/43551287

National Technical Assistance Center on Transition. (2017). Effective practices and predictors. https://transitionta.org/effectivepractices

Odom, S., Brantlinger, E., Gersten, R., Horner, R. H., Thompson, B., & Harris, K. R. (2005). Research in special education: Scientific methods and evidence-based practices. *Exceptional Children, 71*(2), 137-148. https://doi.org/10.1177/001440290507100201

Rittel, H. W. J., & Webber, M. M. (1973). Dilemmas in a general theory of planning. *Policy Sciences, 4*(2), 155-169. https://www.jstor.org/stable/4531523

Sackett, D. L., Rosenberg, W. M. C., Gray, J. A. M., Haynes, R. B., & Richardson, W. S. (1996). Evidence based medicine: What it is and what it isn't. *British Medical Journal, 312*, 71-72.

Stokes, T. F., & Baer, D. M. (1977). An implicit technology of generalization. *Journal of Applied Behavior Analysis, 10*(2), 349-367.

Thompson, B., Diamond, K. E., McWilliam, R., Snyder, P., & Snyder, S. W. (2005). Evaluating the quality of evidence from correlational research for evidence-based practice. *Exceptional Children, 71*(2), 181-194. https://doi.org/10.1177/001440290507100204

Woodward, J., Beckmann, S., Driscoll, M., Franke, M., Herzig, P., Jitendra, A., Koedinger, K. R., & Ogbuehi, P. (2012). *Improving mathematical problem solving in grades 4 through 8: A practice guide (NCEE 2012-4055)*. Washington, DC: National Center for Educational Evaluation and Regional Assistance, Institute of Education Sciences, U. S. Department of Education. https://ies.ed.gov/ncee/wwc/publications_reviews.aspx#pubsearch/

Zirkel, P. A., & Rose, T. (2009). Scientifically based research and peer-reviewed research under the IDEA. *Journal of Special Education Leadership, 22*(1), 36-53.

2

Introduction to Special Education Research

With contributions from Andrew R. Scheef, PhD; Aleksandra Hollingshead, EdD; and Rachel N. Freedman, MA, MS, BCBA, LABA

INTRODUCTION

This chapter begins with a description of how researchers develop ideas into experiments by detailing strategies to ensure research is relevant, meaningful, and viable. In order to determine the relevance of a research project, researchers must conduct a thorough review of previous studies to ensure the project makes a strong connection to the body of existing literature. Meaningful research has high levels of social validity; it is valued by consumers. The viability of a research project relates to logistics and the extent to which researchers have the means to complete the experiment. To guide the development of research experiments, recommendations are provided for developing high-quality research questions and making decisions about research design. Because special education research is often conducted as a team, this chapter identifies considerations researchers make when selecting members and delegating responsibilities. This chapter also includes strategies to search for external funding to support research and develop strong proposals to help procure resources. Once research is complete, authors need to find outlets to publish their work. With this in mind, a description of the publication process and recommendations for selecting potential journals are included. A case study is included to support a deeper understanding of these chapter components.

Hott, B. L., Brigham, F. J., & Peltier, C.
Research Methods in Special Education (pp. 17-37).
© 2021 SLACK Incorporated.

CHAPTER OBJECTIVES

→ Explain how research experiments can be developed so that they are relevant, meaningful, and viable.

→ Describe the key features of high-quality research questions.

→ Identify strategies and considerations when selecting a research design.

→ Describe factors that researchers may consider when recruiting others to join a research team.

→ Explain strategies for seeking and writing grant proposals to fund research.

→ Describe the publication process and identify strategies for selecting potential outlets for research manuscripts.

KEY TERMS

- **Conceptual Framework:** A theory that is developed through consideration of previous studies, and frames a new study.
- **Descriptive:** Describes variables as they occur in the environment.
- **Experimental:** Examine functional (i.e., causal) relation between independent and dependent variable(s).
- **Gatekeeper:** The individual or individuals who prevent or grant a researcher access to potential study participants.
- **Impact Factor (IF):** A metric used as a proxy to identify the quality of a journal, determined by the frequency in which articles in the journal are cited by others.
- **Inclusive Research:** Research that includes direct involvement of individuals with disabilities in the development, execution, and/or analysis.
- **Logic Model:** Process based on theory of change used for program development and evaluation; key elements include required resources, program activities, outputs, and outcomes.
- **Qualitative Research:** Research methodology that features systematic analysis of written, spoken, or observational data with results that rely heavily on written narrative or other artistic media.
- **Quantitative Research:** Research paradigm that is characterized by the use of statistical methods to present findings that are represented numerically to support or reject claims.
- **Relational:** Examines the relation between variables.
- **Replication:** Broad term to describe a research study conducted in the same or similar manner as a previous study.
- **Request for Proposals (RFP):** Document developed by grantors (those offering grants) that describes the nature and requirements of the grant.
- **Research Questions:** Questions that serve as central components to a research experiment; they precisely describe what a researcher aims to answer, understand, or explore.
- **Social Validity:** The extent to which the goals, procedures, and potential effects of a research study are relevant to and valued by consumers.
- **Validity:** The extent to which a study presents a sound argument to support a claim or finding.

CASE STUDY

Mr. deGrom lives a double life. By day, he is a special education teacher at an elementary school, providing specialized instruction and supports for students with disabilities. He enjoys his work in the school and appreciates the opportunity to do meaningful work in the field. By night, he becomes a part-time student himself, working on earning his doctorate at a local university. When he started the degree, he was curious about special education research, but his coursework has heightened his interest. He is, of course, thinking about potential research experiments for his dissertation, but Mr. deGrom is also thinking of the future. The combination of his doctoral special education coursework and his experiences in the classroom have left him with a wealth of ideas for research experiments. Due to time limitations, Mr. deGrom needs to gain a greater focus on exactly what he wants to research.

DEVELOPING IDEAS

Graduate students enter degree programs with varied outlooks on the trajectory of their individual research agendas. Perhaps you find yourself overwhelmed with the number of ideas you have for research experiments? Maybe you entered the degree program laser-focused on an idea for a large, longitudinal research experiment? Perhaps the goal of examining one particular intervention is what led you to enroll in a doctoral program? Then again, other students may begin this phase of their professional life without a clear idea or understanding about the specific kinds of research that will fuel their curiosity. It is not uncommon for novice researchers to enter graduate programs in any of these situations.

Although ideas for research may develop through engagement with existing literature or exploration of a specific theory, many researchers begin their career conducting research that aligns with personal experience. Because a large amount of time and effort will be dedicated to an experiment, researchers benefit from selecting broad topics with which they feel they have a connection. With experience comes knowledge and understanding, which should not be discounted when developing ideas for research. For example, a graduate student who had a large amount of experience with academic interventions for students with disabilities read an article and became quite interested in sex education instruction for students with low-incidence disabilities. For novice researchers, such as this student, it is perhaps best to draw on personal knowledge and experience when developing early research experiments rather than starting an experiment with limited background. However, potential research experiments should be ones in which the researcher may remain objective, even if there is a personal connection to the topic.

When determining the nature of experiments to undertake, researchers may also find themselves drawn toward specific methodologies. This text covers a variety of methodologies, most of which fall into one of two broad categories of empirical research: *quantitative* and *qualitative*. The former involves research that uses statistical methods to present findings that are represented numerically, while the latter includes systematic analysis of written, spoken, or observational data with results that rely heavily on written narrative or other artistic media (American Psychological Association [APA], 2020). Some research methodologies include both quantitative and qualitative elements, such as mixed-methods research and single case research design. This chapter includes a more detailed discussion about the connection between research questions and research methodologies.

How does one identify research experiments that are relevant, meaningful, and viable? How does a researcher take an idea and develop it into something that can be beneficial to the research community, practitioners, policy makers, and the researcher's own career? The following sections describe issues researchers must consider when pursuing experiments. Table 2-1 highlights guiding questions for researchers.

TABLE 2-1. QUESTIONS TO CONSIDER WHEN DEVELOPING RESEARCH PROJECTS	
QUESTION	**CONSIDERATION**
Is the research relevant?	Does existing literature support the need for the study?
Is the research meaningful?	Is this beneficial to the intended consumers?
Is the research viable?	Do you have the resources necessary to complete the study?

Is the Research Relevant? A Review of the Literature

As research experiments seek to add to existing literature, the task of becoming familiar with related existing studies is essential. Although a more in-depth review of existing research will be conducted to develop the literature review section of a manuscript, scholars must explore these works in the early phases of a study. It is not necessary to start with a specific research question (described later in the chapter); initial reviews of the literature may commence with a general idea for a research experiment. Exploration of existing research will help hone broad ideas into more specific and targeted research experiments. Published studies generally include recommendations from the authors that describe implications and considerations for future research. Researchers may consider using these recommendations for future research to guide their own research experiments, promoting alignment with existing literature.

Research manuscripts generally begin with the statement of a problem; this frames the research and presents a case for the need for the current study. When exploring existing literature to identify experiment ideas, researchers should also begin seeking documentation to support the need for the study. This could involve identifying concerns from previous studies or exploring results from large-scale data experiments to support the notion that a need exists (Chapter 4 includes recommendations for reading research articles). If unable to document the need for a study, researchers should consider focusing efforts on experiments that address a genuine, rather than perceived, need.

In addition to understanding the extent to which the potential research experiment aligns with current literature, a broad overview of existing literature helps researchers increase awareness of existing theories and the degree to which they have been studied. If a topic has been covered in great detail and depth, an additional study may not be relevant to the field. Researchers must develop experiments with an awareness of how a new research experiment will benefit both researchers and practitioners. Researchers often seek to embark on projects that address a gap in the literature, or a research area that has not been addressed by any existing studies.

In other instances, a review of the literature may yield information that shows existing studies are outdated and are not representative of current contexts or have findings that are not generalizable (Chapter 6 includes recommendations for evaluating systematic reviews). In these instances, it may be appropriate for researchers to conduct research in the same or similar manner as an existing study, known as *replication*. Replication studies increase the validity of research findings, and when delivered in different contexts, can provide consumers with a greater understanding of the extent to which results are generalizable. The heart of the evidence-based practice (EBP) movement in special education is identifying interventions that have multiple replications demonstrating that the intervention improves socially significant outcomes for students with disabilities. Although replication studies are less common in some areas of special education research, there have been recent calls in the field for researchers to consider conducting replication studies (Makel et al., 2016). Coyne et al. (2016) provide specific recommendations for researchers interested in conducting replication studies in special education.

While reviewing literature, researchers should begin to develop a conceptual framework for the study. In broad terms, a conceptual framework is a theory developed through consideration of previous studies that frames a new study (Smyth, 2004). Rather than viewing a new study as existing in isolation, a conceptual framework acknowledges and weaves in the tapestry of research that has come before. Maxwell (2012) described a conceptual framework as a preliminary theory of what is being studied based on existing literature that informs the research design by: (a) evaluating goals, (b) developing appropriate research questions, (c) determining methods, (d) justifying the purpose of and need for the study, and (e) identifying potential threats to validity (more on this in the next section). Although it is based on content presented in previous studies, a conceptual framework is newly constructed by the researcher and can be presented visually (e.g., text narrative, figure) or not directly included in the research product.

When conducting reviews of the literature, novice researchers should develop a system for filing and organizing materials gleaned from searches. Implementing a systematic way of organizing resources at an early career stage will be beneficial with current and future research projects. Researchers may choose to use a commercially available platform for resource organization, including Zotero, EndNote, and Mendeley. When selecting a specific platform, researchers should explore expenses (some are available at no cost) and specific features that may be relevant to the user. It may also be valuable to discuss these platforms with other faculty members and explore training and support options that may be available through the library.

Social Validity: Is the Research Meaningful?

When developing ideas for studies, it is essential that researchers consider the value of the experiment to others in the field. A well-designed and implemented research experiment is of little value to the researcher and practitioner communities if it is not viewed in a positive light by the consumers. In a foundational work, Wolf (1978) coined the term *social validity* to acknowledge the importance of society and the consumer in the research process. In research, *validity* broadly refers to the extent to which a study presents a sound argument to support a claim or finding (Polkinghorne, 2007). With social validity, researchers seek to ensure that the study is meaningful to consumers. Wolf explained that putting social validity on par with the objective measurements of a study "will bring the consumer, that is society, into our science, soften our image, and make more sure our pursuit of social relevance" (p. 207).

Although Wolf described social validity as it relates to Applied Behavior Analysis, the description can be applied to research in other areas as well. The author described three areas of consideration when determining the social validity of a study, each of which should be considered in the development phase of a research experiment. The first involves the goals of the study; if these are not valued by society, the research may not be worth pursuing. The second area of social validity involves the extent to which the procedures are socially appropriate. When considering the entirety of the study implementation, are there any phases or components that involve treatments that consumers (including participants) may view as unfavorable, harmful, or logistically impossible to implement in current contexts? Finally, the third area is focused on the social value of the effects of the study as it relates to consumer satisfaction. Research seeks to address a problem; however, if the consumers of research do not view the findings as being valuable or worthwhile, then the study itself is perhaps not of benefit to the community. The degree of improvement needs to be large enough to improve quality of life for the consumer and others in a meaningful way.

Researchers in special education who are committed to developing studies with high levels of social validity may consider involving stakeholders in the process. Direct involvement of those who have first-hand accounts and strong connections to the topic being researched will help ensure that an experiment provides a meaningful contribution to the literature. Special education researchers may decide to work directly with practitioners in a variety of capacities to solicit input and guidance to align the research with the needs in the field. These collaborations may result in action research projects. Action research helps to minimize the research-to-practice gap by not only identifying problems, but exploring potential solutions to solve them by involving the practitioners who are in the classroom (Bruce & Pine, 2010).

When conducting research on interventions to improve educational outcomes for students with disabilities, researchers may consider partnering with individuals with disabilities in the process of planning research studies when feasible. Because of the focus on individuals with disabilities, inclusive research helps ensure the meaningfulness of special education studies. Walmsley and Johnson (2003) described inclusive research as "involv(ing) people who may otherwise be seen as subjects for the research as instigators of ideas, research design, interviews, data analysts, authors, disseminators, and users" (p. 10). Bigby et al. (2014) identified three general roles for individual with disabilities in inclusive research:

1. Advisory: Individuals with disabilities support the development or implementation of research projects
2. Leading and Controlling: People with disabilities are empowered to design and carry out a research project
3. Collaborative Groups: A partnership between researchers with and without disabilities where the unique contributions of each party are equally valued

Exploring Logistics: Is the Research Viable?

Even when a relevant and meaningful research experiment is identified, it may become apparent that the project is not viable due to the logistics required to complete the study. When developing ideas, researchers need to be aware of their available resources to understand if the experiment is worth pursuing. The financial cost of a study is something a researcher must consider. Although many studies cost little to nothing, other experiments may require significant financial commitments. For example, a research study involving a technology-based intervention may have significant financial costs associated with the project. Researchers may want to consider accessing available resources through the university's technology center or assistive technology lending libraries if those exist in their state. In addition, it may be possible to procure funding to address financial limitations (described in greater depth later in this chapter); however, other barriers may limit the extent to which an experiment is viable. For example, even if a researcher procures grant funding to purchase a piece of technology with which to experiment in a classroom-based research study, it may not be viable for a school district to purchase similar technology tools. In other words, a study may be deemed not viable regardless of a brilliant idea and positive research findings.

Particularly with special education research, access to study participants may limit the extent to which a study is viable. Although some studies may involve the analysis of secondary (existing) data sets, much of what special education researchers are interested in studying requires having access to study participants. This may involve recruiting a small number of student participants for a single case research design (see Chapter 9), a small group of interviewees for a qualitative study (see Chapter 10), entire classes for an experimental or quasi-experimental study (see Chapters 7 and 8), or a larger group of participants to complete questionnaires as part of a survey design (see Chapter 13). Each requires the involvement of multiple parties, who may have varying degrees of willingness to support the research. The term gatekeeper describes the individual or individuals who prevent or allow access to potential study participants. Although the term is commonly associated with qualitative research paradigms, it could also be applied to quantitative researchers who need to recruit study participants to complete research experiments. Without a supportive gatekeeper, a research study may not be viable.

Another potential logistical limitation involves the resource of time. When completing a study to fulfill an academic degree requirement, researchers must consider the required duration to appropriately find answers to the questions they seek to explore. Anecdotally, it is recommended that doctoral candidates planning their dissertation research (especially if it is their first fully independent experiment) try to overestimate the duration of the study to accommodate for time spent on overcoming unplanned obstacles, amount of time necessary for data collection and analysis, and requirement to revise the written manuscript prior to submission for a final defense. For example, if a researcher is interested in the effects of a specific variable, the study may require longitudinal data that is not available in the time allotted.

In addition to considering the duration of the study, researchers must confirm they have the necessary personnel to ensure the viability of the study. Although it may be possible for researchers to conduct some studies independently, it is often necessary to call on the skills and expertise of others to complete a project. For example, additional personnel may be required to collect data on interobserver agreements or increase the credibility of analysis in qualitative research. Limited support from additional personnel can impact the viability of a research project.

Mr. deGrom has dabbled with assistive technology (AT) to help his students achieve their academic goals and recognizes its potential as a powerful tool when used correctly. With the support of professionals at his state AT center, he has explored a tool that he believes can significantly improve the writing of his students with disabilities. He has considered exploring this tool as the basis for a potential research project. Mr. deGrom has recognized the relevance of the research by exploring existing literature and finds manuscripts that support the notion that AT can improve student writing, but does not see anything about this specific tool. He knows this research is meaningful; writing is included in the state education standards and through conversations with teachers in his school, he knows that they struggle to support students with disabilities. As he begins to develop potential research questions, Mr. deGrom believes he has ideas for a viable study to explore the writing tool. His one potential concern is the availability of the technology to complete the project.

Categorizing Types of Scientific Investigation

Several approaches have been used to categorize types of research investigations. One useful approach is to think of research as *descriptive, relational, experimental,* or *qualitative* (Cook & Cook, 2016).

- Descriptive research aims to describe variables as they occur in the environment. This may be done through self-report using surveys or direct observation.
- Relational research aims to examine the relation between variables as they occur in the environment. This may be done through correlational research or nonexperimental research designs.
- Experimental research aims to examine if a functional relation is present between an independent variable and dependent variable(s). Worded another way, did the independent variable cause a change in the dependent variable(s) under investigation? This may be done through group design, quasi-experimental designs, or single case research designs.
- Qualitative research aims to provide a thick, rich description of phenomena that occur in the environment. This may be done through case studies, ethnographies, or grounded theory.

An important consideration here is every research design listed is useful in addressing a problem identified in society and improving the outcomes for students with disabilities (Table 2-2).

Developing Research Questions

Once a research idea has been identified as being relevant, meaningful, and viable, researchers must move toward developing specific research questions. Research questions are central components to an experiment; they precisely describe what a researcher aims to answer, understand, or explore. Just like ideas for projects, research questions may begin broader and become further refined as literature is explored. Although a research experiment may have more than one research question,

TABLE 2-2. CATEGORIZING RESEARCH QUESTIONS BY TYPE

Problem statement: Students with disabilities are underperforming in mathematics, particularly in their mathematical problem solving.

Descriptive research	• What instructional practices do special education teachers report using when teaching mathematical problem solving? • What instructional practices are special educators observed using during mathematics instruction? What amount of time is spent on mathematical problem-solving instruction?
Relational research	• Do cognitive profiles predict student's mathematical problem-solving performance? • What mathematical skills predict student's mathematical problem-solving performance?
Experimental research	• Is there a functional relation between schema-based instruction and an increase in mean level in mathematical problem solving of students receiving special education services in a resource room setting? • To what extent does providing instruction on mathematical problem structures improve the problem solving performance of students with disabilities over general strategy instruction on the problem-solving process?
Qualitative research	• How do special education teachers implement schema-based instruction?

it is critical to identify primary versus secondary research questions that will be feasible to address. Many researchers use the last paragraph of the literature review to restate the purpose of the research project and introduce the research questions. The key phrases included in the research purpose, and consequently the research questions, indicate the research methodology employed by the author(s). For example, if the purpose of the research is to examine perceptions of special education teachers in rural areas, the reader can expect the methodology in the manuscript to be qualitative. This practice allows them to connect the findings of the review of literature with the identified gap in existing research with a justification for the current investigation. Anecdotally, when completing peer reviews of papers, we often refer to the stated research questions to ensure that all parts of the paper are well-aligned with these items. Table 2-3 demonstrates examples of phrases used in research statements and questions and their indication of research methodology.

Several considerations must be made to evaluate the appropriateness of a research question. High-quality research questions are specific and focused. For example, researchers should avoid broad questions such as "How effective are behavior management strategies when working with students with autism spectrum disorder?" The field of behavior studies is quite large; researching a large question like this is unmanageable and will not result in the precise kinds of information that good research seeks to provide. Although research questions may seek to understand relationships or differences between variables (mostly quantitative studies), other research questions may be more descriptive or exploratory. In these cases, research questions should lead to focused explorations. For example, answering the question "What do students with disabilities want to do after high school?" is too broad for a successful research project.

TABLE 2-3. RESEARCH PURPOSE AND QUESTIONS IN VARIOUS METHODOLOGIES

KEY PHRASES IN RESEARCH PURPOSE AND QUESTIONS	ALIGNMENT TO METHODOLOGY
Examine effectiveness	Single case or quantitative
Examine perceptions	Qualitative
Explore experiences	Qualitative
Address the feasibility and effectiveness	Mixed methods

TABLE 2-4. WEAK AND IMPROVED RESEARCH QUESTIONS

WEAK RESEARCH QUESTION	IMPROVED RESEARCH QUESTION
How effective are behavior management strategies when working with students with autism spectrum disorder?	Is there a functional relation between the use of behavior-specific praise delivered by paraeducators and an increase in on-task behavior for students with autism spectrum disorder during independent work time?
What do students with disabilities want to do after high school?	What fields of work do students with intellectual disabilities expect to pursue after finishing high school?
Do students with disabilities struggle in school?	How do the results on state common core assessments for middle school students with disabilities compare to students without disabilities?
Does providing multiple means of expression for high school science assessments lead to improved outcomes?	To what extent does providing multiple means of expression for high school science assessments lead to improved learning outcomes?

Good research questions also seek to answer questions or explore topics that are novel and do not represent common knowledge. For example, seeking to design research that answers the question "Do students with disabilities struggle in school?" would not be valuable to the field. In addition to lacking specificity, we already know the answer to this question. Research questions should also be written so that they require interpretation. Perhaps most notably, researchers should develop questions that require more than a "yes/no" answer.

Researchers often address this concern by adding qualifiers such as "to what extent..." to acknowledge that a binary finding does not provide the depth that critical consumers of research desire. Table 2-4 provides examples of weak research questions that have been improved.

Selecting a Research Design

Once a researcher determines a research question worth investigating, the next sequential step is to decide on the research design. Selecting the research design is usually determined by one of two factors: (a) the researchers' expertise and/or preference for a particular design or (b) the nature of the research question. Based on their theoretical and methodological preparation, some researchers will naturally be driven to questions examining participants' experiences, beliefs, or reflections; thus, they will choose qualitative methodology. Others might naturally gravitate toward research questions focused on exploring the effects of an intervention or comparisons between larger groups, and thus will choose quantitative methodologies.

Some graduate programs recommend that the doctoral candidate choose a path or a research track and hone in deeply on a certain research methodology. As a result, some researchers will only conduct quantitative studies, while others solely focus on qualitative data collection and analysis. Consequently, if a researcher received training that focused on quantitative methodologies, it is unlikely they will naturally navigate toward research questions that would be best addressed with qualitative measures.

Conversely, Mertens (2010) proposed that researchers should be pragmatic with a broad base of research methodology knowledge and skills, which allows the research questions to dictate the research design. In other words, a researcher identifies a broad area of research, consults the literature, identifies a gap, formulates a research question, and based on that question determines the most fitting research design. For example, if a researcher wants to address a question of whether a particular behavior intervention is effective for young children diagnosed with autism spectrum disorder, they may want to use single case research design (e.g., Gast, 2010) to conduct research. Similarly, if the focus of the research study is to compare the learning growth between fourth graders using a particular curriculum, then a group design (e.g., Vogt, 2007) is more feasible. Lastly, if the researcher is interested in a comprehensive analysis of certain phenomena, a qualitative methodology (e.g., Hatch, 2002) would be the best match. A more detailed discussion of these methods will be presented later in this text.

There are proponents and opponents of both these approaches. Some researchers advocate for in-depth knowledge and skills expertise in only one research methodology. Others support a broader knowledge base with a recognition that a rigorous study in a less-than-familiar research design may require building a collaborative research team that includes experts in that design. To summarize, early career researchers have two basic choices when it comes to research design: (a) rely on their own expertise and knowledge and allow their methodological strengths to determine the true nature of the research questions, or (b) explore the research question they want to pursue and then align research design to that question, even if it requires recruiting collaborators who are more experienced with specific methodologies.

Research Standards

In 2003, the Council for Exceptional Children (CEC) Division of Research created a task force to develop guidelines for designing, conducting, and reporting high-quality research. The work of this task force resulted in five widely cited manuscripts, with four dedicated to different research designs and one focused on general EBPs and quality of scientific methods. For example, while conducting and disseminating qualitative research studies, authors should ensure that they address qualitative research standards described by Brantlinger et al. (2005). Researchers are encouraged to familiarize themselves with these standards early in the research development because they may provide guidance as to how studies are designed. Authors can then cite these documents to show the connectivity between these recommendations and their current study.

As the EBP movement increased in the field of special education, the CEC provided explicit standards for evaluating experimental research designs (i.e., group, single case) in the document

Council for Exceptional Children's Standards for Evidence-Based Practice (2014). These standards parallel the original special issue published in *Exceptional Children* (2005); however, they also articulated how a practice becomes identified as an EBP for a particular population. Readers are encouraged to reference these indicators *a priori* when in the design stage of an experimental project and when writing up the report for publication.

Although not unique to the field of special education, the WWC has released multiple versions of their standards handbook to guide the development and evaluation of research publications. In addition, they provide a procedures handbook that outlines their approach for evaluating the research supporting specific practices to make decisions regarding the quantity and quality of the evidence base.

You may wonder, which set of indicators should I use? Although beyond the scope of the current chapter, we would recommend that researchers consult both sets in the research development and reporting process. Differences are identified across both sets of rubrics, so consulting both sets of indicators will allow you to develop an experiment with more internal and external validity (see Maggin et al., 2014).

ASSEMBLING A RESEARCH TEAM

Many fields outside of education place a particular value on solo research. At some institutions of higher education, faculty are expected to publish single-author papers and conduct independent research. However, this may not be the case in education, especially not in special education. Special education research is often collaborative in nature. Research teams might include multiple faculty members, K-12 teachers, undergraduate or graduate students, or even individuals with disabilities. Therefore, as long as faculty members can demonstrate that their scholarship portfolios contain a variety of publications, including some where they are the first author, the university might adjust their solo-authored papers expectations. Alternatively, in addition to their dissertation research, early career faculty members and graduate students might want to consider leading research projects and taking the first authorship role on manuscripts to demonstrate their ability to lead.

Reasons for this may relate to the size of the special education field or number of possible students in our population pool. In the field of special education, a larger emphasis is placed on the order of the authors in a manuscript, which indicates the hierarchy of roles in conducting the research. When assembling a research team, the researcher may want to ponder the following questions:

- Is it feasible to conduct this research study alone?
- Do I have enough expertise in the chosen research methodology?
- Do I have colleagues with whom I work well?
- Are there fellow students who would benefit from research experience and could work with me?
- Are there practitioners or individuals that I want to recruit as active research team members?

The feasibility and scope of research, and thus the size of the research team, vastly depends on the chosen methodology. For example, some quantitative studies may involve an analysis of a large pre-existing data set (e.g., National Longitudinal Transition Study-2), in which case it may be feasible for a single author to handle the entire process. Conversely, an experiment using a single case research design in a K-12 classroom may require involving classroom teachers or paraprofessionals as data collectors to ensure consistency of data collection (see Chapter 9). Similarly, a large qualitative study consisting of in-depth interviews may be more feasible to conduct with several interviewers and then several data analysts for the purposes of triangulation and reliability of the findings (see Chapter 10). The next few sections will focus on research team structure and assignments.

Team Member Roles in Data Collection and Analysis

In addition to any research ethics training required by the university, it is the responsibility of the lead researcher to train the team in the data collection protocols. Research team training may vary depending on the chosen research methodology. In a qualitative study, the training might involve collaborative designing of the interview questions and reviewing the protocols for administering these questions (Holstein & Gubrium, 2003). When conducting focus group interviews (Hatch, 2002), the training may include specific behavior requirements for each team member (e.g., refraining from showing any emotional reactions to participants' responses). Such training could be as simple as reviewing the protocols during a single meeting or as involved as conducting several practice sessions until all team members demonstrate consistent behaviors. Conversely, training for a research team collecting data for a single case research design might be much more involved (Gast, 2010), from operationalizing the behaviors to be observed, to practicing the use of data sheets, to ensuring the reliability of data across multiple observers. As much as the task might be daunting at first, it is critical for rigorous study design. Moreover, it is paramount that the researchers document all their procedures in detail and describe them in the manuscript to allow future replication studies.

As soon as the team has concluded the data collection (and sometimes parallel to the data collection), the next step is to divide the roles for data analysis. This step is again dependent on the type of research methodology. In a quantitative study, perhaps only the lead researcher will analyze the data and the other team members verify its accuracy and discuss the implications for the research hypothesis. In a qualitative study, there is a wide range of possibilities, from lead researcher analyzing the data and sending it for triangulation among the team, to collaborative code book and theme development, all the way to constant comparative analysis, which requires all researchers analyzing all of the data simultaneously (Glaser, 1965). In single case research, at least two team members should check the data entry from the data collection sheets (if used) and verify the agreements among the data collectors. For this particular design, it is imperative to include actual calculations of the agreement among data collectors where the higher the percentage of the agreement, the more reliable the findings.

Manuscript Authorship

When working with a team on a research experiment, decisions will need to be made about authorship. APA (2020) provides guidance for determining publication credit, explaining that "authorship is reserved for persons who make a substantial contribution to and who accept responsibility for a published work" (p. 24). Although other fields may vary the order of authorship, in special education research it is generally determined by the level of contribution of each author (greatest to least). The task of delegating responsibilities usually falls on the principal (lead) author, which can feel daunting to an early career scholar. It is essential to have honest and frank conversations about manuscript authorship and the order of the author names early on so that everyone is clear on their expectations. It is the responsibility of the principal author to delegate responsibility and identify specific tasks for each team member to complete. When recruiting co-authors, principal authors should be specific about the order of authors by offering colleagues roles, such as "second author." Institutions of higher education have varying requirements for promotion and tenure for faculty members that relate to the order of authorship. For example, for some research-focused universities, greater weight is placed on first-authored publications.

Mr. deGrom continues to explore existing literature and formulates research questions to better understand how the AT tool might impact student writing. The nature of what he seeks to answer, and the participants he has available, have led him to believe that the research questions are best answered using single case design. In exploring previous studies involving AT and writing, he has recognized that other researchers have used similar methods to answer their research questions. This helps Mr. deGrom feel confident that he has made a wise choice. Recognizing that the data analysis will require additional support, he has recruited peers at the university to join his project. In addition to analyzing data, he has assigned writing tasks to his two co-authors and provides them with clear deadlines and expectations.

For the purposes of this chapter, we define the principal researcher (or author) as the one who initially coined the idea and initiated the research process by inviting co-authors into the project. In most teams, the lead author takes on the majority of the manuscript preparation; however, each team member's strengths and areas of expertise should be carefully considered when dividing the tasks. Some people may be strong in finding and analyzing the literature or formulating the argument for conducting the study. Others may have expertise in the chosen methodology and be very detail oriented; these team members may be best suited to developing the Method section of the manuscript. Whatever the task assignment, the principal author is responsible for preparing most of the manuscript, designing and executing the timelines, and keeping all team members accountable and on task. Some practical strategies for accomplishing this task include using a shared file folder (e.g., Dropbox, Google Drive, OneDrive), scheduling regular check-in meetings, and setting up deadlines for completion of each writing task. Finally, the principal author is responsible for ensuring that the research is rigorous and aligned with the established standards for the chosen methodology (see Table 2-5 for misconceptions and rationale).

FUNDING FOR SPECIAL EDUCATION RESEARCH

Although it is possible to complete some research projects without funding, others will require additional resources. As a graduate student, options for grant funding may be limited to internal funding opportunities (i.e., from the college or university with which one is affiliated) or grants created to support student research projects. Seeking grants as a graduate student will help support research, but also potentially lay the foundation for the acquisition of future grant funding. For example, procuring grant funding as a graduate student may lead to early career grants to continue research that began as a graduate student. These experiences and opportunities support the development of one's research agenda, a key factor in how researchers typically define themselves professionally. Students may also aim to align themselves with faculty who have procured grant funding in their area of interest. These experiences working on grants as a graduate student will help develop an increased understanding of the grant funding landscape.

After completing a graduate degree, additional opportunities for grant funding may exist. Grants are awarded by many different agencies, ranging from local nonprofit organizations or small businesses to large corporations, federal agencies, and international foundations. Within the field of special education, there are many opportunities to apply for grants that align with specific research interests or populations. This may include one or more of the following: (a) specific disability categories (e.g., intellectual disabilities, autism spectrum disorder), (b) research settings (e.g., rural, suburban, or urban public school districts, Bureau of Indian Education schools), (c) types of interventions (e.g., assistive technology, positive behavioral interventions and supports), (d) age of participants (e.g., infant/toddler, transition-age youth), or (e) specific research topics (e.g., STEM, independent living skills). Funding agencies evaluate grant proposals based on a variety of factors, including adherence to the requirements outlined in the Request for Proposals (RFP), alignment of the aims of

TABLE 2-5. COMMON MISCONCEPTIONS AND CLARIFICATIONS ABOUT RESEARCH IN SPECIAL EDUCATION

MISCONCEPTION	BETTER UNDERSTANDING
Special education research is usually conducted by a single author completing a research project independently.	Research conducted in teams is often stronger, and as such most special education research is conducted with teams. Assembling a team allows for the recruitment of individuals who have knowledge and strengths that complement those of the lead researcher, often leading to a project that is of higher quality.
Key stakeholders should never be involved in the research process.	Although it may be true that including people with vested interest in a research study may cause concern (due to conflict of interest), there are situations in which adding these individuals may increase the validity of a study. For example, when conducting an action research project, it is appropriate (and encouraged) to include a classroom teacher as part of the research team. Also, teams may want to consider inclusive research, which seeks to elevate individuals with disabilities from participants to key collaborators with insight and perspectives not otherwise represented on the project.
Research projects are not possible without grant funding.	When exploring the viability of a potential project, researchers should consider the need for external funding. Although it may be necessary for some projects to launch, many research questions can be answered without the need for funding. Of course, colleges and universities appreciate researchers seeking external funding, but it is often not necessary to complete a project.

the proposed research study with the funding agency's mission, clarity and quality of writing, and scope of work. When considering a grant proposal, each reviewer must have a clear idea of how the research study is relevant, meaningful, and viable so that it will improve outcomes for students with disabilities.

Searching for and Developing Grant Proposals

Before developing a grant proposal, it is necessary to conduct a search of RFPs and then carefully select an appropriate funding opportunity. There are several different search engines for finding grants. Based on the terms and criteria of the search query, these search engines will generate a list of open RFPs. It is possible to search previous RFPs in order to develop a sense of previous grants and to gain familiarity with the various formats of proposals that have received funding. Links to search engines, including Pivot, Grants.Gov, and SPIN can be found in the resource list included in Table 2-6.

There are many federal agencies within the United States that award grants on an annual basis. For special education teachers, administrators, and researchers, the U.S. Department of Education offers a wide array of funding opportunities for research and program development. To begin a

TABLE 2-6. ADDITIONAL RESOURCES	
RESOURCE	**DESCRIPTION**
Zotero https://www.zotero.org Endnote https://endnote.com Mendeley https://www.mendeley.com/?interaction_required=true	Reference management software tools that allow researchers to organize resources electronically
https://apastyle.apa.org	APA Style provides support related to APA guidelines
https://community.cec.sped.org/dr/new-item/new-item5	Council for Exceptional Children (CEC) Quality Indicators for Research Methodology and Evidence Based Practices
https://www.cec.sped.org/Membership/Special-Interest-Divisions	Council for Exceptional Children (CEC) Special Interest Divisions
Standards Handbook https://ies.ed.gov/ncee/wwc/Docs/referenceresources/WWC-Standards-Handbook-v4-1-508.pdf Procedures Handbook https://ies.ed.gov/ncee/wwc/Docs/referenceresources/WWC-Procedures-Handbook-v4-1-508.pdf	What Works Clearinghouse Standards and Procedures Handbooks (Version 4.1)
Grants.gov https://www.grants.gov U.S. Department of Education Grant Forecast https://www2.ed.gov/fund/grant/find/edlite-forecast.html Pivot https://pivot.proquest.com SPIN https://spin.infoedglobal.com/Authorize/Login	Resources for finding external funding opportunities
Additional Reading Orlich, D., & Shrope, N. (2013). *Developing a winning grant proposal*. Routledge.	

search for funding opportunities through the U.S. Department of Education, a researcher will need to start with the Grants Forecast (see Table 2-6). Within the Grants Forecast, funding opportunities are categorized by six different departmental divisions: the Institute of Education Sciences; the Office of Elementary and Secondary Education; the Office of Postsecondary Education; the Office of Special Education and Rehabilitative Services (OSERS); the Office of Career, Technical and Adult Education; and the Office of English Language Acquisition. OSERS is an excellent source of grants for research and program development. It may also be possible to find grant opportunities through other federal agencies outside of education that offer funding opportunities that may be relevant to specific research interests (e.g., National Endowment for the Humanities, National Science Foundation). For grant seekers affiliated with a college or university, there may be support staff who are able to identify specific listings of grants. Larger research universities often have an Office of Grant Development or similar department that supports graduate students and faculty members in searching for grants and developing and submitting grant proposals. These individuals have expertise in grant writing and may also be able to suggest specific funding agencies that have previously funded similar research studies.

While searching for RFPs, it is important to evaluate how closely the intended research study fits the listed scope of work. This generally includes the timeframe for conducting the study, from obtaining approval from the university's Institutional Review Board, to recruiting participants, to collecting and analyzing all necessary data. The grant proposal for the research study also includes a budget describing the required funds, which may include items such as personnel, materials, travel, and other expenses. Grant proposals also require a description of a target timeframe for completing the study and providing deliverables to the funding agency. Selecting appropriate RFPs requires individuals to be realistic about the time, personnel, and facilities at the disposal of the researcher. It is necessary to calculate the number of people available to work on the study, for how many hours per week, the estimated cost of all materials needed to complete the study, and the availability of facilities where they plan to carry out the research (e.g., a conference room to provide in-service training to special education teachers or a computer lab equipped with touchscreen monitors for participants).

Even though a successful grant proposal results in the university receiving funding, there are costs and logistical constraints involved in completing the plan of work outlined in the grant proposal. Failing to complete the plan of work or failing to submit deliverables, such as data analyses, written reports, or educational products by the established deadlines results in serious legal and financial repercussions for the researcher and the associated university or other institution. For this reason, it is critical to submit proposals only for grants that are realistically manageable with a high level of quality assurance.

Writing a Successful Grant Proposal

The ability to write successful grant proposals allows researchers to make a sustainable, systems-level impact on the lives of students with disabilities and the professionals who educate them. The process of writing a grant proposal is complex; having a faculty member or other collaborator with substantial experience in writing and reviewing grant proposals provide feedback on the proposal throughout the various stages of writing and revising is highly recommended. As such, starting as early as possible is recommended. Grant writers should also work to use written language that is specific and explicit. The tone of the writing should instill confidence that the project is strong and that this specific team is well-equipped to manage the project. Przeworski and Salomon (1988) identified four questions that reviewers of grants generally consider, which should be in the minds of grant proposal authors. These questions include: (a) what will be learned that is not already known or supported with research?, (b) why is this worth knowing or understanding better?, (c) how will researchers be able to show that the goals were achieved?, and (d) have the authors shown that they have the means to realize the project?

It is essential that grant writers follow the RFP exactly as is requested. This cannot be stressed enough; there have been instances of lengthy grant proposals being rejected solely because the formatting of a table was not as described in the RFP. The length, format, and style of the grant proposal varies depending on the selected RFP. However, many RFPs include common sections. As a general rule, an RFP consists of the statement of the problem that the research study aims to address, along with a description of a proposed research study (the plan of work) and the resources required to complete the plan of work (including materials, equipment, facilities, personnel, and budget), and the justification for the required resources (Orlich & Shrope, 2013).

Grant writers may consider using the logic model to help develop ideas for projects that may be funded by grants. The logic model is a team-based process based on theory of change that is used for program evaluation but may also be considered in the development or design phase of a project (McLaughlin & Jordan, 2015). As such, grant writers may consider this model so that the end goals of the project are clearly defined and identified. The key elements of a logic model include: required resources, program activities, outputs (i.e., good or services that result from the project), and outcomes (i.e., the short-term, intermediate, and long-term impact of the program). McLaughlin and Jordan (2015) described five stages associated with the construction of a logic model. These include: (a) having the team collect relevant information from a variety of sources, (b) identifying and defining the target problem and its context with clarity, (c) determining essential program components to address the problem, (d) developing a logic model that shows how program activities or components lead to desired outcomes (theory of change), and (e) validating the model with stakeholders.

WRITING AND PUBLISHING RESEARCH STUDIES

Even special education researchers who have conducted well-designed and -executed studies may struggle getting manuscripts accepted for publication if they are not written in a manner that aligns with standard conventions. In addition, researchers need to be intentional about the selection of potential outlets for their work. The following section provides guidance for researchers in writing and publishing written manuscripts that summarize a completed research study.

Preparing the Manuscript

Although many novice researchers may be aware that the Seventh Edition of the *American Psychological Association Publication Manual* (APA, 2020) includes information pertaining to writing mechanics, crediting sources, and formatting reference lists, it also provides other writing resources for authors. For example, the manual provides guidance for authors related to the structure and content of the manuscript. In addition, guidance is provided for clear and concise writing (including bias-free writing), as well as grammar and word usage. Authors are strongly encouraged to familiarize themselves with the APA Publication Manual for guidance in all phases of the writing process.

To become familiar with the specific requirements of a journal, researchers should look for "author guidelines" or "submission guidelines" on the journal's webpage. These guidelines may vary from journal to journal and include page count, abstract length, abstract structure, and submission format. Although most journals that relate to special education follow APA guidelines, there are occasionally journals from other disciplines that cross over into special education that may follow a different formatting style (e.g., American Medical Association). Whatever the style of the journal, authors must aim to follow the guidelines closely throughout the manuscript because written works that deviate from standard formatting may raise red flags with journal editors or reviewers.

Finding a Publication Outlet

When developing a manuscript, authors may consider potential journals and write with the specific outlet(s) in mind. To determine the extent to which a journal is a good fit, authors should explore the aims and goals of the journal. These are generally available on journal websites. The website usually includes descriptions of the types of articles published by the journal, which researchers should consider. For example, although all researchers are responsible for translating research to practice, some journals only publish practitioner-focused works (e.g., *Beyond Behavior, Intervention in School and Clinic, TEACHING Exceptional Children*), and do not consider manuscripts that present new research. Authors should be aware that some journals offer both research and practitioner-focused articles (e.g., *Learning Disabilities Research & Practice*); thus, it is important to review the journal information to better understand the types of featured manuscripts. Authors also should review manuscripts previously published in the journal to better understand the types of works they desire. This may be especially valuable when considering a journal that does not focus on special education. If this journal has not included previous content related to supporting students with disabilities, it may not be a good fit. Reviewing the members of the editorial board (usually included on journal websites) also may provide insight into the types of scholarly work valued by the publisher. Authors may consider contacting an editor with an abstract of a manuscript to receive feedback on the appropriateness of the topic for the specific journal.

When looking for potential outlets for special education research manuscripts, authors may consider exploring the CEC flagship journals. In addition to *Exceptional Children*, nearly all the 18 special-interest divisions publish a journal focused on the mission and specialization of the group. Another recommendation for finding potential homes for manuscripts involves reviewing the titles of journals in the published research that was described in the literature review. Recognizing that there is at least some connection between these manuscripts, these journals may be open to publishing new research about this specific topic. Also, when considering potential outlets, authors may explore the geographic emphasis of the journal. This can be done by reviewing previously published manuscripts and by reviewing the members of the editorial board. For example, if an author is seeking a home for a manuscript that features research specific to the context of the United States, an international journal or a journal with editorial board members who all come from another country may not be a good fit.

When considering potential journals, there also is value in understanding the quality of the journal. Some of the more prominent journals have a calculated impact factor (IF), a metric used to assess the quality of the journal by calculating the number of article citations from the publication. Many special education journals are not large enough to have an IF, and the ones that do are relatively low when compared to journals in other fields. For example, the highest IF for a special education journal is (at the time of publication) 2.854 (*Exceptional Children*), whereas the *Journal of the American Medical Association* is 51.3. Thus, any IF for a special education journal is an indicator of high quality. The acceptance rate of a journal is also an indicator of quality; lower percentages indicate a higher-quality journal. Many journals also provide a list of abstracting/indexing hosts, which can help consumers understand the quality of the journal. Researchers should be on the alert for predatory or unscrupulous journals; although it may be commonplace for journals in other fields to charge author or publication fees, legitimate special education journals rarely require payment from authors.

In addition to providing guidance in manuscript preparation, the APA manual (APA, 2020) includes an overview of the publication process. Most special education journals follow the double-masked peer review (formerly known as "double blind"), meaning that reviewers are not aware of the identity of the author(s), and vice versa. Journal editors facilitate this process and so they are aware of the identities of all parties. For many journals, editors review newly submitted manuscripts to decide if they should be sent out for peer review. If the manuscript contains fatal methodological flaws, does not meet writing or formatting standards, or does not align with the scope of work for the journal, the editor may decide to spare the efforts of the peer reviewers and reject the manuscript before sending it for review. Journals generally send the manuscripts to two or three peer reviewers, who provide feedback to the authors and make a recommendation for publication. As a response to authors, journal editors provide one of the following decisions: "acceptance," "invitation to revise and resubmit," or "rejection" (APA, 2020, pp. 379-381). Chapter 5 includes more information about the publication process and manuscript review and Chapter 15 addresses the translation of special education research to practice.

Mr. deGrom believed that the AT center would have the technology he needed to complete the research; however, this turned out not to be the case. He also submitted a grant proposal to a state organization. Due to his in-depth exposure to existing literature involving AT and writing, he was able to justify the need for the funds with little difficulty. Mr. deGrom was grateful to receive funding for his project; it was the final barrier to getting started with his research project. Mr. deGrom's planning was outstanding; he completed the research project and was able to document the effectiveness of the AT tool to improve the writing of students with disabilities. He was excited to share his findings with the research and practice communities and began the process of developing and submitting manuscripts.

Summary

Research in the field of special education is essential for establishing EBPs and bridging the research-to-practice gap to support academic, social, and postsecondary success for students with disabilities. Research in special education must be relevant, meaningful, and viable. Without considering these criteria, research projects may never move from the planning phase to becoming realized. Even worse, such projects may do more harm than good. Reflecting on relevance, meaningfulness, and viability of a project idea combined with a solid understanding of research methodologies will lead to high-quality research questions and a rigorous research design. Understanding of research team roles, manuscript authorship, and best collaboration practices is also very important. Finally, knowing which research project ideas will require external funding, and how to procure such funding, is essential knowledge for every researcher.

This chapter explored foundational criteria of high-quality research projects, best strategies for developing research questions, collaboration within a research team, and recommendations for seeking research funding. When following a rigorous and systematic protocol for development, execution, and dissemination, research in special education can be exciting, rewarding, and have a significant impact on the lives of individuals with disabilities.

CHAPTER REVIEW

1. Describe strategies researchers use to develop projects that are relevant, meaningful, and viable.
2. Identify considerations when developing research questions. How might these relate to the design of the study?
3. Why might a special education researcher decide to work with a research team? What are some considerations a lead author may need to make regarding a research team?
4. What are essential factors a researcher must consider when seeking and developing grant proposals?
5. Describe strategies for selecting potential journal outlets for research manuscripts.

REFERENCES

American Psychological Association. (2020). *Publication manual of the American Psychological Association* (7th ed.). Author.

Bigby, C., Frawley, P., & Ramcharan, P. (2014). Conceptualizing inclusive research with people with intellectual disability. *Journal of Applied Research in Intellectual Disabilities, 27*(1), 3-12.

Brantlinger, E., Jimenez, R., Klingner, J., Pugach, M., & Richardson, V. (2005). Qualitative studies in special education. *Exceptional Children, 71,* 195-207.

Bruce, S., & Pine, G. (2010). *Action research in special education.* Columbia University: Teacher College.

Cook, B., Buysse, V., Klingner, J., Landrum, T., McWilliam, R., Tankersley, M., & Test, D. (2014). Council for Exceptional Children: Standards for evidence-based practices in special education. *Teaching Exceptional Children, 46*(6), 206–212. https://doi.org/10.1177/0040059914531389

Cook, B. G., & Cook, L. (2016). Research designs and special education research: Different designs address different questions. *Learning Disabilities Research & Practice, 31*(4), 190-198. https://doi.org/10.1111/ldrp.12110

Coyne, M. D., Cook, B. G., & Therrien, W. J. (2016). Recommendations for replication research in special education: A framework of systematic, conceptual replications. *Remedial and Special Education, 37*(4), 244–253. https://doi.org/10.1177/0741932516648463

Gast, D. L. (2010). *Single subject research methodology in behavioral sciences.* Rutledge.

Glaser, B. (1965). The constant comparative method of qualitative analysis. *Social Problems, 12,* 436-445.

Hatch, J. A. (2002). *Doing qualitative research in education settings.* State University of New York Press.

Holstein, J. A., & Gubrium, J. F. (2003). *Inside interviewing: New lenses, new concerns.* Sage.

Johnson, E. S. (2015). Increasing rural special education teacher candidates' ability to implement evidence-based practices: A program description of the Boise State University TATERS program. *Rural Special Education Quarterly, 34*(1), 5-9. https://doi.org/10.1177/875687051503400103

Maggin, D. M., Briesch, A. M., Chafouleas, S. M., Ferguson, T. D., & Clark, C. (2014). A comparison of rubrics for identifying empirically supported practices with single-case research. *Journal of Behavioral Education, 23*(2), 287-311. https://doi.org/10.1007/s10864-013-9187-z

Makel, M. C., Plucker, J. A., Freeman, J., Lombardi, A., Simonsen, B., & Coyne, M. (2016). Replication of special education research: necessary but far too rare. *Remedial and Special Education, 37*(4), 205–212. https://doi.org/10.1177/0741932516646083

Maxwell, J. A. (2012). *Qualitative research design: An interactive approach* (Vol. 41). Sage.

Mayan, M. J. (2009). *Essentials of qualitative inquiry.* Left Coast Press.

McLaughlin, J. A., & Jordan, G. B. (2015). Using logic models. In K. E. Newcomer, H. P. Hatry, & J. S. Wholey, *Handbook of program evaluation* (4th ed., pp. 62-87). Wiley.

Mertens, D. M. (2010). Philosophy in mixed methods teaching. *International Journal of Multiple Research Approaches, 4*(1), 9-18.

Orlich, D., & Shrope, N. (2013). *Developing a winning grant proposal.* Routledge.

Polkinghorne, D. E. (2007). Validity issues in narrative research. *Qualitative Inquiry, 13*(4), 471-486.

Przeworski, A., & Salomon, F. (1988). Some candid suggestions on the art of writing proposals. Social Science Research Council. Retrieved from https://s3.amazonaws.com/ssrc-cdn2/art-of-writing-proposals-dsd-e-56b50ef814f12.pdf

Smyth, R. (2004). Exploring the usefulness of a conceptual framework as a research tool: A researcher's reflections. *Issues in Educational Research, 14*(2), 167-180.

Walmsley, J., & Johnson, K. (2003). *Inclusive research with people with learning disabilities past, present, and futures.* J. Kingsley Publishers.

Wolf, M. M. (1978). Social validity: the case for subjective measurement or how applied behavior analysis is finding its heart 1. *Journal of Applied Behavior Analysis, 11*(2), 203-214.

Vogt, W. P. (2007). *Quantitative research methods for professionals.* Pearson.

Conducting Research in Applied Settings
Practical Strategies for Forming Effective Partnerships

With contributions from Reesha Adamson, PhD; Felicity Post, EdD; and Jessica Nelson, EdD, BCBA, LBA

INTRODUCTION

The process for designing a research project can be a daunting task for educators to consider. However, having research that takes place within applied settings is critical to expanding the special education field and to understanding how practices are implemented within routine contexts. For example, the Institute of Education Sciences funds research aimed at investigating the effectiveness of interventions implemented in routine conditions. The construction and design of research questions is important. Therefore, understanding how to address school needs and develop a collaborative partnership focusing on the resources and costs required is vital to success. This chapter outlines the steps necessary for research project development and forming research partnerships. Outlined are components around making a request to schools, implementation of projects, feasibility, and ultimately ensuring that outcomes are shared with participants and educational stakeholders. Key concepts and questions are written for researchers to consider when beginning research, along with how to deconstruct a complex task into individual components.

Hott, B. L., Brigham, F. J., & Peltier, C.
Research Methods in Special Education (pp. 39-53).
© 2021 SLACK Incorporated.

CHAPTER OBJECTIVES

→ Recognize the importance of translating research to practice and how to begin the process.

→ Describe the process for forming research partnerships.

→ Determine feasible interventions and practices in collaboration with educators.

→ Apply evidence-based practices and measures within educational settings.

→ Discuss methods for sharing research findings with participants and stakeholders.

KEY TERMS

- **Attrition**: The loss of study participants due to external factors beyond the researchers' control.
- **Dissemination**: How research findings are shared amongst stakeholders.
- **Empirical Articles**: Data-based articles that have a sound methodology associated with their evaluation of practices.
- **Feasibility**: A simple assessment of the practicality of a proposed plan or practice.
- **Fidelity**: Ensuring that implementation is true to the recommended practice or design of the project.
- **Rapport**: Building a close relationship amongst people through effective communication and trust.
- **Retention**: The ability to keep participants from discontinuing their participation within the study.
- **Social Validity**: The acceptance and satisfaction by participants with an intervention.
- **Stipend**: A financial incentive for completing or working on a project.

FORMING EFFECTIVE SCHOOL PARTNERSHIPS

For individuals who want to conduct research with students and teachers in educational settings, the concept of creating a partnership with a school or district can be intimidating. We will discuss some pieces to consider for conceptualizing research in applied settings and how to ensure that researchers are creating a mutually beneficial structure to support their research agenda and all participating stakeholders.

Researchers must first understand the applied settings that they are entering. It is crucial to understand the priorities of administration and teachers in an educational setting to gain buy-in (the desire by individuals to want to participate in a project and see the value), collaboration (working in tandem with researchers and the research team), and support for research activities (committing time and effort to research activities and priorities). This can be established by creating a partnership with a school or district before research activities begin. To create a partnership, researchers may think about offering their time or volunteering to help support the school community. This may even include offering resources (e.g., training, sharing evidence-based resources such as IRIS Center professional development activities, National Center for Intensive Intervention IEP resources) that may be beneficial to the school in some way. At times, it can even help to become a familiar face within the school setting. Some ways to do this include: (a) volunteer in classrooms, (b) listen to or offer short professional development sessions at staff meetings, (c) enjoy lunch with teachers in the lounge and make conversation, (d) participate in greeting students during arrival or dismissal, or (e) volunteer to support afterschool activities. During this process, it will be important to create connections, which will allow potential research participants to trust the researcher and offer suggestions or recommendations for project implementation.

When beginning a research project within an applied setting, it is critical to consider the specific benefit of the site's participation (see Chapter 4 for a more thorough discussion of research ethics). Explicit communication regarding the potential benefits for the school, teachers, and students during initial meetings will increase the likelihood that stakeholders will want to support the research project. Furthermore, ensuring the potential benefits are in alignment with the priorities of administration (school and district) will also increase the likelihood of buy-in. For example, if a doctoral student has a research agenda focused on implementing positive behavioral interventions across contexts outside of a classroom and aims to replicate a previous project on school buses, it will be critical to know the following: (a) what percentage of students ride the bus versus car riders or walkers, (b) what is the frequency of school bus-related disciplinary referrals, and (c) whether this is a situation the administration feels needs to be addressed. Using information from the connections cultivated at the school will ensure the project is a good fit for the school and identify the types of incentives that will be meaningful for participation. In addition, it is helpful to efficiently explain plans for a project to individuals because school personnel have tight schedules. Providing specific information related to the amount of time, work, and disruption to the typical routine that participating individuals will experience is critical for recruitment. A balance must be struck between ensuring the research plans are systematic and thorough with the feasibility for teachers or students to participate in the research project. Also, it is beneficial to think about additional incentives that can be provided besides the potential benefits of participating, as this may not be enough for some participants. Some possibilities include additional tutoring, classroom support, access to or additional curriculum, or maybe even a small stipend. Many funding agencies, professional organizations, and universities have small grants that support student research and can be used for incentives. Asking professors or colleagues about available funding sources may increase the ability to recruit participants. See Chapter 2 for a more in-depth discussion of research funding opportunities.

Working in school settings to conduct educational research can be challenging. Researchers must consider that some of their participants (i.e., students or educators) will not complete the research project; therefore, plans for ways to increase retention and reduce the attrition rate are important. At times, educators may have medical emergencies, pregnancies, instructional adjustments, or lack of interest that preclude them from completing a project. Students may be noncompliant, or have housing or instructional changes that may prohibit them from participating. It is critical to take this factor into account and over-recruit participants. However, just like factors outside the researcher's control may influence participation, factors within the researcher's control can impact participation as well. Consider how to build rapport with individual participants and establish a connection so that they genuinely want to participate and are willing to complete the tasks at hand. Identify specific targets for building rapport and recruiting participants where you can highlight why teachers should participate and give them a tangible outcome to increase their willingness. Think about what could be offered that will be mutually beneficial to both parties. For example, consider a teacher who struggles with classroom management. The teacher is stressed out and overwhelmed daily by student behavior in the classroom. Implementation of a project that focuses on increasing student compliance would be beneficial to both the researcher and classroom teacher.

Navigating a situation involving implementing a new curriculum or practice that is not already familiar to the educational setting can be tricky. No one wants to be told that they are not doing something well, or that the practices or curriculum they are using are not efficient or effective, especially when individuals may have devoted a substantial amount of time to a practice. Instead, think about focusing on what individuals are doing well, and which interventions and practices you can build off of to get to the interventions or practices that you would like to implement. Possibly consider how you can speak to educators about implementing something in a different way than what they have done before. Focus on the idea that this "new" way may give them a more effective or efficient intervention, practice, or strategy to use. Or that the researcher is providing the educator with another opportunity and tool to support students. Researchers should view their role as a partner with educators. Although researchers are there to be completely objective, it is important to emphasize the partnership when and if any difficulties may arise. The researcher is not coming in as an expert, even though they may know more about a specific intervention. The researcher is considered a partner to solve a problem and to assist in making everyone's life a bit easier, because ultimately both have the same goal—to improve the educational outcomes in the classroom. Working to create a goal that will be beneficial for all individuals is considered *social validity*. This term means that individuals are accepting of an intervention and find it beneficial.

When beginning a research project and preparing for the implementation of an intervention, think about how to roll it out most effectively. Even for adults, research literature suggests that using a Show/Model/Practice With Feedback routine is most effective at increasing fidelity of implementation for teacher interventionists. What will this look like for all individuals involved? How can fidelity of training across participants be supported, and what can be done to increase the likelihood the project is completed successfully without any issues? Be sure that all materials that individuals will need for implementation are available and that educators are not required to create additional materials or to take additional time to set up. Another piece is to make training as easy as possible. This may include thinking about how to give training in the most efficient format and to follow up with quick guides for reference. Ultimately, the goal is to take as much work off of participants as possible because this is typically not part of their job, and you want to make sure that you are respectful of their additional commitment (IRIS, 2010).

Discrete Factors to Consider for Research Implementation

One of the most difficult components for beginning researchers is developing partnerships with schools and communities so they are welcome in the educational environments. A personal connection with an individual can assist with this process. This can be done through a university partnership, a friend who works within the environment, or even through a community connection. A personal connection helps to immediately establish a level of credibility that is difficult to attain otherwise. Pitching a research idea to the known individual is a way to start the process of recruitment. Often, if that individual finds your idea beneficial, they will be happy to make a connection with decision makers within the educational environment. It is important when making a request for research participation that you are efficient in your meeting, very understanding of scheduling limitations, and incredibly organized. Ensure that every piece of information that may be needed is available. Have a basic one- to two-page sheet that describes key components, including:

- Brief introduction of yourself
- Study purpose
- What you are requesting (time and resources in a bulleted list) from each type of participant
- Potential benefits and/or risks
- Your contact information

Include additional information in a packet that you can leave for their review. Follow up as soon as you leave with a thank you e-mail and be sure to set a date to speak again. See Figure 3-1 for a sample email. Table 3-1 outlines potential barriers to building partnerships and how to communicate effectively.

For the next meeting, schedule a phone call or a quick visit. At that time, ask what questions they may have, And answer all of the questions. If they do not consent to participate, ask them if there is anything that is holding them back from participating. If they say yes, take this consideration seriously, as they may have a legitimate concern with the project or format that you have not considered and can adjust, or they may cite environmental factors that make the site unsuitable. Either of these concerns is valid, as the researcher has already invested time in this site. If any factors that are

Dear Principal,

My name is Lauren Adams, and I am a Graduate Student in Special Education at Missouri State University. I am writing to you to determine if you have any potential interest in allowing me to conduct a research study at your school to help improve reading practices.

Study purpose: Identify typical reading practices used by teachers, reading specialists, or other instructional support of students (primarily grade 3-5) identified with and at-risk of emotional and behavioral disorders, the degree to which students benefit from reading practices, and training and professional development needs.

What I ask from administrators:

- Grant permission for me to recruit teachers and students for study participation.
- Recruitment will be done in a manner that does not interrupt or in any way disrupt typical school and teaching practices.
- School identity will be kept confidential.

What I ask from teachers:

- Complete a basic teacher demographic form (approximately 5 minutes to complete)
- Consent to allow me to periodically observe regularly scheduled reading instruction (approximately 6 times per year).
- Consent to allow me to interview participating teachers at a day and time that is convenient to them. The interview will take approximately 30 minutes and will be audio recorded.
- Send a researcher-written letter home with students for purposes of gaining parent consent for student participation. Students with parental consent and student assent will twice complete a brief standardized reading assessment and will be periodically observed during typical reading instruction.
- Teacher and school names will not be attached to any data. Teacher and school identity will be kept confidential.

Potential benefits:

- Teachers will receive information on the degree to which reading practices align with evidence-based practices.
- Teachers will receive recommendations for maximizing reading instructional time.

Risks:

- This study involves collecting information on typical teaching practices so no risks are associated with this project.

If you have any questions or are interested in participating, please contact me at your earliest convenience. I have also included a copy of my vita for you to review. Thank you for your time and consideration.

Lauren M. Adams
Graduate Student in Special Education
Missouri State University
Department of Counseling, Leadership and Special Education
100 Park Central Square
Springfield, MO 65897
(123) 457-7890
ladams@abc.edu

Figure 3-1. Sample email soliciting partnership.

TABLE 3-1. BARRIERS AND CONSIDERATIONS FOR RESEARCH PARTNERSHIPS

BARRIER	CONSIDERATIONS
Time commitment	Often, participants may not have the time to give for a project. It may be important to have varied levels of participation to encourage more involvement from participants based on their availability.
Project complexity	Sometimes projects are too complicated for implementation. Be as concise as possible and practice explaining it to others so that everyone understands the project purpose, their role, and what is expected.
Feasibility with existing professional development priorities	Projects may not be compatible with other professional development activities. Understand that an administrator's job is to help ensure that all teachers do not have too many obligations placed on them.
Other district/ school initiatives	District and school initiatives may compete for time and resources with the project. Be aware of these issues before you begin.
Resource commitment	Resources are necessary for all projects; make sure that you have the resources that you need to be effective.
Participant gain	Outline for participants why participation is important for them.
Recruitment support	Recruiting participants, especially students, will primarily fall on school personnel because they have established connections with families. It is critical to think about how to support recruitment and how to ensure that the needed sample size is obtained.

limiting participation cannot be remedied, politely accept that this may not be a good time for the project and ask about contacting them again in the future for participation in other projects.

Brief Introduction of Yourself

It is important to share why you want to implement the project. Is it for fulfillment of a specific class, part of the expectation of a university program, or is it for an entirely different reason? Sharing the research purpose can help educators form connections, understand the ask, and foster understanding that motives for research and acceptance within the school environment are genuine. Be brief within these statements by sharing three to four sentences about the request for participation.

Study Purpose

Next, share the purpose of your study. This should be a short paragraph about what is being investigated and why it is important. This is the chance to "hook" individuals on the need for the project and their participation. Many times, this is the only portion that they read before they ask questions, so it is critical that the study purpose is strong and logical.

What You Are Requesting

When making a request, decision-makers will want to know what sort of commitment the project requires, so it is important to lay out the time and resources that will be needed for project implementation. This will be quite detailed. It is important to be as specific as possible. Being transparent regarding approximate total time commitments is critical. Making an ask for 1 hour from educators is very different from asking for 10 hours of time. Consider if the requested time commitment is going to be proportionate to expected outcomes and benefits to the learning environment. Think about these "asks" as direct, measurable quantities. Start each sentence with a verb directly describing what is needed. Lay out the time and resource commitment for each participant (i.e., administrators, teachers, students).

Potential Benefits or Risks

Outlining the risks and benefits for decision-makers allows them to know explicitly what they may get out of participation, but also if there are any direct risks for participation. It is important to be completely forthcoming within recruitment, as this will help to reduce attrition and is part of your ethical obligation when conducting research with human participants. See Chapter 4 for a more detailed discussion of research ethics.

Contact Information

Finally, include your contact information and affiliation. It is important to give them multiple efficient ways to contact you so that they may ask questions at any time during your study. If the project is part of a class or under direct supervision, the supervisor's contact information must also be included. Researchers are responsible for their conduct throughout the project, and if there is any sort of a violation, participants need to know who to contact.

Other Factors to Consider

Outside of the request, there are larger factors that should be kept in mind when developing a research project for implementation. First, consider the research question. What is going to be the most efficient way to answer this question? Think about the smallest number of participants needed to answer the question. Begin on a small scale, then build and refine your intervention or questions based on what you have learned. See Chapter 2 for additional resources to support developing quality research questions. Initiating a project that has never been attempted before on a large scale can be problematic (e.g., measures are not effective, critical information is missing that is needed to answer research questions). Think small when developing questions and think about efficiency because researcher time is a valuable resource.

When considering recruitment, think about the incentives that are offered. How do these incentives align with the project and are they something research participants want? If there is a monetary incentive, what are possible funding options to help support this endeavor? Think about how to tie incentives to recruitment. Is this something that the researcher will give to participants only at the completion of the project or throughout? For short projects with minimal participation requirements, giving incentives at the end of the project may be fine, but for larger, more time-intensive projects, spacing out incentives may help to ensure continued interest and retention of participants. The incentive should match the individual's time and commitment.

It is important to consider what environment is going to be the most effective for implementation. Schools have multiple learning environments and classroom structures to consider, including general education, co-teaching settings, and self-contained settings. There are benefits and barriers to all of these environments, and this should be carefully considered. In addition, researchers should think about the benefits of rural versus urban contexts and which environment best fits the question that is being asked.

Finally, and probably most importantly, think about the cost of implementation. Consider the amount of time not only for participants, but also for the researcher. Often, individuals try to take on too much. Consider focusing on two to three research questions at most and think about how to be efficient in collecting data to support these questions.

CASE STUDY

Susan is a third-year graduate student at Graham University. She is interested in furthering her research experience and has been given an opportunity to be part of a research team that includes two College of Education faculty members. These two faculty members recently applied for grant funding made available to them through their local grant office. They will work closely with the grant office throughout their research project to ensure proper fulfillment of all grant expectations and to answer any questions they may have. The research team has a scheduled meeting to begin discussing the feasibility of their research project so that they may reach out to a local school as a potential research partner.

During their conversation, the research team creates a feasibility checklist that includes all necessary factors for successful completion of their research project. This checklist will be used to guide the conversation with the school staff at their meeting on Wednesday of the coming week. The team is sure to include all factors that will play a role in their research to determine whether or not the school is a good fit for the project and if the project is feasible for the school team.

On Wednesday, the research team sits down with the principal, two third-grade teachers, and the school social worker to talk through the project, as they will be the key players working side-by-side with the research team on implementation. After explaining their research idea, they talk through all factors on their feasibility checklist to determine if moving forward is a good plan. The checklist includes an opportunity for the school team to identify what resources are already available and what will be needed as a result of this project and to determine outcomes, direction for stakeholder input, a schedule for implementation, training, and discussions related to buy-in of stakeholders. This conversation is a starting point for the project.

After meeting with the research team, the school team designs a survey for all stakeholders to complete in relation to the project. Stakeholders will include parents, staff, and students. This will allow the school team to determine interest regarding the project and foresee any potential issues in implementation. They also revisit the feasibility checklist to fine tune any items that may not have been previously discussed to ensure they have not overlooked any critical elements.

After obtaining stakeholder input, potential outcomes, and thoroughly examining all factors related to feasibility, the school decides to move ahead with participation in the project. They contact the research team to tell them that the project seems to be feasible within their current school setting and that they are interested in moving forward as a team. Shortly thereafter, research begins.

FEASIBILITY

The development of a partnership with schools is just as important as the intervention. There are numerous considerations when selecting interventions or practices. Before adopting an evidence-based practice (EBP), one must determine feasibility. Feasibility is a simple assessment of the practicality of a proposed plan or practice. It is an analysis that takes the factors of a project or practice into account in order to determine the likelihood of successful completion. When determining feasibility in education, one might ask: Do we have the people, tools, technology, and resources necessary for this project or practice to succeed? Closely examining feasibility helps to determine the pros and cons of a project or practice before a lot of precious time is invested. Questions to ask include:

- What existing resources are available for implementation?
- What new resources are necessary for implementation?
- What training is necessary for staff?
- What ongoing supports are needed?
- What are the anticipated outcomes of implementation?
- What amount of time is necessary for training and implementation?
- How am I going to gather stakeholder input?
- What required technology is needed?
- What required staff is necessary for implementation?
- What is the schedule and timeline for adoption?
- How will I encourage buy-in of staff and other various stakeholders (motivation)?
- How will I address resistance of staff and other various stakeholders?
- How will implementation work with current systems?

Although complex feasibility studies are not commonplace in education, the goals that often guide such efforts should be considered. First, determine all aspects of a potential project. Brainstorm and troubleshoot any potential problems that may arise as a result of implementation. After considering all relevant factors, determine if the research is viable and worth implementing within an educational setting. Although every project is unique in terms of required resources and application, there are key factors that should be considered with every potential project. These factors include:

- Existing resources available for implementation
- New resources necessary for implementation
- Training required for staff
- Ongoing supports
- Anticipated outcomes of implementation
- Amount of time necessary for training and implementation
- Stakeholder input
- Required technology
- Required staff for implementation
- Schedule and timeline for adoption
- Buy-in of staff and other various stakeholders (motivation)
- Resistance of staff and other various stakeholders
- Implementation within current systems

Resources

When examining feasibility, new and existing resources must be reviewed (Figure 3-2). Devising a checklist with all materials necessary for practice implementation and including a column for anticipated cost is an ideal way to highlight what already exists within a school and what needs to be purchased. Resources may include, but are not limited to, people, materials, and time. Despite the existence of some resources on the original checklist, some resources are nonrenewable and must be replenished from time to time; thus, the cost of resources that eventually must be replaced and any new resources necessary for implementation must be included on the resource list.

Materials Necessary for Implementation	Associated Costs (Available within school, must be purchased, can be borrowed for community or university resources)	Notes and Possible Funding Sources

Figure 3-2. Checklist for review of new and existing resources.

Training

In addition to the cost of training, consider the amount of time necessary to train staff. Various models exist for training. Choose to use time set aside for professional development to train staff, whether it be for a full day or a shorter amount of time. Another option may be to send a core group of staff to an off-site training with the expectation that the core group will then train the rest of the staff. A third option includes training all staff in rotation at different times. Regardless of choice, consider the cost of substitute teachers if schools are required to provide training during the course of a school day.

Ongoing training should also be considered. Some research may require ongoing training that does not offer a "one and done" type of model. Recognizing the importance of ongoing training is an important consideration, as educators cannot be expected to retain all that they learn in one training session. Many times, after a training session is attended and new knowledge is obtained, educators need time to implement and practice what they have learned in order to formulate new questions and deepen their understanding. This leads to further training for answering questions and extending learning already obtained.

Often, teachers are exposed to new ideas with many more waiting on the horizon. Rather than a deep and rich approach to learning with extended training, schools provide one training on a specific practice and then quickly move on to the next. This does not allow for the meaningful learning that results from depth and not breadth when adopting a new practice. Instead, teachers absorb what they can, knowing that their next training will be on something different. Imagine what would happen if educators received ongoing training regarding an EBP that was adopted within their school. If teachers knew that an ongoing commitment was required and expected, their approach to learning would look much different from the learning that occurs when new ideas are coming from all directions.

Ongoing Supports

Training for teachers is simply not enough. Expecting teachers to spearhead a new idea with one round of exposure is unfair and unrealistic (Danielson et al., 2007). With such an approach, many teachers tend to revert back to old practices out of a desire for comfort and ease and do not implement expected practices with fidelity. When expecting teachers to do something new, time should be taken to determine necessary ongoing supports for implementation. Some supports that may be considered include collaboration opportunities, brainstorming sessions, observation and feedback, further training, mental health checks, professional development, and assistance. The list of ongoing supports should be created with the help of those responsible for implementation. Teachers and any other educators responsible for delivery should be asked what they will need to make this project happen within their classrooms. After all, they may think of necessary supports that you simply overlook.

Anticipated Outcomes

When proposing a research project, schools must determine the anticipated outcomes for all stakeholders. How will this project improve the academic/social/emotional/behavioral growth of students? How will this practice increase communication with parents/guardians? What are the anticipated changes that will happen as a result of project implementation? Creating a list of these outcomes along with schools will help to determine if the project is feasible and worth the time and effort necessary for successful implementation.

Time

Time is a coveted resource in education. Because of this, educators must be purposeful in how they choose to spend the time they have with their students. In considering time, it must be determined how much time educators will spend away from their students to receive ongoing training and support, the amount of time necessary to successfully deliver the project elements, and the time required to determine whether or not outcomes were met. Many times, proposed practices can be included in what is already being done with only minor tweaks to time. Although this is ideal, some proposed projects will require much more time on behalf of those responsible for delivery, so time is an important resource that must be examined closely.

Stakeholder Input

When proposing a research project, various stakeholders should be solicited for input. This feedback will help provide a clear idea of the values and expectations held by those most affected by the project. Insight provided will help cast a light on the necessity of moving forward or slowing down in terms of decision making. Casting a targeted net to stakeholders allows for all parties to provide educational input when it matters. Stakeholders should include teachers, students, parents, and any other party responsible for delivery of the potential practice.

Required Technology

Although it may not be required, technology is another resource that must be considered. If technology is part of what will be expected, is it technology that already exists within the school setting or will it need to be purchased? The cost of maintenance must also be considered because updates and potential fixes will always be necessary. In addition, broadband and security measures should be discussed.

Required Staff

Thought also must be given to the staff necessary to deliver all elements of the project. Ensure that expectations are realistic in terms of what teachers are already being asked to do and what will be required for the research project. Are existing staff members available when needed to implement parts of the project with fidelity? Will the project tasks spread them too thin? Are additional staff necessary for successful implementation?

Schedule and Timeline for Adoption

A proposed schedule and timeline should be provided for the project so that teachers have time to prepare for what is coming next. If teachers can look ahead, they are much more likely to be compliant in terms of expectations and may not feel overwhelmed. Teachers also need to know the amount of time a project will take on an everyday basis so that they can work the project into their daily schedule and appropriately prepare students.

Buy-In and Resistance of Staff and Stakeholders (Motivation)

An important part of any research project is the motivation of stakeholders. Determining up-front how invested teachers are in your proposed project will help you focus energy and time on building necessary working relationships. Directly asking teachers their thoughts, reservations, and ideas about a proposed project will help keep your work transparent and will allow you time to address any misinformation, stress, or confusion. Knowing who is motivated will help to determine project leaders. Those who are not as motivated may require your attention for encouragement, brainstorming, and reassurance.

Implementation Within Current Systems

Although teachers already have a lot on their plate in terms of expectations, ongoing research is critical for advancement of the field. Finding ways to incorporate research into existing systems allows for better reception and implementation overall. It is in your best interest to determine if the project complements what is already being done in a school setting so that it can be highlighted for stakeholders. A complete overhaul of what is already in place will result in stress and resistance, while a project that requires minimal change will be far better received.

After a thorough examination of all of these factors, you, along with school personnel, can make an informed decision about whether or not the adoption of a particular research project is feasible and in the school's best interest. With limited funding, increasing demands placed on teachers, and often a lack of ongoing support necessary for sustained implementation, a purposeful, well thought-out, and realistic approach to adoption is necessary.

COLLABORATION

Many times, student researchers are asked to collaborate on projects with faculty members, full-time researchers, or educators of another capacity. Working together with professors can allow you a unique insight into the research process and organization. These experiences may not be paid, but do provide value when it comes to implementing your own projects. Collegial relationships can lead to productive brainstorming sessions and research opportunities. Once the topic of research is determined, funding sources can be determined or the team can move forward with a research plan if funding is not necessary.

A simple way to access research that has been previously conducted is to subscribe to a professional journal that highlights topics of interest. Journals also can be obtained by visiting a university library or becoming a member of professional organizations. Chapter 5 provides a list of special education journals. It is common practice, at the end of each research article, to recommend further areas of research. These recommendations can assist with determining a research idea.

TABLE 3-2. COMMON MISCONCEPTIONS AND CLARIFICATIONS ABOUT BUILDING PARTNERSHIPS

MISCONCEPTION	BETTER UNDERSTANDING
Recruitment of participants will be easy.	Participants may be reluctant to try something new. It is important to highlight the value of the project but also to support building rapport.
I can follow a strict schedule for data collection.	Part of the reality of working in applied settings is that absences will and do occur. Know when to discontinue data collection. Be flexible and allow more time than needed for data collection, that way if a participant is having an off day, time is available to reschedule, or if a participant is absent, a plan is in place.
I know the principal so I am sure I can do research in this setting.	There are multiple reasons why a specific project may not be right for a setting. Sometimes projects do not align with other initiatives, and sometimes the time commitment is not available. Go into meetings prepared to present projects and keep an open mind when someone says no. Find out why, but carefully consider if this is a valid reason. You want to have sites available for the future and other projects, so getting a no this time, may not mean a no next time.
Professional development days and planning time are built into district and school schedules.	Using planned professional development time and planning periods for your project may not be feasible. Many times these days are planned months and even years in advance. Consider how participants can be incentivized to give their own time for participation. An example would be conducting training for participants during lunch time where you provide the lunch.

SUMMARY

This chapter provided a framework and understanding for developing and implementing applied partnerships in educational settings. Specific considerations focusing on feasibility, social validity, and cost should be considered before starting a project. It is critical to understand that projects may not always work in every setting, but also that the issue may lie with the specific design of the project that was proposed. Consider how projects can be beneficial for you as the researcher but also for the setting, and encourage a partnership between yourself and the research site. Common misconceptions and additional resources are provided in Tables 3-2 and 3-3.

TABLE 3-3. ADDITIONAL RESOURCES

RESOURCE	DESCRIPTION
External Funding https://www.grants.gov/	A searchable website of grants and other funding opportunities.
High Leverage Practices https://highleveragepractices.org/	A website of practices that are considered evidence based and include training and current research.
Institute of Educational Sciences https://ies.ed.gov/	The premiere research institution of education. There are numerous projects, professional development training, and resources for researchers.
IRIS Modules https://iris.peabody.vanderbilt.edu/	Explicit modules of training and instructional practices within education including resources.
Meme generator: https://imgflip.com/memegenerator Also an app on Android and Apple devices	An online tool for creating one sentence statements to promote research outcomes and supports.
National Center for Intensive Interventions https://intensiveintervention.org/	A clearinghouse of resources and trainings.
Positive Behavior Intervention and Supports https://www.pbis.org/	A clearinghouse of resources and trainings around behavior.
Social Media: A Guide for Researchers: https://derby.openrepository.com/ bitstream/handle/10545/196715/ social%20media%20guide%20for%20 screen.pdf?sequence=6&isAllowed=y	A document specifically outlining how to use social media as a resource.
What Works Clearinghouse https://ies.ed.gov/ncee/wwc/	Interventions and resources about determining evidence base and specific practices.

CHAPTER REVIEW

1. What steps must be taken to determine the feasibility of a research project for schools?
2. Discuss strategies for developing effective research partnerships.
3. In what ways can you disseminate your research findings?
4. What discrete factors must you consider for research implementation?

REFERENCES

Brown, J. M., & Schmidt, N. A. (2009). Sharing the insights with others. In N. A. Schmidt & J. M. Brown (Eds.), *Evidence-based practice for nurses: Appraisal and application of research* (pp. 399-417). Sudbury, Mass.: Jones and Bartlett Publishers.

Cann, A., Dimitriou, K., & Hooley, T. (2011). *Social Media: A guide for researchers.* London: Research Information Network. https://derby.openrepository.com/

Cooper, A. (2014). The use of online strategies and social media for research dissemination in education. *Education Policy Analysis Archives, 22*(88). http://dx.doi.org/10.14507/epaa.v22n88.2014

Danielson, L., Doolittle, J., & Bradley, R. (2007). Professional development, capacity building, and research needs: Critical issues for response to intervention implementation. *School Psychology Review, 36,* 632-637.

Dudley-Brown, S. (2012). Dissemination of translation. In K. M. White & S. Dudley-Brown (Eds.), *Translation of evidence into nursing and health care practice* (pp. 263-253). New York: Springer Pub. Co.

Gelinas, L., Pierce, R., Winkler, S., Lynch, H., & Bierer, B. (2017). Using social media as a research recruitment tool: Ethical issues and recommendations. *Am J Bioethics, 17*(3):3-14. http://dx.doi.org/10.1080/15265161.2016.1276644

Gruzd, A., Staves, K., & Wilk, A. (2012). Connected scholars: Examining the role of social media in research practices of faculty using the UTAUT model. *Computers in Human Behavior, 28*(6), 2340–2350. http://doi.org/10.1016/j.chb.2012.07.004

High Leverage Practices. (2019). https://highleveragepractices.org/

IRIS Center. (2019). https://iris.peabody.vanderbilt.edu/

IRIS Center for Training Enhancements. (2010). Fidelity of implementation: Selecting and implementing evidence-based practices and programs. www.iris.peabody.vanderbilt.edu/fid/chalcycle.htm.

National Center for Intensive Interventions. (2019). https://intensiveintervention.org/

Positive Behavior Intervention and Supports. (2019). https://www.pbis.org/

U.S. Department of Education, Institute of Education Sciences, National Center for Education Evaluation and Regional Assistance, What Works Clearinghouse.

Wilson, P. M., Petticrew, M., Calnan, M. W., & Nazareth, I. (2010). Disseminating research findings: what should researchers do? A systematic scoping review of conceptual frameworks. *Implementation Science, 5,* 91. https://doi.org/10.1186/1748-5908-5-91.

Ethical Considerations in Special Education Research

With contributions from R. Nicolle Carr, PhD, BCBA-D

INTRODUCTION

Research has a history nestled in deception and coercive practices that many would now consider immoral or illegal. However, that rocky foundation led to systemic changes that now direct and regulate research to ensure subjects, researchers, and selected topics are all protected and appropriate. For example, beneficence, autonomy, and justice should be at the forefront of all decisions, from topic selection to sample procurement to conducting of the actual research. Contained within those parameters is understanding the nuances of informed consent, which span disclosure, confidentiality, debriefing, and coercion. Researchers work to answer questions through systematic analysis, while also ensuring they are not putting their participants at risk. Due to the nature of the questions often asked within special education, this chapter evaluates ethical issues that often arise, such as risk-benefit analysis, confidentiality, and working to answer socially valid questions. Submissions to the Institutional Review Board (IRB) for permission to conduct a study must show the research is needed, participants are protected, and that the benefits of the potential findings outweigh the risks. Ethics are often assumed to be the same as morals, rules, or laws. However, when that assumption is made, vital mistakes can follow that compromise the integrity of otherwise valid research.

Hott, B. L., Brigham, F. J., & Peltier, C.
Research Methods in Special Education (pp. 55-70).
© 2021 SLACK Incorporated.

CHAPTER OBJECTIVES

+ Provide details of experiments that involved deception and coercion prior to implementation of formal methodological ethics.
+ Summarize the three main ethical principles that came from the Belmont Report.
+ Write an informed consent form with the needed information.
+ Conduct a basic risk-benefit assessment.
+ Explain the role of the Institutional Review Board.

KEY TERMS

- **American Psychological Association (APA) Ethics Code**: In 1953, established guidelines were made into the formal code to drive research and protect welfare of participants.
- **Anonymity**: During the research process, personally identifying information is not gathered about the participants and is therefore unknown even to the researcher.
- **Autonomy**: Finding from the Belmont Report; ensures each person (or person acting on their behalf) provides consent as an autonomous agent. Informed consent protects for this.
- **Belmont Report**: Written in 1979; stipulated three main areas of concern for research: beneficence, respect for autonomy, and justice.
- **Beneficence**: Finding from the Belmont Report; ensures benefits of research outweigh the risks. Approval from the IRB protects for this.
- **Coercion**: An act that occurs under pressure or duress; to include involuntary participation in a study, completion of forms or specific behavior/answers within the study.
- **Confidentiality**: Ethical and professional responsibility to protect personally identifiable information of participants.
- **Debriefing**: After an experiment, explaining to the participant the overall study purpose and disclosing any deception.
- **Deception**: When vague, false, or missing information is utilized to mislead the research participants regarding the purpose of the study.
- **Greater Than Minimal Risk/At Risk**: Study participants are at a greater emotional or physical risk than during typical routine.
- **Informed Consent**: Approval given with full comprehension of an experiment's risks and purpose by a competent adult.
- **Institutional Review Board**: All federally funded institutions have a board that reviews all research for risk–benefit analysis, social validity, and protection of sample.
- **Justice**: Finding from the Belmont Report; ensures the burden of the research is not placed on any one group, but risks and benefits are distributed across the sample.
- **Minimal Risk**: Study participants are at no greater risk of physical or emotional harm than a regular day or routine activity.
- **Plagiarism**: Using another study or researcher's words as one's own without credit to the original writer.
- **Vulnerable Populations**: Participants for whom informed consent requires additional steps, such as individuals under 18 years, those with developmental disabilities, or unborn fetuses.

ETHICAL RESEARCH

The only topic that sounds more mundane to most people than research methodology is ethics. But here we are, diving neck deep into a topic that many do not fully understand, or think is based only on making good decisions: ethics of research methods. Surely by now the other chapters have given a glimpse behind the mystique of methodology. However, before implementing any of the knowledge from those other chapters, ethical implementation is essential. This chapter provides the basic considerations related to the American Psychological Association's (APA) ethical code. This is not the quintessential bluebook to ethical design but will get a new researcher started in the right direction and asking the right questions.

There are two consistent areas where ethics are violated as it relates to research. One is during the actual research process: gathering the sample, conducting socially valid research, and doing no harm in the process. The second area is related to what happens with the information obtained from the study, whether for publication or didactic purposes. From the questions asked to the data that sprang from it, possible ethical violations should be at the forefront of obtaining, using, and reporting the results of research. Research with humans, the most likely participants in educational research, will result in a unique need to protect the participant and the data.

It is assumed by many that morals, laws, and ethics are the same. They are not. For example, friends can debate about John engaging in moral behavior when he cheated on his wife, but that does not mean it is unethical or unlawful behavior. School personnel can debate if Crystal is allowed to hit a peer after weeks of being bullied in the cafeteria. This act of retaliation might be unlawful, but its morality or ethics can be debated. Laws are defined by regulatory agencies over members of that society and morals are based on the culture in which they exist as ideas of right versus wrong. Ethics, as noted here for research purposes, are not a philosophy but a set of rules and/or guidelines determined by governing boards such as the APA, the Behavior Analyst Certification Board (BACB), American Medical Association (AMA), or other leading association or governing body for a specific field.

The ethical codes that now govern many fields were not born of man wanting to do right by others from the field's inception. Instead, they were often born from tragedy, death, and deception. The good news is that these stakeholders wanted to do better and improve the direction of their discipline. The bad news is that for those who were part of these events, they are already over. The damage is done. The ethical code was too late.

HISTORY REPEATS ITSELF

Unfortunately, there have been enough bad apples that Amdur and Bankert (2011) were able to fill an entire handbook with questionable research studies across various fields—not just special education. These instances span hundreds of years and are not given their full depth here, though it is highly recommended to seek out each instance for additional details (e.g., Algahtani et al., 2018; Bickman & Zarantonello, 1978). One of the older events occurred when the Fernald State School in Massachusetts failed to safeguard or have protocols for treatment of its patients over 200 years ago. This resulted in inhumane and impoverished conditions for its residents until the facility finally closed and all residents were relocated (D'Antonio, 2004). Although it would be easy to chalk this one incident up to a power hungry leader running a large institution without appropriate oversight, this is far from the worst case in contemporary history.

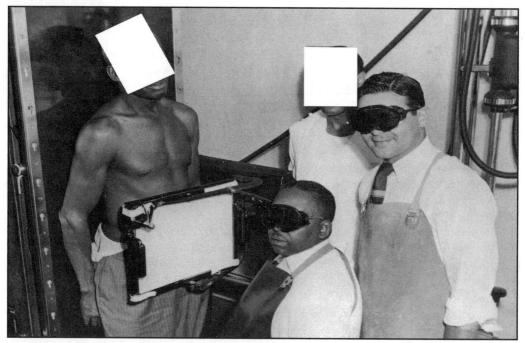

Figure 4-1. Participants in the Tuskegee Syphilis Study sometime around 1932. (Photograph #7852 reproduced from the CDC.gov website CDC/Betty Hooper.)

Tuskegee Syphilis Study

One of the longest running studies that failed its participants was the Tuskegee Syphilis study. From 1932 through 1972, over 400 Black men were part of a longitudinal study on the effects of untreated syphilis from contraction through death. In exchange for participation, they received free health care, funeral costs, and food. In an area of significant poverty, these benefits were nearly impossible to walk away from. However, if the participants were to seek outside medical treatment at any point, it voided the agreement, and they were eliminated from the study. The men were deceived regarding the purpose of the study and, though treatment was available, the participants were not provided access to it. Instead, the men often suffered significant medical problems such as blindness and insanity. Doctors found a cure for syphilis in the 1940s and continued the deception-based experiment for another 30 years (Figure 4-1).

Miami Sunland Scandal

About the time Tuskegee was being shut down, another issue was starting in Miami, Florida, spanning the late 1960s into 1972. Sunland was a residential placement for individuals with developmental disabilities. The director of the program, Dr. E., was unqualified for the job, practiced outside his boundaries of competence, and failed the clients at his facility with high rates of physical and de-humanizing acts of makeshift punishment. This scandal led to the Blue Ribbon Committee in Florida (Bailey & Burch, 2016), which resulted in a set of ethical guidelines that later became the BACB's Code of Ethics for practicing Board Certified Behavior Analysts (BCBAs).

Nuremberg Trials

The Nuremberg Code was written in 1947 following trials related to war crimes and biomedical "research" in World War II concentration camps. According to those on trial, the procedures were an attempt to understand what happens to the body under exposure to various diseases, temperatures,

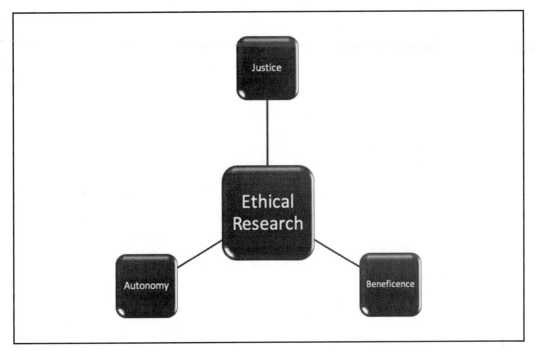

Figure 4-2. Diagram of each area needed for special education research to be considered ethical.

poisons, and drugs (Weindling, 2004). Many atrocities were exposed during those trials and compelling changes were needed moving forward. Perhaps one of the most important changes was the development of the Nuremberg Code, which had 10 principles directed at future studies with human participants in the medical profession, putting high importance on the idea of informed consent (Katz, 1996).

Milgram Obedience to Authority Experiments

In 1953, the APA put forth its own version of these principles that related directly to social sciences and psychological research with human participants. It would seem this would stop unethical experiments from occurring; however, in 1963, Stanley Milgram conducted his infamous research on obedience at Yale. In Milgram's study, participants were told to give progressively stronger shocks to a person in another room for incorrect responses. The shocks were fake and the person in the other room was a confederate (member of the research team); however, this information was unknown to the participant in the study and the result was high levels of personal stress both during the study, thinking they were inflicting pain on another, and later with the knowledge that they had the capacity to do so. Somewhat of a replication was completed years later in Australia with the same long-term trauma response from its participants (Brannigan, 2013).

The Milgram study would have a hard time passing the ethical review process from the IRB with today's rules in place. In 1974, the National Research Act demanded the creation of IRBs and the formation of the National Commission for the Protection of Human Subjects of Biomedical and Behavioral Research to ensure integrity of research and ethical treatment of human participants. The Commission met to discuss multiple areas of concern, but those most related to research methods in the social sciences are risk–benefit analysis for using human subjects, guidelines for selecting human participants, and informed consent. From this Commission came the 1979 Belmont Report and its three main findings of respect for autonomy, beneficence, and justice (Figure 4-2).

- Autonomy: People have the right to choose to participate or have someone act on their behalf to determine if they should participate and thus are treated as autonomous agents. Protected populations include individuals who are under 18 years old, incarcerated, developmentally disabled, or pregnant. In education, researchers often work with students who fall under more than one of these categories. In these cases, additional permissions must be secured from guardians, lawyers, parents, or other responsible parties all working on behalf of the participant. The informed consent process helps to ensures this requirement is met.
- Beneficence: Researchers have an obligation to do no harm and weigh the risks versus benefits before engaging in research. The IRB process is to ensure this requirement is met—that the risks to the physical, psychological, and social aspects of the person are minimized.
- Justice: This requirement is to ensure the burden and risks of the research do not fall to one group or demographic within the sample. Similarly, the benefits should also be spread across participants. When justice occurs, researchers avoid exploitation of any one group.

Special education research must ensure appropriate and humane treatment of its participants and social validity of the topics. Consider Case Study 1. How should Ahmed go about ensuring autonomy, beneficence, and justice criteria are met in his study?

CASE STUDY 1

Ahmed is about to finish his last year of graduate school. All that stands between him and his dream of being a doctor is the dissertation. After working for 3 years in a transition-focused graduate program, Ahmed is curious if task analysis and visual prompts can decrease the time needed to train high school students entering job placements at Goodwill Donation Centers. Ahmed has decided to do a single case research design; therefore he only needs about five high school students to implement his study. He wants to take his baseline data in the classroom over the second half of first semester and then teach the skill first half of second semester. Students start attending their work location just after spring break. As a whole, the study should take 1 year, all occurring during the school day. While this seems long, his dissertation advisor at the University of Sunshine tells him that it is typical. Ahmed is expecting that the task analysis and prompts will be able to decrease some re-learning that has to occur once at the job placement. Ahmed wants to ensure none of his participants miss out on this opportunity to learn faster, so he is implementing a multiple baseline design. To decrease the chance that compensation is mistaken as reinforcement by his students for appropriate behavior, a potential confound, Ahmed will not be providing compensation for participation in the study.

DURING THE RESEARCH PROCESS

The APA adopted the current version of the ethical code that many in the social sciences follow. Although the code highlights many areas related to clinical practice, their stance on research covers areas of concern for the fields of education, behavior analysis, school administration, and many others. This is obvious when comparing the codes in related fields such as Applied Behavior Analysis (ABA) and psychology (Figure 4-3). Overall, there are 10 sections to the APA's Code of Ethics; Section 8 relates specifically to research and is composed of 15 guidelines.

Institutional Review Board

Every federally funded institution (thus, every public university) has an IRB to review research conducted within the institution, funded or not. Aside from universities, private research groups,

American Psychological Association Ethical Code Section 8		Behavior Analyst Certification Board Ethical Code 9	
8.01	Institutional Approval	9.0	Behavior Analysts and Research
8.02	Informed Consent to Research	9.01	Conforming with Laws and Regulations
8.03	Informed Consent for Recording Voices and Images in Research	9.02	Characteristics of Responsible Research
		9.03	Informed Consent
8.04	Client/Patient, Student, and Subordinate Research Participants	9.04	Using Confidential Information for Didactic or Instructive Purposes
8.05	Dispensing with Informed Consent for Research	9.05	Debriefing
		9.06	Grant and Journal Reviews
8.06	Offering Inducements for Research Participation	9.07	Plagiarism
		9.08	Acknowledging Contributions
8.07	Deception in Research	9.09	Accuracy and Use of Data
8.08	Debriefing		
8.09	Humane Care and Use of Animals in Research		
8.10	Reporting Research Results		
8.11	Plagiarism		
8.12	Publication Credit		
8.13	Duplicate Publication of Data		
8.14	Sharing Research Data for Verification		
8.15	Reviewers		

Figure 4-3. Comparison of APA codes to BACB codes. ([Left] Reproduced from the American Psychological Association, https://www.apa.org/ethics/code. [Right] Behavior Analyst Certification Board. All rights reserved. Reprinted and/or displayed by permission granted in 2020. The most current version of this document is available at www.BACB.com. Contact the BACB for permission to reprint and/or display this material.)

hospitals, and clinics may also have an IRB. There are a minimum of five members on the committee whose job is to use their background and expertise to protect the welfare and privacy of human participants. One member of the board must be from outside of the institution and at least one other member is focused on the non-science concerns of the submissions. Evolution of this process continues to occur; for example, an online tutorial covering basic research ethics or nuances of human subject research may be required as part of the process.

One of the main jobs of the IRB is to determine if the subjects are protected from physical and psychological harm. The IRB evaluates submissions based on the level of review required, which is based on the level of risk involved. The three levels of evaluation are Exempt, Expedited, and Full Review, and each level requires a different number of reviewers. The exempt category does not mean the study will bypass review or document submission, only that a full board review is not required. The other two levels of subsequently increasing scrutiny occur when the level of risk is greater than minimal. Blackwood et al. (2015) state that the main contingencies issued by IRB boards are not due to the content within the submission, but rather the completeness of the submission (documents are missing) or clarity of the research proposal.

Let's say a professor wants to take data via direct observation of how many students use the wheelchair ramp outside the engineering building versus the education building. This would not require approval if the professor is only taking frequency data, never speaks to those who use the ramp, and uses the isolated data (4 people used ramp A and 10 used ramp B) for demonstration purposes in class. If, however, after the students used the ramp the researcher approached them for a quick interview and later used that data at a presentation, there is a need for a higher level of review. The questions asked and what is being done with the data determines what level of review is needed. An illustration of research receiving exempt status might be a doctoral student who is curious about the main teaching strategies used for students with dyslexia in schools and sends out an anonymous survey to a teacher organization where no information other than years teaching was requested. This would not require Full Review approval because no one can be identified by the data.

On the other hand, if Dr. Wyclef wanted to take data on the students in his classroom to determine if their reading fluency is differential when reading on paper versus tablet, this could be considered minimal risk research. There is no greater harm in this study than if the students were experiencing a reading activity during a regular school day; the research would most likely receive Expedited status. However, if Dr. Wyclef wanted to present the research at a conference later in the year and provide demographic data of age and gender, this could increase the risk level slightly. Finally, consider an experimenter who wants to evaluate the effect of a token economy on decreasing aggressive behaviors in high school students with autism when coupled with a punishment procedure (versus a control group that only used the token system). Given the aggressive nature of the students, the use of punishment and possible emotional reactions to that intervention, this would garner a greater than minimal risk label, and thus more careful consideration by the full review board.

Many IRBs have a process where a graduate student can ask permission to attend a review session to observe this process. The first step when attempting to conduct a research study is to submit an IRB protocol. The main goal of an IRB is to determine if the research is ethical, the benefits outweigh the risks, and if the rights of the participants are being protected. After review of submitted material, the review board will provide the research summary with a mark of Exempt, Expedited, or Full Board review. Most universities and research institutions have a standard form to submit. The submission of this form is the first formal step toward completion of a study.

Informed consent is required to ensure the safety and welfare of both the participant and researcher. This form educates the participant on the involved risks, benefits, and expectations of the study. Specific details required within the consent form include:

1. Purpose of the study
2. Expected duration/commitment from the participant
3. Risks involved in the study
4. Benefits to the participant or society
5. Description of compensation
6. Limits of confidentiality and maintenance of records
7. Assurance that voluntary participation can be discontinued at any time without repercussions
8. Contact information for debriefing and follow-up at a later date

The participant must sign the consent form without coercion (or have a legal guardian sign the form on their behalf if part of a vulnerable population such as students under the age of 18) and be provided a signed copy. The researcher should maintain the records for a minimum of 3 years (or as determined by the state of residence and type of study). At its conclusion, informed consent is only truly informed if it is signed by a competent person without duress who can fully comprehend all eight areas outlined above (Tai, 2012). Even so, researchers should also seek out assent from participants who might not meet all of those qualifications. This process should be a periodic check-in with participants to ensure continued understanding and desire to be a part of the study, even if they are not the ones who signed the actual consent form. Many IRBs will require the proposed assent process as part of the submission.

As an exercise, develop a consent form for Case Study 1 including the eight requirements listed, or see the sample consent form in Figure 4-4.

Research deception can be controversial and require additional steps within the IRB process. Even so, there are studies where full disclosure could lead to inaccurate outcomes, and without misleading participants regarding certain social or behavioral phenomenon, validity may be limited. Alternatives to deception can sometimes include honest studies, surveys, and role playing to gain information indirectly. If deception is determined to be the best modality to gain data, alternatives

Sunshine University Institutional Review Board
Informed Consent for Educators to Participate in a Research Study

Project Title: xxxxx
Principle Investigators: xxxxx
Department: Department of Educational Psychology

You are being asked to volunteer for this research study. This study is being conducted to xxxxx. You were specifically selected as a possible participant because of your xxxxx. Please read this form and ask any questions you may have before agreeing to take part in this study. Participants must be over the age of 18 to participate in the study.

Purpose of the Research Study: The purpose of this study is to xxxxx. Researchers will use the information gained to xxxxx.

Number of Participants: Up to xx participants are expected to complete this survey.

What I Will Be Asked to Do: If you agree to be in this study, you will be asked to xxxxx.

Length of Participation: We estimate the survey to take approximately xx minutes.

Risks of Being in the Study Are: Multiple specific pieces of demographic information could lead to participants' potential deductive re-identification.

Benefits of Being in the Study: There are no benefits from participating in this study.

Compensation: Five $50 gift cards will be randomly drawn for the participants who complete the whole survey within the allotted time indicated in the recruitment email. You may choose to enter your email address to be entered into the drawing for the gift card. You may also decline to enter into the drawing and still participate in the survey.

Confidentiality: To reduce the potential for re-identification, the researcher will not specifically name you or programs with non-public information (that of which cannot be found on the program website) in publications. Research records will be stored securely, and only approved researchers will have access to the records.

What Will Happen to My Data in the Future: After removing all identifiers, we might share your data with other researchers or use in future research without obtaining additional consent from you.

Voluntary Nature of the Study: Participation in this study is voluntary. If you withdraw or decline participation, you will not be penalized or lose benefits or services unrelated to the study. If you decide to participate, you may choose to withdraw at any time.

Contacts and Questions: If you have concerns or complaints about the research, contact xxxxx@xx.edu.

If you have any questions about your rights as a research participant, concerns, or complaints about the research and wish to talk to someone other than individuals on the research team, or if you cannot reach the research team, you may contact the University of xxxxx's Campus Institutional Review Board at xxx-xxx-xxxx or irb@xx.edu. Contact the researcher(s) listed above if you have questions or if you have experienced a research-related injury.

Statement of Consent: I have read the above information. I have asked questions and have received satisfactory answers. I consent to participate in the study. Please print this document for your records. By providing information to the researcher(s), I am agreeing to participate in this research. This research has been approved by the xxxxx.

_____ I agree and consent to participate and am over the age of 18.

_____ I do not wish to participate/I am not over the age of 18

Signature   Date

Figure 4-4. Sample consent form. (Adapted with permission from Andrea Suk.)

must be explained as non-viable to the review board and prove that no other method of research could glean the same information. The researcher also must ensure the risk is minimal, contributions to the field are substantial, and the truth will be told immediately at the conclusion of the research during a debriefing session (Boynton et al., 2013). One of the IRB's criteria for rejecting a study proposing deception is if the committee believes potential participants would say no to participating if told the truth.

Deception is not simply lying to a participant in the study. Deception can be indirect (full truth not given up front) or direct (false feedback provided to the subject unknowingly). It is direct deception that has the most potential for risk and thus is most frequently denied in a research application to the IRB.

- **Indirect Deception**: An undergraduate arrives at a study his teacher told him about for extra credit. He checks in, is given a clipboard, and told to sit in a waiting room where a researcher will come for him shortly. As he is reading the consent form, it explains the study will only take about 30 minutes and is to evaluate reaction times when loud noises are played through headphones in a room that is either absent or full of distractions. During this process, a second student walks in the room to check in with his hands full and drops all of his textbooks on the ground. For some trials, the waiting room is full of other people (also confederates) and for other trials the participant is alone. The real research question is to evaluate helping and apathy behavior during crowded situations. Once the study is over, this is explained to the participant in a brief conversation where he is allowed to ask questions and be provided additional information on the research topic, if desired.

- **Direct Deception**: Students arrive at a lab on campus known for research on depression and anxiety. Their professor is offering extra credit if they participate in a survey. The consent form explains they will take a survey with a depression scale. One undergraduate is told his depression score is a 14 out of 15—the highest score received by any student so far. His actual score was a 7. The researcher wanted to see the participants' duration of persistence on a difficult series of math problems while thinking they have high (or low) levels of depression. During the debriefing process, the researcher tells the student that his score of 14 was fake, but the risk from the potential momentary increase in anxiety and stress would need to be considered over the benefit of what would be learned from the study.

Debriefing involves the disclosure of the research purpose following the completion of participation. Often, it is used to answer any questions and, if deception was used, to explain the misleading aspects of the study. Two categories of debriefing include *dehoaxing* and *desensitization*. During dehoaxing, the misleading nature of the experiment is disclosed, and desensitization occurs when information about participants is discussed and processed with the experimenter (Holmes, 1976). In dehoaxing, any fake instrumentation may be examined or confederates might be introduced to rectify any false beliefs the participants had about the research environment. When the participants leave, there should not be any question as to what was real and what was contrived within the study. In desensitization, the participants' emotional and psychological state must be returned to its original state, or better, before participants leave, usually by explaining that their behavior in those specific circumstances was expected or even similar to others who participated. This might include offers of therapy in the future or immediate and continued processing of information. Smith and Richardson (1983) found that the act of debriefing was often enough to override negativity participants had about the research experience. However, when negative information was "learned" regarding likability, attractiveness, or other personal attributes, Miketta and Friese (2019) found debriefing did not fully restore participants to their original scores. Researchers should consider this information carefully when designing an experiment, especially the deception and debriefing process.

THE COLLECTED DATA

One of the main purposes of research is to provide truthful and objective data that, theoretically, answer the original research question. Researchers can misstep in a variety of ways from that goal to include plagiarizing, fabricating, or falsifying data. *Plagiarism* is the use of someone else's ideas or words as their own without giving credit to the original author. *Fabrication* is using fictitious data for any part of the data set. *Falsifying data* is manipulation of the collected data to better support one's hypothesis or otherwise manipulate the findings or direction of the results (Benos et al., 2005). If any of these areas of misconduct are noted, federal funding could be suspended and retractions of articles (current and past) required. In one of the more egregious plagiarism fiascos, as many as 180 retractions were required from a single researcher due to fabricated data (McHugh & Yentis, 2019), and the full set of retractions took almost two decades from some of the journals. Even worse, bad research can result in a loss of the public's trust or even changes to public policy and oversight based on this incorrect information. Imagine if research showed that reading program A was significantly better than reading program B and entire school districts made the change to this new program. If the data are false, the students in these schools are now learning with a subpar program, putting them at a disadvantage. Or, if the fabricated data was in the medical field and new hospital policies were developed around those findings, devastating results to patients may occur.

The old adage "There are lies, damn lies, and statistics" is attributed to Mark Twain. It implies what veteran researchers work to avoid—showing bias at any point in the research process, from sample selection to data presentation. Although most researchers work hard to avoid such a mistake, there are also cases of plain fabrication. It should be obvious that researchers cannot make up their data. If a student moves mid-year while serving as a participant in a longitudinal reading program, the researcher does not fill in the missing datapoints for the days the child is absent. In a real-life example, in early 2020, the COVID-19 coronavirus hit America and many schools in Oklahoma cancelled the last 9 weeks of academic instruction at the school building and moved to distance learning. A graduate student in the final weeks of data collection for her dissertation was unable to finish gathering data.

Researchers cannot guess, estimate, or otherwise fill in empty cells. Depending on the situation, a participant could be dropped and only the available data would be used, the study could be restarted, or the missing data explained in a footnote. Bottom line, there are procedures to account for missing data. Although beyond the scope of this text, it is important to understand how to treat missing data and what analyses will be conducted. These inaccuracies should be reported when communicating results. Finally, if a researcher realized some of the data in the sample were incorrect, it would need to be corrected, thrown out, or retracted.

There is more to false data than simply entering made-up numbers in the data sheet. It may include not counting all of the data points because the outliers skew the results, or starting with a sample of ten and finishing with seven but not explaining that two participants dropped out because of the psychological stress from the study. When participants drop out or data are not used, it must be noted. Another example involves taking true data but changing the visual display to skew how it is perceived. This might include using graphs with distorted spacing, confusing color schemes, a figure caption that changes the point of the information, or use of sizing/spacing to imply inaccurate results. In his 1954 book, *How to Lie with Statistics*, Darrell Huff explained how statistics can deceive based on biased sampling, truncated axes, or even using the wrong type of graph.

Most researchers have heard the word plagiarism since they were in high school and yet many do not fully understand what it is or how to avoid it. Roig (2015) notes four ways to avoid plagiarism: (a) using quotations around any direct quote, (b) using citations if the writer is not sure if material is common knowledge, (c) use citations when paraphrasing and summarizing as well as quoting, and (d) paraphrasing, which means to take the idea as a whole and rewrite it in your own words. A good rule of thumb: if an author has to open a resource to write the sentence, a citation should be used. Often, students will attempt to paraphrase early in their career by simply removing/changing a few words within a sentence; however, this does not show understanding of the material or true paraphrasing.

Although institutions may consider intention behind plagiarism when determining consequences, academic peers and journal editors are not as forgiving. Using the words and ideas of another person or piece of work without credit to that author, akin to both stealing and lying, is not a place where ignorance will set a young (or veteran) researcher free. The Office of Research Integrity and its members during a session on the topic of plagiarism have considered such violations in light of multiple criteria (U. S. Department of Health and Human Services, n.d.) to include the experience of the researcher, intent of use, history of prior offenses, and prevalence.

One area of plagiarism that many novice researchers are unaware of is self-plagiarism. If a paper is published or data are presented, it must be cited each time afterward, even if the same author is writing the new article and is writing about their own prior research. This prohibits a single researcher from publishing the same research in multiple journals. With some institutions offering cash incentives for high numbers of publications per year or tenure at universities being based on publications, the desire to stretch a single data set is great. However, researchers must resist using the copy + paste function with the same data to make the same conclusions within multiple publications.

CASE STUDY 2

Mr. Brown is a high school special educator with 10 years of experience as a teacher and case manager for students with disabilities. Teaching and living in a rural small town, he was accustomed to running into both families and his colleagues out in the community. One day, Mr. Brown was grocery shopping with his family and he ran into Mrs. Hall, the English 10 teacher at his school. Some of the students on his caseload were enrolled in her course that semester. They had been communicating via email regarding two students who were currently failing Mrs. Hall's class, and Mr. Brown had some concerns about implementation of IEP accommodations. He saw this as a good opportunity to talk face-to-face. In aisle 6 of the local grocery store, Mr. Brown approached Mrs. Hall for a discussion. The two educators discussed all three students enrolled in English 10, and specifically about the two students who were currently failing. Comments shared between the teachers included: "Sarah just doesn't seem to care. She uses her learning disability as an excuse to not do her work. I am at my wits end!"; and "In order for Eric to be more successful, you need to accommodate more for his laborious writing—he needs at least double the time as his classmates to write notes because of his fine motor problems. Or you could always provide him a copy of notes. It is listed on his IEP." The conversation went on for about 20 minutes. As this was the only grocery store in town, many familiar faces walked by during this impromptu educational discussion.

What would be a more appropriate course of action for Mr. Brown to convey this information to Mrs. Hall? What should Mrs. Hall have done in this situation?

OTHER IMPORTANT CONSIDERATIONS

One aspect that most members of the educational and medical community are already aware of is confidentiality (e.g., FERPA, HIPAA). *Confidentiality* is the ethical and professional responsibility to protect client and participant information. It is important enough to appear in both the section on Research (subsection 8) within the APA code and have its own section called Privacy and Confidentiality (subsection 4). In schools, this might relate more to the idea that teachers cannot walk through a grocery store and talk with a fellow shopper about a student in their class (see Case Study 2) where it is easy to overhear what is said. Similarly, using a case study for didactic purposes at a presentation and giving too many details also falls under this area. For example, there are a limited number of second graders with Down Syndrome at Sunnyside Elementary School who utilize the Picture Exchange Communication System (PECS). There is a chance a member of the audience may be able to identify the participant in the case study using such specific information. Instead, generic terms like "an elementary school in rural Louisiana" can help to conceal identity.

Confidentiality and anonymity related to experimental methods are integral to consider from the first stages of development. There is a difference between anonymity and confidentiality. Confidentiality refers to the participant's identifying information being kept separate from the data and not that the data being obtained will be kept confidential. If it were, there would be nothing to report. *Anonymity* is the correct term to suggest that the data will be reported but the identity of the person reporting it will be unknown to anyone, even the researcher. If asking subjects about sexual habits, domestic violence, drug use, mental health, or other highly personal information, the chance of truthful information and overall participation appears to increase when respondents believe information to be anonymous rather than confidential (Murdoch et al., 2014). Therefore, one option is to not ask for any personal identifying information before conducting the interview or study. If that information is needed, such as in longitudinal research, researchers must note how they will code and store the information separate from the individual's personal demographic information.

There are three ways to think about and plan for confidentiality: (a) separating participants' information from their data, (b) ensuring those who know about the study are not publicizing its results, and (c) when presenting details of the study, ensuring this material stays protected. A study may be considered above minimal risk if the type of information being collected could wreak havoc if privacy is not maintained. One method to provide confidentiality is to code the information so that the data are maintained in one place, connected to a code, which identifies a subject whose identity is maintained in a second secured location. Researchers may also use a pseudonym; a consideration is to let the participant select their own pseudonym so a nickname or other related name is not accidently selected. When these levels of precautions are needed, informed consent should clearly explain limitations of privacy (Wiles et al., 2006). There are times when confidentiality may be broken, such as finding out a participant has plans to hurt themselves or others, a legal authority requests the information, or the subject gives permission to do so. It is imperative that this is conveyed to the participant during the informed consent process.

SUMMARY

Overall, ethics should remain at the forefront of every researcher's thoughts from start to finish of the study. In the beginning, this includes ensuring samples are not biased, participants are treated fairly, and decisions about risk and deception are minimized. As the study continues, decisions about data collection, presentation, and maintenance must be made to ensure privacy is maintained but results are correctly presented. All in all, ethics span all areas of research and the content here is only a starting point for further investigation. See Table 4-1 for common ethics misconceptions, and Table 4-2 for additional resources.

TABLE 4-1. COMMON MISCONCEPTIONS AND CLARIFICATIONS ABOUT ETHICS IN RESEARCH

MISCONCEPTION	BETTER UNDERSTANDING
Ethics are common sense.	Common sense is subjective and based on many personal factors and experiences. Ethics are often based on guidelines or codes put forth by an organization to create a uniform set of expectations. If you are unsure about an ethical code or guideline, find mentors or seek out your IRB members to ask for clarification.
Research methodology inherently contains good ethical protocols.	Appropriate research methodology should be mindful of, and plan for, ethical implementation from the outside. This includes how participants are gathered, what type of consent is needed, which data sets are included, and how they are presented.
Deceiving participants is the best way to gather truthful data.	There are many ways to gather truthful information, deception of the study's main purpose being only one. Role playing, survey, stressing anonymization, and/or confidentiality are other ways to gather truthful data.

TABLE 4-2. ADDITIONAL RESOURCES

RESOURCE	DESCRIPTION
Ethical Principles and Professional Practice Standards for Special Educators from the Council for Exceptional Children can be found here: https://www.cec.sped.org/Standards/Ethical-Principles-and-Practice-Standards	A source from the Council for Exceptional Children to describe in greater detail the policies, procedures, and practices that align with their standards.
Rosenberg, N. E., & Schwartz, I. S. (2018). Guidance or compliance: What makes an ethical behavior analyst? *Behavior Analysis in Practice, 12*(2), 473-482. https://doi.org/10.1007/s40617-018-00287-5	Discussion of difference between requirements and good practice along with presentation of a decision-making model for ethical dilemmas.
The Code of Ethics followed by the National Association of Special Education Teachers can be found here: https://www.naset.org/index.php?id=2444	A source from the National Association of Special Education Teachers that includes those guidelines recommended for the highest level of ethical practice.

Chapter Review

1. Is it possible for Milgram, or other controversial researchers from the past, to have conducted his study using current ethical requirements and learn the same information as the original experiment? If not, does that mean it was worthwhile to conduct? If so, why?

2. Do you think the results of the Belmont Report were good enough? Were the changes to the ethical requirements too strict or not strict enough? Could more have been done?

3. Which of the required information in an informed consent form is most important and why? What could happen if that one section was left out?

4. What can be done to decrease the chance of plagiarism from your co-researchers or students?

5. How is confidentiality maintained?

References

Algahtani H., Bahjunaid, M., & Shirah, B. (2018). Unethical human research in the field of neuroscience: A historical review. *Neurological Sciences, 39*(5), 820-834.

Amdur, R. J., & Bankert, E. A. (2011). *Institutional Review Board member handbook*. Jones and Bartlett.

Bailey, J., & Burch, M. (2016). *Ethics for behavior analysts* (2nd ed.). Routledge.

Benos, D. J., Fabres, J., Farmer, J., Gutierrez, J. P., Hennessy, K., Kosek, D., Lee, J. H., Olteanu, D., Russell, T., Shaikh, F., & Wang, K. (2005). Ethics and scientific publication. *Advances in Physiology Education, 29*(2), 59-74.

Bickman, L., & Zarantonello, M. (1978). The effects of deception and level of obedience on subjects; ratings of the Milgram study. *Personality and Social Psychology Bulletin, 4*(1), 81-85.

Blackwood, R. A., Maio, R. F., Mrdjenovich, A. J., VandenBosch, T. M., Gordon, P.S., Shipman, E. L. & Hamilton, T. A. (2015). Analysis of the nature of IRB contingencies required for informed consent document approval. *Accountability in Research, 22*(4), 237-245.

Boynton, M. H., Portnoy, D. B., & Johnson, B. T. (2013). Exploring the ethics and psychological impact of deception in psychological research. *IRB, 35*(2), 7-13.

Brannigan, A. (2013). Stanley Milgram's obedience experiments: A report card 50 years later. *Society, 50*, 623-628.

D'Antonio, M. (2004). *State boys rebellion*. Simon and Shuster.

Holmes, D. S. (1976). Debriefing after psychological experiments: II. Effectiveness of post-experimental desensitizing. *American Psychologist, 31*(12), 868-875.

Huff, D. (1993). *How to lie with statistics*. W. W. Norton & Company.

Katz, J. (1996). The Nuremberg code and the Nuremberg trial: A reappraisal. *Journal of American Medical Association, 276*(20), 1662-1666.

McHugh, U. M., & Yentis, S. M. (2019). An analysis of retractions of papers authored by Scott Reuben, Joachim Boldt and Yoshitaka Fujii. *Anaesthesia, 74*(1), 17-21.

Miketta, S., & Friese, M. (2019). Debriefed but still troubled about the (in)effectiveness of post-experimental debriefings after ego threat. *Journal of Personality and Social Psychology, 117*(2), 282-309.

Miller, F. G., Wendler, D., & Swartzman, L. C. (2005). Deception in research on the placebo effect. *PLoS Medicine, 2*(9), e262. https://doi.org/10.1371/journal.pmed.0020262

Murdoch, M., Simon, A. B., Polusny, M. A., Bangerter, A. K., Grill, J. P., Noorbaloochi, S., & Partin, M. R. (2014). Impact of different privacy conditions and incentives on survey response rate, participant representativeness, and disclosure of sensitive information: a randomized controlled trial. *BMC Medical Research Methodology, 14*(90). https://doi.org/10.1186/1471-2288-14-90

Richman, W. L., Kiesler, S., Weisband, S., & Drasgow, F. (1999) A meta-analytic study of social desirability distortion in computer-administered questionnaires, traditional questionnaires, and interviews. *Journal of Applied Psychology, 84*(5), 754-775.

Roig, M. (Revised 2015). *Avoiding plagiarism, self-plagiarism, and other questionable writing practices: a guide to ethical writing*. Office of Research Integrity, U.S. Dept. of Health and Human Services.

Rutherford-Hemming, T., Vlasses, F. R., & Rogers, J. K. (2012). Practice makes perfect: Tips for successful Institutional Review Board submissions. *The Journal of Continuing Education in Nursing, 43*(5), 203-208.

Smith, S. S., & Richardson, D. (1983). Amelioration of deception and harm in psychological research: The important role of debriefing. *Journal of Personality and Social Psychology, 44*(5), 1075–1082. https://doi.org/10.1037/0022-3514.44.5.1075

Tai, M. C. (2012). Deception and informed consent in social, behavioral, and educational research (SBER). *Tzu Chi Medical Journal, 24*(4), 218-222.

Tuskegee Study—Timeline—CDC (2020, March 2). https://www.cdc.gov/tuskegee/timeline.htm

U. S. Department of Health and Human Services (n.d.). Handling misconduct. https://ori.hhs.gov/handling-misconduct

Weindling, P. (2004). *Nazi medicine and the Nuremberg trials.* MacMillian Publishers.

Wiles, R., Crow, G., Heath, S., & Charles, V. (2006). Anonymity and confidentiality. Economic and Social Research Council, National Centre for Research Methods, Working Paper Series. 3-17.

Identifying, Locating, and Evaluating Educational Research

With contributions from Kathleen M. Randolph, EdD, BCBA-D; Beth A. Jones, PhD; and Lynn E. Gates, MLIS

INTRODUCTION

This chapter provides the reader with the skills needed to identify different types of research and information for interpreting and reading the parts of a research article. Ways to use library databases to search for relevant information and articles are discussed in detail. Multiple exemplars and details for utilizing the university library to obtain information for student research are provided, along with additional resources and questions students should ask when conducting research. Additionally, this chapter will provide resources for evaluating research articles and ways to identify instances of bias in the evidence base.

Hott, B. L., Brigham, F. J., & Peltier, C.
Research Methods in Special Education (pp. 71-87).
© 2021 SLACK Incorporated.

CHAPTER OBJECTIVES

→ Identify the sections of a research article and the content that should be reported.
→ Use library databases to locate research.
→ Distinguish between research and practitioner articles.
→ Evaluate research articles.
→ Evaluate bias in the evidence base.

KEY TERMS

- **Abstract**: Short synopsis of the article to follow; provides readers with an overview of the material presented in the full article.
- **Boolean Operators**: AND, OR, and NOT. AND and NOT will help narrow the search, OR will broaden it. AND ensures that all search terms are found, NOT will exclude terms from being found, and OR will look for any search terms.
- **Databases**: Electronic collections of information, generally journal articles. They can be subject-specific or broader, and multidisciplinary.
- **Discovery Layer**: The first place (i.e., landing page) to visit on a library's website.
- **Discussion**: Offers a nontechnical interpretation of the results without offering new ideas (Huck, 2004).
- **Introduction**: First section of the manuscript; it establishes the relevance of the topic and outlines the work of previous scholars pertinent to the topic.
- **Method**: Gives information on how the study was conducted; includes descriptions of study participants, materials, and the procedures the authors used to carry out the study.
- **Results/Findings**: Results of the study or article are summarized, displayed, and quantified for the reader.

CASE STUDY

Kaylee is a preservice special education teacher who is taking a research course for future educators. The culminating project in the course is a research project where students look at a problem in their area of education. The professor, Dr. Luna, provided the students with a list of 15 possible topics, and from that list, Kaylee is interested in the overrepresentation of Black males in special education. Dr. Luna also provided the students with multiple articles in their chosen topic area so they could learn about the topic with readily available information. In the past, Kaylee has conducted internet searches and relied on publicly available websites. She knows that she can't depend on wiki-type sites where users can change the information without verifying it. She wants to learn more about the websites and journals she can trust for information that is reliable, but she does not know quite where to start, nor does she know who to contact to get started.

RESEARCH ARTICLES

A research article is a new and original work that no one else has conducted previously, with the aim of contributing knowledge to a given field of study. The research article may evaluate primary data (i.e., collected by authors) or secondary data (i.e., data collected by others) to address the research questions. Research articles provide the best source of rigorously tested data that can provide informative and actionable information to help educators inform their practice (Dunfon, 2005). A practitioner article is an informative text that translates research findings to practice. The article may provide step-by-step guidelines on how to implement an EBP in the classroom (e.g., self-regulated strategy development) or it may focus on providing essential content knowledge that would inform practice (e.g., defining and diagnosing dyslexia). We will focus here on articles purposed to disseminate research findings; with many different types of research methodologies, it is important to know the purposes and correct application of each.

Kaylee realizes that there are gaps in the research that she has been provided, and she needs to find additional articles and support for her research. She conducts an internet search but the sources don't seem to be trustworthy, and she is struggling to locate resources. She knows that the librarian is scheduled to be a guest speaker in her research course and looks forward to learning about accessing additional resources through the university library.

Locating Research

When it comes to doing research, the university library is the ideal place to start. In addition to books, libraries purchase and subscribe to many online resources that assist in conducting research. It is always recommended to start at the university library's home page to access these sources so that you are identified as a user of the subscribing library, specifically when using the university wireless connection. Check with a university librarian to identify the process for accessing items when not on campus through a proxy server.

The first place to visit in a search is the library's catalog, referred to as the *discovery layer*. Many libraries use discovery layers because they search across multiple databases, including the library's physical holdings, journal subscriptions, eBooks, and streaming videos. Searching here provides a good overview of a topic, but because it is pulling together results from many different sources, there will be a lot of results that are not relevant to the search. Although results can and should be narrowed, it is harder to do a targeted search in a discovery layer. It is often better to move to individual databases.

Databases

Databases are electronic collections of information, mostly journal articles. They can be subject-specific or broader, and multidisciplinary. A single database will collect articles or information on articles from many different journals, compile that information (many times they also add relevant metadata), and then make it searchable for researchers. Using a subject-specific database can help target the search because it collects articles from the most relevant journals for that discipline. Libraries frequently subscribe to many of their databases through a third-party platform vendor. This means that searching looks and works the same, even when searching two different databases. Pay attention to the advance search in these cases, because the data and information in the database comes from the database (not the platform), which has different options for searching. Some platforms allow users to search multiple databases at once. If you are taking advantage of this, be aware that it is generally searching the lowest denominator. For example, if one database has metadata for a field, such as practitioner, but the other does not, it cannot search on practitioner for the database that does not have the information.

Databases can be divided into different categories, providing different types of access to articles. Full-text databases will contain a complete version of the article, chapter, book, or dissertation found while searching. Abstract or citation index databases collect abstracts or citations from selected journals, and the library should have a way (i.e., a link) to redirect to the full text of the article if they subscribe to it, or another database that has it. Hybrid databases will contain both full-text and abstracts or citations; the library will be able to provide a link to the full text if it isn't in their database, or it can be accessed through an interlibrary request. There are also many specialized databases that collect very specific formats or types of articles, such as streaming video, literature reviews, or case studies.

Every library subscribes to databases that are appropriate for their university's fields of study. This means that the databases students can access will vary depending on the institution. Questions about databases should be directed to the reference or research assistance desk and those individuals can help locate databases and recommend one or more that would be a good place to start research. Some of the more common databases held by libraries are detailed in the following paragraphs.

EDUCATION RESOURCES INFORMATION CENTER

The Education Resources Information Center (ERIC) is the first choice of many when doing research for education-related topics. ERIC is sponsored by the Institute of Education Sciences under the U.S. Department of Education. It contains both full-text and citations to high-quality research from over 1,935 sources, which include journals, books, conference papers, technical reports, and policy papers. ERIC can be accessed freely at https://eric.ed.gov/. The library also may provide access to ERIC through one of their database vendors. The content provided is the same; the only difference is how search options are accessed. One benefit of accessing ERIC from the library databases page is for titles that are not available as full text through ERIC. The library should have a direct link to the full text of the article if they have access to it through another database or subscribe to the journal (ERIC, 2019; Institute of Education Science, n.d.).

PSYCINFO

PsycInfo, created and maintained by the American Psychological Association (APA, 2020), is a multidisciplinary database that collects abstracts from almost 2,500 journals. It is also possible to find selected abstracts from relevant dissertations, books, and book chapters in PsycInfo. Because its main focus is the behavioral and social sciences, many of the articles have more of a scientific base, there is crossover with education, and it can be a good place to find information. Libraries subscribe to PsycInfo through a database platform vendor; depending on the library, the platforms might look a little different, but the content will be the same. A benefit of accessing PsycInfo through the university library is that even though the content in PsychInfo will be abstracts and citations, the library's link resolver will be able to go directly to the article if the library has access to it through a different database or journal subscription (APA, 2020).

In addition to the subject-specific databases, libraries subscribe to several broad, multidisciplinary databases, such as Academic Search Premier or OmniText Full Text. These larger databases have some of the same problems as library discovery layers, because they do have a lot of articles from a lot of different sources. On the positive side, because of their size, they frequently can acquire articles from journals that the smaller subject-specific databases cannot. Larger databases are frequently full-text or hybrid databases and are generally hosted by the platform vendor the library uses to subscribe to databases, which makes searching consistent with many of the other databases at the university library.

SOCIAL SCIENCES CITATION INDEX

The Social Sciences Citation Index (SSCI), part of Clarivate Analytics' Web of Science and Elsevier's Scopus, includes citation indices that contain high-impact factor journals. It is possible to limit a search to just the SSCI when searching if the library has subscribed to the full Web of Science.

Both SSCI and Scopus have good tools built in to help analyze search results and limit them by discipline. They also provide information (e.g., number of times cited) on articles and journals that help determine the article impact. Like PsycInfo, SSCI and Scopus will not have the full text of the articles they index, but the library has a link resolver to direct to full-text if they have access to it (Scopus, 2020; Web of Science Group, 2020).

Sometimes, despite all the databases and journals to which a library subscribes, they do not have the article needed. When this happens, students can place an Interlibrary Loan (ILL) request with the library for that article. The library asks other libraries all around the United States, and potentially the world, to send them a copy of the article, and then provide it to the requester. In addition to requesting articles, students can request book chapters, books, and frequently DVDs or other media. Many libraries have their link resolver set up so that if it cannot find the article in any of the databases, it will automatically link to the ILL form and fill in the information. In general, students should never have to pay for an article needed for research.

Refining Searches

There are a few things to remember when doing research and searching for articles. First, one is never enough. Researchers should not stop after one search, one set of keywords, or the first page of results. Second, no search or source is perfect. Research is unique and no single database can meet everyone's needs. Searching in different places with different searches will provide a variety of relevant articles. This also means that when a research topic has several components, an article that discusses all of the parts may not exist, and students will instead need to look for articles that discuss various combinations and summarize to bridge the gaps in what was found. Third, searching databases and other library resources is not like searching Google; searches use a variety of keywords and filters to refine results rather than sentences.

When starting a search, identify the keywords, which are words or short phrases that help define the topic. The best way to find keywords is to start with the research questions and pull out the major words, generally the nouns. Next, start thinking about other terms that mean the same thing, as well as narrower and broader terms. The main keywords are specific, but you can narrow or broaden the search if finding too much or too little, and having these extra keywords ready will help. When having trouble thinking of these, looking in a thesaurus, encyclopedia, or Wikipedia will help, or spend some time brainstorming with other students, your professor, or a librarian. Also, note how textbooks and other articles refer to the topic. Create lists of terms to use and keep adding to it, make notes on which terms have been especially useful, and remember that the language scholars use to write about a topic changes over time, so one term that finds a lot of material from a specific time period may no longer be used (Kraemer Family Library, 2020; UTA Libraries, 2020). See Chapter 6 for information on conducting systematic reviews.

KEYWORDS

Databases will be able to help identify keywords. To help make searching easier, each one has created controlled vocabulary used to assign terms to each record. Look for these terms in the record for an item; they may be referred to as Subjects or Descriptors and are generally hyperlinked so that a quick search for other articles that have the same term can be done. When different authors use different terminology to refer to the same idea (e.g., cat, feline, kitty, kitten), the database will assign one generic term to all of them. A database's advanced search can be used to search for various combinations of the controlled terms; look in the dropdown menu for descriptor or subject, or combinations of the controlled term with keywords. Just remember that different databases, even if accessed through the same platform, may use a different controlled vocabulary.

FILTERING RESULTS

Once a result list is generated, use the filters or limiters provided by the database to help bring down the number of results. The available filters will depend on the database; some common filters are date, peer review, full-text, academic journals, discipline, subject, language, and location.

The options are endless; choose one or several filters. Generally, start with the date filter, especially when given a date range by a professor. If researching the historical context of a topic, do not limit by date; if looking for recent developments, limiting to the past 5 or 10 years would be beneficial. Limiting by peer review or academic journal will generally provide similar results when searching for high-quality research. Not every academic journal is peer-reviewed and not every peer-reviewed journal is an academic journal. The discipline filter will be particularly helpful when searching in a multidisciplinary database; it can help eliminate all of the physics or business articles when limited to education. The location filter can be both helpful and problematic; essentially, it depends on how consistently records have a location identified or if the authors mention or use a location as part of their research. Finally, the full-text filter can be misleading; when selected, it is limited to articles that are only available as full-text in that database. This excludes articles to which the library has access in another database or through a journal subscription, or are available through ILL.

When searching, you may find that even when using the filters, there are still too many or too few results, or too many irrelevant results. In addition to using the broader or narrower terms when figuring out keywords, there are a few other strategies to consider. The first and simplest is to enclose the phrase in quotation marks. This instructs the database to search for those words together as a phrase, rather than looking for both words independently. After that, start using Boolean operators to narrow or broaden the search. Most databases have set up their advanced search pages to make this easy, typically with a drop down between two search boxes. Boolean operators are AND, OR, and NOT. AND and NOT will help narrow the search; OR will broaden it. AND ensures that all of search terms are found, NOT will exclude terms from being found, and OR will look for any search terms. If NOT is used in a search, make sure that it is the last thing used. Anything after the NOT will be excluded. If excluding multiple things, use AND and OR after the NOT to make sure everything is excluded. Parentheses can be used to set apart unique sections of the search phrase, which will narrow or broaden a search in a very targeted manner. See Figure 5-1 for a visual representation of how Boolean operators work.

Another way to find relevant articles is to use citation chaining to find more articles using one you have already located that closely matches the topic. *Citation chaining* is typically identified as forward and backward chaining. Backward chaining tends to be a little easier, which involves looking at an article's reference page to see what articles were cited and then looking up any that are relevant to current research. Continue backwards through the articles located the information is outdated or no longer relevant. *Forward chaining* involves looking for articles that cite the article already located. SSCI, Scopus, and Google Scholar are all very helpful for forward chaining (IUPUI University Library, 2019).

If you encounter difficulties finding articles or other resources that help with research, the university library has many resources to assist. Librarians create many tutorials and LibGuides that explore different parts of the research process, how to use specific resources, and discuss relevant research trends specific to individual disciplines. If more personalized assistance or help with a specific question is needed, contact the university library's reference or Research Assistance Desk. Most reference services have multiple ways to contact them, including phone, email, chat, text, or in person. However, if the question is indepth, it may be referred to a subject librarian (librarians who specialize in a discipline). These librarians meet with students one-on-one and delve deeper into questions, as well as assist with discipline-specific resources. Subject librarians are typically listed on the university library's website. The librarians are there to help with research, so contact them before getting frustrated. They will be able to direct you to the best resources and provide various tips and tricks to get the most out of your research.

Kaylee develops a plan for identifying articles by abstract, and then begins to comb through the articles provided by Dr. Luna. Kaylee used the information provided about the different types of research from Chapter 2 during the first few weeks of the research course. She is interested in finding out more information about the number of students in special education overall, and identifying the number of

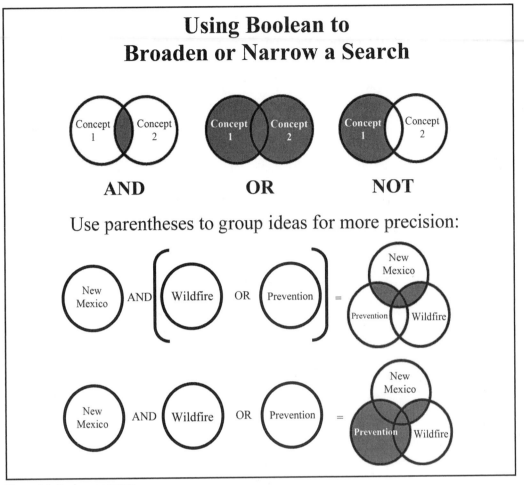

Figure 5-1. Boolean operators.

students of color, specifically Black male students, receiving special education services in the United States. She starts out by reviewing literature reviews and meta-analyses, and then she looks at different studies that examine the numbers of Black students identified with emotional and behavioral disabilities (EBD). She quickly realizes it is necessary to understand the different parts of a research article so that she can pinpoint the important information in the article and identify the parts of the article she can use to identify additional resources.

INTERPRETING A RESEARCH ARTICLE

Regardless of the type of research employed in a study, authors should always provide background information on previous work done in an area, clarify for the reader how their work contributes to the knowledge base on their particular topic, describe the method and procedures that they used, provide their findings, and discuss their findings (and the limitations of their findings) in the context of the previous literature (Dunfon, 2005). Accordingly, the resulting research article should have the following consistent sections, some of which will contain pertinent subsections: (a) Abstract, (b) Introduction, (c) Method, (d) Results/Findings, (e) Discussion, and (f) References (Huck, 2004).

Abstract

The Abstract is a short synopsis of the article. The purpose of the abstract is to provide readers with an overview (i.e., summary) of the material presented in the full article (Fuchs & Fuchs, 1993). Reading the abstract to determine what was being studied, the study design and method, and the results of the investigation helps readers to decide if the manuscript is related to their interests (Huck, 2004).

Introduction

The Introduction of an article is the first section of the manuscript; it establishes the relevance of the topic and outlines the work of previous scholars pertinent to the topic. This section sets up the purpose for the present study and enumerates the research questions or hypotheses the authors sought to investigate. The Introduction should contain context, purpose of the article with research questions addressed, how the study adds to or addressed gaps in the current literature base, and study rationale (Fuchs & Fuchs, 1993).

Background

All research articles should begin with a review of the existing literature on the topic of interest. This should include work from peer-reviewed sources and inform the reader regarding relevant work that has been done previously. Even if there is a dearth of literature on a topic, authors should cite seminal work in the area and clearly pinpoint areas that need further investigation.

Statement of Purpose

The purpose of the study should be targeted at the gaps in the body of the preceding literature. The statement of purpose should align with the research questions.

Research Questions/Hypotheses

The research questions or hypotheses typically follow the literature review and purpose. Authors either explicitly state the questions they sought to answer (i.e., Does exposure to training in assistive technology increase preservice teachers' familiarity with available technology?) or they will state their questions in the form of hypotheses about what they think they will find (i.e., Training in assistive technology will increase preservice teachers' familiarity with available technology). The research questions should be aimed at answering something new and be answered by the end of the article (Dunfon, 2005).

Method

The Method section of an article is where the authors provide detailed information on how the study was conducted. A thoughtful description of the study participants, the materials used to conduct the study, and the procedures the authors used to carry out the study are included. This section should provide enough detail that the study could be replicated and align with applicable design quality indicators (Huck, 2004).

Participants

The authors should describe the participants of their study. This should include a description of how participants were selected, how many participants there were, and the demographic characteristics (e.g., ethnicity, gender, age) of the participants. Demographic data are typically reported using descriptive statistics. For example, the mean age of the sample that was 22 years of age with a standard deviation of 5 years 2 months would be reported as ($M = 22$, $SD = 5.2$). This description is needed because the participants of the study can impact the results and the generalizability of the results (APA, 2019; Huck, 2004).

Materials

In this section, the authors tell the reader how they defined each variable and the measures (i.e., tools, instruments) they used to assess that variable. Researchers can use tools that have already been created and used by others, or they can create their own. If the authors are using previously created measures, they should cite the data showing that it measures what it is intended to measure (i.e., validity). If researchers use measures they have created, they should provide information on how they know the instrument measures what it is intended to measure (Dunfon, 2005).

Procedures

The specifics of how a study was conducted are enumerated in the Procedures section. The authors should explain what the participants did or what was done to them. Again, this portion of the article should give sufficient detail so that the study could be replicated. The Procedures section should answer these questions: (a) where was the study conducted? (in general terms as to not break confidentiality), (b) who conducted the study?, (c) what was the order of events?, and (d) did any of the participants drop out (i.e., attrition) before completing the study? (Huck, 2004). See Table 5-1 for a list of common terms.

Results/Findings

The Results of an investigation can be presented in any combination of three ways: (a) in the text only, (b) summarized in tables, and/or (c) presented in graphical displays or figures (APA, 2019; Huck, 2004). Often, authors organize their presentation of results by their specific research questions to facilitate organization and understanding (APA, 2019). To correctly interpret the results of a study, no matter the format in which they are presented, the reader must be familiar with the terminology and symbols researchers employ.

Discussion

In contrast to the Results/Findings section, which presented a technical report of the findings, the Discussion section should offer a nontechnical interpretation of the results without offering new ideas (Huck, 2004). The Discussion section should provide direct answers to the research questions stated in the Introduction of the article. According to Huck (2004), not only is the Discussion a place for authors to discuss how results turned out, but to offer commentary on why they think the results turned out as they did.

Implications

In this subsection of the Discussion, the authors will explicitly state the scope of their study, including any limitations. As researchers often must work within the limits of real-life contexts while complying with the ethical procedures for conducting research, it is only expected that research studies will have parameters that must be clearly articulated for the reader. Therefore, the authors should address the factors that could not be controlled for, as well as the generalizability of their investigation.

Future Research

Often the final section of the Discussion addresses additional questions that were unanswered or arose from the present study. This section states ideas for future investigation and is a great place to consult when reviewing the existing literature on a topic in order to plan future work. Namely, future researchers can utilize the ideas presented here to help identify a truly novel research idea and ensure that it is situated in the context of previous works. If they are interested in publishing in the journal, they should consult the author guidelines.

TABLE 5-1. HELPFUL TERMS FOR INTERPRETING AND EVALUATING RESEARCH METHODS

TERM	DEFINITION
Interrater agreement/ Interobserver agreement	The degree of agreement between two or more reporting on the same observational session; agreement is 100% if the researchers had the same results for the variables coded/rated. There are several ways to code interobserver agreement including total count, mean or exact count-per-interval, or trial-by-trial (Cooper et al., 2019).
Procedural fidelity	The extent to which an intervention is implemented as planned (Gresham, 2005); the degree to which an interventionist consistently and completely implements intervention component (Sanetti & Kratochwill, 2009).
Social validity	Measures that provide an understanding of what was acceptable and what was unacceptable to consumers used to inform researchers of adaptations that need to be made for implementation (Schwartz & Baer, 1991).
Mean (M)	The average value of all responses to one question (Dunfon, 2005); also used to describe the average age of the participant sample.
Standard deviation (SD)	The distribution of responses in relation to the mean; higher SD values indicate more variance from the mean (Dunfon, 2005).
p value (p)	The result yielded by a formula applied by researchers to determine if results are due to chance or actual correlation; typically, the p value of $< .05$ is used to determine statistical significance (Dunfon, 2005).

References

The final section of a research article is the References section. This is where all sources cited in-text are provided. References can be very helpful when readers would like to know more about an individual study that was referenced or delve into the topic at a deeper level (APA, 2019; Huck, 2004). Readers can use the references to locate more information or additional studies that support their research.

Kaylee visits the library's search page while the university librarian is walking her through the search process. She applies the Boolean operators and finds that she is able to locate articles that support her original theory about the overidentification of Black males in special education. She finds additional support and federal websites that provide more information and datasets featuring the number of students receiving special education services in the United States, which was then broken down into demographic categories.

Evaluating Research Articles

Prior to being published in a journal, manuscripts undergo a rigorous review process to ensure they are accurate, written correctly, use sound methods, and overall will convey effective research that readers of the article can understand and potentially replicate in the future. Research articles

TABLE 5-2. CHECKLIST FOR EVALUATING A RESEARCH ARTICLE

CHECK	CATEGORY	EXPLANATION
☐	Abstract	Scan abstract to ensure the content is relevant.
☐	Introduction	Includes thorough literature review. Study purpose and research questions are stated.
☐	Method	Includes participant demographics and description. Design aligns with the research questions. Method adheres to research quality indicators.
☐	Results/Findings	Addresses research questions. Data analyses are appropriate. Data are presented clearly.
☐	Discussion	Details limitations, future research, and presents a conclusion.

should be read critically and evaluatively to allow for their productive use and dialogue in future research, where readers are learning from the article in its entirety (Finlay, 1997). Readers should then break down the article to ensure comprehension of all aspects of the article so they can identify the type of article (e.g., empirical, practitioner, op eds), the type of research (e.g., single case, group design, or literature review), and the outcomes and implications of the article. Readers should be able to summarize an article by discussing the important sections of the article (i.e., methods, limitations) with the potential for replication as the ultimate goal of each article. For additional tips on evaluating a research article, see Table 5-2.

Peer Review

The peer review process is one that is intended to provide fair and unbiased review of a manuscript once it is submitted to a journal, and is supposed to provide feedback to improve and enhance the manuscript so it can be published. Peer review is used to evaluate manuscripts and grant submissions for scientific processes across disciplines (Starck, 2017). Peer review evaluates all aspects of the manuscript for accuracy, authenticity, and mechanics, and if the manuscript is publishable and acceptable within that specific discipline. The peer review process typically follows this pattern:

- Authors research then conduct a study, or write a practitioner-focused manuscript
- Authors identify a journal and follow the author guidelines for intended submission
- The corresponding author submits the manuscript for consideration for publication in the journal
- Editors identify reviewers based on their self-identified expertise areas
- Reviewers read, review, and provide comments to enhance the manuscript
  - They focus on the entire manuscript, including the organization, data, and conclusions to ensure that it is valid, reliable, and replicable
- Editors return the manuscript to the authors with their own and reviewer feedback
- Authors revise the manuscript according to the feedback provided by the reviewers and resubmit the manuscript (i.e., revise and resubmit)
- Editor and reviewers review again and decide whether to accept or ask for another round of revisions

- Manuscripts are either accepted or rejected after the revise and resubmit requests
- Accepted manuscripts are published, typically first online, and then in print (if the journal is printed)

The preceding section describes an ideal peer-review scenario. The peer-review process brings a level of legitimacy to published articles that non–peer-reviewed articles may not possess.

Identifying Reputable Journals

Reputable journals in academic fields are generally listed in directories, whether they are open access or subscription-based (e.g., Cabell's list, Ulrich's serials directory). Reputable journals often have an impact factor (some may not), acceptance rate, are accessible via major databases (e.g., ERIC, PsycInfo), publish regular issues on a predictable schedule (e.g., quarterly, monthly), and are peer reviewed. Table 5-3 includes reputable, peer-reviewed research and practitioner journals in special education.

Reputable journals have an editorial board listed on their website, a defined scope for the journal content that aligns with the articles that are published. Policies (i.e., peer review and editorial) along with a publication ethics statement are publicly posted on their website. Think-Check-Submit (2020) is a website that provides feedback on different types of publication opportunities, and "helps researchers identify trusted journals and publishers for their research. Through a range of tools and practical resources, this international, cross-sector initiative aims to educate researchers, promote integrity, and build trust in credible research and publications" (Think-Check-Submit, 2020).

Bias in the Evidence Base

When research teams complete studies, the typical process includes submitting the study in a publishable manuscript to a reputable journal. However, some studies that do not have intended outcomes, have null effects, or result in something other than what the researchers intended may not be published (Cook & Therrien, 2017). This is otherwise known as publication bias, which is "what occurs whenever the research that appears in the published literature is systematically unrepresentative of the population of completed studies" (Rothstein et al., 2005, p. 1). Replication and bias have been called to the forefront in special education, as well as the evaluation of studies to ensure they are unbiased and replicable (Cook, 2014).

This could result in possible bias in the evidence base, which essentially means that researchers are only publishing what they consider to be an intervention with ideal outcomes (Gage et al., 2017). A serious concern for this occurs specifically in studies that explore EBPs. EBPs are interventions, systems, or programs that meet standards for research and make marked gains with the populations to whom they are applied (Cook & Odom, 2013; Cook et al., 2008). EBPs are supported through both experimental single case design and group design, and determined by meeting the following standards in high-quality studies: two group design (i.e., randomized or quasi-experimental design) studies, five single case design studies, or a combination of one group design and three single case studies (NPDC, n.d.). EBPs meet rigorous standards in the fields in which they are applied (e.g., Horner et al., 2005; Kratochwill et al., 2013).

The overrepresentation of students of color in special education is not a new notion. First recognized by Dunn (1968) and continuously discussed in literature since then (e.g., Skiba et al., 2013; Skiba et al., 2008), the problem persists and lacks solutions. Students of color (e.g., Black or Latinx students), often referred to and included with the term culturally and linguistically diverse (CLD), are identified with a disability considered to be more subjective (i.e., emotional/behavioral disability, intellectual disability, and learning disability) at more than twice the rate of their White peers (Bean, 2013; Sullivan & Bal, 2013). The causes are attributed to bias in testing, quality of education received prior to being referred, confusion during the special education referral process, lack of classroom management on the referring teacher's part, teacher bias, social differences and cultural mismatch

TABLE 5-3. EXAMPLES OF REPUTABLE SPECIAL EDUCATION JOURNALS

ORGANIZATION	NAME OF JOURNAL	WEBSITE
Council for Exceptional Children (CEC)	*TEACHING Exceptional Children* (practitioner) *Exceptional Children* (research)	https://cec.sped.org/ Publications/CEC-Journals
Subdivisions of CEC		
Council of Administrators of Special Education (CASE)	*Journal of Special Education Leadership*	https://www.casecec.org/ journal
Council for Children with Behavioral Disorders (CCBD)	*Beyond Behavior* (practitioner) *Behavioral Disorders* (research)	http://www.ccbd.net/ publications/
Division on Autism and Developmental Disabilities (DADD)	*Education and Training in Autism and Developmental Disabilities*	http://www.daddcec.com/ etadd.html
Division for Communicative Disabilities and Deafness (DCDD)	*Communication Disorders Quarterly*	https://journals.sagepub. com/home/cdq
Division on Career Development and Transition (DCDT)	*Career Development and Transition for Exceptional Individuals* (CDTEI)	https://community.cec.sped. org/dcdt/publications/ dcdtpublications
Division for Culturally and Linguistically Diverse Exceptional Learners (DDEL)	*Multiple Voices*	https://www. multiplevoicesjournal.org/loi/ muvo
Division for Early Childhood (DEC)	*Young Exceptional Children* (practitioner) *Journal of Early Intervention* (research)	https://www.dec-sped.org/ journals
The Association for the Gifted (TAG)	*Journal for the Education of the Gifted*	http://cectag.com/resources/ journal-for-the-education-of-the-gifted/
Innovations in Special Education Technology (ISET)	*Journal of Special Education Technology*	https://www.isetcec.org/ journal-of-special-education-technology-jset/
Teacher Education Division (TED)	*Teacher Education and Special Education*	https://journals.sagepub. com/home/tes
Division of International Special Education and Services (DISES)	*Journal of International Special Needs Education*	http://www.dises-cec.org/

between students and teachers, or the possibility that it is related to school climate or culture (Skiba et al., 2013; Sullivan & Bal, 2013). Though IDEA (2004) and subsequent legislation attempted to make strides in focusing on and reducing disproportionality in special education, the problem continues to exist. More recently, disproportionality has been highlighted as a concern based on the lack of students of color as participants in intervention studies (CEC-DR, 2015).

Excluding CLD students from the body of research hints that there may be bias in the evidence base. Including CLD students in EBP research helps demonstrate that the practice can be applied across students from different backgrounds and provides a stronger evidence base for the practice. The Council for Exceptional Children–Division of Research (CEC-DR, 2015) highlighted the issue and the importance of including CLD students in research. Additionally, suggestions were provided for increasing CLD students in EBP research, including recruitment, information dissemination, support for CLD families, including CLD individuals on research teams, access to items that diverse families may not otherwise have (e.g., technology), infusing CLD issues in research, including student background information, communicating with CLD families as part of research outreach, and providing training to research teams to utilize EBPs with CLD students and their families (CEC-DR, 2015). Including diverse students in EBP research is imperative in that the research can be applied to students from all backgrounds and ensures that the EBP is truly backed by evidence. When looking at studies and conducting research, be sure to look at the demographics of the participants to ensure that it is provided.

SUMMARY

This chapter provided the background on identifying, locating, and evaluating educational research. Like Kaylee, most researchers may not realize that the university library has many search tools and support to help researchers find reputable research articles. The library is the first place for researchers to start searching because there are resources, both in-person and virtual, that will support the researcher's search to ensure they are using the correct databases and maximizing their search potential. Identifying the pertinent parts of an article is necessary when locating articles, particularly to other researchers to replicate the study, or for researchers who want to design similar studies, and evaluate their effectiveness. Reputable and reliable journals are the first place researchers should start their research, and where they will find the most valuable research to practice information.

Locating EBPs in the research and understanding their importance is imperative in special education because they form the basis for quality instruction. Focusing on the evidence base, with the ability to recognize bias in the research, will ensure equity in research in future research teams. It is important to use the tools provided to examine the evidence base with a critical eye, and reach out to the professionals for help when it is needed. Table 5-4 includes common misconceptions, and Table 5-5 includes additional resources.

CHAPTER REVIEW

1. Identify the librarian at the university library who can assist in special education research.
2. Name three ways to identify reputable journals.
3. Why is it important to involve participants from diverse cultural and linguistic backgrounds in research?
4. List and describe the essential components of a research article.

TABLE 5-4. COMMON MISCONCEPTIONS AND CLARIFICATIONS ABOUT RESEARCH

MISCONCEPTION	BETTER UNDERSTANDING
Selecting one database when using the library resources to find related resources.	Conducting a thorough search of library databases requires utilizing all relevant databases possible to maximize the results of the search.
Submitting research to a journal is a quick process and involves a short time period from submission to acceptance.	Submitting a manuscript to a journal is a process that requires patience and persistence. Often, an author (or team of authors) will receive several rounds of revise and resubmit requests, along with feedback from reviewers on each draft of the manuscript.
Demographic characteristics are not important when conducting research.	Demographics (e.g., race, ethnicity, gender) are important in demonstrating that an intervention works with participants from multiple backgrounds, and can be applied to individuals with multiple demographic characteristics.

TABLE 5-5. ADDITIONAL RESOURCES

RESOURCE	DESCRIPTION
Conducting Literature Reviews https://iupui.libguides.com/c.php?g=473648&p=3421357	This site provides basic information for conducting a literature review.
Peer Review and Scholarly Publishing https://libguides.uccs.edu/c.php?g=694087&p=4919267&_ga=2.155346875.1287445555.1584236986-892820366.1581446797	This site provides an overview of peer-review and publishing processes.
Think-Click-Submit https://thinkchecksubmit.org/	This site provides assistance with determining appropriate journals to submit scholarly work.

REFERENCES

American Psychological Association (2019). *Publication manual of the American Psychological Association* (7th ed.). Author.

American Psychological Association. (2020). PsycInfo. https://www.apa.org/pubs/databases/psycinfo/?tab=3

Astalin, P. K. (2013). Qualitative research designs: A conceptual framework. *International Journal of Social Science and Interdisciplinary Research, 2*, 118-124.

Bean, K. F. (2013). Disproportionality and acting-out behaviors among African American children in special education. *Child and Adolescent Social Work Journal, 30*(6), 487-504.

Cook, B. G. (2014). A call for examining replication and bias in special education research. *Remedial and Special Education, 35*(4), 233-246. https://doi.org/10.1177/0741932514528995

Cook, B. G., & Odom, S. L. (2013). Evidence-based practices and implementation science in special education. *Exceptional Children, 79*(2), 135-144.

Cook, B. G., Tankersley, M., & Harjusola-Webb, S. (2008). Evidence-based special education and professional wisdom: Putting it all together. *Intervention in School and Clinic, 44*(2), 105-111.

Cook, B. G., & Therrien, W. J. (2017). Null effects and publication bias in special education research. *Behavioral Disorders, 42*(4), 149-158. https://doi.org/10.1177/0198742917709473

Cooper, J. O., Heron, T. E., & Heward, W. L. (2019). *Applied behavior analysis* (3rd ed.). Pearson.

Council for Exceptional Children-Division for Research (CEC-DR). (2015). Increasing the involvement of culturally and linguistically diverse students in special education research 2015. https://higherlogicdownload.s3.amazonaws.com/SPED/b7acd4b4-bc4d-4c1f-a7d4-efab3d52da44/UploadedImages/Position%20Papers/White%20Paper%20-%20CLD%20in%20Research%202015.pdf

Dunfon, R. (2005). How to read a research article. https://cpb-us-e1.wpmucdn.com/blogs.cornell.edu/dist/f/575/files/2015/12/How-to-Read-a-Research-Article-1tweh7l.pdf

Dunn, L. M. (1968). Special education for the mildly retarded—Is much of it justifiable? *Exceptional Children, 35*(1), 5-22.

Ediqo. (2016). Eight indicators of a reputable open access journal. https://www.ediqo.com/blog/8-indicators-of-a-reputable-open-access-journal/

ERIC. (2019). 2019 ERIC year in review. *ERIC*. https://www.eric.ed.gov/pdf/ERIC_Year_Review_2019.pdf

Finlay, L. (1997). Evaluating research articles. *British Journal of Occupational Therapy, 60*(5), 205-208. https://doi.org/10.1177/030802269706000504

Fuchs, L. S., & Fuchs, D. (1993). Writing research reports for publication: Recommendations for new authors. *Remedial and Special Education, 14*(3), 39-46.

Gage, N. A., Cook, B. G., & Reichow, B. (2017). Publication bias in special education meta-analyses. *Exceptional Children, 83*(4), 428–445. https://doi.org/10.1177/0014402917691016

Gresham, F. M. (2005). Response to intervention: An alternative means of identifying students as emotionally disturbed. *Education and Treatment of Children, 28*(4), 328-344. http://pent.ca.gov/pos/rti/rtialternativemeans_gresham.pdf

Horner, R. H., Carr, E. G., Halle, J., McGee, G., Odom, S., & Wolery, M. (2005). The use of single-subject research to identify evidence-based practice in special education. *Exceptional Children, 71*(2), 165-179.

Huck, S. W. (2004). *Reading statistics and research* (4th ed.). Pearson.

Individuals with Disabilities Education Act (IDEA). (2004). https://sites.ed.gov/idea/

Institute of Education Science. (n.d.). ERIC: Education Resources Information Center. https://ies.ed.gov/ncee/projects/eric.asp

IUPUI University Library. (2019). Literature reviews: A self-guided tutorial: Citation chaining. https://iupui.libguides.com/c.php?g=473648&p=3421357

Kraemer Family Library. (2020). ENGL 1410: Writing and AI: Search tips. https://libguides.uccs.edu/c.php?g=866783&p=6263629

Kratochwill, T. R., Hitchcock, J. H., Horner, R. H., Levin, J. R., Odum, S. L., Rindskopf, D. M., & Shadish, W. R. (2013). Single-case intervention research design standards. *Remedial and Special Education, 34*, 26-38.

Leary, H., & Walker, A. (2018). Meta-analysis and meta-synthesis methodologies: Rigorously piecing together research. *TechTrends, 62*, 525-534.

National Professional Development Center on Autism Spectrum Disorder (NPDC). (n.d.). What criteria determined if an intervention was effective? https://autismpdc.fpg.unc.edu/what-criteria-determined-if-intervention-was-effective

Rothstein, H. R., Sutton, A. J., & Borenstein, M. (2005). Publication bias in meta-analysis. In Rothstein, H. R., Sutton, A. J., Borenstein, M. (Eds.), *Publication bias in meta-analysis: Prevention, assessment, and adjustments* (pp. 1-7). Wiley.

Sanetti, L. M. H., & Kratochwill, T. R. (2009). Toward developing a science of treatment integrity: Introduction to the special series. *School Psychology Review, 38*, 445-459.

Schwartz, I. S. & Baer, D. M. (1991). Social validity assessments: Is current practice state of the art? *Journal of Applied Behavior Analysis, 24,* 189-204.

Scopus. (2020). Elsevier. https://www.elsevier.com/solutions/scopus

Skiba, R., Albrecht, S., & Losen, D. (2013). CCBD'S position summary on federal policy on disproportionality in special education. *Behavioral Disorders, 38*(2), 108-120.

Skiba, R. J., Simmons, A. B., Ritter, S., Gibb, A. C., Rausch, M. K., Cuadradro, J., & Chung, C. G. (2008). Achieving equity in special education: History, status, and current challenges. *Exceptional Children, 74*(3), 264-288.

Starck, J. M. (2017). Scientific peer review: Guidelines for informative peer review. *Springer Spektrum.* https://doi.org/10.1007/978-3-658-19915-9

Sullivan, A. L., & Bal, A. (2013). Disproportionality in special education: Effects of individual and school variables on disability risk. *Exceptional Children, 79*(4), 475-494.

Think. Check. Submit. (2020). Choose the right journal or publisher for your research. https://thinkchecksubmit.org/

UTA Libraries. (2020). Research Process: Step by step: Identify keywords. https://libguides.uta.edu/researchprocess/keywords

Web of Science Group. (2020). Web of Science. Clarivate Analytics. https://clarivate.com/webofsciencegroup/solutions/web-of-science/

Yilmaz, K. (2013). Comparison of quantitative and qualitative research traditions: Epistemological, theoretical, and methodological differences. *European Journal of Education, 48*(2), 311-325.

Systematic Literature Reviews

With contributions from John William McKenna, PhD

INTRODUCTION

Talbott and colleagues (2018) estimated an increase of 2,700% of published systematic review or meta-analyses in the field of special education from the year 1990 to 2015. This trend is likely due to the critical role of reviews of the literature to inform practice and policy, and identify areas for needed research. A variety of terms are used to describe methodology that involves reviewing the literature: (a) literature review, (b) research review, (c) scoping review, (d) systematic reviews, (e) research synthesis, and (f) meta-analysis. These terms are often conflated to mean the same thing, which impacts the credibility of our science. In this chapter, we will use the terms *narrative literature review, scoping review, systematic review,* and *meta-analysis* to define four distinct types of reviews, each of which include a different purpose, rationale, and methodology. In the field of special education, there has been an increasing prevalence of systematic reviews and meta-analyses published over the last 30 years (Gage et al., 2017; Talbott et al., 2018). Similar to primary studies (i.e., single case research designs, group designs), the methodological rigor of the experiment is critical to protecting the validity of research findings. There are several quality indicators developed for systematic reviews and meta-analyses published in the literature (i.e., MARS [APA, 2010]; MECIR [Higgins et al., 2020]; PRISMA [Moher et al., 2009]; Quality Indicators for Reviews of Research in Special Education [Talbott et al., 2018]) that researchers planning a review of the literature should consult to maximize the internal validity of their design.

Hott, B. L., Brigham, F. J., & Peltier, C.
Research Methods in Special Education (pp. 89-111).
© 2021 SLACK Incorporated.

CHAPTER OBJECTIVES

→ Clarify the purpose for a narrative literature review, scoping review, systematic review, and meta-analysis.

→ Generate research questions that can be addressed through research synthesis.

→ List the methodology steps for conducting a scoping review, systematic review, and meta-analysis.

→ Identify published standards that can be used to evaluate the methodology of systematic reviews and meta-analyses.

→ Explain how publication bias impacts results from scoping reviews, systematic reviews, and meta-analyses.

→ Identify the impact that scoping reviews, systematic reviews, and meta-analyses can have on policy, practice, and future research.

KEY TERMS

- **Boolean String**: A list of keywords and phrases used in electronic database searchers to identify studies that are relevant to research questions.

- **Grey Literature**: A term used to describe literature that is not published in an academic journal. Examples include dissertations, conference proceedings, preprints, or studies that have not yet been published.

- **Internal Validity**: The ability of an experiment to explain away the impact that confounding variables may have on claims made about the results of a study.

- **Interrater Reliability**: A process used to establish consistency across multiple independent raters during the decision-making processes. Interrater reliability is often reported as percent agreement, although other methods can be used (e.g., Cohen's kappa).

- **Meta-Analysis**: Meta-analytic techniques are employed after conducting a systematic review, and they are used to quantitatively estimate the effect of an intervention, or relation between variables, across a literature base.

- **Narrative Literature Review**: A tool used to summarize the critical points or aspects of a particular topic. These types of reviews are used to frame the purpose of a research study (i.e., introduction written before method section of a scientific manuscript) or they can be a stand-alone product.

- **Primary Study**: In the context of a scoping review, systematic review, or meta-analysis, a primary study is one that met inclusion criteria and was included in the synthesis.

- **Publication Bias**: A term used to describe the phenomenon that published literature is systematically unrepresentative of the population of studies completed in the field. In the context of scoping reviews, systematic reviews, and meta-analyses, *publication bias* refers to the issue that the primary studies that met inclusion criteria are systematically not representative of all studies conducted that would meet the inclusion criteria.

- **Scoping Review**: A tool used to explore what literature is available on a particular topic. These types of reviews are used to categorize the literature and identify types of evidence provided for a topic with the goal of pointing to major gaps, or unknowns, in the literature.

- **Systematic Review**: A tool used to systematically search, identify, select, and evaluate a literature base meeting a specified criterion. These types of reviews have a transparent methodology that involves the evaluation of the methodological quality and the systematic analysis of study characteristics. The aim of a systematic review is to provide actionable advice for policy and practice, while also illuminating unknowns in the current literature.

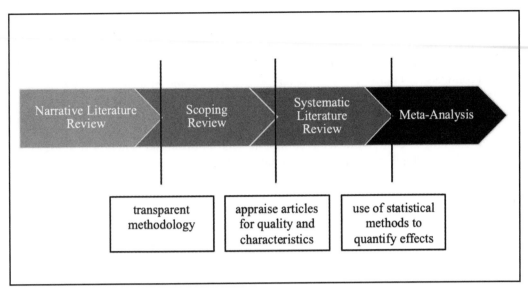

Figure 6-1. Distinguishing between the types of reviews.

CATEGORIZING REVIEWS OF THE LITERATURE

A critical skill to consume and produce reviews of the literature is the ability to categorize reviews by their type based on the purpose, research questions addressed, and methodology employed. Misalignment between a stated purpose, research questions addressed, and the methodology employed impacts the internal validity of the conclusions one can draw from the study. An issue that compounds this decision-making process is the use of the terms literature review, scoping review, systematic reviews, and meta-analysis interchangeably. Below, we define four major types of reviews of the literature, the intended purpose for the type of review, and the research questions they can appropriately address (Figure 6-1).

Narrative Literature Review

A *narrative literature review* is a tool used to synthesize the available literature. This type of review can serve a multitude of purposes. One application of a narrative literature review is the introduction of a primary study (e.g., single case research design, group design, survey). The authors state the problem to address, cite relevant related literature, and then highlight the purpose and need for the current study. The authors typically aim to address four goals in a narrative review: (a) synthesize current literature, (b) critique the current literature, (c) integrate literature across related topics, and (d) identify a primary issue for the field to address (Cooper, 2010). A second application of a narrative literature review is to unpack a theoretical model for a specific phenomenon. The authors typically aim to: (a) describe and critique current experimental work related to the topic, (b) evaluate competing theories on the topic, and (c) provide a justification for a new theoretical model or approach to address the phenomenon (Cooper, 2010).

Readers of narrative literature reviews as stand-alone documents or narrative literature reviews used to frame the purpose of a research study are cautioned. Narrative literature reviews do not provide a systematic approach for selecting primary studies to include in the synthesis. When writing a narrative literature review, the author decides which primary studies to include in the synthesis, which adds a layer of bias to the process. Examples of introductions to primary studies are replete in the literature, so we suggest that readers identify an experimental study that aligns to their specific research agenda for an exemplar.

For example, in the published literature is Carr's (2007) review that aimed to define and provide examples of how to apply positive behavioral interventions and supports (PBIS) in real-world contexts. At that time, discussions surrounding quality of life (QOL) were replete in the literature (see Felce, 1997; Turnbull et al., 2003), with many advocating that this should be the central framework the field considers for improving outcomes for individuals with and without disabilities. Carr's article first described current research in the QOL literature on how the latent constructs of happiness, helpfulness, and hopefulness are defined and the ways in which PBIS researchers could provide operational definitions of observable and measurable variables that would be couched within these domains. This provided a justification for the important role PBIS can play in improving the QOL for students with and without disabilities in school contexts. Carr extended his discussion by identifying specific barriers that school districts have faced in the large-scale implementation of PBIS frameworks. He identified five related sciences and disciplines that the field could draw upon when thinking about tackling these challenges: (a) organizational management, (b) community and ecological psychology, (c) cultural psychology, (d) biomedical science, and (e) positive psychology. The potential impact of this article was to outline a justifiable argument for the use of PBIS frameworks as a scientific technology to improve the QOL outcomes for students. In addition, Carr suggested that the field rely on knowledge from other disciplines to inform large-scale implementation of PBIS models.

Scoping Review

A *scoping review* is a tool used to map out what literature is available for a particular topic (Tricco et al., 2016). This type of review can serve multiple purposes. One utility of conducting a scoping review is to highlight the types of research questions that have been asked and the empirical evidence available on a particular topic. The results of a scoping review highlight major gaps, or unknowns, in the literature. This can aid in building a systematic line of research to address unknowns in the literature. In addition, results from a scoping review can be used to identify a need for a systematic review or meta-analysis on a specific topic within the broad area included in the scoping review.

Scoping reviews differ significantly from narrative reviews. First, the purpose of a scoping review is different from a narrative literature review. A scoping review aims to identify what evidence is available on a topic, whereas a narrative review aims to build an argument or theory out of existing literature. Second, a scoping review employs a systematic methodology that is reported in a transparent manner. Authors are explicit in their systematic search process, how articles were included in the review, how data were extracted from articles, and demonstrate adequate interrater reliability at each step of the process. This systematic process and transparent reporting increases the internal validity of the design and can reduce the likelihood of bias.

Cheng and colleagues (2018) provide an example of a scoping review. The team explored the evidence available on strategies to support individuals with an intellectual disability (ID) to obtain and maintain employment. The authors provided inclusion and exclusion criteria to articulate why articles were included in the review: (a) peer-reviewed publications from 2001 to 2015, (b) include participants 18 years and older identified with an ID, and (c) clear description of the intervention or strategy and data collected on its effectiveness for dependent variables related to obtaining or maintain work. The authors provided a description of their methods for the systematic search procedure and the title/abstract and full-text screening procedures. The researchers coded studies (e.g., read articles in their entirety to identify specific information) to determine: (a) the purpose and type of support used (i.e., natural, employment support services, instructional approaches), (b) participant characteristics and country of origin, (c) experimental design used, and (d) a description of key findings reported by the team. The authors identified 22 studies that met inclusion criteria. Findings suggest natural supports (e.g., using coworkers to providing social reinforcement) show promising results for individuals with an ID. However, the authors identified a needed line of research, which was research investigating the best ways to ensure natural supports work as intended: (a) building social skills for individuals with an ID and (b) training employees in how to be a successful natural support. Employment services were also identified as a potential influence in recruiting and maintaining employment. The last major finding was that the individualized placement and support approach has a substantial research base in helping individuals with mental illness obtain and maintain employment, but no studies investigated this approach for individuals with an ID.

Harrison and colleagues (2019) published a scoping review on the research related to the inclusion of students identified with emotional and behavioral disorders (EBD) in general education settings. The authors provided operationally defined criteria for inclusion: (a) included participants with EBD or participants who provided services to students with EBD, (b) focused on school setting (i.e., K-12) in a general education environment in the United States, (c) published (academic journals or dissertations) or posted (i.e., grey literature) between date restriction of 1997 to 2018, and (d) used one of the following methodologies: quantitative, qualitative, single case research design, systematic review, or meta-analysis. The authors provided a description for the search process and included a flow map (i.e., similar to suggestion from PRISMA [Preferred Reporting Items for Systematic Reviews and Meta-Analyses]) to visually display the process. The authors also described the iterative process in which they engaged to develop coding guides to chart the data. The team identified 30 studies to include in their review. Results were displayed in concept maps to highlight what has been investigated related to this topic and the research questions that cannot be answered given the current evidence. The authors highlighted the concerning finding that only four primary studies investigated practices or strategies that improve academic and behavioral outcomes for students with EBD in general education settings. This was recommended as a needed line of research.

Systematic Review

A systematic review is a tool used to systematically search, identify, select, and evaluate a literature base meeting a specified criterion (i.e., Campbell Collaboration, PRISMA). Systematic reviews have a transparent methodology that involves search procedures, evaluation of the methodological quality, extraction of information from studies, and the systematic analysis of extracted data. Systematic reviews can provide useful information to a variety of stakeholders. First, depending on the scope of the systematic review, it could carry major implications for legislation or policy. One example of a systematic review informing policy and legislation is the National Reading Panel's (2000) final report. The systematic review identified that effective reading instruction should include five components: phonemic awareness, phonics, fluency, vocabulary, and comprehension. The Individuals with Disabilities Education Act (2004) included language that states students cannot be identified with a specific learning disability (LD) for reading if they did not have access to high-quality reading instruction that included the components of phonemic awareness, phonics, fluency, vocabulary, and comprehension. Furthermore, states are currently passing legislation related to the screening, identification, and remediation of academic deficits for students at risk of or identified with dyslexia (Youman & Mather, 2018). The legislation being passed draws heavily on findings from the National Reading Panel's (2005) report. Second, results of a systematic review could provide immediate actionable information for practitioners (e.g., teachers, principals). Third, similar to scoping reviews, a systematic review often will identify unknowns in the literature, which is informative to the research field.

Systematic reviews share similarities with scoping reviews; however, they also share important distinctions. First, two characteristics shared by these methodologies are the systematic process and transparency in reporting the search process and the coding, or data extraction, from primary studies. As is shown in Figure 6-1, this separates these two methodologies from narrative literature reviews. Furthermore, both scoping reviews and systematic reviews have the potential to identify needed areas of future research to address socially important questions for the field of special education. Systematic reviews differ in several ways. First, systematic reviews include more restrictive parameters for study inclusion, thus providing a detailed analysis and synthesis of a narrower literature base. Second, systematic reviews evaluate the methodological quality of primary studies to estimate the internal validity of their designs. Last, due to the parameters set, a systematic review often involves more extensive coding, or extraction, of variables in the primary studies.

Common and colleagues (2020) provide an example of a systematic review. The focus of the review was on a teacher's use of practices to increase students' opportunities to respond (OTR) during whole group instruction. This systematic review includes two unique characteristics. First, the authors evaluated the methodological quality of the studies using the Council for Exceptional Children Standards for Evidence-Based Practices in Special Education (2014) to determine if the practice met the threshold to be considered an evidence-based practice (EBP). These types of systematic reviews have become more prevalent in the literature as the EBP movement in special education has increased (see Cook & Odom, 2013). Another unique feature of the systematic review was that the authors computed effect sizes (i.e., between-case standardized mean difference, Log Response Ratio) for studies that met the quality indicator threshold. The reason this study is classified as a systematic review, rather than a meta-analysis, is because in a meta-analysis effect sizes across studies are aggregated to estimate an overall effect (i.e., omnibus effect) and investigate heterogeneity (i.e., variability) of effects across studies.

The authors provided a transparent description of the systematic search process along with the Boolean string that was used. The authors included many components (i.e., ancestral search, hand searching) in their systematic search process that increased the validity in concluding all available literature was obtained. The inclusion criteria were clear: (a) experimental studies (i.e., group or SCRD), (b) intervention was teacher-delivered OTR in a whole-group instructional setting with K-12 students, and (c) a student-level dependent variable categorized as academic or behavioral. The authors used a comprehensive coding guide to extract data from studies. In addition, they evaluated the methodological quality of studies using the Council for Exceptional Children Standards for Evidence-Based Practices in Special Education (2014). Results suggest teacher's use of practices to increase students' OTR was a potentially EBP. The authors highlighted the need for additional research because there are many variables (e.g., type of response, incorporation of technology, type of dependent variable) that were systematically different across the literature base and could impact effects.

Morin and colleagues (2018) provide another example of a systematic review. The aim was to evaluate all intervention research using high-tech augmentative and alternative communication (AAC) devices to determine if it met the threshold to be considered an EBP. Similar to Common et al (2020), the current review evaluated the quality of studies to make an EBP determination; however, these authors used the What Works Clearinghouse Design Standards (Version 4.0; 2017).

The manuscript author who performed the systematic search was a research librarian who specialized in systematic searches in the medical field. The Boolean string and entire search process were cited in the companion article (see Ganz et al., 2017). To be included in the review, the authors provided clear guidelines: (a) participants with complex communication needs comorbid with autism spectrum disorder (ASD), (b) collected dependent variables dealing with communication (i.e., receptive, expressive, AAC use, joint attention, social play, imitation), (c) AAC was an independent variable, and (d) use of a single case experimental design. The authors first used the What Works Clearinghouse Design Standards (Version 4.0, 2017) to determine the internal validity of the design. In addition, the authors constructed a second coding guide that focused on external validity by pulling from other publications (i.e., CEC, 2014; Horner et al., 2005; Reichow et al., 2008). A unique feature of this systematic review was the authors did not provide any data related to study characteristics because the goal was merely to determine if studies meeting parameters classified AAC as an EBP for the specified population. The authors determined AAC met the threshold to be considered an EBP for individuals with ASD and complex communication needs. The authors also commented on a need for additional research, mainly the collection of extended maintenance and generalization data.

Meta-Analysis

Meta-analytic techniques are employed after conducting a systematic review. *Meta-analysis* is a quantitative technique used to estimate the effect of an intervention, or relation between variables, across a literature base meeting a specified criterion (e.g., article selection criteria). Aggregating effects across studies allows the team to provide an overall estimate (i.e., omnibus) for the entire literature base. Often, the team will identify dispersion around the estimated omnibus effect (e.g., variability in outcomes across included studies), which warrants an investigation to identify if the variance can be explained by systematic differences in study characteristics. This is often investigated by conducting moderator analyses, which can be thought about through three questions:

1. For whom is the intervention most or least effective? This question aims at investigating whether differences in participant characteristics across studies can explain variance in intervention effects.

2. By whom is the intervention most or least effective? This question aims at investigating whether differences in interventionist characteristics across studies can explain variance in intervention effects.

3. Under what conditions is the intervention most or least effective? "Conditions" is defined broadly here. First, the team may evaluate whether effects are differential across geographical regions, settings, and/or locations in which the intervention was implemented. Each of these aspects could include specific variables of interest to the team. Second, the team may evaluate whether effects are differential based on specific characteristics or components related to the intervention that differed across studies. Third, the research team may investigate if an intervention is more effective when implemented by researchers than school-based practitioners. Lastly, the team may evaluate whether effects are differential based on the measurement procedures used in the study (e.g., dependent variable[s] collected, instruments used).

Ciullo and colleagues (2020) published a meta-analysis that serves as an example of the process. The aim of this meta-analysis was to evaluate all experimental studies that implemented an intervention in a social studies context to improve outcomes for students identified with an LD. An important issue that research teams conducting meta-analyses in the field of special education will confront is deciding what to do with group design and single case research designs. Currently, the combination of single case research designs and group designs into one model to provide an estimate of intervention effects is controversial because we do not have statistical techniques that can appropriately model this process. The research team opted to exclude single case research designs and focus exclusively on the group design literature. The authors conducted a systematic search that included a six-pronged approach: (a) electronic database search, (b) hand search, (c) review of previous systematic reviews, (d) Google Scholar Search, (e) ancestral search through reference list of primary studies, and (f) author specific-search. Due to the broad parameters (e.g., writing, social studies, LDs), the authors created a coding guide to investigate systematic differences that may be present across studies. The authors also evaluated the methodological rigor of studies using the What Works Clearinghouse Design Standards (Version 3.0; 2014). The omnibus effect was Hedges' $g = 0.76$ (0.10). The authors attempted to reduce the impact of publication bias through a three-pronged approach: (a) they explicitly included grey literature in their systematic search, (b) they constructed a funnel plot to evaluate if publication bias may be a concern, and (c) ran a statistical test (i.e., Egger regression test) to examine whether publication bias may be impacting their data. The authors identified high variability in effect sizes reported per study around the omnibus effect size. To attempt to explain this dispersion, the authors conducted 14 separate moderator analyses on variables representing for whom, by whom, and under what conditions. The authors then selected variables that were identified as statistically significant by simple contrasts and entered them into a meta-regression model. None of the variables were statistically significant when entered into the model.

Barton and colleagues (2017) provide another example of a meta-analysis. The meta-analysis focused on evaluating technology-aided interventions for students with ASD. The authors faced a similar decision as Ciullo and colleagues (2020)—what to do with single case research designs and group designs. Barton and colleagues (2017) opted to include all studies, but when using meta-analytic techniques, the authors kept the group design and single case research design data separate. The authors aimed to update a similar review that was published 2 years prior by using more advanced statistical techniques. The systematic search procedure aligned with Cochrane and PRISMA's recommendations for conducting an updated systematic review or meta-analysis. The authors provided inclusion/exclusion criteria. The research team conducted four different types of coding: (a) study characteristics, (b) quality coding using the What Works Clearinghouse Design Standards (Version 3.0, 2014), (c) a modified version of the Cochrane's risk of bias tool (Higgins et al., 2008) for group design and a similar tool geared toward single case research designs (Reichow et al., 2017), and (d) all single case research design data were digitized from graphs and summary statistics were extracted from group design studies. To estimate intervention effects, the authors used a two-step approach for the single case research designs: (a) visually analyze graphs to determine if a functional relation was present and (b) calculating the between-case standardized mean difference effect size. The authors also conducted moderator analyses on two variables: (a) the type of intervention and (b) the outcome domain. For the group design studies, the authors calculated an effect size and conducted moderator analyses on the same two variables. Results suggest that computer-assisted instruction is an EBP for students with ASD. Neither AAC nor virtual reality were identified as an EBP. The omnibus effect size for group designs was Cohen's $d = 0.66$ (0.10) and the BC-SMD for single case research designs was 1.97 (0.48).

Conducting a Systematic Review

A variety of recommendations have been provided to define the approach to conducting a systematic review. Cooper (2010) provides a seven-step framework for conducting a systematic review: (a) formulating the problem, (b) searching the literature, (c) gathering information from studies, (d) evaluating the quality of studies, (e) analyzing and integrating the outcomes of studies, (f) interpreting the evidence, and (g) presenting the results.

Beginning a systematic review, or meta-analysis, often feels like rolling the dice. DICE can be used to help us remember the four broad steps to conducting a systematic search:

1. Define parameters
2. Investigate the literature
3. Code studies
4. Evaluate, interpret, report

Following is a step-by-step description of what should occur at each step in the process. Table 6-1 contains a procedural checklist that includes the process for conducting a systematic review. Table 6-2 contains a list of frameworks to use to set parameters for a systematic review. Table 6-3 contains a list of common misconceptions or mistakes made as part of the systematic search process, along with advice on how to avoid these. Table 6-4 contains a list of resource categories by (a) quality indicators, (b) tools for screening titles/abstracts, (c) SCRD data extraction tools, and (d) effect size calculators.

TABLE 6-1. PROCEDURAL CHECKLIST FOR CONDUCTING SYSTEMATIC REVIEWS

DICE	TASKS TO PERFORM
Define parameters	• Identify the problem to address • Identify previous narrative literature reviews, scoping reviews, systematic reviews, or meta-analyses conducted in the topic area • Define parameters using an appropriate framework (e.g., PICO)
Investigate the literature	• Identify key terms from parameters and prior reviews • Refine Boolean string • Run systematic search • Screen titles and abstracts • Screen full texts • Conduct ancestral search of included primary studies • Conduct first author forward and backward search • Other searching procedures (hand search, preprint search) • Evaluate interrater reliability for each step in the process • Record data for each step in the process • Generate flow chart to depict process
Code studies	• Create and refine coding sheet • Select or revise indicator(s) for methodological evaluation • Conduct visual analysis (for SCRDs only) • Digitize data (if calculating an effect size, for SCRDs only) • Extract summary statistics (if calculating an effect size, group only) • Evaluate interrater reliability for each coding process
Evaluate, interpret, report	• Evaluate sample characteristics • Evaluate study effects • Use meta-analytic techniques (if this is the goal) to combine effects across studies, evaluate dispersion, conduct moderator analyses • Interpret findings

Define Parameters

The first step in the process is to identify a worthwhile topic to investigate. The research team needs to consider two problematic approaches: (a) identifying a problem and topic area with limited research and (b) identifying a topic area with an abundance of research. Choosing to conduct a systematic review on a topic with limited research ultimately is not informative to the field, so the research team may opt to conduct a primary study to contribute to the literature base.

There are exceptions to this rule. One example of this was Maynard et al. (2019), who conducted a Campbell Collaboration review. Trauma-informed approaches at the school level were growing in popularity, so the team investigated what empirical evidence was available. The authors found zero studies that met inclusion criteria, which highlighted the need for empirical research on this approach to inform practice.

FRAMEWORK CODE	PARAMETERS
TABLE 6-2. DEFINING PARAMETERS	
	Intervention
PICO	Population, Intervention, Comparison, Outcome
PICOS	Population, Intervention, Comparison, Outcome, Study Type
PICOT	Population, Intervention, Comparison, Outcome, Timeframe
PICOC	Population, Intervention, Comparison, Outcome, Context
	Measurement and Testing
PICOT	Population, Index Test, Comparison, Outcome, Target Condition
PPIRT	Population, Prior Tests, Index, Reference Standard, Target Condition
	Observational
PEO	Population, Exposure, Outcome
PCO	Population, Context, Outcome
PICo	Population, Interest, Context
See Pollock and Berge (2018) for additional information.	

The reverse situation can also be true. If the team sets broad parameters (e.g., math practices for elementary students in school settings), there will be too many articles that could meet inclusion criteria, making the project insurmountable for the team. This is the "apples and oranges" critique for systematic reviews and meta-analyses. If the team includes studies that differ substantially along a host of variables, the synthesis portion of the project is not informative. The authors would be better off refining their proposed research questions and then adjusting some parameters to identify a more targeted and manageable sample of articles that are more similar among specified variables. In the above-mentioned example, the researchers could narrow their initial query by mathematics practice type (e.g., problem solving, fact fluency), grade level (e.g., early elementary grades, upper elementary grades), school setting (e.g., general education classroom, resource room), and student type (general education, students with LDs in mathematics, students who are English Language Learners).

When research teams think about setting parameters, using a framework (see Table 6-2) aligned with the purpose for the review will keep the study in alignment. We provide an example for how this process may unfold. Virtual manipulatives have increased in practice and our team wants to investigate their effects to provide empirically driven recommendations to teachers and the field. We are interested in investigating the effects of mathematics interventions that used virtual manipulatives for students identified with a disability. We searched for prior reviews focused on mathematics manipulatives to identify whether one already existed and to determine what contribution our project can add to the literature. We identified several prior reviews; however, they either focused on manipulatives more broadly (i.e., concrete and virtual) or studied virtual manipulatives without focusing specifically on outcomes for students with disabilities. Given the focus of the project, our team selected a framework aligned with intervention reviews. We selected PICO and set the parameters as follows: (a) population: K-12 students identified with a disability, (b) intervention: mathematics intervention that used a virtual manipulative as the primary component, (c) comparison: baseline or comparison condition did not use virtual manipulatives, (d) outcome: included a mathematical outcome and unique data for students identified with a disability. With our parameters set, we moved to the next stage in the review process.

Investigate the Literature

Investigating the literature is a critical step in the methodologic process. Prior evaluations of published systematic reviews or meta-analyses in the field of special education have identified missing elements in the systematic search process. Failing to run a thorough systematic search will lead to a final pool of studies that is not inclusive of the entire literature base, which raises threats to the internal validity of the study and inhibits confidence in conclusions drawn from the study. Another possibility is that authors may carry out the recommended procedures but fail to transparently report the process. This inhibits replicability and also threatens the conclusions one can draw from findings because of the missing information related to the search process. Due to the complexities with running a thorough systematic search, we highly recommend identifying personnel with expertise in this area at your institution, such as research librarians.

The first step is to identify key terms that will be used for the systematic search. Key terms are selected by identifying all possible terminology that could be used to define each parameter (e.g., PICO) for the study. It is helpful to identify multiple primary studies that fit the parameters of the systematic review and identify the terminology used in the abstract to describe the parameters of interest. It also can be beneficial to locate systematic reviews or meta-analyses related to your current parameters to identify what the authors used for key terms.

Once key terms are identified, the authors need to create a Boolean string to use when searching databases. When setting up the Boolean string, it can be helpful to use truncations (*), which will include all words up to the asterisk. For example, instead of searching for disability, disorder, disabilities, disorders you can just search for disab* OR disor*. These truncations will catch disability, disabilities, disabled, and disorder. Placement of the asterisk is important because placing it too early in the word will catch a lot of irrelevant terms. For example, dis* would catch disaster, distaste, distemper, etc.

Once the Boolean string is created, the authors will run the search through multiple databases that are likely to include the academic journals fitting the discipline. In the field of special education, common databases include: (a) Education Resources Information Center (ERIC), (b) Academic Search Complete, (c) PsycInfo, (d) PsycArticles, (e) ProQuest Dissertations, and (f) Web of Sciences. Although not exhaustive, our main goal here is to highlight the need to search multiple databases to which your university has access and would likely include academic journals that fit your discipline.

The open science movement in the field of special education continues to grow. This can increase the likelihood that research teams conducting systematic reviews will be able to capture grey literature (i.e., completed studies that are not currently published in an academic journal). Authors are publishing preprints of articles that are not yet submitted to journals or are currently under review for publication. During the systematic search process, it could be beneficial to seek out this grey literature by searching platforms that house preprints: (a) EdArxiv (https://edarxiv. org/), (b) PsyArXiv (https://psyarxiv.com/), and (c) Open Science Framework (OSF; https://osf. io/preprints/). Another route used to locate grey literature is to email first authors of articles included in the review to inquire if they have other articles that are not published that meet inclusion criteria.

Once all references are identified as part of the initial search, the team must engage in screening of titles and abstracts. There are open source and paid resources that teams can use to organize this process (see Table 6-4). However, the critical aspect here is for authors to train all screeners to ensure they are well versed in the inclusion/exclusion criteria based on the parameters of the study and calibration is established across personnel used for screening. Typical practice is to track frequency of articles that "pass" screening and articles that are "removed" from screening at the title/abstract step. However, some indicators (i.e., MECCIR) recommend cataloging the APA citation for each study included and excluded at this step for transparency's sake. Interrater reliability (IRR) should be conducted on a minimum of 25% to 33% of titles/abstract screening; however, more is always better. After completing title/abstract screening, the research team will need to download full texts of all studies that cleared the first stage for full-text screening. At this stage, the team will screen the full texts of all articles and identify why a study is removed (i.e., which parameter specified did the article not meet?).

The research team has now identified a number of studies that have met the inclusion criteria and will be included in the systematic review. The next step is to conduct an ancestral search. One step of the ancestral search involves evaluating the reference list of each primary study to determine if any cited studies would meet inclusion criteria for the systematic review. This process can be streamlined using a database (i.e., Scopus). Another step of the ancestral search process involves evaluating the reference list of related systematic reviews or meta-analyses to determine if studies included in those reviews meet the parameters for the current systematic review. It is also recommended to conduct a forward search, which involves finding all studies that have cited the primary study included in the review to determine if the citing study meets inclusion criteria. A first-author search is also recommended to determine if the first author of each primary study has other studies that may meet inclusion criteria. A final step in this process is to hand search the table of contents for academic journals of all included articles, and any other journals that could potentially publish an article meeting the parameters of the review, to identify potential articles. We recommend reporting this information in a flow map (see Figure 6-2 for a template provided by PRISMA).

Code Studies

Once a final pool of studies is identified as meeting inclusion criteria, the team engages in coding. *Coding* involves systematically evaluating and extracting data from studies, and typically is a two-stage process: (a) stage 1 involves an evaluation of the methodological rigor and (b) stage 2 includes coding for study characteristics. For systematic reviews involving single case research designs, a third step usually includes the visual analysis of graphs to determine whether a functional relation was present and the magnitude of effect. Coding for meta-analyses will also involve the extraction of summary statistics (i.e., group design) or digitizing data from time-series graphs (i.e., single case research designs) to use for meta-analytic techniques.

For stage 1, it is critical to carefully consider the selection, or adaptation, to methodological quality indicators. Maggin and colleagues (2014) applied nine quality appraisal rubrics to self-management interventions used in a previous systematic review (Briesch & Chafouleas, 2009) and found overlap, but not high levels of correspondence across all rubrics. The authors concluded that the use of multiple rubrics would likely increase the breadth in evaluating all aspects of internal and external validity pertaining to a primary study. A critical decision to make is whether to remove or retain studies that rate poorly based on their methodological quality. In many of the EBP determination reviews, authors exclude studies with poor quality from the quantitative synthesis; the What Works Clearinghouse Procedures Handbook (Version 4.1, 2020) removes studies that fail to demonstrate a minimal level of internal validity. Similar to screening procedures, it is critical that all coders are trained and demonstrate adequate calibration before coding commences.

For stage 2, authors must develop a coding guide (see Figure 6-3 for examples of variables to code) to extract relevant information on how studies differed on a host of relevant variables based on theory and prior empirical research. Variables can be categorized under the subheadings *for whom* (participant characteristics), *by whom* (interventionist characteristics), and *under what conditions* (context, setting, intervention characteristics, measurement characteristics). It is also common to code for source information such as date of publication, type of publication, and author team/organization, as these could serve as a potential area of emphasis for the team. Similar to screening procedures, it is critical that all coders are trained and demonstrate adequate calibration before coding commences.

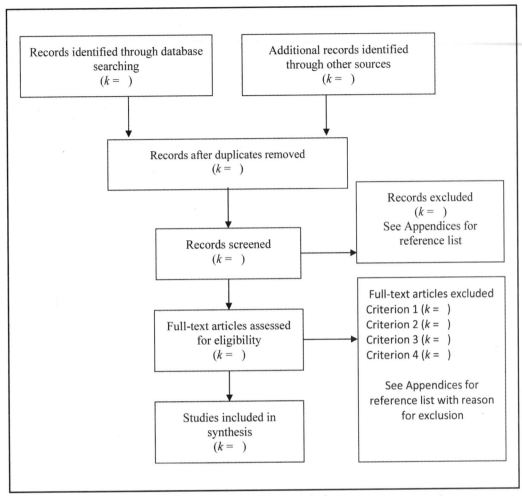

Figure 6-2. Summary of systematic search process using PRISMA standards.

Evaluate, Interpret, Report

The final step in the process is to evaluate, interpret, and report results to a broader audience. The research questions should be the guide the synthesis. Typically, the team will aim to provide an overarching summary statement about the effects of the practice across studies before diving into systematic differences identified through the variable coding process. This will allow the team to provide pertinent information for current practitioners about the caveats on using the practice to allow for a transparent description of the external validity of the practice to varying participants (for whom), interventionists (by whom), and environments (under what conditions). Furthermore, this process may highlight gaps in the literature that the field will need to address through additional primary studies.

CASE STUDY

Ms. Jenkins, a doctoral student in a special education program, was interested in finding out more about research-based instructional and behavior support practices for students with emotional disturbance (ED) who are educated in general education classrooms. She aimed to identify specific

For Whom

Sample Variable Code: Disability Status

Read through the article to determine the disability category specified for the student participant.

1 = autism spectrum disorder only

2 = autism spectrum disorder and intellectual disability

3 = other

COMMENTS: Please provide more specificity for any code of 3. If a participant has additional categories or labels, please list them.

By Whom

Sample Variable Code: Role of Interventionist

Read through the article to determine if the interventionist is a paraprofessional , preservice teacher, in-service teacher, or member of the research staff.

1 = **paraprofessional** (consider aides or staff as paraprofessionals)

2 = **preservice teacher** (individual enrolled in a teacher preparation program)

3 = **in-service teacher** (individual leads their own classroom or is the primary individual responsible for designing/delivering intervention)

4 = **research staff** (include graduate students, researchers)

5 = **other/multiple/not specified**

COMMENTS: Please provide more specificity for any code of 5. If a participant serves multiple roles (i.e., is the classroom teacher but also on the research staff), please code as 0 and specify this.

Figure 6-3. Sample coding menu. *(continued)*

interventions or practices for teachers to implement, so a systematic review was more appropriate than a scoping review or narrative literature review. Ms. Jenkins was interested in this area because she is a specialist at the district level in charge of providing support to faculty working in elementary schools, and her staff continues to face significant challenges in this area. She hopes to perform a systematic review to identify practices on which to focus in future teacher professional development activities. The following research question was created to inform this review: What are research-based practices for improving the academic, behavioral, and social skills performance of students with ED who are educated in inclusive classrooms?

Ms. Jenkins uses PICOS as a framework, given that the focus of the systematic review is on intervention effects (P = Population, I = Intervention, C = Condition, O = Outcomes, and S = Study Type). She operationalizes this framework in the following manner:

Under What Conditions

Sample Variable Code: Setting

Read through the article to determine the setting of the study.

1 = general education classroom

2 = resource classroom (i.e., students spend a portion of the day)

3 = self-contained classroom (i.e., students spend entire day)

4 = separate school (i.e., the location is a separate school for individuals with disabilities)

5 = other (examples may include clinic, homebound, hospital bound)

COMMENTS: Please provide more specificity for any code of 5 and/or type any questions/concerns about this variable code.

Sample Variable Code: Group Size

Read through the article to determine the size of the group of students who received intervention.

1 = whole group (i.e., all students in the classroom received intervention)

2 = small group (i.e., a subset of students from the whole class received intervention)

3 = one-to-one intervention (i.e., only one student received intervention)

0 = other/multiple/not specified (i.e., group size not listed in the codes above, multiple group sizes used, or the article does not provide this information)

COMMENTS: Please specify the number of students receiving intervention in whole group or small group.

Figure 6-3 (continued). Sample coding menu.

P: The literature review will focus on students with ED in grades K-5. Ms. Jenkins is interested in these grades because they align with the grades served at her school.

I: The literature review will focus on instructional and behavior support practices. The review will focus on both because students with ED require high-quality academic instruction and behavioral supports to benefit from school.

C: The review will focus on general education classrooms, or inclusion. It will focus on this condition or setting because the review must focus specifically on the identified problem of school practice (e.g., inclusive instruction for students with ED).

O: The review will focus on academic, behavioral, and social outcomes. It will focus on all three because special education services must confer appropriate benefit in these areas to students with disabilities.

S: Ms. Jenkins wants to cast a wide net to identify manuscripts that are relevant to her literature review. She will include intervention studies that use group designs or single case research designs.

With the parameters defined, she specified the inclusion and exclusion criteria:

- *Criterion 1: Include students in grades K-5 identified with ED through the IDEA (2004)*
- *Criterion 2: The independent variable was an instructional practice or behavior support*
- *Criterion 3: The intervention was implemented in the general education environment; data were collected in the general education environment*
- *Criterion 4: The dependent variables could be categorized as academic, behavioral, or social skills*
- *Criterion 5: The study used a causal design, either a group design (i.e., randomized controlled trial, quasi-experimental design) or a single case research design*
- *Criterion 6: Unique data for the students with ED are provided*
- *Criterion 7: The article is printed in English*

Before beginning the search, Ms. Jenkins must decide which search terms are likely to identify relevant articles. Words that are relevant or describe inclusive instruction for students with ED must be identified. First, she considers "inclusive instruction," "inclusion," "general education," and "mainstream" because these are words that all have been used as key terms in abstracts for studies that would meet her specified criteria. Next, she considers the population "emotional disturbance," "emotional and behavioral disorder," "behavioral disorder," "emotional disorder" because these are similar words and typically used to define this population of students. Ms. Jenkins is not focusing on specific interventions, so no key terms are used for the search. In addition, she opted not to try to list all potential key words for the methodology employed because studies may not reference the specific methodology in the title or abstract, which would inhibit her from locating these studies that would otherwise meet inclusion criteria. She creates a Boolean phrase to string these search terms together using truncations (*; e.g., search for dis* will pull disability, disabilities, disorder) and word order (w1; e.g., general w1 education will pull general education, education in general classroom). The following Boolean string was used ("inclusive w1 instruction" OR "inclus*" OR "general w1 education") OR "mainstream") AND ("emotional dis*" OR "emotional and behavioral disord*" "behavioral dis*," "emotional disorder").

Ms. Jenkins performs a thorough systematic search that includes the following components: (a) search data bases using the Boolean string, (b) title/abstract screening with interrater reliability, (c) full text screening with interrater reliability, and (d) a multi-pronged ancestral search process. The result of this process was a pool of articles that met her inclusion criteria that need to be coded for quality of experimental design and study characteristics. She uses the Council for Exceptional Children Standards for Evidence-Based Practices in Special Education (2014) to appraise the quality of the experiments. To develop the coding menu for study characteristics, she uses the following framework to inform the coding process: for whom, by whom, under what conditions.

For whom: This review focuses on students with ED, so information on student characteristics would be extracted: gender, ethnicity, primary language, grade level, age, clinical diagnoses, SES status, and information on previous academic, behavioral, and social skills performance.

By whom: This refers to the characteristics of the person or persons who are providing the intervention or using the instructional practice. This information is important because the qualifications, level and/or type of experience, or other characteristics of the person providing the intervention or method may be critical to its success. The following descriptive information on the "interventionists" were coded: professional position, highest level of education, certifications/licensures, years of experience teaching, gender, and ethnicity.

Under what conditions: This refers to the characteristics of the setting in which the intervention or instructional practice was provided. It also can refer to characteristics of the intervention or instructional practice. The following characteristics were coded: district type, class size, information on any support staff in class, instructional area, frequency and duration of the intervention, and information on any supports provided to interventionists to ensure fidelity (e.g., that the practice was implemented with sufficient quality and consistency). This information is helpful because it provides important context on the conditions in which the intervention was implemented. When performing the review, Ms. Jenkins can compare this contextual information to the characteristics of her school. This information can help her determine the optimal conditions that are needed for an intervention to be successful, and to identify supports that may be necessary for the intervention to be successful at her school.

PROTECTING INTERNAL VALIDITY: OTHER FACTORS TO CONSIDER

Publication bias refers to the degree to which a body of research is representative of the overall pool of related studies. In essence, publication bias focuses on the following question: To what degree is the sample of primary studies (e.g., studies that were identified during the search procedures) representative of the population of primary studies (e.g., all relevant primary studies)? Sometimes, researchers performing systematic reviews may employ procedures that adversely affect the quality of their sample of studies, such as when they only search for peer-reviewed articles. Peer-reviewed studies are considered rigorous because they have been evaluated by other professionals prior to their publication. In fact, some researchers have referred to the peer-review process as the "gate-keeper" for the field of special education (see Mitchell et al., 2017). However, sometimes studies are not accepted for publication due to reporting null effects or because they do not report statistically significant differences between groups. This phenomenon, the tendency for peer-reviewed journals to publish studies reporting an effect, has been referred to as the "file drawer effect" (Rosenthal, 1979). Also, there are well-constructed and executed studies that go unpublished because the author went into a field other than academia. For example, a dissertation study completed by a school administrator may go unpublished because publication may provide little professional or personal benefit. Thus, this type of study would not appear in a peer-reviewed journal. Lastly, researchers may be less likely to submit a study for possible publication when no effect is found (Driessen et al., 2015). This may occur due to a perception that it will not be accepted for publication or due to confirmation bias (see Cook & Therrien, 2017). That is, some researchers may not attempt to publish a study that conflicts with their preconceived notions or beliefs. Also, researchers may self-select which of their studies to submit for possible publication based on the presence and magnitude of an intervention effect. Collectively, these factors can affect the degree to which peer-reviewed research accurately represents a field of empirical evidence.

Publication bias, or basing systematic reviews on a collection of studies that is not representative, can adversely affect the decisions made by various stakeholders. When making decisions regarding the provision of special education services, stakeholders are encouraged to use research evidence to inform this effort (Cook et al., 2016). In order to make the best decisions possible, practitioners must have a degree of confidence in the research they use as "lessons learned" for addressing a given problem of school practice. The research they use should be as representative of their school and the needs of their students as possible. If practitioners were to rely on research that is not representative, such as a systematic review with publication bias, they may make poor or less beneficial decisions.

For example, publication bias can adversely affect the calculation of effect. If there are primary studies reporting null or small effects that are omitted from the analysis due to being unpublished, the systematic review will overestimate the effectiveness of an intervention or instructional practice. This is an issue because school-based practitioners are likely to make decisions about how to allocate precious resources partly on the benefits they can anticipate from employing a practice or intervention. Thus, practitioners rely on accurate estimates of effectiveness and relative effectiveness (e.g., comparing one practice to another) when making high-stakes decisions. This potential issue also holds true for state- and federal-level stakeholders, as they also are likely to make decisions based on empirical evidence.

Publication bias also can adversely affect the accuracy with which we determine efficacy of a practice. Some studies state that a practice was effective when it was not. This is referred to as a "false positive" (e.g., Simmons et al., 2011). If studies reporting null, mixed, or small effects remain unpublished and a systematic review was based only on published studies, the review may falsely conclude that a practice is promising or effective based on the relatively few studies reporting positive effects and the exclusion of unpublished studies with very different findings. Again, this situation can adversely affect the decisions made by various stakeholders if they rely on a systematic review with publication bias.

You may be wondering, what can we do to reduce publication bias from impacting our systematic review? First, the research community has recognized that publication bias is a significant issue (see Cook & Therrien, 2017; Gage et al., 2017). With this in mind, journal editors are strongly encouraged to publish well-designed studies reporting negative, null, mixed, or small effects. The journal *Behavioral Disorders* did a two-part special series (volume 42 issue 4 and volume 43 issue 1) devoted to publishing articles with null effects in the field of emotional and behavioral disorders. Although this is an important development in the field of special education, it does not account for the presence of well-designed, relevant studies that are unpublished. To address this issue, researchers performing systematic reviews are strongly encouraged to include the grey literature in their search procedures. Grey literature refers to manuscripts that are not commercially published. Manuscripts considered grey literature could include dissertations, conference proceedings, technical reports, working papers, and preprints. A study preprint is a manuscript in its current form prior to peer review and publication in a journal. There are various platforms in which researchers can submit a preprint of their study, such as EdArXv (https://edarxiv.org/), PsyArXiv (https://psyarxiv.com/), and OSF (https://osf.io/).

Preregistration and Registered Reports

Additional methods are available to researchers seeking to improve the internal validity of their systematic reviews. Researchers may elect to preregister their systematic review. This process involves providing a publicly available description of the study, including an explanation of the research methods that will be used prior to starting the investigation. Preregistration provides some benefits to researchers and consumers of research. First, preregistration is another way for researchers to make their studies accessible to others. As long as researchers later include their results and study findings, the complete study is available to others regardless of whether it is published in a peer-reviewed journal. Please note: primary studies can also be preregistered, making this another potential source of grey literature to include in systematic reviews. Second, preregistration requires researchers to establish their research questions prior to conducting the systematic review, which enhances the study's internal validity. Third, preregistration provides an opportunity for researchers to document when they make changes to their research methods, which also improves a review's internal validity. For example, a research team may perform an analysis based on a theory and/or previous research and obtain an unexpected finding. The team then decides to perform an exploratory or secondary analysis to further explore this unexpected finding. By preregistering their study, primary and secondary analyses are appropriately labeled as such. By providing this level of transparency, consumers of research may also have a greater level of confidence in study findings.

There are a number of different preregistration options for researchers to consider. These include PRISMA (http://www.prisma-statement.org/Protocols/Registration), Prospero (https://www.crd.york.ac.uk/prospero/), the Campbell Corporation (https://campbellcollaboration.org/), and OSF (https://osf.io/). These online repositories have some similarities. For example, researchers report the purpose of the study, article selection criteria, search procedures, analyses to be performed, and intended analysis methods when preregistering with PRISMA.

Completing a registered report is another option available to researchers. This process involves submitting a study protocol to a peer-reviewed journal for consideration for publication. In essence, researchers submit a manuscript introduction and method section for peer review. Upon conclusion of the review process, researchers receive feedback on their proposed methodology before carrying out the study. If the manuscript is considered acceptable, the authors are given "in principle acceptance," which means the manuscript will be accepted if the authors carry out the proposed methodology and the results and discussion align with the research questions and methodology. This provides an incredible opportunity for the researchers to refine their research methods and perform a more rigorous investigation (Hardwicke & Ioannidis, 2018). Primary studies and systematic reviews can be submitted as a registered report. In regard to intervention studies, preregistered reports help address concerns with confirmation bias by basing acceptance on the introduction and method sections. Thus, the presence of null, mixed, or small intervention effects cannot result in a manuscript rejection. Many journals in the field of special education accept preregistered reports, including *Remedial and Special Education* and *Exceptional Children*.

SUMMARY

One way to conceptualize reviews of the literature is to categorize them as narrative literature review, scoping review, systematic review, or meta-analysis. Each type of review has a specific rationale and purpose that impacts the methodology and process for conducting. It is critical to evaluate the purpose of the review and methodology to determine whether the design has sufficient internal validity to address the research questions posed. The increase in published systematic reviews and meta-analyses in the field of special education has provided useful information for research, practice, and policy; however, it also has led to a critical reflection on methodological procedures employed and recommendations for increasing the internal validity of designs. In this chapter, we highlighted critical methodological procedures to employ when planning, conducting, and reporting results for a scoping review or systematic review.

CHAPTER REVIEW

1. What are the key methodological differences between a narrative literature review and a systematic review? How do these differences affect the conclusions that can be drawn from the project?
2. Given your research agenda, define parameters for a systematic review focused on evaluating intervention effects using the mnemonic PICOS. Pretend you identified a limited amount of research on the topic and revise your parameters to include a broader literature base.
3. True or False: A meta-analysis should only be employed after conducting a systematic search. Please justify your response.
4. Why is it critical to evaluate the internal validity of the primary studies included in a systematic review or meta-analysis?
5. Identify four to five ways a researcher can attempt to capture grey literature for inclusion in a systematic review or meta-analysis.
6. A researcher conducts a systematic review and identifies that publication bias is impacting her study. Articulate what this means.

TABLE 6-3. COMMON MISCONCEPTIONS AND CLARIFICATIONS ABOUT SYSTEMATIC SEARCH PROCEDURES

MISCONCEPTION	BETTER UNDERSTANDING
Using the term *literature review* to define narrative literature review, scoping review, systematic review, and meta-analysis.	Each type of review defined in this chapter has distinct differences in their purpose and methodology. Precision is the epitome of science, so using the precise terminology to define the research project is important.
Believing systematic reviews can only be performed on experimental studies.	A systematic review is defined by the inclusion of articles fitting prespecified parameters. There are examples in the literature of research projects focused on evaluating studies that used observational approaches, correlation approaches, evaluation of the psychometric properties of an instrument, and even qualitative methodologies. The important element is to use an appropriate framework to set the parameters. See Pollock and Berge (2018) for examples.
Excluding all documents that are not published in an academic journal.	This decision is sometimes framed as an attempt to retain "high-quality" research. However, this decision is undoubtedly increasing the risk of publication bias impacting findings. Grey literature should be included in the scoping review, systematic review, or meta-analysis. To address the quality of the experimental design, researchers can evaluate the methodology by using or adapting indicators published for this purpose (i.e., Council for Exceptional Children Standards for Evidence-Based Practice in Special Education, What Works Clearinghouse Design Standards).

TABLE 6-4. ADDITIONAL RESOURCES

SOURCE	LINK OR REFERENCE
	Quality Indicators for Systematic Reviews and Meta-Analyses
PRISMA	http://prisma-statement.org/prismastatement/Checklist.aspx
MECIR	https://community.cochrane.org/sites/default/files/uploads/inline-files/Version%20March%202020%20Final%20Online%20version%20CLEAN_2.pdf
MARS	https://wmich.edu/sites/default/files/attachments/u58/2015/MARS.pdf
Talbott et al. (2018)	Talbott, E., Maggin, D. M., Van Acker, E. Y., & Kumm, S. (2018). Quality indicators for reviews of research in special education. *Exceptionality, 26*(4), 245-265. https://doi.org/10.1080/09362835.2017.1283625
	Article Screening Tools
Abstrackr	http://abstrackr.cebm.brown.edu/account/login
Colandr	https://www.colandrapp.com/signin
Covidence	https://www.covidence.org/home
Refworks	https://www.refworks.com/refworks2/
Rayyan	https://rayyan.qcri.org/welcome
	SCRD Data Extraction Tools
GetData	http://getdata-graph-digitizer.com/
WebPlotDigitizer	https://automeris.io/WebPlotDigitizer/
	Effect Size Calculators
Declercq et al. (2018)	http://34.251.13.245/MultiSCED/
Pustejovsky (2016)	https://jepusto.shinyapps.io/scdhlm/
Pustejovsky & Swan (2018)	https://jepusto.shinyapps.io/SCD-effect-sizes/
Vannest et al. (2016)	http://www.singlecaseresearch.org/
Wilson (2001)	Online Version https://campbellcollaboration.org/escalc/html/EffectSizeCalculator-Home.php Excel Version http://mason.gmu.edu/~dwilsonb/ma.html

REFERENCES

American Psychological Association. (2010). *Publication manual of the American Psychological Association* (6th ed.). Author.

Barton, E. E., Pustejovsky, J. E., Maggin, D. M., & Reichow, B. (2017). Technology-aided instruction and intervention for students with ASD: A meta-analysis using novel methods of estimating effect sizes for single-case research. *Remedial and Special Education, 38*(6), 371-386.

Briesch, A. M., & Chafouleas, S. M. (2009). Review and analysis of literature on self-management interventions to promote appropriate classroom behaviors (1988–2008). *School Psychology Quarterly, 24*(2), 106-118.

Carr, E. G., & Horner, R. H. (2007). The expanding vision of positive behavior support: Research perspectives on happiness, helpfulness, hopefulness. *Journal of Positive Behavior Interventions, 9*(1), 3-14.

Cheng, C., Oakman, J., Bigby, C., Fossey, E., Cavanagh, J., Meacham, H., & Bartram, T. (2018). What constitutes effective support in obtaining and maintaining employment for individuals with intellectual disability? A scoping review. *Journal of Intellectual & Developmental Disability, 43*(3), 317-327.

Ciullo, S., Collins, A., Wissinger, D. R., McKenna, J. W., Lo, Y.-L., & Osman, D. (2020). Students with learning disabilities in the social studies: A meta-analysis of intervention research. *Exceptional Children*. Advance online publication. https://doi.org/10.1177/0014402919893932

Common, E. A., Lane, K. L., Cantwell, E. D., Brunsting, N. C., Oakes, W. P., Germer, K. A., & Bross, L. A. (2020). Teacher-delivered strategies to increase students' opportunities to respond: A systematic methodological review. *Behavioral Disorders, 45*(2), 67-84.

Cook, B., Cook, S., & Collins, L. (2016). Terminology and evidence-based practice for students with emotional and behavioral disorders: Exploring some devilish details. *Beyond Behavior, 25*(2), 4-13.

Cook, B., & Odom, S. (2013). Evidence-based practices and implementation science in special education. *Exceptional Children, 79*(3), 135-144.

Cook, B., & Therrien, W. (2017). Null effects and publication bias in special education research. *Behavioral Disorders, 42*(4), 149-158.

Cooper, H. (2010). *Research synthesis and meta-analysis: A step-by-step approach* (4th ed.). Sage.

Council for Exceptional Children. (2014). *Council for Exceptional Children Standards for Evidence-Based Practices in Special Education*. Author.

Driessen, E., Hollon, S. D., Bockting, C. L., Cuijpers, P., & Turner, E. H. (2015). Does publication bias inflate the apparent efficacy of psychological treatment for major depressive disorder? A systematic review and meta-analysis of US National Institutes of Health-funded trials. *PLoS One, 10*(9), e0137864.

Felce, D. (1997). Defining and applying the concept of quality of life. *Journal of Intellectual Disability Research, 41*(2), 126-135.

Gage, N. A., Cook, B. G., & Reichow, B. (2017). Publication bias in special education meta-analyses. *Exceptional Children, 83*(4), 428-445.

Ganz, J. B., Morin, K. L., Foster, M. J., Vannest, K. J., Genç Tosun, D., Gregori, E. V., & Gerow, S. L. (2017). High-technology augmentative and alternative communication for individuals with intellectual and developmental disabilities and complex communication needs: A meta-analysis. *Augmentative and Alternative Communication, 33*(4), 224-238.

Hardwicke, T., & Ioannidis, J. (2018). Mapping the university of registered reports. *Nature Human Behavior, 2*, 793-796.

Harrison, J. R., Soares, D. A., & Joyce, J. (2019). Inclusion of students with emotional and behavioural disorders in general education settings: A scoping review of research in the US. *International Journal of Inclusive Education, 23*(12), 1209-1231.

Higgins, J. P. T., Altman, D. G., & Sterne, J. A. C. (2008). Assessing risk of bias in included studies. In J. P. T. Higgins & S. Green (Eds.), *Cochrane handbook for systematic reviews of interventions* (pp. 187–241). John Wiley.

Higgins, J. P. T., Lasserson, T., Chandler, J., Tovey, D., Thomas, J., Flemyng, E., & Churchill, R. (2020). *Methodological expectations of Cochrane intervention reviews (MECIR)*. The Campbell Collaboration.

Horner, R. H., Carr, E. G., Halle, J., McGee, G., Odom, S., & Wolery, M. (2005). The use of single-subject research to identify evidence-based practice in special education. *Exceptional Children, 71*(2), 165-179.

Individuals with Disabilities Education Act, 20 U.S.C. § 1401 et seq. (2004).

Maggin, D. M., Briesch, A. M., Chafouleas, S. M., Ferguson, T. D., & Clark, C. (2014). A comparison of rubrics for identifying empirically supported practices with single-case research. *Journal of Behavioral Education, 23*(2), 287-311.

Maynard, B. R., Farina, A., Dell, N. A., & Kelly, M. S. (2019). Effects of trauma-informed approaches in schools: A systematic review. *Campbell Systematic Reviews, 15*(1-2).

Mitchell, B. S., Adamson, R., & McKenna, J. W. (2017). Curbing our enthusiasm: An analysis of the check-in/check-out literature using the council for exceptional children's evidence-based practice standards. *Behavior Modification, 41*(3), 343-367.

Moher, D., Liberati, A., Tetzlaff, J., & Altman, D. G. (2009). Preferred reporting items for systematic reviews and meta-analyses: the PRISMA statement. *Annals of Internal Medicine, 151*(4), 264-269.

Morin, K. L., Ganz, J. B., Gregori, E. V., Foster, M. J., Gerow, S. L., Genç-Tosun, D., & Hong, E. R. (2018). A systematic quality review of high-tech AAC interventions as an evidence-based practice. *Augmentative and Alternative Communication, 34*(2), 104-117.

National Reading Panel. (2000). Report of the National Reading Panel. Teaching children to read: An evidence-based assessment of the scientific research literature on reading and its implications for reading instruction. U.S. Department of Health and Human Services.

Pollock, A., & Berge, E. (2018). How to do a systematic review. *International Journal of Stroke, 13*(2), 138-156.

Reichow, B., Barton, E. E., & Maggin, D. (2017). Risk of bias assessment for single case designs. Unpublished manuscript, Anita Zucker Center for Excellence in Early Childhood Studies, University of Florida, Gainesville.

Reichow, B., Volkmar, F. R., & Cicchetti, D. V. (2008). Development of the evaluative method for evaluating and determining evidence-based practices in autism. *Journal of Autism and Developmental Disorders, 38*(7), 1311-1319.

Rosenthal, R. (1979). The file drawer problem and tolerance for null results. *Psychological Bulletin, 86*(3), 638-641.

Simmons, J., Nelson, L., & Simonsohn, U. (2011). False-positive psychology: Undisclosed flexibility in data collection and analysis allows presenting anything as significant. *Psychological Science, 22*, 1359-1366.

Talbott, E., Maggin, D. M., Van Acker, E. Y., & Kumm, S. (2018). Quality indicators for reviews of research in special education. *Exceptionality, 26*(4), 245-265.

Tricco, A. C., Lillie, E., Zarin, W., O'Brien, K., Colquhoun, H., Kastner, M., Levac, D., Ng, C., Sharpe, J. P., Wilson, K., Kenny, M., Warren, R., Wilson, C., Stelfox, H. T., & Straus, S. E. (2016). A scoping review on the conduct and reporting of scoping reviews. *BMC Medical Research Methodology, 16*(1), 15.

Turnbull III, H. R., Turnbull, A. P., Wehmeyer, M. L., & Park, J. (2003). A quality of life framework for special education outcomes. *Remedial and Special Education, 24*(2), 67-74.

What Works Clearinghouse. (2014). *What Works Clearinghouse procedures and standards handbook* (Version 3.0). Institute for Education Sciences.

What Works Clearinghouse. (2017). *What Works Clearinghouse standards handbook* (Version 4.0). Institute of Education Sciences.

What Works Clearinghouse. (2020). *What Works Clearinghouse standards handbook* (Version 4.1). Institute of Education Sciences.

Youman, M., & Mather, N. (2018). Dyslexia laws in the USA: A 2018 update. *Perspectives on Language and Literacy, 44*(2), 37-41. https://doi.org/10.1007/s11881-012-0076-2.

7

Correlational Designs

With contributions from Sharon Sullivan, PhD

INTRODUCTION

Correlational research is one of the oldest research techniques. It is unique in research methodology because it presumes no specific causal or directional relationship between the variables employed. A fundamental tenet of research methodology is that correlation is not causation. That is a problem for individuals seeking to establish a causal relationship, but it is a benefit when researchers are unable or unwilling to manipulate the variables because doing so would clearly harm individuals. Nevertheless, situations arise in which events can be paired with each other and the strength of their relationship tested. These situations are ideal for correlational designs.

When working with correlational research, one can expect to find graphic displays of the data (scatterplots), statistical indicators of the strength of the relationship (correlation coefficients), and statistical indicators of the extent that the relationship is meaningfully different from zero (reported as a p value). Finally, an indicator of the amount of variance accounted for by the relations between the variables (a coefficient of determination or r^2 value) is commonly reported. In addition to these quantitative tools, a number of qualitative analyses are applied to correlational data. These include visual inspection of the scatterplot for things like outliers (unusually extreme values) and the linearity of the data.

When working with correlational research, as with any design, it is always important to ask, "but what else could be going on?" The fewer alternative explanations that are available to us, the more confident we can be in our conclusions.

Hott, B. L., Brigham, F. J., & Peltier, C.
Research Methods in Special Education (pp. 113-130).
© 2021 SLACK Incorporated.

CHAPTER OBJECTIVES

→ Identify reasons that a researcher would employ a correlational design rather than an experimental approach.

→ Define a correlation coefficient.

→ Interpret the strength of correlation coefficients.

→ Interpret the statistical significance of correlation coefficients.

→ Describe some of the problems in the interpretation of correlational research.

KEY TERMS

- **Assumption**: Conditions or characteristics of the data that are "assumed" to be in place by the statistical procedure selected. Failure to meet assumptions often causes the analysis to be imprecise or incorrect.

- **Coefficient of Determination**: Indicated by the symbols R^2 or r^2 and pronounced "r squared," the proportion of the variance that can be attributed to the relation between the two variables.

- **Confidence Interval**: A measure of the uncertainty of our measurement. If repeated samples were drawn from the population, the confidence interval provides a range that a given proportion of those samples would represent. The differences among them would be considered to be sampling error or measurement error.

- **Correlation**: Descriptive statistics that assess the relationship between pairs of variables.

- **Correlation Coefficients**: Descriptive statistics that describe the strength of the relationship between a pair of variables.

- **Dichotomous Variable**: A variable that can take on one of two values, such as on/off.

- **Equal Interval Scale**: Possesses a constant or equal interval between each value on the scale but lacks a meaningful zero or point of origin. Standard scores that are reported for most psychological construct variables (e.g., intelligence, reading ability) are examples.

- **Linear**: A data set in which it is possible to draw or imagine a straight line running through the middle of the data.

- **Lurking Variables**: Variables that are unknown, and thus, not controlled for in the research design or data analysis. Such variables are usually extraneous to the question under consideration but can dramatically influence study results.

- **Ordinal Scale**: Rank ordering of data without consideration of the distance between the data points. Percentile ranks are common examples; also, anything described using "ordinal" numbers such as first, second, third. Ordinal scales have naturally occurring orders and the difference between points is unknown or unimportant.

- **r**: Lower-case r is the abbreviation used to indicate Pearson Product Moment Correlation coefficient.

- **Ratio Scale**: A scale in which the distance between each point of the scale is equal and possesses a meaningful zero point or origin point. Age is an example of a variable on a ratio scale; temperature is not because zero is a value on the scale that means something other than the absence of temperature.

- **Scatterplot**: A chart that uses a single dot to represent values for two different numeric variables. The position of each dot on the horizontal and vertical axis indicates the values for an individual data point. Such values are sometimes called Cartesian coordinates.

- **Spurious Correlations**: An observed relationship between two variables that appears to be meaningful but is actually nonmeaningful. Often, spurious correlations are coincidental or related to some unobserved or unconsidered lurking variable.
- **Trendline**: Line imagined or drawn through the data set to provide a clearer picture of the data. It is most frequently used on a scatterplot of ordered pairs of data to help determine if a relationship exists between the two variables.

CORRELATIONAL RESEARCH

A fundamental understanding in research and epistemology (the study of knowledge) is that correlation does not equal causation. Things that happen at the same time or in a specific temporal sequence may be related to each other in some way or they may just be coincidence. This presents a bit of a problem for researchers who would like to be as certain as possible about what they have learned in their work. That problem has led some scholars to dismiss the utility of correlational research, but that dismissal is premature. There are conditions in which correlational research is the best or only way to examine the question. Many of these conditions have to do with the nature of the things to be examined.

There are two general conditions where correlational research is particularly useful. The first is when researchers hold no belief that the statistical relationship is a causal one. Neither variable is considered to cause the other, so there is no independent variable to manipulate. Under this assumption, neither the terms *independent variable* nor *dependent variable* are applicable. The other reason that researchers would choose to use a correlational study rather than an experiment is that the statistical relationship of interest is thought to be causal, but the researcher cannot manipulate the independent variable because it would be impossible, impractical, or unethical to do so.

An example of a situation that researchers would never wish to create occurred in Flint, Michigan. In 2015, tests found dangerous levels of lead in residential drinking water (CNN, 2019). It is well known that exposure to lead is related to a variety of physical and cognitive problems in children and adults. Despite the tragedy of this event, the effects of estimated exposure and its impact over time can be evaluated by following the people who were exposed to the contaminated drinking water over time. One statistical tool that enables us to describe the relationship of amount of exposure to subsequent outcome is a correlation. In a situation such as occurred in Flint, we can be generally certain that the lead exposure was a causal agent, but no ethical scientist would consider exposing randomly selected individuals to specified doses of lead to see where thresholds of detrimental outcomes might lie.

There are other times when we wish to examine the relationship between two variables. To describe a systematic relationship in which, as one variable changes, another variable changes with it, a correlational study will work well. For example, if a teacher wished to know if there was some systematic relationship between the number of words read per minute and reading comprehension, a correlational study would make sense. Such a study would require that the teacher or researcher have decent measures of oral reading fluency and a similarly useful reading comprehension measure for each student. Then, a series of steps is followed to determine the relationship between the two variables. Each of these steps will be described later in the chapter.

Before we move on, take a look at the case study for this chapter. Would it be ethical for Veronica to provide or withhold opportunities within an existing program to generate data? What variables might she consider in her study?

CASE STUDY

Veronica is the coordinator of a university-based program for individuals with intellectual disabilities. Students in this program are involved with many aspects of university life including options for living in the university residence halls, support for enrollment and participation in university classes, and coaching from designated staff members to develop independent living and employment skills. The students in this program are pursuing individual goals and not the prescribed course of study for a standard university degree. Also, due to specific circumstances, students in the program engage in the various opportunities with different levels of intensity. For example, some students who live near the university live at home rather than in the university residence halls. Other students are reluctant to participate in the full range of employment and independence activities that the program provides. Some students engage in university classes only in their personal areas of interest while others sample the curriculum widely. Veronica knows that it is impossible to require or prohibit students to engage in some activities but not others. Nevertheless, she is seeking ways of yielding data-based recommendations to incoming students and their parents regarding better ways to take advantage of the university program.

WHAT IS CORRELATION?

Correlation coefficients are descriptive statistics that describe the relationship between pairs of variables (Coleman, 2008). There are a variety of correlation measures available, but the most common is the Pearson Product-Moment Correlation Coefficient (PPMCC). That is the type of correlation that we address in this chapter.

PPMCCs are typically abbreviated with the lower-case letter "r" that is also displayed in italics. This correlation describes linear relationships. A linear relationship exists when we can draw or imagine a straight line through the data. The data for a correlation would have two variables: one on the X or horizontal scale, and one on the Y or vertical scale. The X and Y values are used to create a single data point showing the values of each measure in the same way that latitude and longitude are combined to indicate a single location on earth. The formula for calculating the r correlation coefficient compares the distance of each datapoint from the imaginary line drawn through the data to measure how closely the relationship between the variables can be fit to the line.

The relationship between some variables is more of a curve than a straight line. If a straight line will not describe or fit the data, we must turn to other correlations that are beyond the scope of this chapter.

Good correlational studies combine both qualitative analyses and quantitative analyses. Each of these aspects provides the researcher with different and complementary forms of information.

Qualitative Analysis of Correlational Data

In a qualitative sense, one produces a scatterplot of the two variables, one variable on the horizontal or X axis and one on the vertical or Y axis. Many readers will recognize this activity from their days in elementary school placing pairs of values on a chart using Cartesian coordinates.

The idea is exactly the same here. Each pair of values produces a single point on the scatterplot. We do this because there is evidence that people are not very good at perceiving patterns in large tables of numbers, but they can more readily do so when the values are presented in a graphic display (Bennett et al., 2000; Cleveland, 1985; Tufte, 2001). Lomax and Hahs-Vaughn (2012) presented a

TABLE 7-1. NUMBER OF CHILDREN AND PETS IN FIVE FAMILIES

FAMILY	CHILDREN (X)	PETS (Y)
1	1	2
2	2	6
3	3	4
4	4	8
5	5	10

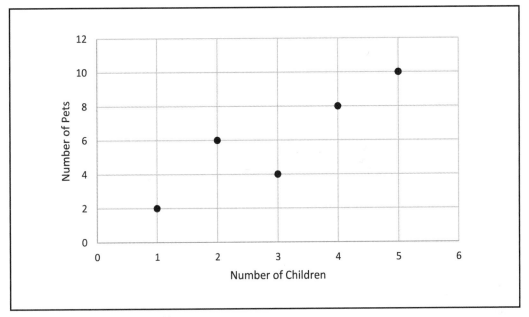

Figure 7-1. Scatterplot of data in Table 7-1.

table of number pairs that describe the relationship between the number of children in a small group of families and the number of pets owned by the families (Table 7-1).

The numbers in the first column, Family, simply serve as identifiers and so are not employed in statistics or in the graphic display of the data. This is a small data set and one of the variables (number of children on the X scale) increases in a very even and systematic manner. Therefore, most people can simply scan the data set and conclude that there is a relationship such that families with more children also have more pets. With larger and more complex data sets, such easy accessibility will not often be the case. That is why we go to the trouble of plotting the data and calculating correlation coefficients.

When we place the pairs of values for children and pets on the graph, the relationship becomes more easily visible (Figure 7-1).

There are a few things that we can see by examining our scatterplot. First, the data on each axis rises together. That is, as the number of children increases, the number of pets increases. That rise in the pattern from left to right is an indication of a positive correlation. If the pattern of the ordered pairs is sloped upward from the left and toward the right as in this example, the correlation between the two variables is positive. If the pattern of the ordered pairs is sloped downward from the left and toward the right, the mirror image of this example, the correlation between the two variables is

Figure 7-2. Trendline.

negative. If there is no slope to the data, there is a neutral relationship that indicates that the variables are unrelated to each other.

A second way to examine the data is to draw a straight line through the middle of the data points to describe the relationship between the variables. Figure 7-2 shows the same scatterplot with this line added. We call this line a trendline or a line of best fit. There are specific techniques that create the line in a way that minimizes the distance of each of the points from the line to the greatest extent possible. Most computer graphing programs have an automatic feature that creates this line accurately and quickly.

When the data can be described by a straight line such as in Figure 7-2, we call it a *linear trend*. Basic correlation coefficients work quite well with linear data sets. When the data becomes curvilinear, more complex procedures are required, so examining the scatterplot provides a first clue that we are on the right path in our examination of the data. We are only addressing linear correlations in this chapter.

The third aspect of the scatterplot that we can examine qualitatively is how closely the data points for each data pair fall from the trendline. The data points for families with one, four, and five children fall nearly on the trendline. The data points for the families with two and three children, however, fall a little bit away from the trendline. We call that distance between the trendline and the actual location of the score a *residual*. The trendline is a prediction of where the data points would fall in an error-free system of measurement. The residual is the difference between the prediction and the actual reported data. The closer the data points fall to the trendline, the stronger the statistical relation described by the correlation coefficient.

Quantitative Analysis of Correlational Data

The most common quantitative measure of correlation is the PPMCC, or simply Pearson's correlation (Coleman, 2008). Pearson's correlation is denoted by the letter r. Before we can be confident the r will be a good statistic to use, we have to ensure that a few important conditions are met. We call these conditions *assumptions*, because calculation of the statistic "assumes" that these conditions are met.

Assumptions About the Data

First, computing Pearson's *r* requires that the data for each of the two variables is linear. We examined the scatterplot to make that determination. People who take statistics classes also find that there are other tools to establish linearity. For this introduction, we will rely on visual analysis of the scatterplot. It is worth taking at least one statistics class to obtain the additional tools if one intends to conduct or understand more rigorous research.

Second, the data for each measure must be on an ordinal (e.g., percentile ranks), equal interval (e.g., standard scores), or ratio (e.g., age) scale of measurement. This aspect of a correlational study is clearly a part of the design of the study. Researchers can, *a priori*, ensure that their measures meet these criteria as well as possess adequate indicators of reliability and validity. There is little statistical hope for a poorly designed study.

An additional requirement of using a Pearson *r* in a study is that the data are roughly normally distributed. We can plot our data using bar graphs to make sure that most of the scores fall in the middle of the range and there is no "stacking up" of the data at the upper end or the lower end of the range. That stacking up on one end of the distribution or another is called skew. *Skew* is a violation of the assumption of normality. One of the best ways of ensuring that the data yielded will fit the requirements of the statistic is to conduct a pilot study with a similar but (usually) smaller group of participants (Creswell, 2008).

Calculating the Statistic With Computers

The purpose here is to give a brief summary of how the correlation coefficients are likely to be computed in research settings, not to provide a statistical exposition of the methods and particulars. Calculating a correlation coefficient by hand or with a simple calculator can be complex. Fortunately, many calculators are able to carry out this analysis with comparative ease. However, it is unlikely that a hand calculator approach will be desirable in most research settings because it is often difficult to carry out all of the data storage and checking procedures necessary in a small calculator.

There are numerous statistical tools available on many personal, school-owned, and university-owned computers. Some of these produce more information than others. For example, Microsoft Excel easily produces a Pearson *r*, but it provides no indication of statistical significance (discussed in the next section). The major advantage of Excel is that it is easily accessible on many personal and school-owned computers and is inexpensive.

SPSS (IBM Corp., released 2017) is a statistical computing package that is commonly employed in statistical training in the behavioral sciences. It will easily produce correlation coefficients and also calculate the statistical significance of the relationship. The enhanced amount of information produced is a major advantage. The disadvantage of SPSS is the cost. Many universities and research organizations hold licenses for this program, but individuals may find the cost to be prohibitive.

Recently, a high-powered statistical application called "R" (R Core Team, 2017) has become quite popular among researchers. R is syntax driven. That is, one must type commands into the computer. Some people report that, at first, it is a little more difficult to operate than SPSS, which is menu-driven. However, with a little coaching, many people find that R is reasonably straightforward and its benefits of being up to date and free make it very appealing. R will produce statistics and graphs easily after one has learned the required syntax.

Interpreting the Statistic

Correlation values range between -1.00 and +1.00. More positive values (those more closely approaching +1.00) indicate a stronger direct relationship. More negative values (those approaching -1.00) indicate a stronger inverse relationship. It is important to note that the direction (positive or negative) of the correlation is not the indicator of the strength. A value of -1.00 is the same strength as a value of +1.00. A value of -0.86 is a stronger relationship than a value of +0.72. The strength of

TABLE 7-2. STRENGTH CATEGORIZATIONS OF CORRELATION COEFFICIENTS

STRENGTH	LOWER BOUNDARY	UPPER BOUNDARY
Strong	0.60	1.00
Medium	0.40	0.59
Weak	0.20	0.39

Note: The same ranges apply to coefficients with negative valences. Each value would be preceded by a minus sign to denote that the relationship was negative.

Adapted from Coleman, J. S. (2008). Correlation. In N. J. Salkind & K. Rasmussen (Eds.), *Encyclopedia of educational psychology* (pp. 193-194). Sage.

the relationship is determined by the absolute value of the coefficient. Values that fall closer to zero signify that the variables are less or not meaningfully linked.

Correlation coefficients also have the benefit of being considered to be effect sizes (Borenstein, 2009a, 2009b). Effect sizes are, in essence, measures of practical significance. Statistical significance is related to the number of people considered in the sample. Effect sizes have the advantage of being somewhat independent of sample size.

STRENGTH OF THE RELATIONSHIP

Some researchers employ a categorical approach to determining the strength of the correlation coefficient. Caution in using this approach is advised because the categorization of the strength of correlation coefficient values varies by discipline and area of inquiry. In fact, some authors (e.g., Glass et al., 1981) have persuasively argued that there is little value in associating effect size measures with descriptive adjectives such as "strong," "medium," or "weak." Regardless of this advice, *r* values in the behavioral sciences are often categorized according to the levels shown in Table 7-2.

There are two additional ways to help interpret a correlation coefficient: a test of statistical significance and a computation called the *coefficient of determination*. Statistical significance tests are generally computed by more professional statistical software, but the coefficient of determination can be easily calculated by hand or with a calculator.

SIGNIFICANCE OF THE RELATIONSHIP

The test of statistical significance provides an indication that the correlation coefficient, regardless of its strength, is different from zero. This is an important consideration because some data sets can produce misleading results due to their size and other aspects.

The significance test employs the traditional alpha level of .05. That is, any computed test of significance with a value of .05 or less is considered to be "statistically significant." We designate this value as "p" in our research reports. In brief and overly simplistic terms, that means that it is an outcome that is unlikely (had a low probability) to have occurred by chance or sampling error.

The correlation coefficient for the number of children and number of pets was calculated in SPSS and found to be .90. This is a very strong relationship, and readers who recall our early scatterplots will be unlikely to be surprised by this strong correlation coefficient. It looks strong in the graph and the statistic indicates that the appearance, in this case, is correct. SPSS also reported the statistical significance of the correlation coefficient as 0.037 ($p = .037$). That is good news because it tells us that our relationship is meaningfully different from zero. The simple interpretation of the .037 p value is that the chances that this relationship is simply based on sampling error are 37 out of 1000. Social science researchers often assume that 5 out of 100 ($p = .05$) is sufficient to support the conclusion of statistical significance.

ACCOUNTING FOR VARIANCE

The final measure to consider for interpreting our correlation coefficient is the coefficient of determination. That sounds complicated, but this is the easiest to compute and interpret of all the statistics associated with correlational research. The coefficient of determination is simply the r value squared. In fact, it is most often referred to as r^2 or r squared. It tells us the amount of variability in one value that is shared by the other (Field, 2017). Another way to explain r^2 is that it is the amount of variability accounted for by the relationship between the two variables. Note that while two variables may share a great deal of the variability in the measures, it is still the case in correlational research that neither variable is presumed to cause the other (Field, 2017).

In the case of our children and pets example, the data appeared to be linear with no observable pileups at either end of the chart. The correlation coefficient was .90, a value that falls in the "strong" range. Further, it was found to be statistically significant ($p = .037$). Squaring $r = .90$ yielded $r^2 = .81$, indicating that the relationship between number of children and number of pets accounted for 81% of the variability in the data. Eighty-one percent is quite a large value for r^2. So, in this data set, we found a strong correlation that was statistically significant and accounted for 81% of the variability in the two data sets. Not bad! But, recall that this is a made-up data set intended to make it easy to show what is happening in the analysis. Research in real-life settings is always more difficult to conduct and analyze than data that was made up to illustrate a procedure! Nevertheless, it is well worth the effort.

PROBLEMS WITH INTERPRETING CORRELATIONAL RESEARCH

Spurious Correlations

Researchers and research consumers must consider correlation coefficients with caution. An association between two variables does not demonstrate causation, and, in some cases, spurious relationships may be found between variables that defy logical explanation. For some amusing demonstrations of this warning, take a look at Tyler Vigen's (2015) book, *Spurious Correlations*. Among the random events that seem to have strong relationships are positive and strong correlations between: (a) amount of tea consumption and number of people killed by misusing a lawnmower (.93), (b) number of potatoes used for frozen French fries and number of instances of Garfield (the comic strip cat) eating lasagna (.97), and (c) estimated revenue from all bingo games and the number of homes with indoor houseplants (.89). It seems clear that these are simply random events with an ebb and flow that mirrors some other completely unrelated event. In other words, meaningless coincidence. Other spurious correlations may be the result of the influence of some lurking variable.

Think back to the case study once again. Can you suggest any possible relationships that Veronica might encounter that could turn out to be spurious? How might you consider the outcomes to eliminate or reduce the risk that you were reporting a spurious correlation?

Lurking Variables

There are other correlations that appear, on the surface, to be simply coincidental but have an underlying meaningful relationship. Two examples of these relationships follow. Both of the statements are true, but each is incomplete. Try to determine the missing element that would allow these superficially preposterous claims to be rational before you read the explanations that follow them.

A. There is a positive correlation between foot size and spelling ability.
B. There is a negative correlation between cancer and divorce rates in adults.

We can restate example A as: the bigger one's feet, the better one's spelling. We can restate example B as: the more likely one is to develop cancer, the less likely one is to become divorced. It seems preposterous that foot size "causes" spelling ability or vice-versa and it is. It is equally preposterous that developing cancer protects one from divorce or vice-versa. Another possibility is that there is some other variable that is behind each of the relationships. In each of these cases, the third (lurking) variable is age.

In example A, we know that when we are very young, we have small feet and little if any spelling ability. However, as we begin to mature, our feet grow larger and we also acquire the ability to spell an increasing number of words properly. Even this is a generalization, because simply aging does not impart spelling ability. There is also a ceiling level where the relationship breaks down, i.e., at some point, one's foot growth is no longer associated with spelling ability and vice-versa. Spelling bee champions can relax. There is little threat that circus clowns (who often are observed to have enormous shoes and, presumably, enormous feet) will become a serious competitive threat simply by virtue of their shoe size.

In example B, we find the same lurking variable, age. Statistically speaking, marriages are more likely to fail in the earlier years than they are in the later years, and one is more likely to develop cancer later in life. Of course, this is in no way a claim that young people never develop cancer or that lengthy marriages are invulnerable to failure. However, younger people are more likely to become divorced and less likely to develop cancer than are older people and vice-versa.

Possible Relationships Among Correlated Variables

The spurious correlations presented earlier and these two examples of the influence of a variable outside of the direct comparison suggest that logical claims made in correlational research are sometimes problematic. In fact, that complaint is often true. We know that correlations consider only two variables at a time, but the world in which we live is complex and there are many influences in any relationship among variables. Some of the possible relationships between a pair of variables (A and B) are listed below:

- A causes B
- B causes A
- A and B are consequences of a common cause, but do not cause each other
- A and B both cause C
- A causes B and B causes A (a bidirectional or cyclic causation)
- A causes C which causes B (an indirect causation)
- There is no connection between A and B (i.e., the correlation is a coincidence)

The bottom line here is that no meaningful conclusion regarding the existence of a cause and effect relationship or its direction if it exists can emerge from the observation that A and B are correlated. Even if a correlation coefficient is strong, statistically significant, and explains a great deal of the variance between the two phenomena considered, determining any cause and effect relationship requires more investigation.

Return once more to the problem facing Veronica in our case study. Think about the possibility of lurking variables that might interfere with a solid conclusion. Can you think of a potential way of ruling out the lurking variable?

EXAMPLE OF CORRELATIONAL RESEARCH

Good examples of published correlational research using the analyses described here are becoming increasingly rare. Part of the reason for that is an increased understanding of the complexity of research in the special education profession. Earlier publications that used more basic designs have given way to more sophisticated analyses such as multiple regression, path analysis, and hierarchical modeling, to name but a few. These models can handle more than two variables and also can estimate the proportion of variance that is uniquely related to any single variable (Paris, 2013).

Test et al. (2009) provided an excellent example of research using correlational outcomes. The research that they conducted was a meta-analysis. A meta-analysis is a statistical analysis and summary of individual studies to allow the findings to be integrated (Cooper et al., 2009). Meta-analytic studies are important because they provide a more reliable estimate of the effect under consideration than can any single study.

Test et al. surveyed the literature published between 1984 and March 2009 to locate publications regarding secondary transition that used correlational analysis. Initially, 162 articles were identified for possible inclusion in the study. After screening the articles to remove articles that were inappropriate for statistical analysis (e.g., position papers, program evaluations, program descriptions), 63 articles remained for consideration. These 63 articles were further screened using a set of quality indicators so that only reports that were of sufficient integrity were included. The final screening procedure for quality indicators reduced the number of articles to be included to 22. These 22 articles reported studies that included over 26,000 students across all disability conditions. Two statistics were chosen to integrate the findings across studies, r and r^2. The authors identified 16 evidence-based predictor outcomes with positive correlations between the predictor and improved postschool outcomes across the areas of education, employment, and/or independent living. Table 7-3 presents a brief summary of these positive indicators.

Researchers must be careful when interpreting these findings. Although there is a positive correlation between the predictors and the outcomes indicated, we cannot presume a causal relationship. For one thing, there are too few effect sizes to support strong conclusions. Also, there are a number of other factors that may be in play in the findings. For example, inclusion in general education has one of the more substantial effect sizes, but it could be that students with stronger abilities are more likely to be included and for longer times than students with disabilities that result in greater impairment and, thus, greater need for support. As such, the students with stronger abilities would be more likely to have more positive outcomes than would their peers with greater needs.

In addition to these effect sizes based on positive correlations between predictors and outcomes, Test et al. reported negative correlations (these are correlations, not effect sizes) between the amount of time that a student spent in general education and the amount of support needed for independent living. That is, as time included goes down, need for support goes up. Another negative correlation was reported for receiving support from vocational rehabilitation (VR) and mental health/mental retardation (MH/MR) agencies and postschool employment. One should be careful to interpret this correctly. Rather than indicating that involvement with VR or MH/MR agencies hinders employment, it is far more likely to be an indicator that such involvement is a proxy for the severity of the individual's disability with people who have more serious needs seeking more regular involvement with such agencies.

QUALITY INDICATORS IN CORRELATIONAL RESEARCH FOR SPECIAL EDUCATION

Despite the epistemological issues that surround it, correlational research serves a useful purpose, but only if it is conducted well so that we can believe the claims that are made by any given study. Thompson et al. (2005) explained a variety of quality indicators that apply to correlational research. Many of these apply to the more complicated designs and analyses (e.g., Structural Equation Modeling, Hierarchical Linear Modeling) and are outside the scope of this discussion. However, a number of these apply to the kinds of research described here. Three areas of quality indicators appear to have great application to correlational research: measurement issues, issues of practical and clinical significance, and confidence intervals.

Table 7-3. Effect Sizes of Positive Correlations Between Predictors and Post-Secondary Outcomes

PREDICTOR	PREDICTED OUTCOME	N EFFECTS	STRENGTH[+] [^] [#]
Career Awareness	Education	1	.27, .23
Community Experiences	Employment	1	.39
Exit Exam Requirements/High School Diploma Status	Employment	1	.06 R^2
Inclusion in General Education	Education	3	.27-.74 (.53)
Interagency Collaboration	Education	2	.26-.45 (.31)
	Employment	1	.31
Occupational Courses	Education	1	.47, .57
	Employment	1	.09
Paid Employment/Work Experience	Education	2	.22, .54
	Employment	5	.22-.54 (.26)
Parental Involvement	Employment	1	.03 R^2
Program of Study	Employment	1	.08, .09
Self-Advocacy/Self-Determination	Education	1	.21
	Employment	1	.70-.86 (.72)
Self-Care/Independent Living	Education	1	.27
	Employment	2	.42, .53
Social Skills	Education	1	.47, .53
Student Support	Education	1	.82, .85
	Employment	2	.31-.56 (.42)
Transition Program	Education	3	.26-.61 (.45)
	Employment	1	.46
Vocational Education	Education	2	.21-.53 (.47)
Work Study	Employment	3	.22-.55 (.41)

+ Studies reported multiple effects sizes that were not integrated in Test et al. (.xx, .xx)

^ Reported as range .xx-.xx and median (.xx)

Predictors for which effect sizes could not be calculated are omitted from this table.

Adapted from Test, D. W., Mazzotti, V. L., Mustian, A. L., Fowler, C. H., Kortering, L., & Kohler, P. (2009). Evidence-based secondary transition predictors for improving postschool outcomes for students with disabilities. *Career Development for Exceptional Individuals, 32*(3), 160-181. https://doi.org/10.1177/0885728809346960

Measurement Issues

Measurement issues include reporting reliability coefficients for all of the measured variables, particularly for published tests. These values can be estimated from prior studies or test manuals. Far too many studies employ measures that are presumed, without evidence, to be reliable, valid, or appropriate to the sample under consideration. Certain measures may be reliable or valid for some purposes or samples but not others (Thompson, 2003). The responsibility for developing the evidence of the appropriateness of the measures in this quality indicator falls upon the researcher.

Another measurement issue that is critically related to correlational studies is that the quality of the measures employed (reliability and validity) are considered in the interpretations of the study outcomes (Thompson et al., 2005). Score reliability and validity issues can either bolster or undermine the claims that the researcher wishes to make regarding study data. Again, it is the responsibility of the researcher to address the issues.

Issues of Practical and Clinical Significance

Effect sizes are the major indicators of practical significance and should be reported regularly. "An effect size is simply an objective and (usually) standardized measure of the magnitude of the observed effect. The fact that the measure is standardized allows us to compare effect sizes across different studies that have measured different variables or have used different scales of measurement (so an effect size based on speed in milliseconds could be compared to an effect size based on heart rates) …APA recommends reporting these effect sizes, so it's a habit well worth getting into" (Field, 2017, p. 79). Such a definition supports the earlier contention by Thompson et al. (2005) that research, including correlational research, should report and clearly identify one or more effect size statistics for each study primary outcome.

An additional quality indicator for correlational research is that authors interpret study effect sizes for selected practices by directly and explicitly comparing study effects with those reported in related prior studies (Thompson et al., 2005). This requirement obligates the researcher to have read and understood other studies in the field of interest. The previous research is usually presented in the introductory section of the research report, but a high-quality study will reconsider the previous results in light of the findings reported in the study. It is, perhaps, an interesting side note that the common structure of current research reports where previous research is summarized and then method and so forth are described was developed by Louis Pasteur (Stokes, 1997).

Another important quality indicator that Thompson et al. (2005) suggest is that authors explicitly consider study design and effect size statistic limitations as part of effect interpretation. That is, researchers have some obligation to set limits about how far one can generalize or trust their findings across other situations. This obligation requires researchers to be deeply engaged in the realities of the conditions and phenomena they wish to investigate.

Confidence Intervals

Confidence intervals are available for nearly every statistic and it is important that they be reported, even though they are somewhat rare in much of the literature. A *confidence interval* describes the impact of random error on the statistic. Many people mistakenly state that a confidence interval provides information about how confident we can be that our statistic captures the "true" or population parameter. Individuals making this mistake will often say things such as, "we can be 95% certain that the true score lies between N and N." Such a statement would only apply to a study regarding the entire population rather than a sample. If we were dealing with the entire population instead of a sample, we would not need a confidence interval because there would be no sampling, hence no variability related to sampling error (Thompson, 2002).

A confidence interval when provided for a correlational study gives us a range of values that could be expected to occur randomly around the computed value should the study be performed repeatedly with different samples. Confidence intervals are symmetrical because they are related to the random nature of sampling error. That means they extend in both ways from the observed *r* value. An illustration of two different confidence intervals is presented in Figure 7-3.

Figure 7-3. An illustration of two different confidence intervals.

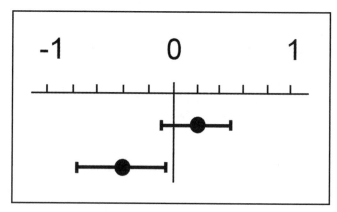

Figure 7-3 shows two *r* values as round dots with the confidence interval spans shown as arms extending each way from the dot. The range of values for the correlation extends from -1 to +1, with the value of zero at the midpoint. The confidence interval for the uppermost value has a confidence interval that includes zero. If a confidence interval includes zero, it is nonsignificant. The lowermost value has a wider confidence interval, but because it does not span zero, it is considered to be significant. Using confidence intervals to represent the significance of inferential statistics is an increasing common and useful practice (Cumming, 2012).

It may be noted that using confidence intervals in this way is simply another way of conducting statistical significance testing (i.e., determining that our observation is reliably different from zero). Thompson et al. (2005) suggested that the width of the confidence intervals can be compared across different studies to obtain a deeper understanding of the variability of measures across different samples and circumstances. More narrow confidence intervals suggest greater precision in measurement or greater consistency in the relationship, while larger confidence intervals suggest less measurement precision of consistency in the relationship. Therefore, providing confidence intervals is a fruitful first step to enable oneself and subsequent researchers to better integrate the data from different studies.

CORRELATION STATISTICS IN ADDITION TO THE PEARSON R

Thus far, we have examined correlational research from the perspective of studies involving two linear variables. Under such circumstances, the Pearson *r* statistic is the better approach. However, there are many other correlation statistics that can be used with other forms of data. Table 7-4 provides examples of other correlational tools and the kinds of data with which they are used.

Having these additional tools opens up a wide variety of elements that can be included in correlational research. For example, point biserial correlations allow the researcher to examine the relationship between some continuous variable such as response to word reading fluency intervention with a dichotomous variable such as the reader being male or female. There are many other possible combinations of such variables. It is important to recall the lesson from Vigen's collection of spurious correlations discussed earlier in this chapter and avoid calculating correlations without considering why such a correlation might be meaningful and/or non-spurious.

TABLE 7-4. EXAMPLES OF CORRELATION STATISTICS AND THEIR USES

CORRELATION STATISTIC	PURPOSE
Spearman's rho (ρ_s) coefficient	Used when both variables are ordinal.
Kendall's tau (τ) coefficient	A non-parametric measure of rank correlation (i.e., the similarity of the orderings of the data when ranked by each of the quantities).
Phi coefficient (φ)	Used when both variables are dichotomous.
Crammer's phi	Used when there are more than two categories in the variables being correlated.
Rank biserial	Used when one variable is dichotomous and the other is ordinal.
Point biserial	Used when one variable is dichotomous and the other is on an equal interval or ratio scale.

SUMMARY

This chapter has provided a limited view of what can be done with correlational research. Although the kinds of studies described here are increasingly being replaced by more complicated and sophisticated multivariate designs, there is still a place for solid correlational research in the toolbox of a skilled researcher, as well as for the critical consumer of research. Correlational research includes a set of tools used when one wishes to analyze relations between variables. They are particularly valuable tools when researchers assume that there is no causal relation between the variables or when the researchers would be unwilling to establish the experimental conditions that would enable them to demonstrate a causal relationship. See Table 7-5 for common misconceptions about correlational research.

Correlational research analysis involves both qualitative analysis of graphic displays and quantitative analysis of statistical data. Each form of analysis makes important contributions to understanding the data generated by a given study and to ensuring that the data meets the assumptions necessary for good statistical analysis.

As researchers work to improve the quality and the quantity of useful educational research, they should adhere to the quality indicators that are available for their unique form of research. Correlational researchers must be particularly concerned with the reliability and validity of the measures that they employ, as well as any unique aspects of the situations from which the data were generated to aid in placing each individual study within the larger context of other studies related to the same or similar topics.

As beginning researchers dig deeper into the research base in their areas of interest, they should bear in mind that there is no perfect study and that the entire research endeavor is a quest for continuous improvement of design, analysis, reporting, interpretation and application. In addition to this effort, there is also what physicist Richard Feynman called "the pleasure of finding things out" (Feynman & Robbins, 1999). Learning and understanding new things can be a particularly rewarding outcome of conducting research. See Table 7-6 for additional resources.

TABLE 7-5. COMMON MISCONCEPTIONS AND CLARIFICATIONS ABOUT CORRELATIONAL RESEARCH

MISCONCEPTION	BETTER UNDERSTANDING
Correlation can show causation.	Although correlation is necessary for causation, it is insufficient. There are other reason things can co-occur.
Strong correlations are always meaningful.	Not necessarily. The correlation could be spurious or based on a particularly unusual sample.
Statistically significant correlations are always meaningful.	While it is true that a non-significant correlation is probably not meaningful, significance is affected by the sample size. Large samples can yield significant outcomes because of their size.
Correlation studies have so many epistemological issues that they should be avoided.	Sometimes, a correlational study is the only way available to study a given outcome because one would not want to establish the conditions studied experimentally. Additionally, correlations are very useful in considering preliminary results and within other kinds of studies to show relationships.

CHAPTER REVIEW

1. Describe a situation other than the ones provided in the chapter where you would choose to conduct a correlational study because experimental manipulation would be impossible or unethical.

2. Let's conduct a thought experiment. Imagine that we had data from a number of students that paired the number of days that they were absent from school with their end-of-year GPA across their classes. It turns out to be a linear relationship.
   a. Do you expect the GPA to increase or decrease as the number of absences increase?
   b. Would the relationship you imagined in part "a" be an example of a positive or a negative correlation?
   c. Would you expect individuals with fewer absences to show more variability (i.e., a wider cloud of dots around our imaginary line) than those with more absences? Why?
   d. Imagine that the analysis found a nonsignificant relationship between absences and GPA. Provide an interpretation of that outcome in plain language.
   e. Imagine that the analysis found a significant relationship between absences and GPA. Provide an interpretation of that outcome in plain language.

3. Identify the pairs of variables that a classroom teacher might consider that are correlated. Try to include positive correlations as well as negative correlations.
   a. Order them from most important to least important based on your opinion of the importance of the relationship. Provide a brief explanation for why you ranked the variable pairs where you did.

4. Find an example of poorly interpreted correlational data in your educational resources or in the popular media. Identify the problem in the interpretation and why it makes little or no sense.

5. Differentiate among these three means of interpreting the statistical values produced in correlational research:
   a. Strength of the relationship
   b. Significance of the relationship
   c. Amount of variance accounted for by the relationship

TABLE 7-6. ADDITIONAL RESOURCES	
RESOURCE	**DESCRIPTION**
Special issue in *Exceptional Children*	Thompson, B., Diamond, K. E., McWilliam, R., Snyder, P., & Snyder, S. W. (2005). Evaluating the quality of evidence from correlational research for evidence-based practice. *Exceptional Children, 71*(2), 181-194. https://doi.org/10.1177/001440290507100204
Special issue in *Intervention in School and Clinic*	Cook, B. G., & Cook, L. (2008). Nonexperimental quantitative research and its role in guiding instruction. *Intervention in School and Clinic, 44*(2), 98-104.
Journal of Educational Research and Reviews article	Asamoah, M. K. (2014). Re-examination of the limitations associated with correlational research. *Journal of Educational Research and Reviews, 2*(4), 45-52.

6. Choose two variables that are available to you in your classroom and create a scatterplot showing their relationship. Be careful to use only numbers that are not personally identifiable to maintain confidentiality.

   a. Does your data appear to be roughly linear?

   b. Are there any potential outliers (extreme values)?

   c. Does your scatterplot indicate a positive, negative, or non-meaningful relationship?

   d. Does the relationship appear to be strong, moderate, or weak? (This is a bit of a qualitative analysis so you should be able to explain why you made the choice that you did.)

REFERENCES

Bennett, R. E., Morley, M., Quardt, D., & Rock, D. A. (2000). Graphical modeling: A new response type for measuring the qualitative component of mathematical reasoning. *Applied Measurement in Education, 13*(3), 303-322.

Borenstein, M. (2009a). Effect sizes for continuous data. In H. M. Cooper, L. V. Hedges, & J. C. Valentine (Eds.), *The handbook of research synthesis and meta-analysis* (2nd ed., pp. 221-236). Russell Sage Foundation.

Borenstein, M. (2009b). *Introduction to meta-analysis.* John Wiley & Sons.

Cleveland, W. S. (1985). *The elements of graphing data.* Wadsworth Advanced Books and Software.

CNN. (2019, December 13). Flint Water Crisis Fast Facts. https://www.cnn.com/2016/03/04/us/flint-water-crisis-fast-facts/index.html

Coleman, J. S. (2008). Correlation. In N. J. Salkind & K. Rasmussen (Eds.), *Encyclopedia of educational psychology* (pp. 193-194). Sage.

Cooper, H. M., Hedges, L. V., & Valentine, J. C. (Eds.). (2009). *The handbook of research synthesis and meta-analysis* (2nd ed.). Russell Sage Foundation.

Creswell, J. W. (2008). *Educational research: Planning, conducting, and evaluating quantitative and qualitative research* (3rd ed.). Pearson/Merrill Prentice Hall.

Cumming, G. (2012). *Understanding the new statistics: Effect sizes, confidence intervals, and meta-analysis.* Routledge.

Feynman, R. P., & Robbins, J. (1999). *The pleasure of finding things out: The best short works of Richard P. Feynman.* Perseus Books.

Field, A. (2017). *Discovering statistics using IBM SPSS statistics* (5th ed.). Sage.

Glass, G. V., McGaw, B., & Smith, M. L. (1981). *Meta-analysis in social research.* Sage.

IBM Corp. (Released 2017). IBM SPSS Statistics for Windows, Version 25.0. IBM Corp.

Lomax, R. G., & Hahs-Vaughn, D. L. (2012). *An introduction to statistical concepts* (3rd ed.). Routledge.

Paris, J. (2013). *Fads and fallacies in psychiatry.* RCPsych Publications.

R Core Team. (2017). R: A language and environment for statistical computing. R Foundation for Statistical Computing. Author. https://www.R-project.org/.

Stokes, D. E. (1997). *Pasteur's quadrant: Basic science and technological innovation.* Brookings Institution Press.

Test, D. W., Mazzotti, V. L., Mustian, A. L., Fowler, C. H., Kortering, L., & Kohler, P. (2009). Evidence-based secondary transition predictors for improving postschool outcomes for students with disabilities. *Career Development for Exceptional Individuals, 32*(3), 160-181. https://doi.org/10.1177/0885728809346960

Thompson, B. (2002). What future quantitative social science research could look like: Confidence intervals for effect sizes. *Educational Researcher, 31*(3), 25-32. https://doi.org/10.3102/0013189X031003025

Thompson, B. (2003). *Score reliability: Contemporary thinking on reliability issues.* Sage.

Thompson, B., Diamond, K. E., McWilliam, R., Snyder, P., & Snyder, S. W. (2005). Evaluating the quality of evidence from correlational research for evidence-based practice. *Exceptional Children, 71*(2), 181-194. https://doi:10.1177/001440290507100204

Tufte, E. R. (2001). *The visual display of quantitative information* (2nd ed.). Graphics Press.

Vigen, T. (2015). *Spurious correlations.* Hachette Books.

Experimental Designs

With contributions from Wilhelmina van Dijk, PhD

INTRODUCTION

This chapter introduces experimental designs, with a specific focus on randomized controlled trials (RCTs), often considered the gold standard design for establishing causality in intervention research. Two features are essential to RCTs: randomization and the use of multiple experimental conditions. This chapter provides an explanation of the purpose of random assignment and how it differs from random sampling. It also reviews several different methods of randomization—simple assignment, matching, and stratification—and explains their differences and reasons for use. The chapter provides step-by-step instructions on the mechanisms for random assignment, including random number tables and various software. Information on the function and selection of control conditions is provided. We review the most commonly used designs, their main elements, and what types of questions they might answer. Finally, the chapter touches on several issues to consider while designing, conducting, and reporting RCTs. These issues include the loss of participants during the study, ethical considerations about withholding treatment to participants in control groups, and promotion of quality and transparency in designing RCTs and reporting their outcomes.

Hott, B., Brigham, F., & Peltier, C. (Eds.).
Research Methods in Special Education (pp. 131-147).
© 2021 SLACK Incorporated.

CHAPTER OBJECTIVES

→ Identify the two distinct parts of a randomized controlled trial.
→ Explain the differences in purpose between random selection and random assignment.
→ Identify and diagram the main experimental designs.
→ Explain the reasoning behind matching and stratification methods.
→ Describe the function of a control group.

KEY TERMS

- **Attrition**: The complete loss of a participant during the course of a study. *Loss* refers to participants not completing the intervention phase of a study, even if they were assigned to a control group.
- **Matching**: Placing participants into pairs or small groups based on specified characteristics that may interact with the intervention, before random assignment occurs, to increase the possibility of equivalence of the conditions. Groups contain as many participants as there are conditions.
- **Probabilistically Similar**: Through random assignment, two groups are equated on the expectation of group means and thus are probabilistically similar. The expectation of group means is the mean of the distribution of all possible sample means.
- **Random Assignment**: Using a procedure to assign participants to a condition based on chance, where each participant has an equal chance of being assigned to the same condition, and the probability of being assigned to a condition is greater than zero.
- **Random Selection**: Using a procedure to identify potential participants for a study based on change from a prespecified population.
- **Randomized Controlled Trial**: A type of experimental design that uses random assignment to divide participants into at least two groups, usually a treatment and a control group.
- **Stratification**: Placing participants into groups based on specified characteristics before random assignment occurs in order to increase the possibility of equivalence of the conditions. Groups contain more participants than the number of conditions.

CASE STUDY

Rosie is an assistant professor of special education focused on helping students who struggle with mathematics in upper elementary school. While she was an advanced doctoral student, she designed a one-on-one tutoring intervention targeting fractions titled A Piece of the Fraction, with help from her advisors. The intervention progresses from fundamental computational skills to applied word problems. To validate the content of the intervention, Rosie first sent all the materials to other experts in the field to gauge their opinion. Then, she tested the intervention herself with one student. Finally, she conducted a pilot study with four students using a single case design. The outcomes of the pilot study showed a functional relation between A Piece of the Fraction and percentage of fractions added and subtracted correctly for all four students (see Chapter 10). She also conducted several small-scale field studies that showed students who participated in A Piece of the Fraction increased their mathematics skills more than the students who did not receive the intervention. Rosie would like to generalize her intervention to a broader population, and she decided that a study using an RCT would be most helpful.

While designing her study, Rosie spent some extra time on her sampling procedures. From her previous field studies, she knows that the effect sizes varied depending on the type of posttest assessment. Some of the effects were small and the statistical tests did not reach significance, and Rosie was not able to conclude that these effects existed. For her RCT, she wanted to make sure her sample was big enough to detect the differences. Rosie worked with a methodologist and they performed a power analysis to figure out how many students she would need in order to detect the smallest estimated effect of the intervention. They determined Rosie needs at least 130 students in each condition.

Rosie then worked to recruit several districts and their elementary schools for her study. She started screening only after she was certain that she would be able to enroll more than the minimum 260 students in her study. She screened all fourth and fifth graders in the elementary schools with a general math test, a more specific fraction test, and a reading comprehension task. The students scoring below the 25th percentile on the general math test and the specific fraction test were eligible to participate in her study and she sent consent forms to just over 300 students. Rosie then used a random number generator to assign the 289 students to either the intervention group or the control group. Finally, she randomly assigned tutors to schools, and the students within those schools to a specific tutor. Rosie felt confident that she had done everything in her power to make sure any differences in math outcomes could be attributed to her intervention.

EXPERIMENTAL DESIGNS

The primary feature of an experimental design study is the use of randomization to assign subjects to conditions. One type of experimental design, an RCT is considered the gold standard in intervention and treatment outcome research (Mosteller & Boruch, 2002). By "gold standard," we mean that the results of an RCT can be taken as strong evidence of the causal effectiveness or efficacy of an intervention or treatment, assuming the RCT was designed, conducted, and analyzed appropriately. By "causal effectiveness," we mean that changes in student outcomes can be attributed to the intervention. The two essential features in RCTs that enable researchers to establish causality are: (a) having at a minimum two groups under study and (b) random assignment of participants (Dooley, 2001). In an RCT, the control group stands in for what would have happened to the treatment group had they not received the treatment. This group is also referred to as the "hypothetical counterfactual" (Shadish et al., 2002) and should be similar to the treatment group.

In special education, behaviors under study tend to have multiple causes. To establish causality of an intervention or treatment, researchers need a way to limit the influences of these causes on their experiment. In other words, researchers are typically interested in studying only one or a few causes and need a way to control for the other causes. In well-executed experimental designs, these other causes are randomly dispersed across the treatment and control conditions. Random assignment controls for the confounding effect of other causes that could occur if randomization does not happen. Each participant is allocated to one of the groups completely by chance and this randomization makes groups, on average, probabilistically similar to each other (Shadish et al., 2002) on all causes, both known and unknown. There are many different mechanisms used to randomized participants, and randomization can happen at different levels.

THE BASICS OF RANDOMIZED CONTROLLED TRIALS

RCTs are characterized by random assignment of participants to treatment and control groups. Before going into the specifics of randomization, it is important to distinguish between random assignment and random selection. *Random selection* refers to identifying participants for a study by chance from a prespecified population. Using random selection helps ensure the generalizability of the study outcomes to the intended population, i.e., it increases the external validity of the study. Random selection is a useful, but not required, aspect of RCTs. Indeed, it is often not possible to randomly select participants for an experimental design study in special education due to the limited number of potential participants in a particular population or because Individual Education Plans require specific service arrangements. Instead, the pool of potential participants is often determined by convenience (e.g., students with reading disabilities attending schools that have consented to participate in a study, or young adults with autism participating in a particular community outreach program). Participants are then selected from this convenience sample using inclusion and exclusion criteria specific to the study.

After participants have been selected and have consented to participate in the study, the critical element of the RCT study happens: dividing the participants into groups using random assignment. The principles of *random assignment* are: (a) using a procedure to assign participants to a condition based on chance, (b) each participant has an equal chance of being assigned to each condition, and (c) the probability of being assigned to a condition is greater than zero. A classic example of a random assignment method is the coin toss. Provided the coin toss is done fairly, each participant will have a probability of .5 (or a 50% chance) of being assigned to either the treatment or control condition. Other ways to randomize are using a random number table or random number generator.

The purpose of random assignment is to make sure that the groups that are created do not have systematic differences, unless this happened by chance. In other words, the different groups within an RCT should be similar on expectation. Having equivalent groups is vital to determine if an intervention or treatment is effective. A systematic difference between groups will act as a confounding variable. A *confounding variable* is an additional (possibly unknown) variable that influences the outcome variable. When groups are different from each other on a specific variable, it is impossible to tease out the effect of an intervention from this systematic difference.

Consider, for example, what happened to Rosie during one of her first field trials where she assigned students on a first-come, first-served basis.

Rosie had limited space in her math tutoring intervention. She wanted to help as many students as possible but had a limited time frame; it is already the end of February. Because she had pretest scores for all children from her screening measures, she decided to fill up the tutoring slots first. The first 25 students returning parent consent forms were assigned to the treatment condition. The remaining 38 students were all assigned to the control condition. After doing the intervention study and running the statistical analysis, Rosie found that the intervention group made statistically significantly greater progress than her control group.

Rosie cannot make the conclusion that her math intervention was the cause for this greater progress. Due to her assignment method, the last 38 students had a zero probability of being assigned to the treatment condition. Even though the individual students within the treatment and control conditions were similar to each other on the essential characteristics based on her selection criteria (e.g., scoring below the 16% percentile on a standardized math test, and scoring above the 50% percentile on a reading comprehension test), there could be a systematic difference between the two groups of students. Consider the following two possible differences. First, it is possible the intervention group consisted of better organized children. These children may have given their parents the consent form the same day, and therefore were selected for the intervention. The students allocated to the control condition may have kept the consent form in their backpack for a number of days before giving it their parents. Students' organizational abilities may also differentially affect their performance. A second possibility for systematic differences is related to the students' parents. It is possible these parents were more responsive. Their responsiveness may have made them more likely to ask about the intervention and what their child learned. Both scenarios introduce confounding variables (i.e., organizational skills and parent responsiveness) that might be correlated to the treatment condition and influence study outcomes. Randomly assigning participants to study conditions avoids the possibility of systematic differences on known and unknown characteristics. Rosie should consider this study a quasi-experimental, rather than an experimental study.

The next academic year, Rosie and her team decided to do a second field study. This time, she used a table of random numbers to assign students to the intervention or control group to make sure there were no systematic differences between groups. After randomly assigning the students, Rosie checked to see if the two groups were equivalent on some basic variables. After comparing the mean scores on the reading comprehension test of the two groups by conducting a t-test, she found out the students in the intervention group scored statistically significantly better on reading comprehension. She was confused, because random assignment should equate the groups, and worried this might influence her results.

Rosie is understandably confused. She expected the groups to be equivalent, but they were not. This is due to the nature of random numbers themselves. As Abelson noted, "chance is lumpy" (1995). That is, the equivalence of groups resulting from random assignment is an expectation but often not a reality. The expectation refers to the equality that would be achieved if an infinite number of people could be randomly assigned. All the "lumpiness" would even out. Often, study samples are smaller and it is possible, especially with smaller samples, that a study may suffer from "unhappy randomization" (Kenny, 1979). Although this is confusing, Rosie should not worry; there are statistical techniques designed to handle such an occurrence. However, she does decide to adapt the random assignment to avoid this situation in her next RCT.

DESIGNS

There are many different RCT designs from which to choose when planning a study. Two features that all designs have in common are the presence of randomization and the presence of at least two groups. In this chapter, we use the common notation for experimental and quasi-experimental designs first used in Campbell and Stanley (1966), where the randomization is represented by R, assessment occasions by O, and interventions or treatments by X. If multiple interventions (or levels of interventions) are used, subscripts are added to X (i.e., X^A, X^{B1}). In schematic representations of designs, each group in a design is represented by symbols on its own line, and the order of events goes from left to right. Because special education research often relies on using pretesting as screening and selection methods and randomization happens after the pretesting occasion, we place R after O and before X. However, it is also possible to perform the randomization before conducting pretests. It is a useful skill to be able to schematize designs in this way, not only when designing your own studies, but also when reading research reports.

Basic Designs

The most basic RCT is a posttest only randomized control group design. This design includes random assignment, one treatment and one control group, and a posttest (Figure 8-1). Based on the assumption that the groups are equivalent before treatment, this design can give evidence of the efficacy of an intervention based on the comparison of posttest performance of the two groups. Sometimes, however, we want to compare the difference between two different interventions, both of which have evidence of efficacy. In this case, the design to use is a posttest only randomized comparison group design. If a researcher wants to test two interventions, neither of which have been validated, designs can be extended to include the two intervention conditions and a control group—the posttest only randomized control and comparison group design. The validity of the causal claims

DESIGN 1	Posttest only randomized control group design					
		R	X	O		
		R		O		
DESIGN 2	Posttest only randomized alternative treatment design					
		R	X_A	O		
		R	X_B	O		
DESIGN 3	Posttest only randomized alternative treatment and control group design					
		R	X_A	O		
		R	X_B	O		
		R		O		
DESIGN 4	Pretest–posttest randomized control group design					
	O	R	X	O		
	O	R		O		
DESIGN 5	Pretest–posttest randomized alternative treatment design					
	O	R	X_A	O		
	O	R	X_B	O		
DESIGN 6	Pretest–posttest randomized alternative treatment and control group design					
	O	R	X_A	O		
	O	R	X_B	O		
	O	R		O		
DESIGN 7	Crossover design					
	O	R	X_A	O	X_B	O
	O	R	X_B	O	X_A	O
DESIGN 8	Switching replications design					
	O	R	X_A	O		O
	O	R		O	X_A	O
DESIGN 9	Factorial design with pretest					
	O	R	X_{A1B1}	O		
	O	R	X_{A1B2}	O		
	O	R	X_{A2B1}	O		
	O	R	X_{A2B2}	O		
DESIGN 10	Dose-response design					
	O	R	X	O	X	O
	O	R		O	X	O

Figure 8-1. Design types for randomized experiments.

made based on any RCT designs is threatened by attrition. If participants drop out of a study, it is important to know if the group of participants that dropped out was similar to the remaining participants. It is also important to find out if participants dropping out of groups are similar to each other. It is clear that researchers employing Designs 1 through 3 will not be able to show the effects of attrition on equivalence, because they have no information on the participants that dropped out. To avoid this problem, it is highly recommended to add pretesting to the RCT designs. Designs 4 through 6 are the corresponding pretest–posttest designs based on Designs 1 through 3. The best pretests typically consist of measures that will also serve as the posttest measures.

Extension Designs

Other useful designs in special education research are the crossover design, switching replications design, and factorial design with pretest (see Figure 8-1). The switching replications design starts with the pretest and randomization. Then, the intervention is provided to the treatment group and after the intervention is completed both groups receive a posttest. Next, the groups are reversed, and the intervention is provided to the previous control group. The switching replications design is a particularly elegant design for special education research. First, it ensures that participants randomly allocated to the control group will also receive the intervention. Denying intervention to participants who would benefit from it is one of the major limitations to randomized trials and can be a potential ethical issue. Second, it provides an opportunity for direct replication of an intervention. Finally, it provides an opportunity to test for maintenance effects by conducting a second posttest to the original intervention group.

The crossover design is an extension of the pretest–posttest randomized alternative treatment design. Equal to the pretest–posttest randomized alternative treatment design, participants complete a pretest and are randomly assigned to receive either intervention A or intervention B. After receiving the randomly allocated intervention and posttest, participants "cross over" to receive the alternative intervention and take a second posttest. This design is useful when treatments are short and have little carryover; otherwise, effects in the second posttest may still be attributable to the first treatment. The crossover design can help answer questions about the efficacy of both treatments by looking at the first round of treatment, and order effects by looking at the second posttest.

Factorial designs are useful when a researcher wants to compare the outcomes related to two or more independent variables (factors) that each have two or more levels. The basic factorial design tests two levels of two factors, and this results in four different groups. Suppose Rosie wanted to further test her mathematics intervention by checking whether the intensity of the intervention, both in group size and in frequency, mattered for the size of the effect. She would then randomly assign all eligible participants to one of the four groups (Tables 8-1 and 8-2). The benefit of using a factorial design is that combinations of interventions or treatments and their interaction can be tested at the same time. Factorial designs need a high degree of control to make sure all cells receive exactly the intended intervention. The more factors or levels a researcher includes in a factorial design, the harder it is to maintain adequate control. As with earlier designs, the factorial design is stronger when pretests are available.

These nine designs represent some of the most common designs in special education RCTs. It is easy to imagine how each of the designs might be expanded by including more assessment occasions or intervention groups. With each expansion, researchers should keep in mind the added cost of the increasing complexity. For example, adding an intervention group also implies adding intervention providers who will need training, adding participants who will need to be assessed both pre- and postintervention, and extra materials. The increasing complexity also adds to the organizational demands of a project. Although complex designs may seem attractive, a well-planned and executed design is always better than a disorganized and overly complicated design.

TABLE 8-1. EXAMPLE OF A 2x2 FACTORIAL DESIGN		
	INTERVENTION SIZE	
Frequency	*One on One*	*Small Group*
Daily	One on One—Daily	Small Group—Daily
3x per week	One on One—3x	Small Group—3x

TABLE 8-2. EXAMPLE OF A 2x2 FACTORIAL DESIGN IN GENERAL DESIGNATION		
	VARIABLE (A)	
Variable (B)	*A1*	*A2*
B1	A1B1	A2B1
B2	A1B2	A2B2

RANDOMIZATION

In its purest form, participants in an RCT are randomly assigned individually to a group, and then each group is randomly assigned to a particular condition. This method is referred to as *simple random assignment* because researchers do not have to conduct any prior matching or stratification of the participants. Although this method is the best way to ensure groups are probabilistically equal, a consequence of this method is that group sizes can often end up being unequal, especially with smaller samples. A rule of thumb is to use simple random assignment with sample sizes of 200 or more. Having equal group sizes is more important in smaller samples because it limits possible problems with statistical analyses, such as decreased power and heterogeneity of variance (Shadish et al., 2002).

Matching

When researchers have small sample sizes, an option is to use *restricted random assignment* to force equal sample sizes. This method is best done through participant matching. This technique is particularly useful if the researcher has variables that might have influence on the outcome of the treatment. In matching, participants are first matched on a specific criterion and placed in groups. The size of the groups depends on the number of conditions. In a treatment and control group design, participants will be matched in pairs. If a study design includes a control and three treatment conditions, participants will be matched in groups of four. In the case of matched pairs, one member of a pair is randomly assigned to a condition. The second member of the pair is assigned to the remaining condition. For example, Landa and colleagues (2011) examined the effect of Interpersonal Synchrony intervention on young children with autism spectrum disorders. They first matched pairs of participants based on their receptive language and social interaction abilities before randomly placing one of the participants into the intervention group. In this case, the matching variables may have had an influence on the effectiveness of the intervention, and researchers took extra precautions to prevent this potential confound.

Besides consulting her methodologist on sample size for her large RCT of A Piece of the Fraction, Rosie also asked about the nonequivalent scores on reading comprehension. The methodologist suggested matching participants on their reading comprehension scores before randomly assigning them to either the treatment or control group. They also decided to change the study design from the pretest–posttest control group design to a switching replications design. After conducting and scoring the pretests, Rosie sorted the scores on the reading comprehension measure of students who had consent to participate from highest to lowest. She then formed pairs, starting with the top two students, and used a random number table to assign the first student of each pair to a condition. After all students were assigned, she compared the two group means on reading comprehension scores and noted that they were not statistically different from each other.

Stratification

In other cases, broader groups can be established through stratification to ensure equal opportunity of being assigned to a condition within a block. Each stratum contains as many participants as meet the criteria. Researchers then take participants from a single stratum and randomly assign those to conditions before moving to participants from the next stratum. For example, Fuchs and colleagues (2009) stratified students into 12 blocks before randomly assigning the students to one of three conditions (number combination intervention; word problem intervention; BAU control). Stratifying was done within site, the type of mathematics difficulty student displayed on a screening assessment, and having an additional word-reading difficulty. As with matching, using variables that might interact with the intervention are the best candidates for stratification. This stratification method increases the probability of equal spread of students with similar characteristics across the three conditions.

Cluster Randomization

A second consideration for randomization is the unit to be randomized. The best way to ensure probabilistic equivalence across conditions is by randomizing participants as the unit of analysis. In special education, this usually means the students. For example, researchers who are examining the effect of an intervention on students' social-emotional skills or the effects of a professional development in essay writing on student outcomes would randomize at the student level. Often, however, researchers are unable to randomize at the student level in special education RCTs. This is especially true: (a) if the student sample is distributed across classrooms, grades, and schools, (b) if the study is conducted for a brief period during the academic year, or (c) if the intervention is delivered by the teacher to the entire classroom. In these cases, researchers often resort to cluster randomization. *Cluster randomization* refers to using a higher order unit for randomization, such as the teacher, classroom, or even school. In this case, the researcher would randomly assign each teacher to either the intervention or control condition, and subsequently, all their students as well.

From a statistical perspective, cluster randomization works similarly to individual randomization. Clusters are expected to be probabilistically similar to each other on expectation. However, this equivalence is enhanced by numbers. In the case of only one cluster per condition, intervention effects are completely confounded with clusters, and any effect on the outcome cannot be attributed to the intervention. Having only a few randomly assigned clusters can have great impact on statistics across conditions. To successfully design and plan a cluster RCT, it is important to take the statistical analysis into account. In this text, we do not cover analyses, but a general rule to keep in mind is that the power to determine an effect, if this effect exists, will be increased by adding more clusters, but not necessarily by adding participants to each cluster. This is because the proper unit of analysis is the cluster, not the student. In many cases, it is better to treat cluster randomized trials with few clusters as quasi-experimental designs.

TABLE 8-3. RANDOM NUMBER TABLE USE	
STEP	**ACTION**
1	Decide which numbers to use to allocate to each condition. In the case of Rosie, she decides a 1 will assign students to the one-on-one tutoring condition, and a 0 will assign students to the BAU condition.
2	Select a random starting point, for example, by turning to a random page, and pointing to a spot without looking. Alternatively, you can use more formal methods to identify the start point. Rosie, for example, rolls a die three times to determine the page, column, and row where she will start.
3	From the starting point, move across the page (either by row or by column) and stop at the first occurrence of either a 0 or a 1. The first participant will be assigned to that condition. Rosie's starting point shows her the numbers 71647 45663 78435 03762 80789 59749. Her first number is 1, and the first participant is assigned to the tutoring condition. The second and third participant are assigned to the BAU condition.
4	Continue moving through the table until all participants have been assigned to a condition.

Randomization Methods

Researchers use randomization often and usually specify different variations on randomization, such as stratification or matching. However, in manuscripts, the exact method used for the random assignment is not routinely stated. Most statements regarding randomization in manuscripts are limited to "participants were randomly assigned to ..." Providing more details about the mechanism is important to give readers and reviewers the opportunity to evaluate the appropriateness of the method. Evaluation of the mechanism should include information about the mechanism used and its implementation.

Several traditional, mechanical methods to randomize exist, including the coin toss, spinners, urns with numbered balls, and dice rolls. These traditional methods are, in general, good options. However, it is possible that they have unintentional systemic biases. For example, a coin might be heavier on one side, or an urn could have a numbered ball missing. It is also possible for the person randomizing to have specific habits that might incur bias, such as always turning a die to six before rolling. To avoid these systemic biases, it is better to use a random number table or a random number generator. Random number tables can be found in the back of many statistics textbooks or in separate books (e.g., Fisher & Yates, 1943; Hald, 1952). Random number tables are generally considered nonbiased and reliable (Shadish et al., 2002). Table 8-3 contains detailed instructions on how to use a random number table.

Many statistical software packages also have built-in functions to generate a random number list and assignment mechanisms. Such packages include SPSS, SAS, Excel, and the randomizr (Coppock, 2019) package in R (R Core Team, 2019). When using statistical packages to randomize, it is important for the researcher to understand the code or syntax to avoid faulty randomization. If researchers are unsure what statistical packages are doing, it is better to use random tables or consult a colleague with knowledge of the software. Finally, randomization works best if everyone involved understands how and why it works, and if implemented by a member of the research and evaluation team, including information about the individuals responsible for the implementation (Shadish et al., 2002).

CONTROL CONDITIONS

The second important feature of RCTs is the use of two or more groups. Including a control group helps to ensure the observed difference in a skill is due to the intervention, and not due to other changes that happened during the intervention. For example, when testing a language intervention for young children, researchers need to take the natural language growth of children into account. In other cases, participants in an intervention may be primed to do better on a posttest because they have taken a pretest. Control groups who are tested at the same time as intervention groups are subject to these same threats. Comparing the difference in outcome between groups will give a more precise estimate of the effect of an intervention. Control groups in special education often take one of two forms:

1. A business as usual (BAU) control group. This group receives the normal, day-to-day instruction or treatment. Most often, this means the control group receives no intervention at all.

2. A comparison intervention control group. This group receives an intervention that is different from the targeted intervention. The differences can be substantial (e.g., a completely different intervention) or small (e.g., the same intervention delivered electronically). In some cases, researchers add a dummy treatment group to control for the extra time or attention an intervention group receives.

Some studies use a combination of the two types of control groups and some studies use multiple different interventions. When designing an RCT, researchers should think carefully about the purpose of the control group. For example, when trying to establish initial efficacy of an intervention, the control group might receive BAU. For questions regarding the difference in effectiveness of two interventions, control groups are more likely to consist of an alternative intervention. In sum, the specific characteristics of the control group are dependent on the specific research question of a study.

To illustrate, Lane and colleagues (2009) conducted a component analysis of a reading tutoring program consisting of five steps to identify which elements in the program were necessary for student success. The researchers used five different groups: (a) the full intervention, (b) no intervention control, (c) the intervention without Step 1B—manipulative letter work, (d) the intervention without Step 3—sentence writing strategy, and (e) the intervention without Step 5—extending literacy. Students were then randomly assigned to one of the five conditions. With this design, researchers were able to assess: (a) if the intervention as a whole was effective to increase students' reading skills, (b) if the intervention as a whole was more effective than the variations missing particular Steps of the intervention, and (c) which of the Steps are more important to promote increased reading skill. They concluded the intervention as a whole was effective, and that both manipulative letter word and sentence writing were critical components to the intervention, whereas extending literacy was not.

In some cases, researchers are more interested in comparing two competing approaches. To determine the difference between dynamic response to intervention (RTI) and typical RTI, Al Otaiba and colleagues (2014) randomly assigned students to one of the two conditions. The intervention conditions were identical, except for when the students were provided with the supplemental intervention sessions. In typical RTI, all students started in Tier 1 after the first screening time and moved up if the subsequent screening indicated insufficient growth. In contrast, in dynamic RTI, students could be placed in Tier 2 or 3 directly after the initial screening. Results of this study showed students in the dynamic RTI group outperformed students in the typical RTI group.

These example papers both described all of the conditions in detail. Often, research articles using a BAU control group may not spend time on detailing the specifics. Not providing these specifics limits the ability of the reader to consider how different the BAU group was from the control group. If there is considerable overlap between instruction in BAU and intervention, this could affect the potential impact of the intervention. Therefore, it is essential to provide detailed information on all conditions in a study.

OTHER CONSIDERATIONS

During the design phase of an experimental study to examine the effectiveness of an intervention or treatment, researchers should pay specific attention to the two main features of experimental studies: randomization and the use of multiple groups. However, there are other noteworthy concerns that may influence the design, execution, analysis, and reporting of a study. Three such concerns are attrition, ethical considerations, and quality and transparency of reporting.

Attrition

Randomization ensures groups are probabilistically equal on characteristics before interventions. Theoretically, this equivalence is present during all stages of a research project, including post-testing. However, this assumption does not hold when studies experience loss of participants after random assignment. *Attrition* is the term used to refer to participants dropping out of a study after random assignment and before posttesting. The nature of the intervention, or length of posttesting, may influence some participants to not fully complete the project (Shadish et al., 2002). Keeping track of allocation and attrition as well as participants' reasons for dropping out is important. Providing this information in a study not only increases the transparency of a project, but also helps to provide evidence that outcomes are not biased.

Many quality indicators for reporting quantitative research, such as the Journal Article Reporting Standards (JARS) of the American Psychological Association (APA; Appelbaum et al., 2018), recommend including a participant flowchart. These flowcharts include information on enrollment and screening procedures (including number of participants not included with reasons), allocation (number of participants allocated and receiving intervention, i.e., treatment attrition), number of participants assessed at follow-up, including discontinued intervention and measurement attrition, and number of participants used in the analysis, with reasons for excluding from sample. One frequently cited exemplar is the Flow Diagram provided by the CONsolidated Standards of Reporting Trials (CONSORT) task force in 2010 (Schulz et al., 2010). Landa and colleagues (2011) included the CONSORT flow diagram in their manuscript on the effectiveness of Interpersonal Synchrony intervention for children with autism spectrum disorders (Figure 8-2).

Ethical Considerations

Although individual randomization with a control group is the gold standard in experimental designs, it is not always desirable to conduct these types of studies. It is considered unethical to withhold potential beneficial treatments from individuals who need and deserve them. Imagine a study aimed to investigate the effectiveness of a year-long intervention to improve early literacy skills of young children at risk for reading difficulties. By using one of the most basic designs, the pretest–posttest randomized control group design, a large number of students would not receive additional intervention to prevent further reading problems. Because we have ample evidence that the reading problems of most students are easier to remediate in early elementary years (e.g., Vellutino et al., 1996, 1998), it is almost impossible to argue no possible harm will come to participants not receiving intervention.

When withholding intervention poses ethical concerns, considering the nature of the control group becomes a crucial part of study design. There are a range of possible solutions. Instead of receiving no intervention, a control group might start off without the intervention, but start receiving it after a short period. This turns the design into a dose-response study (see Figure 8-1). In this design, it is important to hypothesize how much time it will take before the intervention shows an effect, and how much time it is ethical to withhold the intervention to the control group. Additionally, this design gives the opportunity for replication. A different solution is to designate the participants in the control group as wait-list controls. This means that study personnel will ensure the control group receives the intervention, but only after the initial study has been completed.

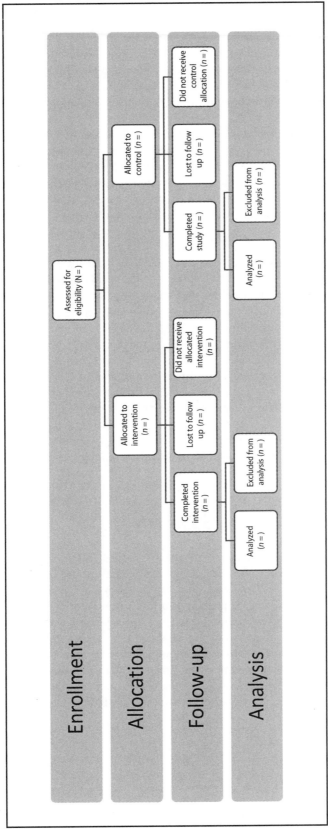

Figure 8-2. Sample participant flow diagram.

Quality and Transparency of Reporting

In an effort to improve the quality and transparency of RCTs in medicine, the CONSORT was established in 1996 (Begg et al., 1996). Over the last 25 years, this field has shown increased quality in reporting of clinical trials (Plint et al., 2006). Besides establishing reporting standards, the medical field also led the way in preregistration of trials, with the FDA Modernization Act of 1997. Preregistration has shown a decrease in large, significant findings and an increase in null results (Kaplan & Irvin, 2015).

In Educational Sciences, the same concerns about quality and transparency arose. In reaction from the field, special education researchers established quality indicators for several types of designs, including experimental design studies (Gersten et al., 2005). These quality indicators can help consumers of research evaluate the quality of reports, as well as aid researchers in designing high-quality studies. Similarly, the Institute of Education Sciences (IES) initiated the What Works Clearinghouse (WWC) to provide the public with reliable information on the efficacy of educational interventions. The WWC has strict requirements for studies to be considered for their reviews that are put forth in their Standards Handbook (What Works Clearinghouse, 2020). Finally, the APA released a detailed list of elements that should be included in a final manuscript reporting the outcomes of an RCT (Appelbaum et al., 2018). Reviewing the standards and indicators of these three sources may be helpful in considering the design, analysis, and reporting of an RCT.

In addition to the development of reporting standards and quality indicators, the special education field is also calling for increased use of preregistration of intervention research, and RCTs in particular (e.g., Cook et al., 2018). *Preregistration* refers to the practice of specifying the parameters of a study before conducting it through clear descriptions of the intervention, hypotheses, and research questions, specifics of study design including data collection, and the data analysis plan (van't Veer & Giner-Sorolla, 2016). The protocols can be uploaded to registries, such as those hosted by the Society for Research on Educational Effectiveness (SREE; https://sreereg.icpsr.umich.edu/), OSF (www.osf.io), and AsPredicted (www.aspredicted.org). These registries also provide templates with guiding questions that can help when designing studies by including considerations for analyses that influence design. Table 8-4 includes a list of common misconceptions associated with experimental research design, and Table 8-5 provides additional resources to consult.

SUMMARY

From the basic description, it may seem that experimental designs are deceptively straightforward because the two defining features are randomization and the use of a control group. A well-designed, well-executed, and well-analyzed study can establish a causal relation between the intervention used and the changes in participant outcomes. As such, experimental designs, and RCTs in particular, are highly sought after. In this chapter, we hope we have illustrated that there are many details to which researchers should pay special attention that can reduce the internal validity of a study. Nonequivalence of groups at the onset of a study, cluster randomization with a low number of clusters, and differential attrition are some of the threats to internal validity. More importantly, when designing an experimental study, researchers must keep ethical considerations in mind. In other words, is the knowledge gained from the intervention worth withholding effective instruction from individuals with special needs?

TABLE 8-4. COMMON MISCONCEPTIONS AND CLARIFICATIONS ABOUT EXPERIMENTAL DESIGNS

MISCONCEPTION	BETTER UNDERSTANDING
Randomization makes sure that groups are equal to each other.	Randomization is based on chance. Chance implies that, even though we expect the two groups to be equal, there is a probability they will not be equal. The higher the number of participants to be randomized, the better the chances.
	Imagine flipping a coin 10 times. It is possible all 10 flips come out "heads," even though we expect "heads" and "tails" to come up approximately the same number of times.
In a cluster-randomized study, a higher number of total participants leads to higher power.	Because the unit of analysis in a cluster-randomized trial is at the cluster level, power (or the ability to detect a null result if it exists) increases by increasing the number of clusters. Consider the following two scenarios of studies, both with 400 participants. In Study A, the participants are clustered in 10 groups of 40 participants. In Study B, the participants are clustered in 27 groups of 15 participants. Study B has higher power, even though the total number of participants is the same as in Study A.
BAU control groups always receive different treatment from the intervention group.	We can only be sure that the BAU control group receives different treatment from the intervention group when both conditions are described in detail. For example, Rosie's math intervention may include several steps that are very similar to the students' regular math instruction. In that case, her intervention may not make a big difference in student achievement, because only a few parts of her intervention are setting it apart from regular classroom instruction. It is important to describe both conditions, and to check for fidelity of implementation in both conditions.

CHAPTER REVIEW

1. Explain the differences in purpose and process for random assignment and random selection.
2. Give an example of a research question for which a BAU control group would be an appropriate choice.
3. Explain which types of student characteristics are unlikely to be important to include as matching or stratification variables.
4. List the two main characteristics of experimental designs.
5. In what situation might it be more appropriate to regard and analyze RCT as a quasi-experiment?
6. How could Rosie have improved her study? Think of both randomization issues and her choice of control group.

TABLE 8-5. ADDITIONAL RESOURCES

RESOURCE	DESCRIPTION
Faul, F., Erdfelder, E., Lang, A.-G., & Buchner, A. (2007). G*Power 3: A flexible statistical power analysis program for the social, behavioral, and biomedical sciences. *Behavior Research Methods, 39*, 175-191. https://www.psychologie.hhu.de/arbeitsgruppen/allgemeine-psychologie-und-arbeitspsychologie/gpower.html	Computer software to perform statistical power analyses. It can be used to determine the sample size needed to detect an effect of a certain size (*a priori* power analysis), or the power a study had (post hoc power analysis). *A priori* analyses are preferred to ensure researchers do not waste resources by performing studies that are not powerful enough to detect potential effects.
https://www.youtube.com/watch?v=sbOBlHcdYg0 https://www.youtube.com/watch?v=Uxqw2Pgm7s8	Animated videos on the theory behind randomization.

Additional Readings

Gersten, R., Fuchs, L. S., Compton, D., Coyne, M. D., Greenwood, C., & Innocenti, M. S. (2005). Quality indicators for group experimental and quasi-experimental research in special education. *Exceptional Children, 71*(2), 149-164.

Kauffman, J. M., & Hallahan, D. P. (2011). Designing rigorous group studies in special education: Common understandings of efficacy, effectiveness, and evidence standards. In J. M. Kaufman & D. P. Hallahan (Eds.), *Handbook of special education* (pp. 48-57). Routledge.

Odom, S. L., & Lane, K. L. (2014). The applied science of special education: Quantitative approaches, the questions they address, and how they inform practice. In L. Florian (Ed.), *The SAGE Handbook of Special Education* (2nd ed., Vol. 1, pp. 369-388). Sage.

REFERENCES

Abelson, R. P. (1995). *Statistics as principled argument*. Lawrence Erlbaum Associates, Inc.

Al Otaiba, S., Connor, C. M., Folsom, J. S., Wanzek, J., Greulich, L., Schatschneider, C., & Wagner, R. K. (2014). To wait in Tier 1 or intervene immediately: A randomized experiment examining first-grade response to intervention in reading. *Exceptional Children, 81*(1), 11–27. https://doi.org/10.1177/0014402914532234

Appelbaum, M., Cooper, H., Kline, R. B., Mayo-Wilson, E., Nezu, A. M., & Rao, S. M. (2018). Journal article reporting standards for quantitative research in psychology: The APA Publications and Communications Board task force report. *American Psychologist, 73*(1), 3–25.

Begg, C., Cho, M., Eastwood, S., Horton, R., Moher, D., Olkin, I., Pitkin, R., Rennie, D., Schulz, K. F., Simel, D., & Stroup, D. F. (1996). Improving the quality of reporting of randomized controlled trials: The CONSORT statement. *JAMA, 276*(8), 637–639. https://doi.org/10.1001/jama.1996.03540080059030

Campbell, D. T., & Stanley, J. C. (1966). *Experimental and quasi experimental designs for research*. Rand McNally & Co.

Cook, B. G., Lloyd, J. W., Mellor, D., Nosek, B. A., & Therrien, W. J. (2018). Promoting open science to increase the trustworthiness of evidence in special education. *Exceptional Children, 85*(1), 104–118. https://doi.org/10.1177/0014402918793138

Coppock, A. (2019). randomizr: Easy-to-use tools for common forms of random assignment and sampling. https://CRAN.R-project.org/package=randomizr

Dooley, D. (2001). *Social research methods* (4th ed.). Prentice Hall.

Fisher, R. A., & Yates, F. (1943). *Statistical tables for biological, agricultural and medical research*. Oliver and Boyd Ltd.

Fuchs, L. S., Powell, S. R., Seethaler, P. M., Cirino, P. T., Fletcher, J. M., Fuchs, D., Hamlett, C. L., & Zumeta, R. O. (2009). Remediating number combination and word problem deficits among students with mathematics difficulties: A randomized control trial. *Journal of Educational Psychology, 101*(3), 561. https://doi.org/10.1037/a0014701

Gersten, R., Fuchs, L. S., Compton, D., Coyne, M. D., Greenwood, C., & Innocenti, M. S. (2005). Quality indicators for group experimental and quasi-experimental research in special education. *Exceptional Children, 71*(2), 149–164.

Hald, A. (1952). *Statistical tables and formulas*. Wiley.

Kaplan, R. M., & Irvin, V. L. (2015). Likelihood of null effects of large NHLBI clinical trials has increased over time. *PLoS One, 10*(8), e0132382. https://doi.org/10.1371/journal.pone.0132382

Kenny, D. A. (1979). *Correlation and causality*. Wiley.

Landa, R. J., Holman, K. C., O'Neill, A. H., & Stuart, E. A. (2011). Intervention targeting development of socially synchronous engagement in toddlers with autism spectrum disorder: A randomized controlled trial. *Journal of Child Psychology and Psychiatry, 52*(1), 13–21. https://doi.org/10.1111/j.1469-7610.2010.02288.x

Lane, H. B., Pullen, P. C., Hudson, R. F., & Konold, T. R. (2009). Identifying Essential Instructional Components of Literacy Tutoring for Struggling Beginning Readers. *Literacy Research and Instruction, 48*(4), 277–297. https://doi.org/10.1080/19388070902875173

Mosteller, F., & Boruch, R. F. (2002). *Evidence matters: Randomized trials in education research*. Brookings Institution Press.

Plint, A. C., Moher, D., Morrison, A., Schulz, K., Altman, D. G., Hill, C., & Gaboury, I. (2006). Does the CONSORT checklist improve the quality of reports of randomised controlled trials? A systematic review. *Medical Journal of Australia, 185*(5), 263–267. https://doi.org/10.5694/j.1326-5377.2006.tb00557.x

R Core Team. (2019). R: A Language and Environment for Statistical Computing. R Foundation for Statistical Computing. https://www.R-project.org/

Schulz, K. F., Altman, D. G., & Moher, D. (2010). CONSORT 2010 statement: Updated guidelines for reporting parallel group randomised trials. *BMC Medicine, 8*(1), 18.

Shadish, W., Cook, T. D., & Campbell, D. T. (2002). *Experimental and quasi-experimental designs for generalized causal inference*. Houghton Mifflin.

van't Veer, A. E., & Giner-Sorolla, R. (2016). Pre-registration in social psychology—A discussion and suggested template. *Journal of Experimental Social Psychology, 67*, 2–12. https://doi.org/10.1016/j.jesp.2016.03.004

Vellutino, F. R., Scanlon, D. M., Sipay, E. R., Small, S. G., Pratt, A., Chen, R., & Denckla, M. B. (1996). Cognitive profiles of difficult-to-remediate and readily remediated poor readers: Early intervention as a vehicle for distinguishing between cognitive and experiential deficits as basic causes of specific reading disability. *Journal of Educational Psychology, 88*(4), 601.

Vellutino, F. R., Scanlon, D. M., & Tanzman, M. S. (1998). The case for early intervention in diagnosing specific reading disability. *Journal of School Psychology, 36*(4), 367–397.

What Works Clearinghouse. (2020). https://ies.ed.gov/ncee/wwc

Quasi-Experimental Designs

Jason C. Chow, PhD

INTRODUCTION

The purpose of this chapter is to provide an overview of quasi-experimental designs and to situate them within the context of experimental research in special education. This chapter aims to distinguish quasi-experiments from randomized designs while highlighting the strengths and opportunities they provide in answering complex research questions in the context of school and classroom ecologies. This chapter includes an overview of three types of quasi-experiments that have utility and promise for special education researchers: (a) regression discontinuity designs, (b) propensity score matching designs, and (c) fixed-effect regression designs. The primary aim is to provide a working knowledge of the purpose and features of each design, and detailed examples of these designs in practice in the field of special education research. By widening the repertoire and solidifying the conceptual understanding of these designs, this chapter will provide an introductory foundation to quasi-experimental research designs.

Hott, B. L., Brigham, F. J., & Peltier, C.
Research Methods in Special Education (pp. 149-164).
© 2021 SLACK Incorporated.

CHAPTER OBJECTIVES

→ Distinguish between quasi-experimental designs and randomized experimental designs.

→ Identify reasons why a researcher might select a quasi-experimental design over a randomized design.

→ Explain the specific comparison that each quasi-experimental design makes to estimate the intervention or program effect.

→ Identify a practical situation and research questions that align with the design features of regression discontinuity, propensity score matching, and fixed-effect regression designs.

KEY TERMS

- **Causal Inference**: Attributing the change in a dependent variable to an independent variable by controlling for confounding variables.
- **Confounding Variables**: Any variables that could potentially be attributed to identified differences across groups rather than the independent variable.
- **Randomized Controlled Trial (RCT)**: An experimental methodology that uses a randomized process to assign participants to group membership.

In educational research, causal inference is central for determining program effectiveness. As with all research designs aimed at isolating the effect of an intervention or program, the strongest studies and support for causal inference making rely on designs that can rule out confounds and threats to internal validity. Although the field relies heavily on randomized experiments to provide causal estimates of effectiveness, there are many situations in which these "gold standard" experimental designs are not feasible or appropriate. Randomized controlled trials rely on the fewest assumptions and, by design, present the fewest confounds (Shadish et al., 2002).

The purpose of this chapter is to introduce quasi-experimental design and provide an overview of three strong quasi-experimental designs that are, under some conditions, able to provide causal estimates for effectiveness. In doing so, I hope to provide a conceptual foundation for interpreting these designs as well as highlight the strengths and potential limitations of three widely used quasi-experimental designs. The primary purpose is to provide the vocabulary and foundational knowledge to apply these concepts to challenging questions in special education research, where producing causal estimates is the end goal.

One guiding question to situate this chapter in the context of quasi-experimental methods is: *In what contexts or under what conditions would it not be feasible or appropriate to use random assignment? These are often when quasi-experimental methods are the best choice.*

RANDOMIZED CONTROLLED TRIALS

In the social sciences, the gold standard for causal inference is the randomized controlled trial (RCT), which is evident in the standards for educational research method quality and design (Gersten et al., 2005; What Works Clearinghouse [WWC], 2020). The random assignment of units (e.g., children, classrooms, schools) to receive an intervention or access a program ensures that, on average, the units that receive the intervention and the units that do not receive the intervention have no systematic differences. Designing a study in which each unit is randomly assigned to a treatment group accounts for many threats to internal validity because the process and result of randomization generates comparable groups prior to the treatment and eliminates many threats to internal validity, including selection bias. As such, RCTs operate under and rely on the least and weakest assumptions and provide the best approximation of causal estimates (Bloom et al., 2005; Glazerman et al., 2003). However, in practice, there are a variety of reasons and situations where random assignment is not feasible. These may include financial constraints, ethical considerations, and logistical challenges such as limited resources, implementation of state or federal policy, or school districts agreeing to introduce a program or intervention under the condition that all students receive it.

Issues and Challenges With Randomized Controlled Trials

When conducting experimental research in special education, researchers often turn to RCTs or single case research designs to answer empirical research questions about cause and effect. Although these designs, if rigorously planned and well-implemented, provide the cleanest route to causal inference, there are situations where they are either not feasible or not appropriate. It is also the case that in some situations, evaluating larger structures and organization-level effects may be of interest and random assignment is not possible nor appropriate.

To illustrate, we can contrast experimental questions around evidence-based practices (EBPs) and the implementation of the Individuals with Disabilities Education Act (IDEA, 2004). Through a large body of high-quality experimental research, we have robust support for the use of EBPs in special education, and it is through these EBPs that the system of special education in the United States aims to provide students with disabilities with a free and appropriate public education (FAPE). Through the systematic process of special education referral and identification, individualized education programs (IEPs) provide educational guidance for special and general education teachers to ensure that students with disabilities are receiving the type of instruction from which they make appropriately ambitious progress toward important educational and behavioral outcomes. Part of this process is turning to the research literature to identify EBPs that meet the unique needs of each student. Whether implementing an EBP that targets specific skills like problem solving for students with mathematics disabilities (Jitendra et al., 2018; Powell & Fuchs, 2018), or more general positive behavior supports like classroom management interventions for teachers of children with behavior disorders (Chow & Gilmour, 2016; Maggin et al., 2017), the research base relies heavily on randomized experiments to provide evidence for effectiveness.

Although the evidence base may be strong for interventions that target specific skills (e.g., word problem solving performance, decoding skills) or specific individual behavior (e.g., teacher implementation of a proactive classroom management strategy), the evidence is largely based on the magnitude of the difference in performance on discrete, skill-specific measures between children who were randomly assigned to receive the intervention and those who were randomly assigned to a business-as-usual (BAU) control group (i.e., the results of an RCT). As such, this evidence and the research studies that produced this evidence are aligned to the nature of the research question: What are the average effects of this intervention on the outcome of interest compared to children who did not receive the intervention? However, in the context of special education practice where random assignment may not be ethical or possible, we may need alternative research designs to evaluate the effectiveness of special education on student outcomes.

Is it feasible and/or appropriate to evaluate the effectiveness of special education using an RCT? Why or why not?

Because special education is a federal provision where students with disabilities are entitled to receive a FAPE, it would not be possible to conduct an experiment where students were randomly assigned to receive services and some were randomly assigned to not receive services (i.e., an RCT). Because students who meet the eligibility criteria for special education services are legally entitled to those services, it would be unethical and inappropriate to design a study aimed at evaluating the effects of special education using random assignment. This is a situation where an RCT is not appropriate, and thus we must rely on different methods to make a causal inference in this context. Well-designed, quasi-experimental designs can be a powerful alternative to a randomized experiment that can address this type of research question in the absence of random assignment. Quasi-experimental designs are often more flexible than RCTs because they can evaluate effects of naturally occurring practice, use existing data for post-hoc analyses, and they are less costly (Jacob et al., 2012).

CASE STUDY

Sam is starting the third year of his doctoral program and has successfully conducted two single case design studies (see Chapter 10) with the support of his advisor, Dr. Button. Sam drafted two manuscripts summarizing outcomes of his studies, received feedback from Dr. Button, and was able to successfully submit both studies for peer review. Sam is working to complete his dissertation proposal and is thinking about scaling his intervention and conducting a small group design study. Sam and Dr. Button meet to discuss study design options, feasibility, and possible methods that align with Sam's research questions. Some of the questions they discussed are outlined in the chapter.

AN OVERVIEW OF QUASI-EXPERIMENTAL DESIGNS

Broadly, quasi-experimental designs can be conceptualized as those that compare the outcomes of units in an intervention group to the outcomes of units in a comparison group without relying on random assignment when determining group membership. All experiments, whether randomized or quasi-experimental designs, aim to test causal hypotheses by demonstrating that the intervention preceded the effect in time (i.e., temporal precedence), and that there are no alternative explanations for how or why the change occurred other than the intervention.

The 19th-century philosopher John Stuart Mills described three critical conditions under which one can plausibly claim that one thing or event causes another (Shadish et al., 2002). Specifically, these critical conditions allow one to move from correlational statements (e.g., relations, relationships, associations) to causal inference and claims. The first condition was temporal precedence. That is, one must be able to prove that the cause preceded the effect in time. The second condition was that if levels of the cause varied in some systematic fashion, there would be corresponding variation in the level of the effect. In other words, if one changed the intervention, they should expect to see a change in outcomes. For example, imagine we were delivering an explicit equal-sign tutoring intervention to improve children's relational understanding and problem solving performance once a week for 30 minutes. If we had theoretically sound reasons to believe that increasing the dosage would further improve outcomes, and we then increased the dosage to three times a week for a total of 90 minutes per week, we would expect the children to display improved problem-solving performance (effect) as a function of increasing the intervention dosage (cause). The third condition, arguably the most important, is that one must be able to rule out all other plausible explanations for the observed connection between the cause and the effect. Put simply, a causal relation may exist if: (a) the cause preceded the effect, (b) the cause is related to the effect, and (c) there is no other explanation for the effect other than the cause.

To illustrate, suppose you were designing an experimental study where the aim was to test the effects of a computer-based mathematics program on the mathematics performance of high school students with autism spectrum disorder (ASD). To satisfy Mills' first condition, you would need to prove that the implementation of the intervention (in this case, the computer-based mathematics program) came before the measured effect in mathematical performance. To satisfy the second condition, you would need to be able to argue based on your theoretical framework that altering levels of the intervention would produce variation in the levels of the outcome. For example, if you increased (or decreased) the dosage of the intervention, you would anticipate larger (or smaller) effects based on our theory. In the equal-sign intervention example in the previous paragraph, you would need to logically connect and explain how and why you would expect improved problem-solving performance by increasing dosage from 30 to 90 minutes per week. Another way to conceptualize satisfying this claim is to demonstrate that outcome measures of the skills an intervention is targeting are improving, while demonstrating that more distal measures (measures that are less related to the intervention) are yielding smaller or no gains. That is, if your intervention is designed to target equal-sign problem solving performance, you can demonstrate that the intervention improves equal-sign problem solving performance more than it does a broad, norm-referenced measure of mathematics (e.g., equal-sign problem solving performance improved more than performance on the norm-referenced mathematics measure). A more extreme example to help solidify this point: If you trained teachers to implement a proactive classroom management intervention (cause), you would logically and theoretically expect to see improvements in student engagement (effect), but you would not logically or theoretically argue to see improvements on mathematics performance to the same degree as you would behavior.

To satisfy the third condition, which is likely the most difficult to satisfy, you must be able to convincingly argue that the change in the mathematics performance of the students with ASD was caused by the computer-based program. You must also be able to convincingly argue that the observed change was not due to other factors such as teachers selecting students who like computers and mathematics to participate in the study, or parents enrolling their child in an additional after-school mathematics tutoring program. In Mills' cause-and-effect language, you would be able to say there was a causal effect if: (a) the intervention came before the change in math performance, (b) the intervention is related to math performance, and (c) there are no explanations for the students' improvement in performance other than the intervention.

The most persuasive way to meet all three critical conditions is to conduct an experiment, which can be defined as an empirical investigation where levels of potential cause are altered by an independent, external entity operating outside the context of the participants, and subsequently, upon completion altering potential causes, outcomes of importance are measured (Murnane & Willett, 2010).

Although studies that use random assignment are considered randomized experiments, studies that do not use random assignment are aptly considered quasi-experimental. Quasi-experimental designs are experiments that employ design features in an effort to mimic experiments absent of random assignment (Cook & Wong, 2008a). In the case of experimental research, randomized experiments (such as RCTs) make up a subset of the broader category of experiments. We consider all other designs that are considered experiments but do not use random assignment quasi-experiments. Again, experiments that do not randomize units do not have the same strength as those that do randomize, because random assignment enables researchers to rule out any factors (other than the intervention) that may influence one group over the other. Figure 9-1 provides a visualization of how randomized and quasi-experiments are situated in the broad scope of experimental designs. It also lists the three designs that this chapter will detail: regression discontinuity designs, propensity score matching designs, and fixed-effect regression designs.

Types of Quasi-Experimental Designs

This section provides an overview of three types of quasi-experiments: (a) regression discontinuity designs, (b) propensity score matching designs, and (c) fixed-effect regression designs. Although the strongest quasi-experimental designs are not as well-suited for causal inference as randomized experiments (Cook et al., 2008), alternatives to the randomized experiment are essential in educational research for ethical, legal, practical, and political reasons (Steiner et al., 2009). It is important to recognize that there are many other designs that fall under the umbrella of quasi-experimental designs (e.g., difference-in-differences, instrumental variables, comparative interrupted time series

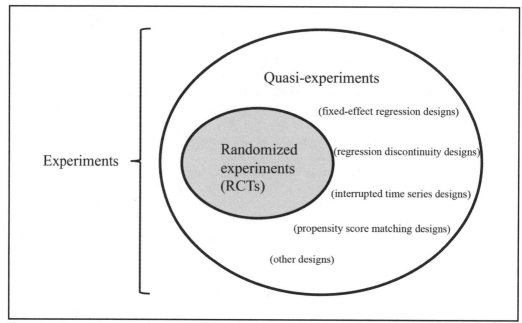

Figure 9-1. How randomized and quasi-experiments fit in the broad scope of experimental designs.

designs). However, this chapter focuses on regression discontinuity, propensity score matching, and fixed-effect regression designs. The primary aim is to provide a working knowledge of the purpose and features of each design, and detail examples of these designs in practice in the field of special education research.

Regression Discontinuity Designs

Regression discontinuity designs are methodologically one of the strongest experimental designs that do not rely on random assignment (Cook & Wong, 2008b; Imbens & Lemieux, 2008). The basic premise of a regression discontinuity is that individuals are categorized into the treatment condition or the comparison condition based on having an observed quantitative characteristic either above or below a predetermined cut point. For example, students' test scores are continuous variables, and a practical cut point is the grade to fail an exam (e.g., a score of 59). From a simplistic viewpoint, regression discontinuity designs argue that students who score a 59 are similar and comparable to students who score a 60 and apply this logic to group students into "comparable" intervention and comparison groups. Upon completion, the researcher then investigates the causal effect of the intervention on an outcome measure by comparing the outcomes of the treatment group to the outcomes of the comparison group. This provides the expected discontinuity (shift) in the regression line precisely at the cut-off point (Figure 9-2), representing the causal effect (Steiner et al., 2009). In theory, the intervention or program being evaluated should provide an additional elevation to the regression of the outcome measure(s) onto the treatment assignment variable, in turn estimating a step-like discontinuity at the cut point (Thistlethwaite & Campbell, 1960).

In typical regression discontinuity designs, intervention effects are estimated as the mean difference on the outcome variable of interest between the intervention and comparison groups at a pre-specified cut-off point. Consider the following hypothetical example. One may want to evaluate the effects of a remedial reading program in a large school district. Per policy, students who fall below a certain cut-off score on the end-of-year reading exam are enrolled in the remedial program the following year. Let's say the cut-off for being enrolled in the remedial program is scoring below a 50 on the exam. One could argue that students who scored a 49 would be similar to students who scored a

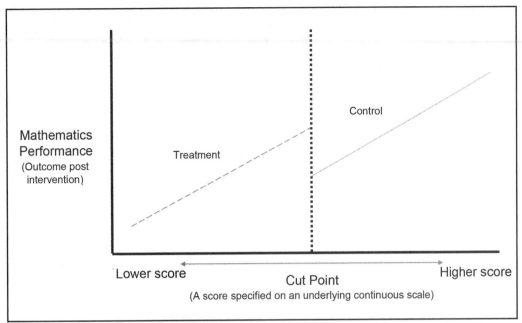

Figure 9-2. Example visualization of a regression discontinuity design where the y-axis represents the average post-intervention outcome score. The cut point (dotted vertical line) represents the average effect of the treatment at the threshold where students either failed (treatment) or passed (comparison) their mathematics class the year prior. Note that the x-axis represents a continuous score, and the cut point represents a score along the continuum.

51. In the context of a regression discontinuity design, the fair comparison would not be to compare all the students who were enrolled in the remedial reading program (scored below a 50) to all the students who were not enrolled (scored 50 or above). A fairer comparison would be to compare the group of students who scored 45 to 49 (enrolled) to students who scored 50 to 54 (not enrolled).

Questions: Why is it a fairer contrast to compare students closer to the cut point (threshold) than to compare all students who were enrolled to all students who were not enrolled? How is comparing students who are close to the cut-off point (more similar to each other) a better approximation of random assignment?

To evaluate the effects of No Child Left Behind (NCLB) using a regression discontinuity design, Wei (2012) used data from the California Department of Education to compare the academic performance of groups of students with disabilities that were above and below the identified threshold (Table 9-1). This study reported no effects for holding teachers and schools accountable for student achievement. The threshold in this study was identified by a score on a continuous variable that was defined as either meeting or failing to meet adequate yearly progress. Specifically, schools were assigned to the treatment group if their score was classified as failing to meet adequate yearly progress. Specifically, schools were assigned to the treatment group (receiving federal sanctions in the case of NCLB) if they failed to meet adequate yearly progress, and schools above the cut point were assigned to the comparison group because they were classified as meeting adequate yearly progress. Because of this, the study could compare the outcomes of students in schools right above the adequate yearly progress cut point to the outcomes of students in schools right below the cut point. This analysis was able to provide knowledge about how a designation of meeting or not meeting adequate yearly progress was related to student achievement. Although this study involved complex procedures and analyses, the purpose of this example is to illustrate the identification of similar groups around a threshold to estimate a plausible comparison.

In another example that applies a regression discontinuity design to answer an empirical special education research question, Coyne and colleagues (2018) tested the effects of a supplemental reading intervention on the reading skills in the early elementary grades in the context of a multitiered

TABLE 9-1. EXAMPLES OF QUASI-EXPERIMENTAL STUDIES USING A REGRESSION DISCONTINUITY DESIGN

AUTHOR(S)	TITLE	JOURNAL	STUDY AIM
Coyne et al. (2018)	"Evaluating the effects of supplemental reading intervention within an MTSS or RTI reading reform initiative using a regression discontinuity design"	*Exceptional Children*	Evaluate the effects of a supplemental Tier 2 reading intervention on reading outcomes in early elementary school.
Jitendra et al. (2018)	"Using regression discontinuity to estimate the effects of a Tier 1 research-based mathematics program in seventh grade"	*Exceptional Children*	Test the effects of a Tier 1 mathematics intervention on the problem-solving performance of students with mathematics difficulty.
Wei (2012)	"Does NCLB improve the achievement of students with disabilities? A regression discontinuity design"	*Journal of Research on Educational Effectiveness*	Estimate the effects of No Child Left Behind accountability on the achievement of students with disabilities.

systems of support (MTSS) framework (see Table 9-1). Participating schools from four school districts were selected by the state department of education to participate in a state-wide pilot reading initiative that focused on the implementation of a supplemental Tier 2 reading intervention. The cut scores the authors selected in this study to identify the intervention group and comparison group were based on previously established progress monitoring benchmark goals. These continuous benchmark scores were then used to identify similar students who did not receive the supplemental Tier 2 intervention to serve as the comparison group in this design. It is important to remember that scores in regression discontinuity designs a specified value or score on a continuous variable. This study is an example of a design where the cut score for assignment to the intervention condition was synonymous with the district-based criteria for enrollment into supplemental Tier 2. Regression discontinuity allows for researchers to partner with schools to estimate the effects of programs in practice, which is rarely possible in the context of an RCT design.

> *Questions: What are the advantages of experimental research questions that can be answered in the context of naturally-occurring educational contexts? What are some trade-offs between researcher-led and practitioner-led research studies?*

Regression discontinuity designs can also be used to evaluate the impact of specific educational programs and curriculum on subgroups of students by retrospectively structuring and analyzing data from a previously conducted RCT. Jitendra and colleagues (2018) used a regression discontinuity design to test the effects of a Tier 1 research-based mathematics program on the problem solving performance of seventh grade students with mathematics difficulty (see Table 9-1). The authors reported that the program, schema-based instruction, was associated with improved performance for students with mathematics difficulty compared to their similar counterparts—students with mathematics difficulty that received BAU Tier 1 mathematics instruction. The threshold defined in this study was a student's score on a continuous pretest measure of mathematics performance, where students scoring similarly in each condition were considered a fair comparison. Put differently, students who had scores above or below the cut point received different treatment, with students scoring below receiving schema-based instruction and students scoring above continuing to receive BAU instruction. In this study, the authors applied a regression discontinuity design to the data from a previous RCT (see Jitendra et al., 2017), where a cut score was used to identify comparable groups (i.e., students in the treatment group who performed very similarly to students in the comparison group on a set of measures). It is important to remember that in regression discontinuity designs, even though cut scores are used to form groups, cut scores are defined by researchers using continuous variables.

When considering whether a regression discontinuity design is appropriate for your research question, an important factor is that the observed variable that determines assignment to the treatment group or the comparison group must be a quantitative continuous variable. Regression discontinuity designs will not work with categorical assignment variables because the regression lines to determine discontinuity (or not) cannot be estimated. For example, Wei (2012) used a cut-off score based on adequate yearly progress, Coyne et al. (2018) used a cut score based on student performance on progress monitoring measures of reading, and Jitendra et al. (2018) developed cut scores based on performance on two measures of mathematics. These are all quantitative continuous variables. Regression discontinuity would not be appropriate for research questions aiming to test for group differences based on categorical variables like race/ethnicity or gender. For more information on designing regression discontinuity designs, see Jacobs and colleagues (2012), who provide an excellent, in-depth practical guide for researchers pursing this methodology.

Just like all research designs, there are important limitations that must be considered and appropriately addressed when using regression discontinuity. For example, regression discontinuity designs are only as strong as the adherence to the cut point identified in the study. Further, when interpreting the average treatment effect of a regression discontinuity analysis, it is usually only appropriate for participants close to the cut point (right above, or right below). For those interested in pursuing the application of regression discontinuity designs to their own research, I recommend consulting the WWC Standards and Procedures (2020).

Propensity Score Matching Designs

Propensity score matching designs statistically pair individuals that receive an intervention or participate in a program with students who are similar in other ways but did not receive the intervention or participate in the program. Conceptually, the goal of propensity score matching is to pair individuals who are as similar as possible on as many demographic and individual characteristics as possible that are correlated with group assignment and the outcome of interest, in an effort to increase the chance that the only difference between the two individuals was that one received the intervention or participated in the program and the other did not. Examples of matching characteristics that would be relevant to special education are variables such as gender, age, cultural background, socioeconomic status, academic achievement, community characteristics, and behavior or social skills. In the majority of designs, covariate selection involves linking variables to theory, but in the case of propensity score matching, large amounts of data are used to generate the most precise score as possible.

Matching methods use observed characteristics (like the ones just listed) and statistical techniques to generate a comparison group. This is different from random assignment because matching methods construct a comparison group to approximate random assignment without actually randomly assigning individuals to groups. Conceptually, a perfect matching procedure would result in everyone who was in the treatment group having a match in the generated comparison group who was virtually identical on all relevant observed and unobserved characteristics (White & Sabarwal, 2014). However, this is a highly unlikely situation. In propensity score matching, instead of matching each individual based on all observable characteristics, individuals are matched on their propensity score. An individual's propensity score can be conceptualized as the likelihood, given an individual's characteristics, that they would participate in a program or intervention. Creating propensity scores using data on individuals' observed characteristics allows a comparison group to be constructed that represents the same average characteristics as the intervention group. This allows researchers to

TABLE 9-2. EXAMPLES OF QUASI-EXPERIMENTAL STUDIES USING A PROPENSITY SCORE MATCHING DESIGN

AUTHOR(S)	TITLE	JOURNAL	STUDY AIM
Ansari (2018)	"The persistence of preschool effects from early childhood through adolescence"	*Journal of Educational Psychology*	Evaluate the short-term and long-term effects of preschool participation on academic and psychosocial functioning.
Morgan et al. (2010)	"A propensity score matching analysis of the effects of special education services"	*Journal of Special Education*	Examine whether participation in special education improved academic and prosocial outcomes, and reduced problem behavior compared to matched peers not receiving special education services.
Sullivan & Field (2013)	"Do preschool special education services make a difference in kindergarten reading and mathematics skills? A propensity score weighting analysis"	*Journal of School Psychology*	Examine the effect of preschool special education services on academic performance in kindergarten.

reduce the matching problem to a single dimension, as opposed to matching individuals on a series of observable characteristics (Heinrich et al., 2010). Here, matching cases on a propensity score is just another method for resampling data to ensure balance on confounding variables (i.e., covariates).

Using data from the Early Childhood Longitudinal Study–Kindergarten cohort (ECLS-K, 1998), Ansari (2018) used propensity score matching to examine short- and long-term effects of participation in preschool on children's academic and social outcomes (Table 9-2). Given the theory behind this study, participants were matched on demographic variables, cultural background, household characteristics, family socioeconomic status, family home-school involvement, and community characteristics. Given the variables that were used to generate the propensity scores, researchers are more likely able to say the effect was causal if the variables included in the score are associated with what might make that child's family select attending preschool. In this propensity score matching design, the featured comparison was between children who attended preschool and similar children who did not attend preschool, and the authors reported that children who attended preschool were associated with stronger academic skills upon kindergarten entry compared to their classmates who did not attend preschool. Further, the improved academic skills of children who attended preschool persisted through early adolescence.

Also using the ECLS-K data, Morgan and colleagues (2010) sought to estimate the effects of naturally delivered special education services on the academic and behavioral outcomes of students with disabilities (see Table 9-2). In this design, the featured comparison was between students receiving special education services and similar students not receiving special education services (i.e., students in general education who were characteristically similar to children receiving special education services). The authors matched children on a wide range of demographic variables and used propensity score matching to generate a comparison of similar children, with the primary difference being that one group of children was receiving special education services. The study reported that students who received special education services exhibited lower achievement scores than the general education matched group, but did display higher growth in learning-related behaviors compared to the general education matched group.

Sullivan and Field (2013) conducted a similar study comparing the outcomes of children who participated in early childhood special education to similar children who did not receive early childhood special education services (see Table 9-2). The authors reported that when comparing outcomes of children who participated in early childhood special education to their matched peers, children who participated had lower kindergarten academic performance in reading and mathematics. To generate propensity scores, the authors used 32 indicators of demographics, prenatal and perinatal factors, parent and home factors, health information, developmental measures, childcare and education, and geographic factors.

An advantage of propensity score matching designs is that they can be conducted after an intervention has been completed. Obviously, if you are conducting an evaluation via an RCT, the design and study must be established prior to conducting the intervention. This allows for post-hoc evaluations of interventions and can be particularly useful for quantifying the effects of naturally occurring programs such as preschool, special education, and early childhood special education. One of the primary shortfalls of this design is that it requires matching based on individuals' observed characteristics, and as such, any unobserved factors that are related to either receiving or not receiving treatment that may impact group membership or participation are not detectable and may bias the results of the study.

It is important to recognize that propensity score matching designs involve numerous stages of variable selection and aggregation and multiple complex statistical procedures. However, the goal of this overview is to provide a conceptual understanding of the purpose of propensity score matching designs. It may be difficult in practice to identify close matches on all the observed characteristics that researchers aim to match. As opposed to matching on all characteristics, propensity scores allow for matching on a set of observed characteristics (Stuart & Rubin, 2007). The example studies in this section are included to approximate random assignment using this method because random assignment was not possible in these contexts. Even though these studies were not testing a comparison between randomized groups, they do compare groups that were designed to be similar, which can be considered conceptually as an approximation of random assignment.

Fixed-Effect Regression Designs

Although multiple regression models are used for a variety of purposes in the social sciences, a specific application of fixed-effect regression can serve as a powerful tool in evaluating program effects. As with regression discontinuity and propensity score matching designs, fixed-effect regression designs can be particularly useful in the context of program evaluation that cannot be tested via random assignment. The benefit of fixed-effect regression designs is that they do not require you to identify a threshold to examine group differences, nor do they require you to conduct a matching procedure. This design is ideal for studying effects within a single group such as a school district or state-level data, or even within a student. It is a strong design for examining within-individual change that occurs as a function of a program or intervention of interest. As such, the focus of the application of fixed-effect regression designs will be on leveraging the design's strengths to study within-person change. These designs diverge conceptually from regression discontinuity and propensity score matching designs, both of which aim to approximate random assignment by generating a fair comparison group. A strength of fixed-effect regression designs is that the comparison from which an effect is estimated can be a within-person comparison, which can eliminate time-invariant confounds—particularly those that researchers are unable to measure. Rather than estimating the difference between two sets of individuals, we estimate the difference between the same individuals under different conditions. This is distinct from correlational regression analyses in that, by design, we are estimating a difference metric that estimates the effect of an intervention or program by comparing an individual's performance on outcomes when they were participating or enrolled to when the same individuals were not participating or enrolled.

TABLE 9-3. EXAMPLES OF QUASI-EXPERIMENTAL STUDIES USING A WITHIN-PERSON FIXED-EFFECT REGRESSION DESIGN

AUTHOR(S)	TITLE	JOURNAL	STUDY AIM
Hanushek et al. (2002)	"Inferring program effects for special populations: Does special education raise achievement for students with disabilities?"	*Review of Economics and Statistics*	Determine the effects of special education enrollment on the outcomes of students with disabilities.
Hurwitz et al. (2019)	"Special education and individualized academic growth: A longitudinal assessment of outcomes for students with disabilities"	*American Educational Research Journal*	Determine the effects of special education enrollment on the outcomes of students with disabilities.

Using fixed-effect models, we can test empirical questions about the effect of an intervention or program on a group of individuals compared to when they do not receive the intervention or program. Here, we are posing a within-individual or within-subjects analytic question. In the context of school-based research, we can use student fixed-effects to compare students' academic performance or behavioral functioning to their own performance at a different time. This method gets rid of the need to match students who did receive special education to similar students who did not. In special education research, fixed-effect regression designs have been used to estimate the impact of special education on student outcomes.

In a study on the effects of special education on the achievement of students with disabilities, Hanushek and colleagues (2002) conducted a fixed-effect analysis by following students who transition in and out of special education programs (Table 9-3). Remember, a primary design feature difference between within-person fixed-effect designs and matching designs is that within-person designs contrast individuals' performance to their own performance under different conditions. Matching designs compare individuals' performance to a matched group formed based on similar characteristics. The authors found that, on average, special education participation improved mathematics performance for students with disabilities, and these improvements were particularly pronounced for students with learning disabilities or emotional disturbance. In their analysis, their models specified the effects of special education as "the difference in achievement gains for students who transition into or out of special education and those who retain the same special education classification throughout the period, controlling for grade and for time-varying differences in teacher and school quality" (Hanushek et al., p. 590).

More recently, Hurwitz and colleagues (2019) conducted a similarly framed analysis that examined whether the participation in special education programming was associated with improvements in the academic performance of students with disabilities over time (see Table 9-3). Similar to Hanushek et al. (2002), the authors used fixed-effect models to compare academic performance of individual students prior to, during, and/or after participation in special education. Converging with and extending on the 2002 findings, Hurwitz and colleagues reported that students with disabilities demonstrated growth in academic performance after participating in special education. Further, the authors found that the trajectories of students who exited special education maintained growth, providing some evidence of the long-term effects of special education participation.

These are two examples of studies that leverage within-person change to answer research questions about participation in special education. In contrast to propensity score matching designs, which use statistical matching procedures to generate a similar group from which to estimate a comparison, within-person fixed-effect designs compare data from intervention or program participation of an individual to data from the same individual under different conditions. This design has practical benefits that are not afforded to other designs like regression discontinuity, because researchers do not need to specify a threshold or adhere to the design elements necessary to assign individuals based on cut scores. Given its strengths, one of the limitations of this design is that while it eliminates time-invariant confounds, it does not necessarily limit time-varying confounds. As such, there is an assumption that participants are similar over time and the design does not account for factors that vary over time.

Additional Considerations and Resources

This chapter provides an introductory overview of three quasi-experimental designs. There are many other factors that warrant consideration when pursuing the design and implementation of a rigorous study. First, just like all other empirical research, scholars who aim to successfully employ quasi-experimental designs should fully understand levels of study quality and how design features and decisions contribute to the strengths and weaknesses of research design. Gersten and colleagues (2005) provide an excellent overview of quality indicators for experimental and quasi-experimental studies in special education. This article can serve as a roadmap for essential elements in study design as well as for critical issues that must be considered when undertaking experimental research in special education. Handley and colleagues (2018) also provide useful definitions and explanations for how to improve quasi-experimental designs in the context of effectiveness and implementation research in real-world settings. For specific information on how quasi-experimental designs measure up to the quality and rigor of randomized experiments in the view of the U.S. Department of Education, the WWC Standards and Procedures documents provide a detailed explanation (2020). The WWC standards and procedures are particularly relevant to regression discontinuity designs in special education research, because these designs are included in their intervention reviews and are also able to meet the WWC standards without reservation (the highest standards for evidence from the U.S. Department of Education).

Validity is one major component of quasi-experimental design that must be considered prospectively when designing any type of experimental study. To claim causal inference, it is essential to demonstrate that a study has high levels of internal validity. Because quasi-experiments employ research designs absent of random assignment, they are unable to rely on the strength that randomization provides to designs like RCTs. As mentioned above, Gersten et al. (2005) provide guidance on designing high-quality quasi-experimental designs; Handley et al. (2018) provide applied examples for how to improve internal validity in quasi-experimental designs in real-world settings. Heinrich et al. (2010) provide guidance on how to assess validity in propensity score matching designs. Specific to regression discontinuity designs, Jacobs et al. (2012) cover a variety of ways to address and increase validity in these designs.

In a digestible yet comprehensive primer on quasi-experimental methods that includes resources for addressing bias and internal validity and is situated in the context of applied educational research, Murnane and Willett (2008) describe how to improve causal inference in education and social science research. Their book covers theory, concept and question development, challenges with design and implementation, and a series of quasi-experimental methods. This excellent resource situates each design in the context of data and research studies, which is recommended for researchers who want to deepen their methodological understanding. Table 9-4 includes a list of common misconceptions associated with quasi-experimental designs, and Table 9-5 provides additional resources to consult.

TABLE 9-4. COMMON MISCONCEPTIONS AND CLARIFICATIONS ABOUT QUASI-EXPERIMENTAL DESIGNS

MISCONCEPTION	BETTER UNDERSTANDING
QEDs cannot attribute causation.	To establish a causal relation, the following conditions must be met: (1) the cause preceded the effect, (2) the cause is related to the effect, and (3) there is no other explanation for the effect other than the cause. QEDs have the capacity to address these issues as long as the methodological procedures take steps to minimize confounding variables.
Propensity score matching can control for all threats to internal validity.	Participants can vary on an infinite number of variables that the researchers are aware or unaware of and related to the experiment. Thus, a randomized process is the gold standard for assignment. However, propensity score matching can be a useful approach as long as the researchers think critically about the theoretical model for their investigation and select critical variables on which to match participants when assigning to groups.

TABLE 9-5. ADDITIONAL RESOURCES

RESOURCE	DESCRIPTION
What Works Clearinghouse Design Standards (Version 4.1) https://ies.ed.gov/ncee/wwc/Docs/referenceresources/WWC-Standards-Handbook-v4-1-508.pdf	Contains standards for QEDs to use when designing an experiment or evaluating findings of an experiment.
Quasi-Experimental vs. Experimental Designs https://www.youtube.com/watch?v=0do6j5KzFl8	This video shares a brief overview of the differences between quasi-experimental and experimental designs.
Cook, B., Buysse, V., Klingner, J., Landrum, T., McWilliam, R., Tankersley, M., & Test, D. (2014). Council for Exceptional Children: Standards for evidence-based practices in special education. *Teaching Exceptional Children, 46*(6), 206.	This article summarizes CEC standards for determining evidence-based practices.

Summary

The goal of this chapter is to provide an introductory foundation to the purposes of quasi-experimental research designs, and to situate these powerful empirical tools in the context of experimental research in special education. Although randomized designs are still the gold standard for causal inference, there are many instances where random assignment is not appropriate and other rigorous empirical methods are needed to evaluate whether an intervention or program is yielding the desired effects. This is particularly salient in the context of special education research, where students with disabilities are entitled to special education services.

Chapter Review

1. Identify two to three contextual situations related to your line of research when a QED may be a more ethical, or appropriate, design than an RCT.
2. Articulate the role of the cut score in determining group membership for a regression discontinuity design.
3. Explain why confounding variables are a larger threat to QEDs over RCTs. What are some ways researchers can minimize threats of confounding variables?
4. Identify a topic related to your line of research that you could implement using a propensity score matching design. What key variables would be critical to consider when matching participants to conditions? Explain why you selected each variable.

References

Ansari, A. (2018). The persistence of preschool effects from early childhood through adolescence. *Journal of Educational Psychology, 110*(7), 952-973.

Bloom, H. S., Michalopoulos, C., & Hill, C. J. (2005). Using experiments to assess nonexperimental comparison-group methods for measuring program effects. In: H. S. Bloom (Ed.), *Learning more from social experiments* (pp. 173–235). New York, NY: Russell Sage Foundation.

Chow, J. C., & Gilmour, A. F. (2016). Designing and implementing group contingencies in the classroom: A teacher's guide. *TEACHING Exceptional Children, 48*(3), 137-143.

Cook, T. D., Shadish, W. R., & Wong, V. C. (2008). Three conditions under which experiments and observational studies produce comparable causal estimates: New findings from within-study comparisons. *Journal of Policy Analysis and Management, 27*(4), 724–750.

Cook, T. D., & Wong, V. C. (2008a). Better quasi-experimental practice. *The Handbook of Social Research*, 134-165.

Cook, T. D., & Wong, V. C. (2008b). Empirical tests of the validity of the regression discontinuity design. *Annales d'Economie et de Statistique*, 127-150.

Coyne, M. D., Oldham, A., Dougherty, S. M., Leonard, K., Koriakin, T., Gage, N. A., Burns, D., & Gillis, M. (2018). Evaluating the effects of supplemental reading intervention within an MTSS or RTI reading reform initiative using a regression discontinuity design. *Exceptional Children, 84*(4), 350-367.

Gersten, R., Fuchs, L. S., Compton, D., Coyne, M., Greenwood, C., & Innocenti, M. S. (2005). Quality indicators for group experimental and quasi-experimental research in special education. *Exceptional Children, 71*(2), 149-164.

Glazerman, S., Levy, D. M., & Myers, D. (2003). Nonexperimental versus experimental estimates of earnings impacts. *The Annals of the American Academy of Political and Social Science, 589*(1), 63-93.

Handley, M. A., Lyles, C. R., McCulloch, C., & Cattamanchi, A. (2018). Selecting and improving quasi-experimental designs in effectiveness and implementation research. *Annual Review of Public Health, 39*, 5-25.

Hanushek, E. A., Kain, J. F., & Rivkin, S. G. (2002). Inferring program effects for special populations: Does special education raise achievement for students with disabilities? *Review of Economics and Statistics, 84*(4), 584-599.

Heinrich, C., Maffioli, A., & Vazquez, G. (2010). A primer for applying propensity-score matching. Inter-American Development Bank.

Hurwitz, S., Perry, B., Cohen, E. D., & Skiba, R. (2019). Special education and individualized academic growth: A longitudinal assessment of outcomes for students with disabilities. *American Educational Research Journal, 57*(2), 576-611.

Imbens, G. W., & Lemieux, T. (2008). Regression discontinuity designs: A guide to practice. *Journal of Econometrics, 142*(2), 615-635.

Individuals with Disabilities Education Act, 20 U.S.C. § 1400 (2004).

Jacob, R., Zhu, P., Somers, M. A., & Bloom, H. (2012). *A Practical Guide to Regression Discontinuity*. MDRC.

Jitendra, A. K., Harwell, M. R., Dupuis, D. N., & Karl, S. R. (2017). A randomized trial of the effects of schema-based instruction on proportional problem-solving for students with mathematics problem-solving difficulties. *Journal of Learning Disabilities, 50*(3), 322-336.

Jitendra, A. K., Lein, A. E., Im, S. H., Alghamdi, A. A., Hefte, S. B., & Mouanoutoua, J. (2018). Mathematical interventions for secondary students with learning disabilities and mathematics difficulties: A meta-analysis. *Exceptional Children, 84*(2), 177-196.

Maggin, D. M., Pustejovsky, J. E., & Johnson, A. H. (2017). A meta-analysis of school-based group contingency interventions for students with challenging behavior: An update. *Remedial and Special Education, 38*(6), 353-370.

Morgan, P. L., Frisco, M. L., Farkas, G., & Hibel, J. (2010). A propensity score matching analysis of the effects of special education services. *The Journal of Special Education, 43*(4), 236-254.

Murnane, R. J., & Willett, J. B. (2010). *Methods matter: Improving causal inference in educational and social science research*. Oxford University Press.

Powell, S. R., & Fuchs, L. S. (2018). Effective word-problem instruction: Using schemas to facilitate mathematical reasoning. *Teaching Exceptional Children, 51*(1), 31-42.

Shadish, W. R., Cook, T. D., & Campbell, D. T. (2002). *Experimental and quasi-experimental designs for generalized causal inference*. Boston: Houghton Mifflin,.

Steiner, P. M., Wroblewski, A., & Cook, T. D. (2009). Randomized Experiments and Quasi-Experimental Designs in Educational Research. The SAGE International Handbook of Educational Evaluation, 75-96.

Stuart, E. A., & Rubin, D. B. (2007). Best practices in quasi-experimental designs: Matching methods for causal inference. In: *Best Practices in Quantitative Social Science*, Edited by Jason Osborne. Thousand Oaks, CA: Sage.

Sullivan, A. L., & Field, S. (2013). Do preschool special education services make a difference in kindergarten reading and mathematics skills? A propensity score weighting analysis. *Journal of School Psychology, 51*(2), 243-260.

Thistlethwaite, D., & Campbell, D. (1960). Regression-discontinuity analysis: An alternative to the ex post facto experiment. *Journal of Educational Psychology, 51*(6), 309-317.

Wei, X. (2012). Does NCLB improve the achievement of students with disabilities? A regression discontinuity design. *Journal of Research on Educational Effectiveness, 5*(1), 18-42.

What Works Clearinghouse. (2020). Standards handbook (Version 4.1). Retrieved from https://ies.ed.gov/ncee/wwc/Docs/referenceresources/WWC-Standards-Handbook-v4-1-508.pdf

White, H., & Sabarwal, S. (2014). Quasi-experimental design and methods. *Methodological briefs: Impact Evaluation, 8*, 1-16.

10

Single Case Research Designs

With contributions from Art Dowdy, PhD, BCBA-D and Joshua Jessel, PhD, BCBA-D, LBA

INTRODUCTION

Single case methods include small *n* applied designs that allow for causal claims. Single case research designs (SCRDs) involve the manipulation of an independent variable and direct observation of the dependent variable for individual cases. The purpose is to determine whether a functional relation is present between the independent variable and dependent variable. A variety of SCRDs are available to researchers, with the three major families of designs including: (a) withdrawal, (b) multiple-baseline, and (c) alternating treatment. To reduce threats to the internal validity of the study, the What Works Clearinghouse (WWC) and Council for Exceptional Children (CEC) published research quality guidelines for researchers to consult *a priori* when designing their study. We will make explicit reference to these indicators at each step of the design process. A critical decision researchers using SCRDs must make is when to introduce, or withdraw, the intervention condition. We provide a discussion on three approaches researchers can use: (a) response guided, (b) fixed-criteria, or (c) randomization. To make decisions regarding a functional relation and magnitude of treatment effects, visual analysis of graphed time series data has been the predominant method used. Quantitative approaches are increasing in prevalence to estimate the magnitude of treatment effect and to use for quantitative syntheses. We discuss the strengths and limitations of commonly used indices. Lastly, we provide guidance on the collection, curation, and graphical display of data to reduce threats to internal validity and provide a transparent and accurate representation of data to a broader audience.

Hott, B. L., Brigham, F. J., & Peltier, C.
Research Methods in Special Education (pp. 165-198).
© 2021 SLACK Incorporated.

CHAPTER OBJECTIVES

→ Identify core features of single case research design methodology.

→ Generate research questions that could be addressed through research design methodology.

→ Identify the core single case research design methodologies and explain how they combat threats to internal validity.

→ Determine whether a functional relation is present using visual analysis of data collected from single case designs.

→ Interpret effect size indices used for single case research designs.

KEY TERMS

- **Alternating Treatment Design**: One of the core designs used in single case research. The core characteristic of this design is rapidly alternating, through a randomized process, between conditions to observe whether a condition is superior.

- **Baseline Logic**: Scientific reasoning used when interpreting outcomes of SCRD that involves four elements: prediction, affirming the consequent, verification, and replication.

- **Condition**: In SCRDs, participants are exposed to different conditions to determine whether behavior changes. Conditions are often labeled using letters (i.e., **A** denotes baseline, **B** denotes intervention). An operational description of the environment and instructions given to the participant are clearly provided so that readers can identify the differences across conditions.

- **Effect Size**: A quantitative metric used to estimate the magnitude of change in the dependent variable and to compare effects across the literature base.

- **Fidelity of Implementation**: An evaluation to the degree (i.e., procedural, quality) the independent variable was implemented as intended at the intended dosage.

- **Functional Relation**: Attributing a change in the dependent variable (i.e., participant's behavior) to the independent variable (i.e., intervention or practice) by reasonable controlling for confounding variables. This signifies a causal relation between the independent variable and the dependent variable.

- **Interobserver Agreement**: An evaluation to the degree two or more observers provide similar data based on their observation of specified behaviors.

- **Multiple-Baseline Design**: One of the core designs used in single case research. The core characteristics of this family of designs involves the repeated collection of baseline data across cases and through a temporal sequence introducing the intervention condition across cases.

- **Single Case Research Design**: The methodology described in this chapter. A variety of terms are used to describe this methodology: single-subjects design, single case experimental design, small *n* design, *n* of 1 design.

- **Steady-State Performance**: Behavior that remains relatively stable with minimal change in trend, level, or variability across time.

- **Withdrawal Design**: One of the core designs used in single case research. The core characteristic of this family of designs involves introducing and withdrawing an intervention and observing how the dependent variable changes across conditions.

SINGLE CASE RESEARCH DESIGN

The utility of SCRDs can be found in a quote from Skinner (1966), "instead of studying a thousand rats for one hour each, or a hundred rats for ten hours each, the investigator is likely to study one for a thousand hours" (p. 21). In the 19th and 20th centuries, researchers started investigating cases of people who exhibited atypical emotional and behavioral patterns. The science of psychology was invented, and a research methodology was needed to communicate findings to the scientific community. This methodology would allow the field to develop knowledge at a faster rate and attract members to the field. The predominant methodology used from the field's inception was the case study method. Case study methodology has contributed significantly to the development of SCRD by: (a) intensive investigation of the individual student and (b) repeated observation or data collection across time (Barlow et al., 2009). The major difference between case study design and SCRD is that the former is grounded in hypothesis generation and is couched as a qualitative or descriptive research methodology. A case study design has numerous threats to the internal validity of the design if attempting to make a causal claim (Kazdin, 1981), thus the need for a design that allows for causal claims if intervening with an individual case.

Similar to other scientific advances, the catalyst for the "invention" of SCRD was an amalgamation of factors. First, current research methodology had limitations for the questions researchers wanted to address. Case study methodology, along with other applied research procedures, had severe limitations to address research questions about causal claims between an independent variable and dependent variable, which forced a need to develop a new methodology. Group design research was used to make causal claims but there were significant concerns, including: (a) cost associated with running a large randomized controlled trial, (b) ability to recruit sufficient number of participants meeting specific criteria, (c) ethical concerns over withholding treatment, (d) averaging effects across groups loses sight of individual participant performance, and (e) without repeated measurement there is an inability to observe trends in participant responsiveness to intervention. Second, Bergin and Strupp's (1970) foundational work argued against process-only investigations or outcome-only studies. Process-oriented investigations focused on reporting how behavior change occurred during treatment sessions, whereas outcome-oriented approaches focused on what change took place as a result of treatment. They proposed the experimental single case approach devoted to isolating mechanisms of change in the intervention process and collecting outcome data over time to observe how behavior responds to the manipulation of the intervention. Third, scholars had begun using this methodology and providing evidence of its use. One example is found by Shapiro and Ravenette (1959), who used an SCRD to investigate the effect of two therapeutic interventions on the intensity of self-reported paranoid delusions. The study was important because it combined the outcome-oriented approach by collecting repeated measurements across time with the process-oriented approach by providing descriptive information about the intervention and how this independent variable was experimentally manipulated by the research team. Despite relying on self-report data rather than direct observation of target behaviors, this is a foundational article that served as a model for developing the SCRDs we use today (Barlow et al., 2009). Last, Skinner (1953) demonstrated the use of single case methodology in experimental analysis of behavior (EAB) with animals. Sidman (1960) drew upon EAB literature, early experiments in applied behavior research, and early work of scholars articulating elements of single case research methodology we use today (Thorne, 1947) to provide a comprehensive outline for a methodology entitled Tactics of Scientific Research. The methodology has continued to evolve, but the foundation was laid for a rigorous methodology capable of determining a functional relation between an independent variable and dependent variable for an individual student.

Critical Attributes of Single Case Research Design

There are several attributes that distinguish SCRDs from other designs and allow researchers to make causal claims. First, all behaviors under investigation are operationally defined and evaluated through direct observation. Second, the dependent variable(s) are measured repeatedly across time to identify changes in behaviors that occur when, and only when, introduced to the independent variable. Third, the dependent variable(s) are measured by more than one observer to evaluate the reliability of the obtained data. In addition, the implementation of the independent variable is measured by an independent observer to ensure it was implemented as intended.

Repeated Measurement

All SCRDs rely on the use of a specific form of scientific reasoning called baseline logic (Cooper et al., 2020). *Baseline logic* includes four key elements that, when combined, aid a researcher in reducing possible threats to internal validity. A confident interpretation of experimental control is dependent on the repeated exposure to a set of contingencies arranged in a systematic fashion. In other words, the more we can repeat a certain outcome in a predictable pattern, the more we can agree that the outcome was a function of what we did. Although the visual analysis of functional relations has historically depended on the subjective notion of convincing similarly trained researchers that control has been demonstrated and replicated (Johnston & Pennypacker, 1993), standardized guidelines to interpreting functional relations have been widely adopted to improve consensus and dissemination among other research and educational communities.

To adequately evaluate the trend, mean level, and variability of the data within a phase, current guidelines suggest a minimum of three data points be collected within a phase, with a minimum of five preferred (CEC, 2014; WWC, 2020). However, the decision of when to stop collecting data within a phase is a dynamic process and requires researchers to use visual analysis to determine when they are comfortable with trend, mean level, and stability. Baseline logic can only be appropriately used when engaging in such a regimented pattern of scientific behavior. Figure 10-1 presents patterns of hypothetical baseline data for visual analysis.

The first element of baseline logic is prediction. *Prediction* refers to the ability of the researcher to determine where a future data point will likely fall within a phase (i.e., baseline or intervention). Researchers can predict the level of future behavior only when there is a stable, steady state of responding that has been obtained in a previous series of data points. *Affirming the consequent* is the second element of baseline logic and refers to a change in the environment resulting in a corresponding change in the predicted steady-state performance of the target behavior. The researcher is assuming that if they manipulate an independent variable, the patterns in behavior are likely to change, and affirming this assumption by obtaining said change. A return to baseline conditions will then allow the researcher to verify that behavior would continue as predicted had there been no introduction of the independent variable. This *verification of previously obtained performance* is the third element of baseline logic and provides an initial level of confidence that the independent variable does in fact affect the behavior. However, the process is not entirely complete until the effects on behavior are replicated with a return to the *manipulation of the independent variable*, the fourth and final element of baseline logic.

Using baseline logic with repeated measures, the researcher is tasked with producing a believable demonstration of control over the dependent variable among colleagues who have similar training in visual analysis. Throughout the years, a set of basic single-subject designs have been developed to aid in the use of baseline logic; however, properly trained researchers can use, combine, and intuitively rebuild designs using the basic elements to establish confidence in their manipulation of the independent variable. That is to say, the basic designs are useful but only insofar as researchers understand the underlying baseline logic that defines their use.

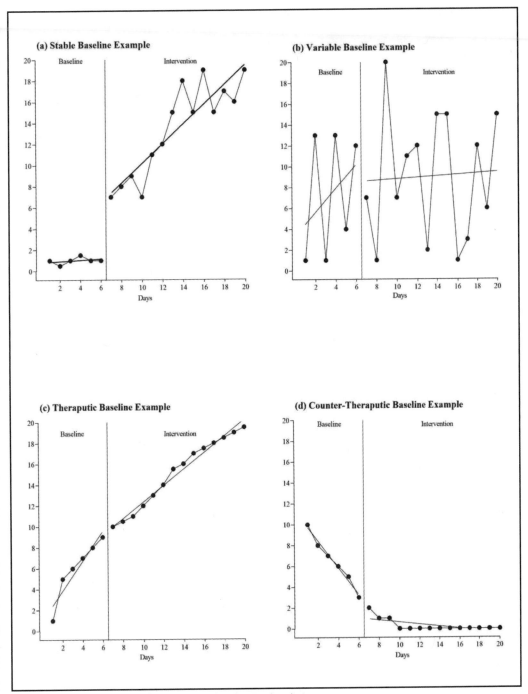

Figure 10-1. Patterns of hypothetical baseline data for visual analysis.

TABLE 10-1. PROVIDING OPERATIONAL DEFINITIONS OF TARGET BEHAVIORS	
VAGUE DESCRIPTION	**OPERATIONAL DEFINITION**
Social greetings: James *recognizes* opportunities to greet his peers.	Social greetings: When in close proximity to a peer (i.e., 2 to 4 feet), James will greet the peer by vocally saying "hello."
Task compliance: When Ariel *understands* and does an activity.	Task compliance: Any instance of completing a demand prior to the second verbal prompt for mastered tasks or initiation at the target prompt using most-to-least prompting for new tasks.
Request break: When Arron *realizes* he is tired of doing work and needs a break.	Request break: Any instance of Arron requesting a break from a task using vocalization, gesture, or picture communication exchange.
Aggression: Jasmine *develops* anger and punches.	Aggression: Any instance or attempt at biting others, hitting others with closed hand, head butting, scratching, pushing, pinching, kicking, throwing objects or furniture within 2 feet of an adult or student, ripping or pulling off others' clothes, and hair pulling.
Dropping: Bridget *refraining* from getting up when asked.	Dropping: Any instance of Bridget dropping to the ground following a demand to transition or asked to complete an activity. Dropping also includes any instance of Bridget refusing to stand and/or walk following a demand to transition (start drop duration following second verbal prompt).

Observable Target Behaviors and Operational Definitions

A vital component to SCRDs is to define target behaviors in a manner that is both observable and measurable (Johnston & Pennypacker, 1993). Both these criteria are critical when developing an operational definition (Table 10-1). Given that behavior is dynamic and occurs over time, three fundamental dimensions should be considered to ensure that the behavior is observable (Cooper et al., 2020). The first dimension is *repeatability*. For a target behavior to be repeatable, it should occur multiple instances over time. Repeatability can also be referred to as *count*. A question to ask to determine if the behavior suits the repeatability dimension is, can the behavior be repeated or counted? The second dimension is *temporal extent*. For a target behavior to suit the dimension of temporal extent, it should occur for an amount of time, even briefly. A question to ask to determine if the behavior suits the temporal extent dimension may be, does the behavior occur over an extended period? The third and final dimension of an observable behavior is *temporal locus*. The temporal locus dimension refers to the time that elapses between instances of a response as it relates to other contextual events. A question to ask to determine if the target behavior suits the temporal locus dimension may be, does the behavior occur at a point of time with respect to other behaviors?

Three dimensions can be measured with respect to an observable behavior: *repeatability, temporal extent,* and *temporal locus*. To provide an example of an observable behavior that meets these three dimensions, imagine a student frequently pushes their assignments off of the desk when asked to complete schoolwork. The operational definition may include pushing items off the desk that fall to the floor. This definition meets all three dimensions of observable and measurable criteria. Occurrences of the defined target behavior can be repeated or counted, thus suiting the repeatability dimension. Data could also be collected on the amount of time the student engaged in the behavior, thus suiting the temporal extent dimension. For example, if the teacher is interested in the amount of time the student engaged in the target behavior (i.e., duration of pushing items off desk), the teacher could track this dimension over time. Data could also be tracked on the time between the occurrences, thus suiting the temporal locus dimension. To achieve this, data could be collected on the time between instances of pushing items off the desk that fall to the floor.

Target behaviors that are assessed, monitored, and analyzed using SCRDs are operationally defined. For a target behavior to be operationally defined, the behavior should be described using observable and measurable terms, while meeting the three dimensions. The example, pushing items off the desk that fall to the floor, meets the criteria to be considered operationally defined. In contrast, if uncertain terms were used to define this target behavior, such as "angry" or "annoyed," the data run the risk of being unreliable. This is due to the abundance of differing specific behaviors and data collector interpretations that could represent "angry" or "annoyed." For example, if the same student's target behavior was defined as angry, the data collector may erroneously collect data on instances of student frowning, instances of the student folding their arms, and instances of when the student pushes items off of the desk. These data would not validly measure the target behavior of focus.

In addition to developing an operational definition, it is helpful to provide examples and nonexamples to support accurate data collection. In the example of pushing items off the desk that fall to the floor, several examples could be provided: pushing a worksheet off the desk, pushing books off the desk, etc. Nonexamples are provided to demonstrate the boundary of the behavior; a nonexample could include the student dropping a pencil out of their hand while sitting at a desk.

Measurement Procedures

Once a target behavior has been operationally defined and described using both examples and nonexamples, the next step is to select an optimal method to measure the target behavior (Table 10-2). Figure 10-2 presents measurement procedures available to the SCRD researcher, which can be categorized as continuous, discontinuous, and indirect measures. Continuous and discontinuous measures are also considered direct measures, meaning the target behavior is observed as it occurs in either a natural or contrived setting. Indirect measures draw on post-hoc data collection and involve making inferences about the target behavior based on other behaviors or environmental events. Direct measures maximize the validity of measurement due to the likely decrease in discrepancy between actual behavioral events and sampled behavior and should be selected over indirect measures when possible (Hersen & Barlow, 1976). Next, we offer a brief overview of applications for continuous, discontinuous, and indirect measurement procedures.

Continuous Measurement Procedures

Often described as the most rigorous and powerful measurement procedure, continuous measurement procedures require the data collector to record each occurrence of the target behavior, often in real time (Sanson-Fisher et al., 1979). Applications of continuous measurement procedures include frequency or count, duration, latency, and magnitude. Frequency or count measurement includes recording separate instances of the target behavior as it occurs. This type of continuous data collection is optimal when the number of times the target behavior occurs is the response dimension of interest (Ledford & Gast, 2018). However, if observations times are unequal, frequency data collection should be converted to response rate (Kazdin, 2011). Rate is often notated as response(s) per minute. Duration recording involves measuring the entire amount of time that the target behavior was performed and is an optimal selection when temporal dimensions of a response are of interest, and when the participant's target behavior varies in the length of time. Participants' proportions of engagement can be determined using duration data recorded by dividing the total duration of the target behavior by the total observation time. Latency

TABLE 10-2. DIMENSIONS OF BEHAVIOR MEASUREMENT

BEHAVIOR MEASUREMENT	REPEATABILITY	TEMPORAL EXTENT	TEMPORAL LOCUS
Count (tally)	X		
Rate or RPM (responses per minute)	X		
Celeration	X		
Duration		X	
Latency			X
Interresponse time			X

measurement is the amount of time that elapses between the onset of a specific cue and the target behavior of interest. This measurement type is optimal when the relation between a certain event and the initiation of a specific target behavior is of interest. Intensity or magnitude of a target behavior is the final application of continuous measurement and is used when the level of the target behavior requires an increase or decrease. Intensity recording often requires automated technology to precisely capture levels of the response. Examples of target behaviors suitable for intensity recording include writing, aggression, or shouting.

Discontinuous Measurement Procedures

Despite the benefits of continuous measurement, these procedures can occasionally be resource heavy, laborious, and impractical for data collectors to obtain reliable results due to uncontrolled circumstances (e.g., teaching a classroom full of students). Therefore, discontinuous measurement procedures may be used because they address several of these barriers. Applications of discontinuous measurement procedures include both interval recording and momentary time sampling. *Interval recording* requires dividing observations into equal lengths, called *observation intervals* (e.g., 10s or 15s). Each interval is scored as positive for an occurrence or negative for a nonoccurrence, across the equal observation lengths. Varieties of interval recording include whole-interval recording, where an interval is scored as positive (occurrence) if the target behavior occurred during the entire interval; and partial-interval recording, where an interval is scored as positive (occurrence) if the target behavior occurs at any point during the interval. A second discontinuous measurement application is *momentary time sampling*, which consists of scoring an interval as positive if the target behavior occurs exactly at the conclusion of the interval. A variation of momentary time sampling is called *planned activity check*, which is designed to track the behavior of a group of participants. During planned activity check, data are collected by counting the number of participants who emit the target response at the elapse of the interval.

Indirect Measurement Procedures

When it is impossible or impractical to collect data on a target behavior of interest using continuous or discontinuous measurement procedures, an alternative option is to use indirect measurement procedures. Researchers should be cautious when employing indirect measurement procedures because the accuracy of obtained data may be comprised due to the lack of direct observation. Generally, there are three applications of indirect measurement procedures, including permanent product recording, self-monitoring, and structured interviews. Self-monitoring and structured interviews have significant limitations and are rarely used in SCRDs, so we will focus on permanent product recording. Permanent product recording involves recording the tangible outcome of a

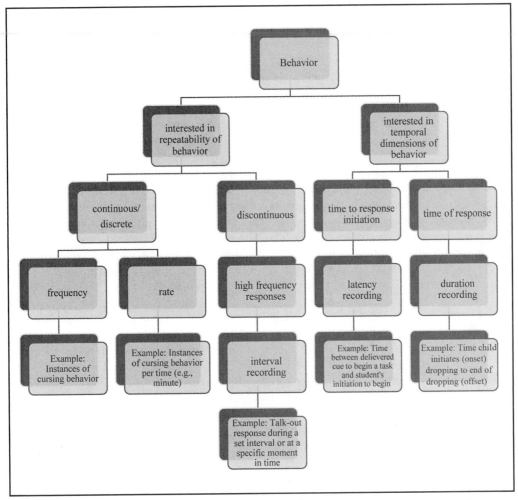

Figure 10-2. Measurement procedures available to the SCRD researcher.

behavior rather than the specific occurrence of the behavior. For example, homework or worksheets may be scored for accuracy, mathematical word problems may be scored for correct steps demonstrated, writing samples may be evaluated for number of included parts and overall quality, or video clips may be viewed at a later date.

Interobserver Agreement and Procedural Fidelity

To determine if a functional relation is present, researchers must demonstrate that the data collected to measure the dependent variable are reliable and the independent variable was implemented as intended. Both factors protect the internal validity of decisions regarding a functional relation (i.e., casual statements) and the magnitude of effect.

Interobserver Agreement

Interobserver agreement (IOA) is used in SCRD to assess the reliability between two observers who collect behavioral data simultaneously, which provides credibility to the obtained data related to the dependent variable. IOA data are often calculated as a percentage to determine agreement. To increase the internal validity in the design, both data collectors should be separated from each other and blind to the treatment condition. Both the WWC (2020) and CEC (2014) guidelines suggest collecting IOA data for a minimum of 20% of sessions per phase and agreement to be above 80%. IOA should be analyzed during the study, rather than post-hoc, to avoid collecting insignificant data over an extended period determined by low agreement. In the event of low IOA scores (e.g., below 80%), researchers must make adjustments before useful data can be obtained. Examples of adjustments may include researchers providing additional observer training or revisiting the operational definition to ensure definitions are clear and specific. A note about IOA: high IOA outcomes (85% to 100%) do not evaluate the accuracy of the measurement system (Cooper et al., 2020), meaning both observers could be collecting inaccurate data but still agree with one another.

Several common methods exist to calculate IOA. Total agreement is often considered the simplest IOA index to calculate but is limited in that it cannot be determined whether the two observers scored the same occurrences of behavior (Poling et al., 1995). To calculate total agreement, the ratio of scored occurrences by both observers is determined by dividing the smaller number by the larger number. Interval agreement is considered a more stringent index for assessing whether the observers are scoring the same behavior at the same time (Page & Iwata, 1986). Agreement or disagreement is determined for each interval (often brief, 10 to 15s) or trial for interval agreement indices, and the number of agreements is divided by the total number of intervals or trials. Two variants of interval agreement exist: (a) exact agreement, in which IOA is collected on observers agreement on the exact number of occurrences within an interval for an agreement to be counted (Hagopian et al., 2005), and (b) block-by-block agreement, in which total agreement is calculated for each interval and the quotients are averaged across the whole session. A third common method to calculate IOA is occurrence agreement, which is commonly used when the target behavior occurs at low rates. Thus, limited occurrences of the target behavior result in few intervals in which the behavior occurs. Occurrence agreement entails dividing the number of intervals in which both observers agreed on the occurrence of the behavior by the total number of intervals in which either observer scored an occurrence (Lerman et al., 2005). The opposite method is nonoccurrence agreement, which is often used for high-rate behavior. The IOA for nonoccurrence agreement is calculated by both observers reporting that the target behavior did not occur during a given interval and the total number of agreements is divided by the total number of intervals in which either observer did not score the occurrence of a response.

Fidelity of Implementation

In addition to ensuring that the data collection related to the dependent variable is reliable, researchers using SCRD also must provide evidence that the procedures of the experiment were implemented as intended. One way to conceptualize fidelity of implementation is to consider the procedural fidelity and treatment integrity. *Procedural fidelity* refers to the extent to which procedures in all conditions of an experiment are correctly implemented, including all baseline and treatment conditions (Ledford & Gast, 2018). *Treatment integrity* refers to the extent that the independent variable is implemented by the interventionist (e.g., special education teacher, paraprofessional, peer) as planned. Low fidelity of implementation increases the possibility of introducing confounding variables into the experiment, making it impossible to interpret outcomes with confidence.

Steps can be taken to ensure high fidelity of implementation (Barnett et al., 2014). First, researchers using SCRD should ensure that precise operational definitions are developed for target behaviors and interventionists can proficiently identify occurrences of the target behavior. Second, interventionists should be trained on and practice each condition and be provided with feedback. Researchers must not assume that interventionists will implement conditions with high fidelity by simply reading the condition description. Third, conditions should be as simple, standardized, and automated as possible. By implementing this step, interventionists will be more likely to accurately implement the condition consistently with relatively little effort. Fourth, fidelity should be assessed and reported for each condition. These data reveal the extent to which the actual implementation of all experimental conditions over the course of the study matches descriptions provided in the method section of the study. Fidelity reporting has increased in recent years (Reed & Codding, 2014), and the CEC (2014) standards explicitly state fidelity of implementation should be evaluated throughout the intervention (i.e., beginning, middle, end) across cases or participants.

Precise Research Questions

SCRDs are the result of combining process-oriented research methodology and outcome-oriented methodology; thus, research questions could be posed to address either of these foci. Due to the applied nature of SCRDs, research questions addressing the social validity of the practice for the student, key stakeholders, or the interventionist may be posed. However, the primary research question for a SCRD study will be focused on determining whether a functional relation is present between the independent variable and dependent variable. A key to improving SCRD research questions related to a functional relation is to focus on precision.

A quick search in the literature for published SCRDs will highlight vague primary research questions. The following stems, or slight variants, can be observed in the literature: (a) What are the effects of [x intervention] on [x dependent variable]?, (b) Is there a functional relation between [x intervention] and [x dependent variable]?, (c) To what extent does [x intervention] improve [x dependent variable]? An issue observed from these research questions is how broad they are, and none specify hypothesized reactions. Time series data collected via a SCRD have several elements that could be observed (e.g., change in mean level, change in trend, change in variability, immediacy of effect, time to criterion). Therefore, if a team asks if a functional relation is present, it leaves readers unsure as to what element of the data the research team considered in making this judgement. Conversely, a research team that asks about the effect of an intervention on a dependent variable would identify changes across all these attributions, but this in isolation does not address whether a functional relation is present. To provide a more precise research question, teams may consider starting with the following stem and altering from there: "Is there a functional relation between [specify independent variable] and [specify characteristic of data and direction in which you hypothesize it will change] on [specify dependent variable] for [specify population]?" See Table 10-3 for sample research questions from the literature.

Basic Single Case Research Designs

Researchers using SCRDs have a variety of designs at their disposal. Like other research methodologies, design selection should align with the research questions. Here, we provide an overview of the three main families of basic SCRDs and identify how these can be combined to address additional research questions.

Withdrawal Design

The withdrawal design provides the most conservative display of functional control. The universal appeal of the withdrawal design comes from its most basic form of logic of repeatedly enacting and eliminating change with the manipulation and removal of the independent variable, respectively. The withdrawal design is essentially the sum of two parts (i.e., baseline and intervention) repeatedly interchanged at the moment steady-state performance is achieved across repeated measures in each condition. The baseline condition is often denoted with the letter (A), the intervention with the letter (B), and any additional treatments using the letters thereafter (ABA design). This process can be repeated as many times as the researcher feels is necessary to demonstrate control over the dependent variable, limited only by concerns of practicality. Described below are some common variations along with their strengths and weaknesses.

The ABA withdrawal begins with the baseline condition, then introduces the independent variable in the intervention, and ends by removing the independent variable and returning to the baseline condition. The ABA design is the withdrawal in its most basic form because it only includes one phase of intervention implementation and one phase where that intervention is removed. Therefore, the ABA design is the most efficient format, but achieves efficiency at the expense of some other

TABLE 10-3. WRITING PRECISE RESEARCH QUESTIONS

STUDY	RESEARCH QUESTION	POSSIBLE REVISION
Bruhn & Watt (2012)	"Is there a functional relation between multicomponent self-monitoring and the academic engagement and disruptive behavior of female middle school students with reading and behavior problems in a targeted reading classroom?" (p. 6)	Is there a functional relation between multicomponent self-monitoring and an increased mean level of academic engagement and a decreased mean level of disruptive behavior of female middle school students with reading and behavior problems in a targeted reading classroom?
Cuenca-Carlino & Mustian (2019)	"To what extent does the SCRD model of instruction for persuasive writing with self-determination instruction improve written performance, self-efficacy in writing, and self-determination knowledge and skills for students with EBD?" (p. 4)	Is there a functional relation between the SCRD model of instruction for persuasive writing with self-determination instruction and an increased mean level change in holistic quality number of essay components for middle school students with EBD?[a]
Garwood et al. (2019)	"What effect does SCRD persuasive writing instruction delivered by a science teacher have on the quick write performance (persuasive parts, total words, and holistic quality) of secondary students with EBD educated in an RTF?" (p. 229)	Is there a functional relation between SCRD persuasive writing instruction delivered by a science teacher and an increasing trend and increased mean level change in total words written on quick write assignments of secondary students with EBD educated in an RTF?[b]
Peltier & Vannest (2018)	"What are the effects of a schema instruction package on students' accuracy in solving word problems?" (p. 278)	Is there a functional relation between a schema instructional package and an increased mean level change on mathematical problem-solving performance for second-grade students identified with EBD receiving instruction in a self-contained setting?

[a]The other dependent variables investigated by the authors (i.e., self-efficacy in writing, self-determination knowledge and skills) were not evaluated using repeated measurement across time. Thus, determining a functional relation is not feasible, so the team would provide a different research question pertaining to these elements.
[b]The authors would write a research question for each aspect of the writing evaluated (i.e., persuasive parts, total words, and holistic quality).

important considerations. First, the ABA design does not fully embody baseline logic because there is no replication of the effects observed when the treatment is withdrawn and introduced; to do so would require an additional intervention phase. Second, the design unnaturally ends during a period when intervention is not in place. From a purely basic perspective, this is not problematic; however, when the participants are children, students, or any at-risk population, the goal is evidently to help the participants of the study, thereby ending on the intervention. That is, applied researchers may use the same SCRD methodology as their counterparts conducting basic research, but applied researchers are bound to adhere to additional principles of social importance (Wolf, 1978). One approach to reduce this limitation is to simply rearrange the conditions to beginning and ending with treatment (BAB design). Doing so may improve the practicality of the withdrawal design, but remains only partially supported by baseline logic.

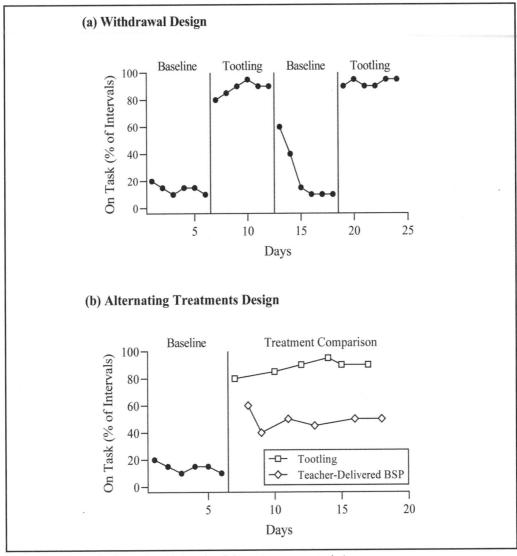

Figure 10-3. Graphs displaying the withdrawal and alternating treatments designs.

The ABAB design includes all elements of baseline logic (prediction, affirming the consequent, verification, replication) by replicating the transition from baseline to the intervention. The ABAB design (Figure 10-3) provides the most direct demonstration of functional control because the isolated change of the independent variable is manipulated twice, ensuring the effects on the dependent variable can be demonstrated at will. From the perspective of a researcher, there can be no better demonstration to eliminate threats to internal validity, and improving confidence that an effect was obtained requires only repeating the replication process (e.g., ABABAB). The WWC (2020) and CEC (2014) guidelines state that a minimum of three demonstrations of experimental control be demonstrated at three different points in time (i.e., the ABAB). However, there are several practical barriers to its use.

First, withdrawing a seemingly effective intervention often can be vexing to interventionists who have observed behavioral progress. Of course, without the withdrawal of the intervention in the ABAB design, there would be no way of knowing if the intervention was effective or if the positive outcome was due to some extraneous variable. Nevertheless, observing a child's behavior return to a previously unfavorable state because of the purposeful decision of the researcher can be difficult. This is particularly critical when considering severe behaviors such as self-injury or aggression, which brings us to our second practical barrier.

For some participants, the behavior of interest may be so severe that returning to baseline conditions creates a level of risk that places those involved in danger of injury. Therefore, not only will caregivers find the withdrawal of the treatment counterintuitive, researchers may also find themselves wanting to avoid previously experienced situations that evoke patterns of severe problem behavior.

Third, some situations are difficult to replicate once a certain repertoire has been taught. For example, a repertoire that produces its own form of automatic reinforcement will now continue to occur regardless of whether the systematically arranged reinforcement in the intervention is withdrawn (Kazdin, 2012). A child may initially avoid the tedious task of learning how to read, but once a proficient repertoire is developed, they may end up nose deep into fantastical stories that stir the imagination. Other repertoires that are taught during an intervention may be a combination of too many moving parts to be able to practically return to baseline performance (Sidman, 1985). Students taught a second language do not completely lose or "forget" the targeted structures of communication over summer vacation. Often, there is simply a transitional period during review sessions that is required to get them back to their original performances.

Alternating Treatments Designs and Multi-Element Designs

Alternating treatments designs (ATD) have been referred to using a variety of terminology: (a) multiple schedule design, (b) multi-element manipulation design, (c) multi-element design, (d) randomization design, and (e) simultaneous treatment design. In the field of special education, the term ATD is used most prevalently. Barlow and Hayes (1979) provided a rationale for the use of this terminology: "alternating treatments design has the advantages of avoiding inaccuracies associated with the above-mentioned terms and, at the same time, describing the essential features of this design, the fast alternation of two or more treatments in a single subject" (pp. 201-202). An example of the ATD can be found in Figure 10-3.

To establish a functional relation for an ATD, the researchers would observe a clear separation between the two treatments in order to determine one is superior for the individual participant. The WWC (2020) states that at four different points in time, the researchers must demonstrate one intervention was superior to the other in order to determine a functional relation. For example, a special education teacher wants to increase the percentage of time a student is on-task during independent work time. She works with a faculty member from the local university to test two separate interventions: (a) tootling and (b) teacher-delivered behavior-specific praise. She aims to identify which intervention is superior so she can continue using it for this student. Figure 10-3 provides a sample graph showing that tootling was superior to teacher-delivered behavior-specific praise at increasing on-task behavior for her student.

The key contribution of the ATD is the ease in which researchers or practitioners can compare the effects of two interventions. To compare effects of two or more different interventions using a withdrawal or multiple-baseline design would be cumbersome. It would require additional sessions and multiple participants to overcome issues with order effects. ATDs also have two primary advantages over withdrawal designs: (1) treatment does not have to be withdrawn, and (2) because of the rapid alteration, useful information about which intervention is superior is known more quickly.

ATDs have several critical attributes that should be included to reduce threats to the internal validity of the design. The fast-paced alternation between two test conditions without waiting for steady-state performance raises the risk of the effects of one condition interacting with the other. These potential interactions create two distinguishable threats to internal validity that could influence the effects of the interventions being evaluated. First, a sequence effect refers to the outcomes of an intervention being dependent on the order in which it occurs in the sequence of conditions. For example, if researchers repeat a pattern with two interventions without variation, they will find it difficult to determine if the effects obtained in intervention B were dependent on first being exposed to intervention A. The second possible interaction in the ATD is the carryover effect, which refers to the intervention from the previous condition continuing to influence behavior in the subsequent intervention. Some interventions could be so powerful that the effects are sustained for some time even after the intervention has been withdrawn. For example, a child who experiences timeout for the first time may begin to behave appropriately in the classroom for quite some time even after the teacher stops implementing it. Although it is impossible to completely eliminate the effects of interactions in an ATD, researchers can illuminate whether one exists by presenting the interventions in a semi-randomized process. An interventionist could flip a coin before each session to ensure that certain sequences are never purposefully arranged. However, no more than two consecutive sessions in a row of the same intervention should be conducted because multiple exposures to a single condition would, contrary to the intended purpose, actually increase the likelihood of a carryover effect occurring. In addition, the more a single condition is consecutively repeated, the more the design becomes indistinguishable from a withdrawal design. If the team is concerned with interaction effects (i.e., learned skills are more likely), a second component to consider would be to lengthen the time between sessions, or the intersession interval.

Multiple-Baseline Designs and the Variants

The logic behind establishing a functional relation for a multiple-baseline design and the variants is demonstrating that a change occurs when, and only when, the intervention is directed at the behavior, setting, or subject in question (Barlow et al., 2009). In other words, the data collected for the dependent variables across cases in the multiple-baseline design should remain stable until the intervention is targeted to that case. At the initiation of intervention, the researchers should expect to see an abrupt improvement in the dependent variable for that case while all other cases in baseline remain steady. Demonstrating this abrupt improvement across three time-lagged cases allows the researchers to demonstrate experimental control at three different points in time and determine a functional relation (Figure 10-4).

Baer and colleagues (1968) were the first to mention the multiple-baseline design technique as a possible replacement for using a withdrawal design. Although withdrawal designs were powerful in reducing threats to internal validity, there were issues raised by the research community that specified the need to establish another design to address additional research questions across various contexts. First, not all behaviors are reversible. When implementing a withdrawal design, a behavior must reverse back to initial baseline levels to adhere to baseline logic establish a functional relation. There are plenty of behaviors that are irreversible because they are considered learned skills (e.g., manding [requesting], decoding, completing mathematical tasks) and will not reverse to baseline levels when the intervention is removed. Second, for certain behaviors it would be unethical to withdraw the intervention and allow the behavior to regress (e.g., aggressive or self-injurious behaviors). Third, some interventions may have carryover effects (e.g., use of pharmacological interventions). Last, the research team may meet resistance from key stakeholders (e.g., teachers, paraeducators, parents, participants) when attempting to withdraw an intervention that is effective. These factors all inhibited teams from using a withdrawal design to establish a functional relation and led to the creation of the multiple-baseline design.

A multiple-baseline design has many distinct features that distinguish it from a withdrawal design. First, a multiple-baseline design consists of a minimum of three cases (i.e., behaviors, participants, settings), whereas a withdrawal design only requires one case. The cases can be comprised of separate participants sharing similar needs, selection of independent yet functionally similar behaviors, or selection of independent settings. Second, a multiple-baseline design demonstrates experimental control by temporally sequencing when the intervention is applied to subsequent cases. For example, a sample schedule could include:

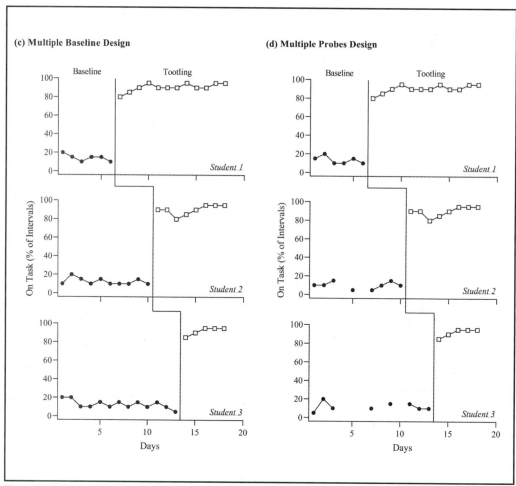

Figure 10-4. Graphs displaying the multiple baseline and multiple probe designs.

- Case 1: Collecting baseline data for 5 sessions and starting intervention on session 6
- Case 2: Collecting baseline data for 8 sessions and starting intervention on session 9
- Case 3: Collecting baseline data for 11 sessions and starting intervention on session 12

The temporal sequencing allows the research team to demonstrate a change in behavior for an individual participant, setting, or behavior is only observed when the intervention is targeted to that individual case. The decision of when to enter a subsequent case into intervention is critical and can make or break experimental control. When the first case enters intervention, the subsequent case's baseline should remain consistent with previous data. The subsequent case should not enter intervention until data suggest the first case has responded or reached a specified criterion. See Figure 10-4 for a sample graph depicting data for effects of a tootling intervention on percent of intervals on task that used a multiple-baseline design across participants.

A slight variation to the multiple-baseline design across participants, settings, or behaviors is the use of the probe technique (Horner & Baer, 1978). In the probe technique, the research team does not collect data every session, but at specific time points to identify if the data pattern remains stable. There are several reasons the probe technique may be used, and in some cases may increase internal validity (Christ, 2007). First, a probe technique requires less data collection, which increases the utility of the design for researchers with limited resources. Second, a probe technique requires less data collection for interventionists, which could save time and energy if using a teacher or paraeducator. Third, instrumentation (i.e., error in the data collection procedures) and testing (i.e., testing impacts student performance) are two threats to internal validity. Thus, using a probe design would require fewer probe sessions to decrease these threats. Last, ethical reasons may be considered. If the testing environment is punishing to the student (e.g., presenting academic tasks the student cannot perform), the student may exhibit problematic behavior to escape the task.

A question that often arises is, "How often should I probe student performance?" The WWC (2020) provided guidelines specific to multiple-probe designs. Table 10-4 includes a description of each indicator and the rationale for how it strengthens the internal validity of the design.

Combination Designs

Behavior is a fluid phenomenon, which is why it is necessary to evaluate changes across repeated measures and rely on the flexibility of SCRDs to adapt to changes. It is the duty of researchers to modify their design procedures to maintain the flow of baseline logic. Demonstrating that the effects can be replicated in a variety of ways only improves confidence that you have reduced threats to internal validity. Furthermore, the limitations of one design can be mitigated by using elements of another design. It is not always a quality one identifies in a researcher, but creativity is required when attempting to combine research designs.

One combination is the inclusion of both withdrawal and ATD elements. Conducting more than one treatment in a traditional withdrawal design is highly inefficient. To replicate the effects of each treatment requires a return to baseline and the patience to wait for steady-state responding before implementing each treatment multiple times. With only two interventions, a researcher would have had to include an additional two phases (i.e., another baseline and intervention comparison) to obtain the same demonstration of control if the design elements were not combined. The number of extra phases continues to multiply in a withdrawal design as more interventions are included in the comparison. Therefore, the combined withdrawal and ATD elements create a more streamlined experimental design. The combination of the withdrawal and ATD also reduces threats of interactions between test conditions likely to be of possible influence in the ATD. The designation of conditions could look something like this: A(B+C)ABAC. The letters in the parentheses refer to the rapid alternation of intervention B and intervention C. The researcher then returns to baseline before replicating each treatment in isolation. If the same effects are observed, we can point to the interventions as the most likely contributor of those outcomes. If different effects are observed during the reversal, we can pinpoint some influence of interaction effects during the ATD.

Jessel and Borrero (2014) provide an example of the withdrawal and ATD combined experimental design when comparing procedures for reducing disruptive classroom behaviors. A common technique is to provide reinforcers after an interval of time in which the disruptive behavior does not occur or occurs at an acceptable frequency. Historically labeled a full-session DRL, the classroom preparation may look like a set of stars on a board that are removed with each occurrence of the target response. If at least one star remains on the board by the end of the class period, the student earns access to preferred items. Although the full-session DRL is suitable for reducing classroom behavior that can be tolerated at low levels but preferred when completely eliminated (e.g., talking out), it has the potential to eliminate appropriate behavior that is only disruptive at high levels (e.g., requesting help or teacher's attention). Jessel and Borrero originally compared two variations of the DRL procedures in a traditional ATD with a baseline. The researchers then extended the design to include separate withdrawals of the procedures to ensure the effects of the two different DRL procedures were replicable alone. This design combination of ATD and withdrawal elements helped the authors categorize the use of different DRL procedures for reducing unwanted classroom behavior in comparison to wanted, while tempered, behavior.

Another example of combining design elements includes the withdrawal and multiple-baseline design. The multiple-baseline design has the added benefit of not requiring the removal of an effective intervention; however, the effects are systematically manipulated across some variation of

TABLE 10-4. WHEN TO PROBE FOR A MULTIPLE-PROBE DESIGN

TIME POINT	RATIONALE	WWC GUIDELINES
Initiation of baseline data collection	Estimate natural frequency of behavior across all cases. This will be used predictively to rule out other plausible variables as the causal agent when attributing change to the IV for each case. If data are not collecting concurrently across all cases, the environmental factors may be different and maturation could be a threat. 3 data points allow the researcher to estimate trend in performance, 1 datum does not.	*Meets* Collect 3 overlapping data points across all cases at the initiation of baseline (i.e., Sessions 1–3). *Meets With Reservations* Collect 1 overlapping data point across all cases at the initiation of baseline (i.e., Session 1).
Baseline data collection prior to implementing intervention for an individual case	Demonstrate similar mean level to the initial baseline data that were collected. 3 data points allow the researcher to estimate trend in performance prior to implementing intervention, 1 datum does not.	*Meets* Collect 3 consecutive data points immediately before introducing the independent variable. *Meets With Reservations* Collect 1 datum immediately before introducing the independent variable.
Baseline data collection for all cases not in intervention when the intervention is implemented for a previous case	Demonstrate similar mean level to all previous baseline data that were collected. The cases in baseline serve as a control for the case in intervention and demonstrate that improvement in the case receiving intervention is due to the independent variable and no other plausible variables.	*Meets* All cases not in intervention must have 1 datum collected when the previous case first received intervention, or meets a prespecified criterion. The datum must be consistent with previous baseline.

Note. The other unique WWC criteria applicable to multiple-baseline and multiple-probe designs is (1) meets standards: minimum of 6 phases (which equates to a minimum of 3 cases) with 5 data per phase, meets with reservations: minimum of 6 phases (which equates to a minimum of 3 cases) with 3 to 4 data points per phase.

different variables (people, places, or things). This does reduce some level of confidence in that there is always one other variable that is changing with the introduction of the intervention. Of course, a simple way to ease doubt would be to conduct additional baselines to replicate the outcomes, but the more baselines are conducted, the less efficient the design becomes. To circumvent this need, the researcher could combine a withdrawal in one baseline and continue the staggered, single introduction of the intervention in the remaining baselines. The combination of the withdrawal and multiple-baseline design is especially adept at identifying whether the effects of the intervention are irreversible. That is, if the researcher conducts a single ABA design and observes continued performance during the return to baseline, there are multiple threats to internal validity that could have contributed to that outcome. However, if the ABA design is repeatedly conducted in a staggered fashion across multiple baselines and the same effects are obtained (i.e., intervention improves performance and this performance maintains after the intervention is withdrawn), then the researcher is able to pinpoint that the intervention is likely to be causing the change. Only that the change is enduring and cannot be readily eliminated.

Jessel et al. (2016) used the combined withdrawal and multiple-baseline design elements to evaluate the difficulty children with ASD were having transitioning to less preferred areas. Caregivers and teachers will often report having difficulties during transitions, especially with students who have more intensive support needs. Difficulties during a transition can range from general noncompliance to extended tantrums or aggressive behavior. Therefore, caregivers may understandably prefer not to withdraw any interventions that appear to be effective. Jessel et al. maintained the systematic replication of the intervention improving transitions across three participants while directly replicating the effects with one participant, thereby limiting exposure to the removal of the intervention.

CASE STUDY

Paulina is a graduate student in a special education doctoral program who has completed the required research methodology courses. She is planning her preliminary research project as part of her program's residency requirements. Paulina has built a partnership with a local elementary school and one of the special education teachers wants her support in identifying an effective intervention to address elopement for two of her elementary students identified with Autism. The teacher conducted a functional behavioral assessment and identified that both students exhibit elopement to escape academic demands. Paulina has a background in behavioral analytic interventions and suggests testing the effects of a break card intervention. The teacher will wear a green bracelet to let the students know it is appropriate to ask for a break and a red bracelet to let the students know it is not an appropriate time to ask for a break.

Paulina opts to use a withdrawal design to evaluate the effects of the intervention because (a) the behavior of elopement is reversible and (b) there are only two students that are exhibiting elopement to escape the task, which limits her ability to use a multiple-baseline design across participants. Paulina plans to conduct some observations in the classroom to create an operational definition for the behavior and identify the most appropriate measurement procedure for the dependent variable.

Other Considerations to Increase Internal Validity

A critical decision made as part of the SCRD process is when to implement, or withdraw, intervention from a case. Researchers use one of three methods: (a) a response-guided approach, (b) a fixed-criteria approach, or (c) a randomization approach. The most prevalent approach selected is a response-guided approach (Kratochwill et al., 2013). In a *response-guided approach*, the researcher collects, graphs, and evaluates data in real time to make decisions regarding the continuation of data collection in a phase, changing to a new phase, or even adjusting the intervention altogether. Hence, the student's response guides the researcher's decision making. In a *fixed-criteria approach* (Kratochwill & Levin, 2014), the researcher sets *a priori* the number of sessions for each phase for each case (e.g., five baseline probes for A1, five intervention probes for B1, five baseline probes for A2, five intervention probes for B2). The schedule is fixed, and student responsiveness does not dictate the researcher's decisions about entering or withdrawing intervention. The last approach used is randomization. The researcher uses *randomization* methods to set the schedule of when intervention is implemented or withdrawn for the participant (Kratochwill & Levin, 2014).

The response-guided approach has been the predominant method used by the field for many reasons. First, the researcher can collect data during baseline that aligns with baseline logic. If a student displays variable data or data with a trend moving in a therapeutic direction, the ability to make a decision regarding a functional relation has serious threats. Second, responding to the data allows the research team to isolate as many variables as possible to pin down what causes variation in the participant's behavior (Sidman, 1960). Last, SCRD was invented as an applied methodology. Thus, researchers have the flexibility to rapidly change the research design to pinpoint what works for the individual student. However, response-guided methods are not flawless. Allison and colleagues (1992) estimated that when visual analysis is combined with a response-guided decision-making process, Type I error rate (i.e., claiming a functional relation was present when it was not present) was as high as 25%. This means there is a 25% chance of determining a functional relation was present, when in fact there was not one. Ferron and colleagues (2003) provided further evidence that Type I error rates increased under response-guided conditions.

The fixed-criteria approach has potential benefits. First, for stakeholders (e.g., teachers, students), it is easier to know the intervention schedule *a priori* rather than having to respond to the research team on a session by session basis. Second, some have suggested a fixed-criteria approach could reduce Type I error rates observed from a response-guided approach (Kratochwill & Levin, 2010). However, concerns are prevalent. If baseline data are unstable or moving in a therapeutic direction, decisions about a functional relation are problematic, and the researcher is unable to respond because they set the schedule *a priori* rather than using a response-guided approach. In addition, if the intervention is not effective for the student, the researcher is left without the ability to rapidly change the design to identify what is effective.

The last approach available to the team is the use of randomization procedures for setting the schedule of the design. This increases internal validity and reduces Type I error rate compared to response-guided method or fixed-criteria approaches (Ferron et al., 2003). Major concerns with randomization designs are the inability to flexibly alter the intervention based on the behavior of participants, as well as the inability to respond to concerning baseline patterns.

Graphical Display

A critical feature of SCRDs is the display of data via time-series graphs (Cooper et al., 2020). The presentation of data via a time-series graph is transparent (i.e., all data are present) but can be misrepresented (Figure 10-5). Visual analysis has received criticism from the field for having low reliability across analysts when determining if a functional relation was present and the magnitude of the intervention's effect (Byun et al., 2017). Early studies have demonstrated low IOA across visual analysts (0.61, De Prospero & Cohen, 1979; 0.55–0.66, Gibson & Ottenbacher, 1988; 0.58, Ottenbacher, 1993). In a more recent review, Ninci and colleagues evaluated IOA of determining a functional relation across visual analysts in 19 published studies (years 1984–2010) and reported the overall mean IOA to be 0.76. The low IOA highlights two critical needs: (1) improving training in structured visual analysis, and (2) the presentation of data in graphs that are transparent and minimize distortion of data.

Prior research has identified two graphical elements with empirical data suggesting they may be analysis-altering, meaning when manipulated they affect a visual analyst's decisions regarding a functional relation and magnitude of treatment effect (Dart & Radley, 2018). The first element with preliminary evidence is the procedure used to scale the ordinate, or y-axis. The current recommendation is to scale the ordinate axis using the full range of possible scores (Dart & Radley, 2017). If you are using a percentage-based scale, the possible range is 0% to 100%, so the ordinate should be scaled from 0% to 100%. If you are using a count-based procedure with an upper bound maximum (e.g., rubric score, number of parts included, number of problems solved correctly), then the full range of

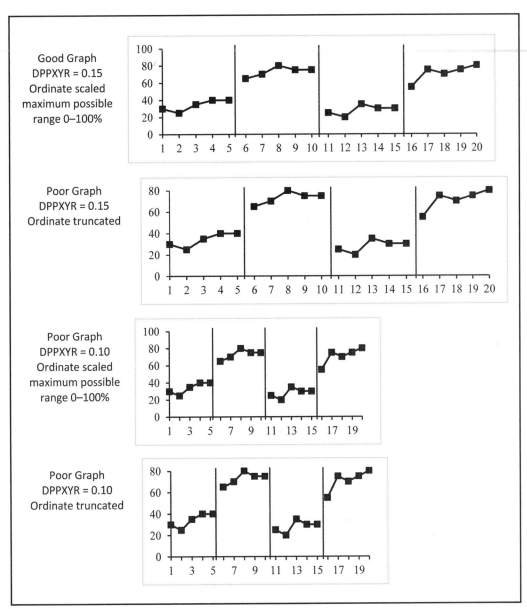

Figure 10-5. Graph construction and the distortion of data.

possible scores should be graphed. When researchers truncated graphs (i.e., 100% is maximum but set to 80%) or increased minimum ordinate value (i.e., minimum 0% but set to 20%), Type I error rates increased. This means analysts were more likely to state a functional relation was present and the magnitude of the effect was larger when evaluating the same data set plotted on the truncated graph compared to the accurate graph. A second preliminary analysis-altering element is the ratio of the x:y axis lengths. Parsonson and Baer (1978) recommended constructing a graph with a y:x ratio between 5:8 and 2:3, which Cooper et al. (2020) still recommend. The authors suggested this ratio would properly display variability in the data. However, no empirical data has been provided to suggest these ratios are appropriate. Radley and colleagues (2018) argued the potential data points to be plotted on the x-axis need to be considered rather than just the x:y axis ratio. They developed the data points per x- to y-axis ratio (DPPXYR) using the formula (length of x/length of y)/possible number of data points to be plotted on x-axis. The team found a DPPXYR between 0.14–0.16 led to the most accurate decision from visual analysts regarding a functional relation and magnitude of treatment effect. DPPXYR below 0.14 led to inflated Type I error (i.e., stating an effect was present when it was not) and DPPXYR above 0.16 inflated Type II error (i.e., stating an effect was not present when it was). See Figure 10-4 for an example of how data can be distorted by manipulating the ordinate scaling and DPPXYR.

Our recommendations are as follows:

- For dependent variables with an upper bound limit, the y-axis should be scaled to represent all possible values. For dependent variables without an upper bound limit, the y-axis should be scaled one tick mark above the maximum observed value.

- When providing labels for the values on the y- and x-axis, ensure it is legible. If you need to label every other tick mark for clarity's sake, that is recommended.

- When placing tick marks on the y- and x-axis, have them face away from the graph (cf. cross or inside).

- Construct graphs with a DPPXYR between 0.14 and 0.16.

VISUAL ANALYSIS

A hallmark of SCRDs is the presentation of data on a time-series graph to make decisions about a functional relation and magnitude treatment effect. Data are evaluated by visual analysts to make these decisions. There are two primary methods for this process: structured visual analysis and masked visual analysis. Following is a step-by-step guide for both approaches.

Structured Visual Analysis

In SCRD, a functional relation between the independent variable and dependent variable is often determined through visual analysis, and this is arguably the most widely used method (Smith, 2012). Visual analysis is a unique difference between group design research and SCRD, in that group design research primarily makes comparisons between treatment and control conditions using parametric and nonparametric statistical procedures. Alternatively, SCRD results in baseline and treatment comparisons for one or more individuals and these comparisons are most often made through visual analysis. Thus, conclusions about the effects of various independent variables on dependent variables are made by visually examining the graphed data. The conditions included in the graph are often analyzed using mean level, trend, and variability when drawing conclusions about the functional relation. Despite the prevalence of visual analysis in SCRD, a drawback to this method is that visual inspection may introduce bias due to its subjective nature and is sometimes associated with poor accuracy and inconsistent IOA (Ninci et al., 2015). Methods have been developed that are intended to be coupled with visual analysis to address this potential bias.

Fisher et al. (2003) developed the dual criteria (DC) and conservative dual-criteria (CDC) methods to assist with visual inspection of SCRD. For the DC method, the mean and trend lines are calculated and determined for baseline conditions and these lines are extended over subsequent data paths or phases. The number of points in the successive data path that fall above or below both lines are counted and compared to an identified value based on a binomial distribution. The CDC method is similar to the DC method; however, the mean and trend lines are increased or decreased by 0.25 standard deviations (Fisher et al., 2003). Research suggests that both the DC and CDC methods are effective tools to supplement visual analysis data and address the drawbacks of visual analysis (Wolfe et al., 2018).

Masked Visual Analysis

A critical decision point in SCRD is when to transition a participant from baseline to intervention (or withdrawal from an intervention), with a response-guided approach being the most prevalent. Despite concerns with Type I error rates being inflated when using a response-guided approach, the primary rationale for keeping this approach is the researcher maintains control in minimizing problematic data patterns within phases that may impact decisions regarding a functional relation (e.g., variable baseline, baseline trending in a therapeutic direction). One suggestion to reduce Type I error rates and maintain the response-guided flexibility is the use of masked visual analysis (Ferron & Foster-Johnson, 1998). Through Monte Carlo evaluation, Ferron and colleagues (2017) demonstrated that masked visual analysis produced decisions regarding a functional relation with an acceptable Type I error rate (i.e., less than 5%) and adequate power (i.e., detecting an effect when it was truly present, above 80%). Masked visual analysis has also been used in the literature across a variety of disciplines: teachers' self-monitoring behavior-specific praise (Sallese & Vannest, 2020), training reading instruction to implement trial-based functional analysis to identify effective intervention to reduce stereotypy in a 13-year old male with autism (Lloyd et al., 2015), improving elementary teachers' well-being through a strength-based intervention (Mccullough, 2015), Effect of Good Behavior Game on decreasing disruptive behavior, increasing academic engagement, and increasing students' writing output (Fallon et al., 2019).

We will provide a brief overview of masked visual analysis. First, the researcher must set parameters for the study (e.g., number of participants, intervention intensity [frequency, dosage], setting characteristics, intervention alteration). Next, specific information related to the masked visual analysis portion of the design must be agreed upon. Examples include: minimum number of sessions per phase, criteria for determining specific characteristics of the data pattern (i.e., trend, outliers, variability), and contingency plans for how to handle problematic data patterns (i.e., variable baseline, baseline trending in a therapeutic direction, missing data). Once study parameters are set, the research team is split into two—the intervention team and the analysis team. The intervention team is responsible for all duties associated with implementing the study (i.e., training interventionists, data collection, IOA, fidelity of implementation, social validity). The analysis team is responsible for the response-guided portion of the study; they tell the interventionist team when they are comfortable with data patterns and to implement intervention:

1. The intervention team will collect the predetermined number of baseline data points and share with the analysis team.
2. The analysis team will determine if data are sufficient for entering a case into intervention. If yes, they notify intervention team and proceed to step 3. If no, they request more baseline data from the intervention team. This process is repeated until analysis team is ready to proceed to step 3.
3. The intervention team randomly selects one case of the multiple-baseline design to enter into intervention, collects the prespecified number of data points across cases, and shares data with analysis team.
4. The analysis team will determine if data are sufficient for entering another case into intervention. If yes, they notify intervention team and proceed to step 5. If no, they request more data from the intervention team. This process is repeated until analysis team is ready to proceed to step 5.
5. Steps 3 to 4 are repeated until all data collection for the experiment is completed.
6. The analysis team "guesses" the order in which participants were entered into intervention (e.g., Participant 3 was entered first, Participant 4 was entered second, Participant 1 was entered third, Participant 2 was entered fourth).
7. A null hypothesis test is conducted (null hypothesis = no effect). The probability of guessing the correct order is divided by the total number of possible orders in which participants could

be transitioned from baseline to treatment. This probability can be represented as a p value. To calculate the total number of permutations, you need to consider the number of cases: for current example, we had 4 cases = 4! or 24. Thus, if the analysis team guesses the correct order of treatment transitions in a multiple-baseline design across participants with four students on the first try, this probability is 1/24 or 0.04 (Type I error of 4%), which is less than a typical alpha of 0.05 (5%). If the analysis team guesses the correct intervention order not on second try, the p value is 2/24 = .083 (Type I error = 8.3%), which is above the alpha level typically set (0.05, 5%). This would lead to the team to reject the null and determine no functional relation.

There are several critical factors to consider if using a masked visual analysis framework. First, to increase power, the research team must include more than three cases. A research team that conducts a multiple-baseline design across three participants can determine a functional relation using a response-guided approach or fixed-criterion approach. However, this is not possible through a null hypothesis test using masked visual analysis. Second, the intervention team must use a randomization process to determine which participants enter intervention. Last, the sharing of data between the intervention and analysis team must be protected because any contamination would ruin the experiment.

Quantitative Approaches as It Relates to Single Case Research Designs

Updates to the WWC (2020) removed visual analysis from the process used to determine intervention effects for SCRDs and replaced it with solely calculating design-comparable effect sizes (D-CES; Pustejovsky et al., 2014; Shadish et al., 2014). Researchers who use SCRDs raised several concerns regarding the role of visual analysis and effect sizes in determining effectiveness of interventions (see Maggin et al., 2020).

- Visual analysis should be the primary method used to determine functional relation. Visual analysis and the estimated effect size do not always agree. A visual analyst may determine no functional relation is present, whereas the effect size would be statistically significantly different from 0. Furthermore, visual analysis is used to examine potential irregularities in data patterns to rule out confounding variables.
- Weaker designs will produce larger effects. Withdrawal designs will produce smaller effect size estimates than multiple-baseline designs across participants, although withdrawal designs are widely regarded as a more rigorous design.
- Ignoring SCRDs. The D-CES can only be calculated for withdrawal designs replicated across at least three participants and multiple-baseline or multiple-probe designs across a minimum of three participants. Thus, a variety of SCRDs (e.g., alternating treatment design, multiple-baseline or multiple-probe design across settings or behaviors, changing criterion) would be excluded from evidence reviews.

Thus, before expanding upon the various statistical options available to researchers, we want to remind readers that visual analysis is inherently important in determining functional relations and the magnitude of intervention effects. Researchers should consider effect size estimates as a way to help corroborate visual analysis (Vannest et al., 2018).

There is no shortage of commentary from the field surrounding the application of effect size metrics to data collected via an SCRD. The first question one may ask is, "What purpose does an effect size serve and why would a researcher in SCRD want to use one?" Hedges (2008) describes an effect size as a way to quantify an estimate of the magnitude of an intervention's effect and then to compare this finding to other related literature. This process also enables the field to conduct meta-analyses of SCRDs to identify quantitatively, for whom, by whom, and under what conditions does the practice work (see Chapter 6).

The field predominantly reports an effect size from one of the following families: (a) nonoverlap indices, (b) within-case parametric indices, and (c) between-case indices. Nonoverlap indices quantify the amount of intervention data improved from baseline. The challenge is each nonoverlap effect size uses a different procedure to compare baseline data to intervention data and quantifying how much "nonoverlap" is observed (see Table 10-5 for description and interpretation guidance). Parker and colleagues (2011a) reviewed 9 nonoverlap indices and applied 7 to a sample of 200 published time series data sets. The authors concluded Nonoverlap of All Pairs (NAP; Parker & Vannest, 2009) and Tau-U (Parker et al., 2011b) had the greatest statistical power, and Tau-U had the greatest sensitivity in distinguishing effects. Another promising feature of Tau-U is that it can account for monotonic trend (i.e., linear, curvilinear) observed during baseline.

Another approach used to quantify effects is within-case indices. These approaches all quantify the change in behavior from baseline to intervention for that individual case. The standardized mean difference using pooled standard deviation (Gingerich, 1984; Kratochwill et al., 1992) and standardized mean difference using standard deviation of baseline are both similar to Cohen's d or Hedges' g, with baseline serving as "control" and intervention serving as "treatment." Another approach used by Maggin and colleagues (2011) was a generalized least squares regression approach. Last, the Log Odds Ratio (Pustejovsky, 2015) and the Log Response Ratio (increasing/decreasing; Pustejovsky, 2018) have both been applied to SCRDs.

The most recent advances are the between-case indices, or as the WWC defined them, D-CESs. These approaches allow researchers to capture within-case and between-case variations in responses on the dependent variable. These provide a metric that is conceptually comparable to group design metrics (i.e., Cohen's d). Plus, these metrics account for the magnitude of change in the dependent variable along the y-axis. The between-case standardized mean difference (see Hedges et al., 2012; Pustejovsky et al., 2014) uses multilevel modeling procedures and can be applied to withdrawal designs (with a minimum of three replications) and multiple-baseline designs across a minimum of three participants.

There are limitations that exist with all of the metrics listed. First, within the family of nonoverlap indices, there is great variability in how these metrics "measure" nonoverlap, with some indices receiving criticism for approaches used (see Maggin et al., 2017). A major concern for the entire family of nonoverlap indices is the magnitude of the effect is not captured, rather just the amount of overlap (e.g., Wolery et al., 2010). Furthermore, in a structured visual analysis framework, overlap is only one characteristic of this process, yet these metrics rely solely on this for quantifying the magnitude of the effect. Nonoverlap indices are affected by design type employed (Chen et al., 2016), the number of data points per condition (Tarlow, 2017), and the observation system employed (Pustejovsky et al., 2019). Second, a major concern for the class of within-case indices is results are not interpretable across cases or studies, which is a key criterion and rationale provided by Hedges (2008) for defining an effect size. Third, a concern for both within-case and D-CES is the fact that SCRD data violate many of the assumptions required for the parametric procedures employed. Autocorrelation is one of the major issues researchers using SCRDs face when attempting to use quantitative approaches for their data because it violates assumptions for the use of parametric procedures. Shadish and Sullivan (2011) provided evidence that it is prevalent in published studies. Using 800 data series from published SCRDs, they estimated the autocorrelation to be 0.20 and if this is ignored it will increase the Type I or Type II error rate, depending on the directionality of the autocorrelation. If researchers could obtain an accurate estimation of the autocorrelation for their data series, they could use different quantitative approaches; however, small data series often lead to inaccurate estimations of autocorrelation.

Given the limitations provided, several implications are relevant. First, researchers must select effect size indices knowing the strengths and limitations of the metric. Furthermore, to increase transparency and ability for replication, the researchers should provide: (a) a description of the effect size selected identifying pros and cons, (b) a clear and concise description for interpreting the effect size (cf. percentage of intervention improved from baseline), (c) a procedural checklist for how the effect sizes were computed (i.e., which data were used, what software was used for calculation, providing syntax if applicable), and (d) a data file providing the raw data, if approved through the

TABLE 10-5. DESCRIPTION OF COMMON EFFECT SIZE PROCEDURES FOR SINGLE CASE RESEARCH DESIGNS

EFFECT SIZE	DESCRIPTION	BENEFITS	DRAWBACKS
Non-Overlap			
Percentage of Non-overlapping Data (PND)	Determined by locating the highest data point in phase A and the number of data points that exceed it in phase B	• Easy to calculate	• Outliers and the number of baseline data points may result in an inaccurate effect size due to unstable data • Ignores baseline trend • Potential for ceiling effects • No known sampling distribution and cannot precisely weight effect sizes • Not comparable to group effect sizes; thus, limiting the audience
Percent Exceeding Median (PEM)	Determined by finding the median of phase A, and then the percent of B phase data points that exceed the phase A median	• Outliers and the number of baseline observations can result in accurate effect sizes with unstable data	• Ignores baseline trend • Is not sensitive to the size of the effect • No known sampling distribution and cannot precisely weight effect sizes • Not comparable to group effect sizes; thus, limiting the audience
Extended Celeration Line (ECL)	Determined by finding the celeration line of phase A, extending it, and then finding the percent of B phase data points that exceed it	• Outliers and the number of baseline observations can result in accurate effect sizes with unstable data • Accounts for baseline trends assuming trend is linear	• Is not sensitive to the size of the effect • No known sampling distribution and cannot precisely weight effect sizes • Not comparable to group effect sizes; thus, limiting the audience

(continued)

TABLE 10-5. DESCRIPTION OF COMMON EFFECT SIZE PROCEDURES FOR SINGLE CASE RESEARCH DESIGNS (CONTINUED)

EFFECT SIZE	DESCRIPTION	BENEFITS	DRAWBACKS
Non-Overlap of All Pairs	Determined by pairing each phase A data point with each phase B data point to make n pairs	• Outliers and the number of baseline observations can result in accurate effect sizes with unstable data • Known sampling distribution and can precisely weight effect sizes assuming independence	• Ignores baseline trend • Is not sensitive to the size of the effect • Not comparable to group effect sizes; thus, limiting the audience
TauU	Determined by pairing each phase A data point with each phase B data point to make n pairs and scaled from –1 to 1 and can correct for trends	• Outliers and the number of baseline observations can result in accurate effect sizes with unstable data • Known sampling distribution and can precisely weight effect sizes assuming independence	• Ignores baseline trend • Is not sensitive to the size of the effect • Not comparable to group effect sizes; thus, limiting the audience
TauU$_{adj}$	TauU$_{adj}$ (adjusted) for baseline trend. Each baseline observation can be paired with all later baseline observations. Baseline trend is determined.	• Accounts for baseline trend • Outliers and the number of baseline observations can result in accurate effect sizes with unstable data • Known sampling distribution and can precisely weight effect sizes assuming independence	• Is not sensitive to the size of the effect • Not comparable to group effect sizes; thus, limiting the audience

(continued)

TABLE 10-5. DESCRIPTION OF COMMON EFFECT SIZE PROCEDURES FOR SINGLE CASE RESEARCH DESIGNS (CONTINUED)

EFFECT SIZE	DESCRIPTION	BENEFITS	DRAWBACKS
Within-Case Parametric Measures			
Within-Case Standardized Mean Difference (SMD)	An effect size measure determined by difference in means between phases and difference is standardized	• Effects described for each case • Comparable to group effect sizes; thus, increasing the audience • Sampling distributions can be determined and precisely weighted	• Ignores trends in baseline and treatment phases • SCRD measurement procedures that are unreliable result in a within-case SMD that is not comparable across studies • Range restriction and potential for ceiling effects
Log Response Ratio (LRR)	An effect size measure that quantifies functional relation in terms of the proportionate change	• Effects described for each case • Comparable to group effect sizes; thus, increasing the audience • Can account for trends • Sampling distributions can be determined and precisely weighted • Can include simple and random effects meta-analytic techniques	• General recommendation to not use with interval-based data (partial interval, whole interval, MTS) until additional research is conducted

(continued)

TABLE 10-5. DESCRIPTION OF COMMON EFFECT SIZE PROCEDURES FOR SINGLE CASE RESEARCH DESIGNS (CONTINUED)

EFFECT SIZE	DESCRIPTION	BENEFITS	DRAWBACKS
Between-Case Parametric Measures			
Between-Case Standardized Mean Difference (BC-SMD)	A hierarchical model that is estimated from single case data that describes variation between participants	• Focal follow-up time addresses models with time trends • Describes average effect across cases • Used to complement within-case parametric measures • Allows for model selection and fit • Comparable to group design effect sizes.	• Must have more than three participants • More flexibility in the model requires additional cases • Only suitable for withdrawal and multiple baseline/multiple probe designs • Assumes normal distributed and interval scale outcomes • Additional research on model selection and fit

TABLE 10-6. COMMON MISCONCEPTIONS AND CLARIFICATIONS ABOUT SINGLE CASE DESIGNS

MISCONCEPTION	BETTER UNDERSTANDING
SCRDs are only conducted with a single participant.	SCRDs can be conducted with only one participant without impairing internal validity. However, the same procedures can be conducted with a limitless number of participants, with each replicated outcome improving the generality of the findings.
SCRDs are quasi-experimental designs because they do not include a control group.	In an SCRD, the participant serves as their control, improving internal validity in comparison to group designs where the differences in genetics and experiences of the multiple participants pose threats to understanding functional relations.
SCRDs and case reports are the same thing.	SCRDs require the methodological rigor of a scientific experiment that can help explain functional relations. Case reports are anecdotal narratives that can only describe observed correlations.
SCRDs are time consuming and cumbersome.	Although SCRDs typically require extended time spent collecting repeated measures with a single participant, an entire experiment can be completed with one participant and is a viable option among teachers with limited resources. Group designs require a collection of data across a large number of participants and specialized training to analyze the data.

Institutional Review Board (IRB), to allow for researchers to compute additional effect sizes or use in future meta-analytic work. Another suggestion made is to select and report more than one effect size index to provide a more global description of the magnitude of intervention effects. Our final suggestion is not unique to SCRD, but we feel it is pressing to reiterate. When interpreting the magnitude of an effect, it is more beneficial to engage in direct comparison to related literature rather than an arbitrary benchmark system (e.g., $d = 0.2$ is small effect, $d = 0.5$ is medium effect, $d = 0.8$ is large effect). Table 10-6 includes a list of common misconceptions associated with single case research designs, and Table 10-7 provides additional resources to consult.

SUMMARY

SCRD is a powerful methodology that allows a researcher to interpret experimental control while enacting meaningful change in the behavior of participants in need of particular interventions. SCRDs share the scientific logic of replicating changes in some targeted behavior based on the systematic manipulation of environmental variables. To improve the critical decision-making process of reducing threats to internal validity, standard guidelines have been developed regarding fundamental attributes such as: (a) behavioral measurement, (b) basic design elements, (c) graphical display, and (d) visual analysis techniques. A comprehensive understanding of the fundamental attributes of SCRD and the supplemental guidelines will help the applied researcher in the development of future research questions that will undoubtedly shape our continued understanding of behavior.

TABLE 10-7. ADDITIONAL RESOURCES	
RESOURCE	**DESCRIPTION**
Generating SCRD Graphs: Graphpad Prism Guidance	Guidance on creating SCRD publication quality graphs using Graphpad Prism. Mitteer, D. R., Greer, B. D., Fisher, W. W., & Cohrs, V. L. (2018). Teaching behavior technicians to create publication-quality, single-case design graphs in Graphpad Prism 7. *Journal of Applied Behavior Analysis, 51*(4), 998-1010. https://doi.org/10.1002/jaba.483
Generating SCRD Graphs: Microsoft Excel	Guidance on creating SCRD graphs using Microsoft Excel. Chok, J. T. (2019). Creating functional analysis graphs using Microsoft Excel 2016 for PCs. *Behavior Analysis in Practice, 12*(1), 265-292. https://doi.org/10.1007/s40617-018-0258-4
Collecting SCRD Data: BDataPro	SCRD data collection software. Bullock, C. E., Fisher, W. W., & Hagopian, L. P. (2017). Description and validation of a computerized behavioral data program: "BDataPro." *The Behavior Analyst, 40*(1), 275-285. https://doi.org/10.1007/s40614-016-0079-0
Suggested Reading	Comprehensive overview of SCRD research. Ledford, J. R., & Gast, D. L. (2018). *Single case research methodology: Applications in special education and behavioral sciences*. Routledge.
	Overview of methodological and statistical advances in SCRD. Kratochwill, T. R., & Levin, J. R. (2014). *Single case intervention research: Methodological and statistical advances*. American Psychological Association.
Graph Construction	Gould, K., Gaither, J., Dart, E., & Weaver, A. D. (2018). A practical guide to single case design graphing. *Communique, 47*(1), 22-24.
Masked Visual Analysis	Byun, T. M., Hitchcock, E. R., & Ferron, J. (2017). Masked visual analysis: Minimizing type I error in visually guided single case design for communication disorders. *Journal of Speech, Language, and Hearing Research, 60*(6), 1455-1466.
ABAI IOA Procedures	https://www.abainternational.org/media/31416/examplespreadsheet.pdf

CHAPTER REVIEW

1. Define baseline logic and how it is used in single case research designs to make decisions regarding a functional relation.

2. What is a functional relation? Articulate how a functional relation is determined using a withdrawal design. Articulate how a functional relation is determined using a multiple-baseline design.

3. Given your research agenda, provide an operational definition of a dependent variable you could measure and the type of data measurement procedure that would be most appropriate.

4. What is interobserver agreement? What is implementation fidelity? Why is it critical to measure both to address threats to the internal validity?

5. What are three commonly used ways to make decisions about moving a participant from baseline to intervention? Articulate the pros and cons of each approach.

REFERENCES

Allison, D. B., Franklin, R. D., & Heshka, S. (1992). Reflections on visual inspection, response guided experimentation, and Type I error rate in single-case designs. *The Journal of Experimental Education, 61*(1), 45-51.

Baer, D. M., Wolf, M. M., & Risley, T. R. (1968). Some current dimensions of applied behavior analysis. *Journal of Applied Behavior Analysis, 1*(1), 91-97.

Barlow, D. H., Nock, M. K., & Hersen, M. (2009). *Single case experimental designs: Strategies for studying behavior change.* Pearson.

Barnett, D., Hawkins, R., McCoy, D., Wahl, E., Shier, A., Denune, H., & Kimener, L. (2014). Methods used to document procedural fidelity in school-based intervention research. *Journal of Behavioral Education, 23*(1), 89-107.

Bergin, A. E., & Strupp, H. H. (1970). The directions in psychotherapy research. *Journal of Abnormal Psychology, 76*(1), 13-26.

Bruhn, A., & Watt, S. (2012). Improving behavior by using multicomponent self-monitoring within a targeted reading intervention. *Behavioral Disorders, 38*(1), 3-17.

Byun, T. M., Hitchcock, E. R., & Ferron, J. (2017). Masked visual analysis: Minimizing type I error in visually guided single-case design for communication disorders. *Journal of Speech, Language, and Hearing Research, 60*(6), 1455-1466.

Chen, M., Hyppa-Martin, J. K., Reichle, J. E., & Symons, F. J. (2016). Comparing single case design overlap-based effect size metrics from studies examining speech generating device interventions. *American Journal on Intellectual and Developmental Disabilities, 121*(3), 169-193.

Christ, T. J. (2007). Experimental control and threats to internal validity of concurrent and nonconcurrent multiple baseline designs. *Psychology in the Schools, 44*(5), 451-459.

Cook, B., Buysse, V., Klingner, J., Landrum, T., McWilliam, R., Tankersley, M., & Test, D. (2014). Council for Exceptional Children: Standards for evidence-based practices in special education. *Teaching Exceptional Children, 46*(6), 206.

Cooper, J. O., Heron, T. E., Heward, W. L. (2020). *Applied behavior analysis* (3rd ed.). Pearson.

Cuenca-Carlino, Y., Mustian, A. L., Allen, R. D., & Whitley, S. F. (2019). Writing for my future: Transition-focused self-advocacy of secondary students with emotional/behavioral disorders. *Remedial and Special Education, 40*(2), 83-96.

Dart, E. H., & Radley, K. C. (2017). The impact of ordinate scaling on the visual analysis of single-case data. *Journal of School Psychology, 63*, 105-118.

Dart, E. H., & Radley, K. C. (2018). Toward a standard assembly of linear graphs. *School Psychology Quarterly, 33*(3), 350-355.

DeProspero, A., & Cohen, S. (1979). Inconsistent visual analyses of intrasubject data. *Journal of Applied Behavior Analysis, 12*(4), 573-579.

Fallon, L. M., Marcotte, A. M., & Ferron, J. M. (2019). Measuring academic output during the Good Behavior Game: A single case design study. *Journal of Positive Behavior Interventions*. Advanced online publication. https://doi.org/10.1177/1098300719872778

Ferron, J., & Foster-Johnson, L. (1998). Analyzing single-case data with visually guided randomization tests. *Behavior Research Methods, Instruments, & Computers, 30*(4), 698-706.

Ferron, J., Foster-Johnson, L., & Kromrey, J. D. (2003). The functioning of single-case randomization tests with and without random assignment. *The Journal of Experimental Education, 71*(3), 267-288.

Ferron, J. M., Joo, S. H., & Levin, J. R. (2017). A Monte Carlo evaluation of masked visual analysis in response-guided versus fixed-criteria multiple-baseline designs. *Journal of Applied Behavior Analysis, 50*(4), 701-716.

Fisher, W. W., Kelley, M. E., & Lomas, J. E. (2003). Visual aids and structured criteria for improving visual inspection and interpretation of single-case designs. *Journal of Applied Behavior Analysis, 36*(3), 387-406.

Garwood, J. D., Werts, M. G., Mason, L. H., Harris, B., Austin, M. B., Ciullo, S., Magner, K., Koppenhaver, D. A., & Shin, M. (2019). Improving persuasive science writing for secondary students with emotional and behavioral disorders educated in residential treatment facilities. *Behavioral Disorders, 44*(4), 227-240.

Gibson, G., & Ottenbacher, K. (1988). Characteristics influencing the visual analysis of single-subject data: An empirical analysis. *The Journal of Applied Behavioral Science, 24*(3), 298-314.

Gingerich, W. J. (1984). Generalizing single-case evaluation from classroom to practice setting. *Journal of Education for Social Work, 20*(1), 74-82.

Hagopian, L. P., Paclawskyj, T. R., & Kuhn, S. C. (2005). The use of conditional probability analysis to identify a response chain leading to the occurrence of eye poking. *Research in Developmental Disabilities, 26*(4), 393-397.

Hedges, L. V. (2008). What are effect sizes and why do we need them? *Child Development Perspectives, 2*(3), 167-171.

Hedges, L. V., Pustejovsky, J. E., & Shadish, W. R. (2012). A standardized mean difference effect size for single case designs. *Research Synthesis Methods, 3*(3), 224-239.

Hersen, M., & Barlow, D. H. (1976). Single case experimental designs. Pergamon Press.

Horner, R. D., & Baer, D. M. (1978). Multiple-probe technique: A variation of the multiple baseline. *Journal of Applied Behavior Analysis, 11*(1), 189-196.

Jessel, J., & Borrero, J. C. (2014). A laboratory comparison of two variations of differential-reinforcement-of-low-rate procedures. *Journal of Applied Behavior Analysis, 47*(2), 314-324.

Jessel, J., Hanley, G. P., & Ghaemmaghami, M. (2016). Interview-informed synthesized contingency analyses: Thirty replications and reanalysis. *Journal of Applied Behavior Analysis, 49*(3), 576-595.

Johnston, J. M., & Pennypacker, H. S. (1993). *Readings for strategies and tactics of behavioral research*. Lawrence Erlbaum Associates, Inc.

Kazdin, A. E. (1981). Drawing valid inferences from case studies. *Journal of Consulting and Clinical Psychology, 49*(2), 183-192.

Kazdin, A. (2011). Single-case research designs: Methods for clinical and applied settings (2nd ed.). Oxford University.

Kazdin, A. E. (2012). *Behavior modification in applied settings*. Waveland Press.

Kratochwill, T. R., Hitchcock, J. H., Horner, R. H., Levin, J. R., Odom, S. L., Rindskopf, D. M., & Shadish, W. R. (2013). Single-case intervention research design standards. *Remedial and Special Education, 34*(1), 26-38.

Kratochwill, T. R., & Levin, J. R. (1992). *Single-case research design and analysis: New directions for psychology and education*. Routledge.

Kratochwill, T. R., & Levin, J. R. (Eds.). (2014). Enhancing the scientific credibility of single-case intervention research: Randomization to the rescue. In T. R. Kratochwill & J. R. Levin (Eds.), *School psychology series. Single-case intervention research: Methodological and statistical advances* (p. 53–89). American Psychological Association. https://doi.org/10.1037/14376-003

Ledford, J. R., & Gast, D. L. (2018). *Single case research methodology: Applications in special education and behavioral sciences*. Routledge.

Lerman, D. C., Parten, M., Addison, L. R., Vorndran, C. M., Volkert, V. M., & Kodak, T. (2005). A methodology for assessing the functions of emerging speech in children with developmental disabilities. *Journal of Applied Behavior Analysis, 38*(3), 303-316.

Maggin, D., Johnson, A. H., Barton, E., & Lane, K. L. (2020, March 1). WWC SCD revisions commentary. Retrieved from osf.io/8zcxd

Maggin, D. M., Lane, K. L., & Pustejovsky, J. E. (2017). Introduction to the special issue on single-case systematic reviews and meta-analyses. *Remedial and Special Education, 38*(6), 323-330.

Maggin, D. M., Swaminathan, H., Rogers, H. J., O'keeffe, B. V., Sugai, G., & Horner, R. H. (2011). A generalized least squares regression approach for computing effect sizes in single-case research: Application examples. *Journal of School Psychology, 49*(3), 301-321.

McCullough, M. M. (2015). Improving elementary teachers' well-being through a strengths-based intervention: A multiple baseline single-case design. (Doctoral Dissertation, University of South Florida). http://scholarcommons.usf.edu/etd/5990

Ninci, J., Vannest, K. J., Willson, V., & Zhang, N. (2015). Interrater agreement between visual analysts of single-case data: A meta-analysis. *Behavior Modification, 39*(4), 510-541.

Ottenbacher, K. J. (1993). Interrater agreement of visual analysis in single-subject decisions: Quantitative review and analysis. *American Journal on Mental Retardation, 98*(1), 135-142.

Page, T. J., & Iwata, B. A. (1986). Interobserver agreement. In Poling, A. & Fuqua, R. W. (Eds.). *Research methods in applied behavior analysis. Applied clinical psychology*. Springer.

Parker, R. I., & Vannest, K. (2009). An improved effect size for single-case research: Nonoverlap of all pairs. *Behavior Therapy, 40*(4), 357-367.

Parker, R. I., Vannest, K. J., & Davis, J. L. (2011a). Effect size in single-case research: A review of nine nonoverlap techniques. *Behavior Modification, 35*(4), 303-322.

Parker, R. I., Vannest, K. J., Davis, J. L., & Sauber, S. B. (2011b). Combining nonoverlap and trend for single-case research: Tau-U. *Behavior Therapy, 42*(2), 284-299.

Parsonson, B. S., & Baer, D. M. (1978). Training generalized improvisations of tools by preschool children. *Journal of Applied Behavior Analysis, 11*(3), 363-380.

Peltier, C., & Vannest, K. J. (2018). The effects of schema-based instruction on the mathematical problem solving of students with emotional and behavioral disorders. *Behavioral Disorders, 43*(2), 277-289.

Poling, A. D., Methot, L. L., & LeSage, M. G. (1995). *Fundamentals of behavior analytic research*. Springer Science & Business Media.

Pustejovsky, J. E. (2015). Measurement-comparable effect sizes for single-case studies of free-operant behavior. *Psychological Methods, 20*(3), 342.

Pustejovsky, J. E. (2018). Using response ratios for meta-analyzing single-case designs with behavioral outcomes. *Journal of School Psychology, 68*, 99-112.

Pustejovsky, J. E., Hedges, L. V., & Shadish, W. R. (2014). Design-comparable effect sizes in multiple baseline designs: A general modeling framework. *Journal of Educational and Behavioral Statistics, 39*(5), 368-393.

Pustejovsky, J. E., Swan, D. M., & English, K. W. (2019). An examination of measurement procedures and characteristics of baseline outcome data in single-case research. *Behavior Modification*. Advanced online publication. https://doi.org/10.1177/0145445519864264

Radley, K. C., Dart, E. H., & Wright, S. J. (2018). The effect of data points per x-to y-axis ratio on visual analysts evaluation of single-case graphs. *School Psychology Quarterly, 33*(2), 314-322.

Reed, F. D. D., & Codding, R. S. (2014). Advancements in procedural fidelity assessment and intervention: Introduction to the special issue. *Journal of Behavioral Education, 23*, 1-10.

Sallese, M. R., & Vannest, K. J. (2020). The effects of a multicomponent self-monitoring intervention on the rates of pre-service teacher behavior-specific praise in a masked single-case experimental design. *Journal of Positive Behavior Interventions*. Advanced online publication. https://doi.org/10.1177/1098300720908005

Sanson-Fisher, R. W., Poole, A. D., & Thompson, V. (1979). Behaviour patterns within a general hospital psychiatric unit: an observational study. *Behaviour Research and Therapy, 17*(4), 317-332.

Shadish, W. R., Hedges, L. V., & Pustejovsky, J. E. (2014). Analysis and meta-analysis of single-case designs with a standardized mean difference statistic: A primer and applications. *Journal of School Psychology, 52*(2), 123-147.

Shadish, W. R., & Sullivan, K. J. (2011). Characteristics of single-case designs used to assess intervention effects in 2008. *Behavior Research Methods, 43*(4), 971-980.

Shapiro, M. B., & Ravenette, A. T. (1959). A preliminary experiment on paranoid delusions. *Journal of Mental Science, 105*(439), 295-312.

Sidman, M. (1960). *Tactics of scientific research*. Authors Cooperative, Inc.

Sidman, M., Kirk, B., & Willson-Morris, M. (1985). Six-member stimulus classes generated by conditional-discrimination procedures. *Journal of the Experimental Analysis of Behavior, 43*(1), 21-42.

Skinner, B. F. (1953). Some contributions of an experimental analysis of behavior to psychology as a whole. *American Psychologist, 8*(2), 69.

Skinner, B. F. (1966). The phylogeny and ontogeny of behavior. *Science, 153*(3741), 1205-1213.

Smith, J. D. (2012). Single-case experimental designs: A systematic review of published research and current standards. *Psychological Methods, 17*(4), 510-550.

Tarlow, K. R. (2017). An improved rank correlation effect size statistic for single-case designs: Baseline corrected Tau. *Behavior Modification, 41*(4), 427-467.

Thorne, F. C. (1947). The clinical method in science. *American Psychologist, 2*(5), 159-166.

Vannest, K. J., Peltier, C., & Haas, A. (2018). Results reporting in single case experiments and single case meta-analysis. *Research in Developmental Disabilities, 79*, 10-18.

What Works Clearinghouse (2020). *What Works Clearinghouse procedures handbook* (Version 4.1). Author.

Wolery, M., Busick, M., Reichow, B., & Barton, E. E. (2010). Comparison of overlap methods for quantitatively synthesizing single-subject data. *The Journal of Special Education, 44*(1), 18-28.

Wolf, M. M. (1978). Social validity: The case for subjective measurement or how applied behavior analysis is finding its heart. *Journal of Applied Behavior Analysis, 11*(2), 203-214. https://doi.org/10.1901/jaba.1978.11-203

Wolfe, K., Seaman, M. A., Drasgow, E., & Sherlock, P. (2018). An evaluation of the agreement between the conservative dual-criterion method and expert visual analysis. *Journal of Applied Behavior Analysis, 51*(2), 345-351.

Survey Research

With contributions from Nathan A. Stevenson, PhD and Andrew L. Wiley, PhD

INTRODUCTION

Surveys occupy a unique niche in special education research. Unlike some other means of data collection, surveys are a flexible and often efficient option for research across a variety of populations and contexts. Surveys can be administered to students, teachers, parents, and other stakeholders to gather critical information about their knowledge, perceptions, thoughts, feelings, priorities, understanding, and other information useful to researchers and practitioners alike. Today, digital survey platforms enable researchers to sample relatively small to relatively large populations and gather meaningful data without leaving the lab or office.

However, for all the advantages of surveys as a research tool, great care must be taken to ensure survey data meet rigorous standards for scientific research. From question and hypothesis to analysis and conclusion, researchers have many decisions to make, each of which impact the data collected and how such data are interpreted. This chapter introduces survey research methods as they pertain to scientific study of special education. An overview of the basic information necessary to conduct survey research is provided, including: (a) guidance on the development and selection of survey instruments, (b) sampling procedures to minimize bias, (c) methods of administration, (d) analytic procedures, (e) considerations for surveying persons with disabilities, and (f) other relevant topics. Definitions of key terms and acronyms are included along with additional resources for further study.

We encourage readers interested in survey methods to use this chapter as a beginning for further study. The texts and examples cited provide critical information necessary to help researchers begin meaningful, scientifically rigorous research. We encourage readers to explore the primary literature cited here as well as other reputable resources.

Hott, B. L., Brigham, F. J., & Peltier, C.
Research Methods in Special Education (pp. 199-216).
© 2021 SLACK Incorporated.

CHAPTER OBJECTIVES

→ Explain the purpose(s) of survey research in the context of special education.

→ Identify and/or develop research questions suitable for investigation with survey methods.

→ Describe the considerations and/or accommodations for conducting survey research with persons with disabilities.

→ Evaluate the quality of survey methods in research literature.

KEY TERMS

- **Construct**: An element or phenomenon of interest, made up of a group of observed items or behavior.
- **Instrument**: Refers to the survey itself, specifically as a tool for measuring a phenomenon of interest.
- **Items**: The individual questions contained in a survey.
- **Pilot Testing**: Administering a newly designed survey to a small group in order to gather useful information for improvements to the survey.
- **Psychometric Properties**: Reported statistics on the reliability and validity of data collected from an instrument.
- **Reliability**: The consistency of measurement for a survey or individual item across time or respondents.
- **Respondent**: Any individual who provides information in response to survey items.
- **Validity**: The degree to which a survey or individual item correlates with other items or variables of established importance.

SURVEYS AS A TOOL FOR RESEARCH

It is likely that readers of this text have previously encountered surveys on several occasions. These may include: (a) customer satisfaction survey following a retail purchase, (b) community planning survey from local government, (c) phone solicited political survey, or (d) one of many others. Surveys can be adapted to specific audiences and carefully crafted to target very narrow areas of interest. When compared to some other methods, surveys are also a cost-efficient and flexible means for collecting data directly from target groups, and are therefore appealing to businesses, nonprofit organizations, and researchers alike.

When used for scientific research, surveys may be quite different from those used for other purposes. Scientific survey research is carefully developed to explore specific phenomena and employed strategically to control for potential confounding variables (e.g., responses from people outside the target group or respondents who merely click through questions without reading thoroughly). Survey instruments must be carefully constructed or selected, then revised, to ensure data are of the highest possible quality. Sampling plans must be designed to minimize potential bias or measurement error, align with the questions of interest, and ensure internal and external validity.

CASE STUDY

In preparation for a newly funded grant aimed at reducing high school dropout for students with disabilities, a public education services agency (ESC) is working with local schools to execute the project. Prior to the start date, the ESC is working with districts to collect baseline data on high school students' social, behavioral, and academic engagement in school. After discussing a number of different strategies, they determine the most efficient and meaningful data collection strategy is a direct survey of students. The ESC team briefly considers creating a new survey that fits their needs but are unsure if creating their own survey will be a valid way to gather data. The team begins by first determining the specific questions they seek to answer and then by examining a variety of existing surveys. The team carefully evaluates each instrument to determine how closely the questions align with those of their current project. They also consider the potential costs of licensing and data collection. Meanwhile, a subset of the project team gathers more detailed information on the estimated time and resources necessary to create a custom survey that meets their needs. Before long, the project team becomes overwhelmed with the range of options. To help weigh the pros and cons of each approach, the team turns to an experienced group of researchers at a local university. Like many public research universities, the university has a center to support teams conducting survey research. For a nominal fee, the university center offers some useful advice and provides the project team with resources that help the team make critical decisions. Ultimately, the project team chooses an existing survey administered online. Though the ESC paid a small fee for use of the survey, the license includes basic data analysis and reporting, which ultimately saves a great deal of time and labor on the part of ESC staff. The survey itself provides important data that align to the project goals and provide useful information to school leaders.

Before beginning the often time-consuming and difficult process of selecting or developing a survey for research, one must be certain a survey is indeed the best tool for the job. That is, the researcher must first assess whether survey methods are appropriate for answering the research question(s). Research questions that are appropriate for survey research include those seeking to gather information from and/or about a specific population. In the case study example above, the team wants to know the degree to which students feel engaged in their school experience. They also recognize that engagement can be represented in many different ways (e.g., social, emotional, academic). Because these questions are primarily about how a large sample of students feel or perceive their own experiences, administering a survey is the optimal method. Other approaches could be used (e.g., qualitative interviews, direct observation of behaviors associated with engagement); however, these methods can be quite costly and time consuming. A survey will enable the researchers to collect useful data from a large target sample to address their research questions.

Appropriate questions may center on various types of descriptive information that can be provided by respondents (e.g., information about special education directors' training, or types of classroom management courses included in teacher education programs). Information gathered through surveys can include respondents' knowledge, attitudes, beliefs, and perceptions related to a wide range of phenomena of interest. It is important to collect demographic information on variables pertinent for the population of interest (e.g., years of experience, type of teaching certificate, geographical locale) to allow readers of the manuscript to gauge the external validity of the reported results and conclusions. As we will see, survey methods are flexible and can be used to answer many, but not all, research questions.

For example, questions about the effectiveness of an intervention typically cannot be answered by asking participants if they thought the intervention worked. On the other hand, survey methods can illuminate important contextual variables related to an intervention, such as whether the participants found the intervention to be helpful and easy to use (i.e., social validity). Numerous surveys have been developed and evaluated through scientific peer-review including the Usage Rating

Profile–Intervention (URP-I; Briesch et al., 2013; Chafouleas et al., 2011) and Primary Intervention Rating Scale (PIRS; Lane et al., 2009). In any case, the point cannot be overstated. Surveys are best used when the data necessary to answer a particular research question are closely aligned with the strengths of surveys as a tool for data collection.

Research Questions and Survey Research in Special Education

Throughout this chapter, we refer to several survey studies to illustrate important concepts and considerations related to designing, conducting, and interpreting survey research. Each example has strengths and limitations that illustrate how researchers navigate the many scientific and practical challenges of conducting survey research in special education.

Examples of Survey Research Studies

Survey research can be used to examine a wide range of questions and phenomena in special education. For example, Hess and colleagues (2008) conducted a state-wide survey to examine teachers' reported use of evidence-based practices (EBPs) for students with autism spectrum disorder (ASD) taught in public schools. Specifically, Hess and colleagues sought to answer the following research questions: "What are the demographic characteristics of the educators serving children with ASD in the public school systems throughout the state of Georgia? [According to teachers] what classroom strategies are being used by Georgia public school teachers for students with ASD enrolled in their classes? Do strategies being used for students with ASD differ by classroom type and grade level? Are the strategies being used considered best practices for students with ASD?" (p. 962).

In another study, Gagnon and colleagues (2018) investigated the implementation of Positive Behavior Interventions and Supports in secure care juvenile justice (JJ) schools by surveying principals of these schools across the United States. Research questions were "How do JJ facilities' current approaches to student behavior align with a multitiered system of support for behavior? What are JJ facilities' activities related to organizational leadership and training for providing behavior supports? What are JJ facilities' approaches to behavioral expectations and consequences? What is the nature of JJ facilities' behavioral responses, monitoring, and oversight? What are JJ facilities' current crisis management policies and procedures?" (p. 5).

Finally, Siperstein and colleagues (2007) surveyed a nationally representative sample of middle school students to understand their attitudes toward the inclusion of students with intellectual disabilities (ID). Their research questions were: How do middle school students without disabilities "picture" peers with IDs' skills and capabilities? What are middle school students' intentions to interact with peers with ID? How do middle school students think inclusion will affect them personally? Do middle school students think their peers with ID can participate in academic and nonacademic classrooms?

SURVEY SELECTION VERSUS SURVEY CREATION

Once the research questions have been defined and deemed appropriate for survey research, researchers must decide whether to select or adapt an existing survey or to develop a new one (Figure 11-1). All efforts to answer research questions using survey methods rest on the careful and purposeful selection or development of the survey instrument. Of the examples we refer to in this chapter, two adapted existing surveys (Siperstein et al., 2007; Stevenson et al., 2019).

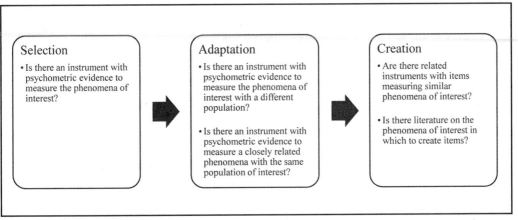

Figure 11-1. Survey selection, adaptation, or creation decision-making process.

Using Existing Survey Instruments

When researchers explore questions with a long history in the field and a robust body of literature firmly established, there may be surveys available that fit the needs of a new project. Naturally, the use of a previously developed and perhaps widely used survey instrument saves a great deal of time and effort that would otherwise be spent developing and piloting a new survey. When used for research purposes, many established surveys are available at little or no cost to researchers. At the time of the ESC study, HSSSE was available free for use in schools. Even when researchers do have to pay licensing fees, the cost may be nominal compared to the costs of developing a new survey.

The use of existing surveys also may be beneficial in helping researchers remain consistent with prior research. By collecting data with the same tool as used in previous studies, researchers can more easily interpret or situate the results of their current study within a larger empirical context. In some cases, researchers also may wish to conduct replication studies, in which case using the same survey and sampling plan is essential. Replication studies are those in which researchers attempt to reproduce the results of previously published studies using the same method as was reported in the original study. Replication studies allow scientists to evaluate the veracity of scientific claims by either confirming or refuting past results.

When choosing among existing surveys, researchers have many things to consider. It is critical that researchers select surveys that are appropriately fit for the population of interest and research questions. This means consideration of the constructs measured by the survey, the method of administration, the reading level and wording of questions, and psychometric properties (if available). To collect useful data, researchers must select an instrument that aligns with the goals and parameters of the research project to the fullest extent possible. We provide a brief example to clarify this decision; if an instrument was used with early childhood educators and related to their beliefs on responding to challenging behavior and the types of practices they use at different frequencies, the survey will need to be adapted to address similar research questions for parents of high school students.

Within the field of special education, there are hundreds of surveys available through public and proprietary sources that have been carefully reviewed and evaluated for consistency, reliability, accuracy, and validity. Many instruments, such as the Student Engagement Instrument (SSI; Betts et al., 2010), have been researched and revised by independent research teams over several years, whereas others lack such scrutiny (Table 11-1).

In the case of the ESC study, the project team recognized that data from studies of the HSSSE independent of the survey development team were scant. This presented an opportunity for the project team to determine if HSSSE was the best survey for their project and independently evaluate the claims made by the HSSSE development team. One particular focus was to evaluate if the data

TABLE 11-1. PSYCHOMETRIC PROPERTIES

PROPERTY	QUESTION ADDRESSED	IMPORTANCE
Reliability		
Test-retest	How reliable are scores if the instrument is administered at two different points in time?	If the intended instrument is meant to be administered at multiple points in time, it is important to demonstrate scores are consistent across measurement occasions.
		It is important to consider the length of time between measurement occasions when designing your methodology.
Internal consistency	How reliable are scores on items in measuring the intended phenomena?	It is important to demonstrate items are measuring the intended phenomena of interest. Thus, items should be correlated if they are intended to measure a similar construct.
Parallel forms	How reliable are scores on two equivalent forms of the same instrument?	If multiple forms are created, it is important to demonstrate each form is consistently measuring the same phenomena.
		This might be relevant when creating parallel forms in different languages or different administrative modalities (e.g., paper and pencil, computer).
Validity		
Content	Are items on the instrument attempting to measure the skills, content, or factors that should be measured given the phenomena of interest?	The instrument must address the phenomena grounded in a theoretical orientation, thus items should tap related content.
Construct	Are scores from items on the instrument measuring the constructs as intended?	Given the content the measure intends to measure (see above), statistical tests can be run to demonstrate items do indeed measure those constructs accurately.
Criterion	Are scores on the instrument predictive of scores on socially significant outcomes in the future?	Often, the instrument is used in a research project to demonstrate scores are correlated with other significant outcomes either in the future (i.e., predictive validity) or at the same time (i.e., concurrent validity).
	Are scores on the instrument correlated with scores on socially significant outcomes at the same time?	
	Are scores on the instrument correlated with scores on a well-established, psychometrically sound similar instrument?	

collected from their project measures subtypes of engagement (i.e., emotional engagement, social-behavioral engagement, and cognitive/academic engagement) with the same reliability and validity as the original investigation.

It is important to note that popularity of an instrument in no way guarantees quality. The quality of each individual instrument must be judged within the context of the research purpose and population of interest. It is simply not possible to make sound comparisons of surveys side-by-side. Impressive looking reports on the psychometric properties (e.g., predictive validity, reliability, etc.) of an instrument do not necessarily indicate one survey is the best choice for a particular strand of research. Though technical adequacy is important, there are other considerations. Researchers may select an instrument with lower technical adequacy than others if the technical limitations are offset by other beneficial features, such as the ease of use by participants, alignment of the instrument with key outcomes of interest, reduction in total time of completion, etc. Researchers must carefully weigh the costs and benefits of each potential instrument and select the one that is best suited to the research question and planned statistical analyses.

Researchers may not find an existing survey that meets all the necessary criteria and choose to adapt an existing survey. By making changes such as adding or deleting questions, changing the format of delivery, or changing the target audience, researchers enable a better fit for the current research. However, any modification to an existing survey should be made with a great deal of caution. In the development process, surveys are carefully crafted to collect specific data, and have typically been revised according to pilot testing, in which the survey is administered to a small group of participants in order to identify potential problems before it is administered to the full pool of participants. Data are then screened for basic psychometric properties such as internal consistency, test-retest reliability, and construct validity. Modifications may change the measurement characteristics (e.g., relation of survey items to meaningful variables of interest, consistency of measurement over time) of that survey. It cannot be assumed that the prior reported statistics are valid. Even a simple change such as rearranging the order of items, which may seem trivial, can fundamentally alter how a survey functions and how data can be interpreted. Any time a survey is modified from its original form, it is highly recommended that researchers pilot and evaluate it as if a new survey had been developed.

For example, in a recent study examining student engagement and predictors of dropout in high schools, Stevenson and colleagues (2019) administered the High School Survey of Student Engagement (HSSSE) using an online survey platform rather than the paper-pencil version originally developed by the Indiana Center for Evaluation and Education Policy. By using a digital platform, researchers were able to efficiently collect data from a large sample of students. However, analysis showed HSSSE was not as strong an instrument as previously reported. It is unclear if the differences were due to the change in delivery methods or some other phenomena. Results indicate further research and possible revision to the survey may be necessary before a digital version of the HSSSE has evidence of providing reliable and valid data for the measurement of engagement.

To further illustrate this point, in their survey of a nationally representative sample of middle school students, Siperstein and colleagues (2007) adapted an existing attitude rating scale (Prognostic Belief Scale; Wolraich & Siperstein, 1983) to create a new subscale called the Perceived Capabilities Scale. The purpose of the adapted scale was to measure how middle school students perceived the skills and capabilities of peers with intellectual disabilities. The researchers conducted pilot testing to determine if the items in the adapted scale reflected skills that middle school students without disabilities typically may exhibit, thus tailoring the items/survey specifically to middle school. Statistical testing was conducted to confirm the internal consistency reliability of the reworded items. Importantly, the researchers did not assume the adapted instrument would have the same measurement characteristics as the existing instrument.

Developing and Using New Survey Instruments

Another option for survey researchers is to develop a new survey. Researchers may choose to develop a new survey for several reasons, including: (a) poor technical adequacy of extant instruments, (b) misalignment of extant surveys to phenomena of interest, (c) formatting or readability that is inappropriate for the population of interest, (d) cost of licensing, and (e) limitations in how the survey is administered. The development of a new survey instrument requires the development of a prototype (or, when adapting an existing instrument, redesigned) survey. The prototype survey is field tested, piloted, and revised to maximize reliability and validity of obtained scores and minimize measurement error (Groves et al., 2011). Field testing usually requires the involvement of content or subject area experts, survey design and evaluation specialists, survey administrators, and respondents.

For example, to examine practices used with students with ASD in public school settings, Hess and colleagues (2008) created their own web-based survey called the Autism Treatment Survey. The first step in creating this survey was to synthesize several authoritative reviews of ASD intervention research, including a previous review conducted to develop a family survey (Green et al., 2006); a guide to EBPs (Simpson et al., 2005), and a report on ASD intervention research by the National Research Council. This synthesis was used to develop a survey with 43 items/practices divided into five categories, with an open response item at the end of the survey for respondents to identify additional practices. The 43 practices or strategies included those that are research-based and those that are not research-based. The initial survey draft was first reviewed by four experts in ASD; the researchers revised the survey based on the experts' feedback. Next, the researchers piloted the survey with a small group of public school teachers and students in a graduate class on ASD. The researchers stated that pilot data were used to assess the reliability and validity of scores obtained from the survey, but specific information about this was not provided.

Gagnon and colleagues (2018) also developed their own electronic survey instrument to examine the implementation of PBIS nationally in JJ schools. Like Hess and colleagues, the first step was to synthesize authoritative sources (in this case, three reliable and valid assessments of PBIS implementation, as well as research on PBIS) to develop an initial set of survey items. Next, the researchers completed four steps to pretest the survey (Dillman et al., 2009). First, a panel of experts in PBIS and JJ reviewed the items. Based on their feedback, items were removed and/or consolidated. Next, four JJ administrators rated each of the initial items using a four-point Likert scale, and these ratings were used to evaluate the content validity of the items/sections. Third, the same administrators were interviewed to evaluate the wording, terminology, clarity, and face validity of the survey. Fourth, the electronic survey was field-tested with six JJ administrators. Note that this is a smaller sample than is recommended for field testing (Dillman et al., 2009), but was necessary given the small size of the population of JJ administrators in the United States (the challenge of small populations may be encountered in other areas of special education survey research).

SAMPLING

Sampling is a key element of most types of research. Unless data are collected from every single member of a population, a sample must be used. When sampling is done with proper care, researchers can use a sample to make meaningful inferences about the population. Improper, haphazard, or biased sampling can lead to invalid or erroneous inferences about the population of interest (Figure 11-2).

Generally speaking, samples should be randomly selected from the population of interest and large enough to make reliable and valid inferences. Random selection helps to minimize the likelihood of sampling bias and allows researchers to more confidently generalize findings to a population. Larger samples are more likely to be representative of the population and enable appropriate

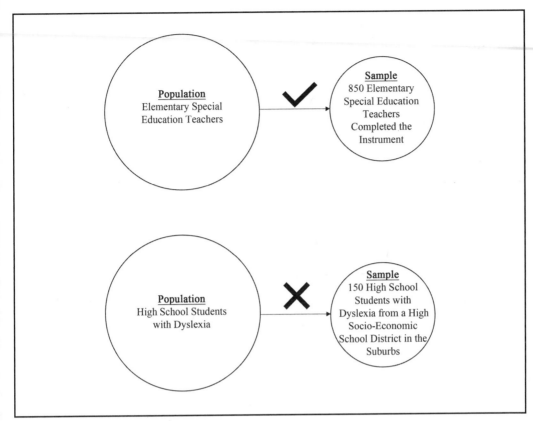

Figure 11-2. Sampling from a population.

statistical analyses of data (e.g., detecting differences between comparison groups). It is preferable to collect the largest possible sample in order to best represent the population of interest and achieve sufficient statistical power.

However, there is a lot more to consider in sampling than merely randomness and sample size. Sampling must be done strategically, with careful consideration of all the potential benefits and drawbacks of each decision. Large sample size can increase the possibility of interpreting chance differences between groups as meaningful (Type I error), when they are in fact due to an unknown phenomenon. In some instances, it may be more beneficial to target a survey at a specific group of participants because those participants share a characteristic that is relevant to the research question. In this case, sample size may be relatively small, but more informative than a more general sample.

Outside of those factors already mentioned elsewhere in this text, the key factors to consider in sampling for survey research are bias (i.e., results that skew in a particular way that is not representative of the population) and response rate (i.e., the percentage of participants that complete the survey relative to the total number surveyed). When data are collected, assumptions that the data are representative of the population must be made cautiously. For instance, when collecting data on high school dropout as in the ESC project example, any survey given to students in school will be biased because the data do not include responses from students who have already dropped out. Therefore, any conclusions will be limited to students at risk for dropout (Stevenson et al., 2019). Questions about the representativeness of a sample must be addressed through the design and implementation of the study, and/or clearly explained as a limitation.

For example, to obtain a nationally representative sample of middle school students in the United States, Siperstein and colleagues (2007) used three-stage stratified random sampling to randomly select "47 school districts from 26 states that represented every geographical region of the country" (p. 438). School districts were stratified by number of schools and then selected randomly. A total of 68 schools (27 suburban, 24 urban, 17 rural) were drawn based on district size (first-stage strata); alternative and vocational schools were not included. Two seventh grade classes and two eighth grade classes were selected to receive surveys in each school. Surveys were completed by hand by students in these classes during regular school hours. The large sample size for this survey ($n = 5837$) contributed to a relatively small margin of error for their survey results (plus or minus 1.4%, 95% confidence interval), as reported by the researchers.

Hess and colleagues (2008) sought to obtain a representative sample of public school teachers who teach students with ASD in the state of Georgia. They were unsuccessful in this endeavor, as they explain clearly when describing the limitations of their study. Their multistep process for recruiting participants included, first, emailing 249 special education directors and ASD specialists in all 159 counties, representing all school districts in Georgia. Three counties declined to participate, and 20 emails did not work. The researchers used standard survey follow-up protocols to maximize responses, including an advance notice to administrators that the link to the survey would be sent in 1 week; an email containing an invitation/explanation and link to the survey; and a third follow-up reminder email to administrators to forward the link to teachers. A total of 234 surveys were submitted electronically over a 3-month period; 49 surveys were excluded from analyses because they were either not completed or were completed by someone who was not currently teaching students with ASD. Of the 103,105 pre-K-12 teachers in Georgia at the time of the study, it was impossible for the researchers to know how many were currently teaching students with ASD. The researchers did note that the surveys they obtained represented rural, suburban, and urban school districts, and all geographic regions of the state.

In their study, Gagnon and colleagues (2018) first created a sampling frame by reviewing a comprehensive national directory of adult and juvenile correction departments. They created and applied criteria to ensure that only secure facilities that provided on-site educational services (301 JJ schools) were included in their sampling frame. Using statistical analyses, the researchers determined the minimum number of survey responses ($n = 169$) with which they would achieve satisfactory measurement accuracy. Because response rates in survey research are typically around 50%, the electronic survey was sent to all 301 JJ schools. Common strategies for maximizing response rates were used, including multiple contacts and reminders, clear directions, clear identification of the sponsoring university on all materials, assurance of confidentiality, and the provision of a gift card for participating. A total of 143 usable surveys were completed by JJ school principals. While the number of returned surveys fell slightly below the target number, the researchers found no statistically significant differences between respondents and nonrespondents in terms of JJ school characteristics and geographic regions, increasing confidence that the results obtained from the sample were representative of the population.

ANALYSES

Once responses are collected, researchers must analyze the data using procedures that align with the type of data collected and the questions of interest. As previously mentioned, surveys can yield many different types of data. Whether running the analyses oneself or with the support of a statistician, it is highly recommended that an analytic plan be developed in the initial planning stages of any research project. Considering how the data will be analyzed in the early stages of project planning will lead to better alignment between questions and results, and reduce misalignment between question, procedures, and analysis.

Following is a brief overview of some basic analytical and statistical procedures researchers may consider when conducting survey research. It is not an exhaustive or detailed list, merely an overview. Readers interested in conducting survey research should consult texts that provide more in-depth information regarding these and other procedures.

Data Preparation and Screening for Assumptions

Like other research involving quantitative data, analysis occurs in phases, beginning with entry and preparation of the data. All data must be carefully examined for completeness, errors, and outliers. Data that contain errors may lead to erroneous results and therefore may be unfit for analysis. Datasets that contain missing values must be examined for nonrandomness and potential bias. Missing values can be handled in a variety of ways depending on the randomness (or lack thereof), quantity of missing values, and potential for bias. From simple listwise deletion of records to advanced procedures such as multiple imputation or use of Full Information Maximum Likelihood, the data must be suitable for analysis, complete to the fullest extent possible, and free of errors.

Hess and colleagues (2008) used a web-based survey that directly imported survey data into a statistical software package, significantly simplifying the data entry, inspection, and preparation process. Gagnon and colleagues (2018) ensured the integrity of the data and data entry by randomly sampling surveys, having two researchers enter the data independently on coded data sheets, and then comparing to assess reliability and accuracy. The coded data sheets were also compared to data entered in statistical software. Finally, the researchers used a codebook throughout data entry to guide and direct the data preparation and entry process.

Once the data have been prepared, it is necessary to conduct statistical tests of assumptions that underlie the method or methods that are used to analyze and draw inferences from the data. For example, if linear regression will be used to examine relationships among survey items or constructs and external variables (i.e., grades, absences, employment status), the data must be examined for normality, multicollinearity, and homoscedasticity (e.g., see Osborne & Waters, 2002). Other statistical methods will require their own tests of underlying assumptions about the variables and data.

Common Analytic Procedures for Survey Data

Whether using an existing survey or a newly constructed instrument, all data should be analyzed strategically and systematically, using relevant statistical procedures. The following is a sampling of statistical procedures commonly used in survey research. The accompanying descriptions are written in simplified terms to give readers a basic understanding of what to look for in quality survey research articles and how to begin thinking about crafting a research plan.

Descriptive Analysis

Descriptive statistics provide basic information about respondents' answers to particular items. For instance, if researchers are trying to estimate the number of special education directors in public schools that are female, simply reporting the percentage of respondents to the survey that selected female may be adequate. No advanced procedures are necessary. Calculating descriptive statistics can typically be completed using spreadsheet software or even a basic calculator. Many online survey platforms include basic descriptive statistics as a part of data reporting.

Descriptive analyses are also a necessary step for conducting more complex analyses, a few of which are described in the following paragraphs. Descriptive statistics such as the mean, median, mode, standard error, and standard deviation provide necessary information about the overall pool of responses and whether or not the dataset meets the conditions necessary for more complex analysis (e.g., data are normally distributed, no substantive evidence the data are skewed positive or negative).

Internal Consistency

Internal consistency examines the degree to which items within a survey (or subsections of a survey) are correlated with one another. Tests for internal consistency give researchers an estimate of how well the survey is measuring the construct of interest across items. Internal consistency is often assessed using Cronbach's alpha statistic (Cronbach, 1951). Analysis of internal consistency can help researchers identify poor-quality survey questions or those that seem to be measuring a construct the researchers did not intend to measure.

Factor Analysis

Rather than examine the correlation between each individual item and an external variable, factor analysis allows researchers to group items in meaningful sets that estimate a single variable or construct. Exploratory Factor Analysis (EFA) is typically used for newly developed surveys, although we caution researchers that this approach is rarely appropriate given the context of a project. Confirmatory Factor Analysis (CFA) is used for existing surveys to confirm that factor structure is the same or similar to what has been published in technical reports or other peer-reviewed studies (Cole, 1987).

General Linear Model

General linear model (GLM) is a framework for examining and describing the effect, change, or relation between an independent variable (or variables) and a dependent variable (Werts & Linn, 1970). Many common statistical procedures, including Analysis of Variance (ANOVA), Analysis of Co-variance (ANCOVA), and regression analysis, fall under the general umbrella of GLM, as do many others. If a survey were given examining years of teaching experience and students' satisfaction with the course experience, GLM would be a suitable choice for modeling the relation between teacher experience and course satisfaction.

Multilevel Modeling

Multi-level modeling is a form of statistical modeling that enables researchers to examine data that are nested within existing groups, and therefore unable to use random assignment or random selection (e.g., students within classes, within grades, within schools, within districts; Woltman et al., 2012). Multi-level modeling is helpful for teasing out the variance of a dependent variable that is attributable to the independent variable(s) rather than variance attributable membership in a nested group.

Analyses Used in Example Survey Research Studies

Gagnon and colleagues (2018) used descriptive analyses and statistics organized by their research questions. They first reported the demographic characteristics of survey respondents as well as characteristics of the JJ schools where they worked (e.g., size, security levels, age, and grade ranges). The remaining data analyses focused on JJ school administrators' responses to survey items, reported primarily as percentages and numbers of administrators indicating whether their school implements a PBIS framework, as well as specific critical elements of PBIS. Responses to open-ended survey questions were analyzed using qualitative methods that included categorizing and coding topics and themes. The reliability of the process for descriptively coding open-ended responses was assessed through random checks. Overall, these descriptive analyses provide an estimate of the extent to which secure-care JJ schools across the country are implementing PBIS and its key components.

Similarly, Siperstein and colleagues (2007) first analyzed their data by presenting descriptions of student responses to survey questions, grouped by attitude subscales. They also used t tests to examine differences in responses by gender, extent of contact with persons with intellectual disabilities, and other individual and school characteristics. Effect sizes (Cohen's d) were calculated to obtain standardized mean differences between groups. Hess et al. (2008) descriptively analyzed respondent characteristics (gender, education level, years of experience, class type), as well as the frequency with which respondents reported using the 43 strategies (again, both research-based and not research-based) included in their Autism Treatment Survey. Next, Hess and colleagues examined differences by classroom type and grade level. To do this, they identified the most frequently used (by percentage) strategies in general education classrooms, special education classrooms, "mixed" classrooms, as well as across grade levels (preschool, elementary, middle, and high school). Finally, the practices that Georgia teachers reported using most frequently were categorized according to Simpson et al's (2005) levels of research support (scientifically based, promising practice, limited support, not recommended, not rated).

Because of their large sample size, Siperstein et al. (2007) were able to analyze their survey data using structural equation modeling. Using findings from previous studies, the researchers developed an *a priori* model of relationships between multiple variables (demographics, exposure to people with ID, perceived competence of people with ID, expectations about the personal impact of inclusion) and the attitudes of nondisabled middle school students toward the academic and social inclusion of students with ID. Survey data and structural equation modeling methods were used to assess the overall model and the statistical significance and strength of relationships among variables in the model. A key finding was that perceptions and beliefs about students with ID, as well as expectations about the personal impact of inclusion, had a bigger influence on negative and positive attitudes toward inclusion than exposure to or contact with people with ID.

CONSIDERATIONS FOR SURVEYING PARTICIPANTS WITH DISABILITIES

Surveying individuals with disabilities requires special consideration. Individuals with disabilities are one of many subpopulations afforded special protections when participating in research. As discussed in Chapter 4, federal regulations administered by the U.S. Department of Health and Human Services (Subpart A of Part 46: Basic HHS Policy for Protection of Human Subjects) state that children, prisoners, pregnant women, and anyone with diminished capacity for decision making, including persons with disabilities, are afforded special protections as members of uniquely vulnerable populations (U.S. Department of Health and Human Services, 2018). Additional safeguards must be taken to avoid coercion and to ensure informed consent is provided willingly by the participant and/or parent, legal guardian, or representative with appropriate legal authority. Researchers may need to have consent forms available in written and auditory formats, enlarged print, braille, or simplified text. We strongly suggest researchers work closely with officials in charge of protection of human subjects in research (Institutional Review Boards) at their local institutions to ensure appropriate supports and informed consent are provided in the most appropriate format.

Appropriateness of Survey Methods

In addition to addressing ethical concerns related to consent, beneficence, and confidentiality, researchers must determine whether survey methods are appropriate considering the characteristics and accessibility of a survey for prospective participants with disabilities. Most importantly, researchers must confirm that participants have the requisite skills needed to understand the questions and to accurately and independently communicate their responses, with or without augmentative or alternative communication methods. Collecting responses that do not accurately convey the thoughts and feelings of respondents with disabilities is indefensible from both an ethical and research perspective. Of particular concern is the use of alternative communication techniques that may falsely attribute responses to the individual with a disability (e.g., facilitated communication; rapid prompting; see Travers et al., 2014). Ensuring that individuals with disabilities understand the meaning of survey questions is equally important. This can be difficult (sometimes deceptively so) for individuals with and without disabilities. Great care must be taken in the design and administration of surveys to individuals with identified deficits in reading. Furthermore, even accommodations such as read aloud may not allow individuals to access the survey if they have deficits in expressive or receptive language. Surveys must be presented in formats that can be accessed by people who are blind or have low vision and individuals who are deaf or hard of hearing.

In the case of HSSSE, the project team determined that it was appropriate (and consistent with federal law) for students with disabilities to be allowed to use the accommodations included in their Individualized Education Program (IEP) when completing the HSSSE. This means that students would have access to accommodations such as having the directions read aloud, use of screen-reading/text-to-speech software, extended time, and periodic breaks, among others, provided such accommodations were included in their IEP.

Participants With Communication Difficulty

Despite the limitations and considerations presented previously, one should not assume that a disability automatically disqualifies an individual from participating in survey research. Omitting individuals with disabilities, even extensive ones, is a disservice to such individuals and creates an unnecessary gap in the scientific record. If all ethical and methodological requirements can be satisfactorily addressed, obtaining valid and reliable survey data from individuals with disabilities seems a necessary and valuable way to advance research in special education. Done properly, survey methods can and should be used to investigate research questions related to the knowledge, thoughts, feelings, and experiences of students with disabilities.

MISCONCEPTIONS, MISUSES, AND LIMITATIONS

Though survey research is a powerful and flexible research tool, it is important that anyone involved in such research be aware of misconceptions, misuses, and limitations (Table 11-2). Producers and consumers of survey research should regard each of the following items as red flags that signal potentially serious flaws or problems. Producers and consumers should be aware of these pitfalls and avoid them whenever possible. This is not an exhaustive list; rather, these are some of the more common red flags associated with survey research.

Conflating Correlation and Causation

Possibly the single biggest misstep in social science research is the conflation of correlation and causation. *Correlation* refers to a relation between two variables. Correlation occurs when change in one variable co-occurs with change in another variable. *Causation* is a phenomenon in which change in a variable is a result of change or manipulation of another variable (Holland, 1986). Correlation itself does not indicate the cause of the change. Causation must be inferred by carefully controlled experimental studies in which specific variables are manipulated to produce a specified outcome. In the case of surveys, there is no such manipulation. Therefore, any conclusions drawn from survey data are limited to correlations. Even if/when the survey itself seeks information on the causes of a phenomenon, researchers must be very cautious in making any claims of causation from survey data.

Ignoring Bias and Nesting Effects

It cannot be assumed that survey respondents always provide truthful, unbiased data. Depending on the type of question, and perceived consequences of a particular response, respondents may be tempted to provide responses that do not necessarily reflect objective truth. When asked about their own behavior or knowledge, respondents may be more likely to provide answers that reflect favorably on themselves and/or less favorably on others. We are not suggesting all, or even most respondents answer dishonestly; however, we suggest researchers know the population of interest and carefully think through strategies to reduce bias in the obtained data.

TABLE 11-2. COMMON MISCONCEPTIONS AND CLARIFICATIONS ABOUT SURVEY RESEARCH

MISCONCEPTION	BETTER UNDERSTANDING
Stating a reliable or valid instrument exists.	The properties of reliability and validity are reserved for the obtained scores, not the instrument. This is critical because believing an instrument is valid or reliable may lead a researcher to assuming the scores obtained are reliable or valid despite the fact the sample may not match prior research.
Conflating correlation and causation.	Correlation refers to a relation between two variables, whereas causation is the establishment of a functional relation between an independent and dependent variable. This means the researchers demonstrated the manipulation of an independent variable, while holding all else constant, and are attributing change in the dependent variable to the independent variable.
Deleting respondents who do not complete the entire survey (i.e., listwise).	This approach is common because many statistical programs use this as a default setting to deal with missing data. However, this can lead to bias in the data. If the skipped items are not random and due to systematic reasons, then these respondents are being eliminated despite this correlation. We caution researchers to carefully check their sample size through statistical software with the sample size they believe they obtained to ensure listwise deletion is not being used without their knowledge. We also suggest readers consult other literature on more advanced methods for dealing with missing data (e.g., multiple imputation, full information maximum likelihood).

One example is a survey study conducted by Harvey and colleagues (2015), who surveyed teacher education program training of preservice teachers and Response-to-Intervention (RTI). Data collected from the survey revealed an interesting pattern often seen in other areas of research. When asked to rate their own knowledge of RTI, faculty in special education generally rated their personal knowledge as very high. The same faculty rated their colleagues within their own program highly on knowledge of RTI, but not as highly as they rated themselves. Likewise, respondents rated their colleagues in their college or department but outside their program (i.e., School Psychology) as knowledgeable, but less so than their immediate colleagues within the department. In each case, the further the subject was from the respondent within the organizational hierarchy, the lower respondents tended to rate their expertise. Because the study was based on a survey and not an observation of skill or assessment, it is not clear if special education faculty do in fact have superior knowledge of RTI over their colleagues in other programs. It is also unclear if the difference in knowledge of RTI is a result of bias or nesting with groups. In either case, researchers must be mindful of these possibilities when crafting the research design and data analytic strategy.

Faux Mixed Methods

Researchers involved in mixed-methods research aim to study certain phenomena of interest through strategic use of mixed methods in a way that capitalizes on the strengths of quantitative and qualitative methods in a single, cohesive research design. Unfortunately, the term *mixed methods* is often taken as a short for any study with qualitative and quantitative elements. As discussed in Chapter 13, mixed-methods research is not a catch-all term for studies that include both quantitative and qualitative data. One cannot simply add an interview to an experimental study and call it mixed methods without undermining the core function of mixed-methods research. Similarly, adding some open-ended items to a quantitative survey does not constitute mixed methods. Mixed methods is a synergistic blend of rigorous quantitative and qualitative techniques that maximize the potential for useful scientific data around a single question or phenomenon. As Creswell (2002) describes, "The two forms of data [quantitative and qualitative] are integrated in the design analysis through merging the data, explaining the data, building from one database to another, or embedding the data within a larger framework" (p. 215). Essentially, mixed methods provides a useful means of gathering meaningful scientific data when parsing studies into distinct quantitative and qualitative investigations falls short. This means researchers must be thoughtful and strategic in their use of quantitative and qualitative techniques, such that the overall study design is crafted to capitalize on the strengths of each data source and minimize any potential weaknesses. When survey methods are used in service of mixed-methods research, it must be essential to answering the research question and incorporated into the initial research design.

Cherry-Picking Survey Items

On occasion, researchers may be interested in examining a particular subcomponent of an existing instrument with little or no interest in the rest of the survey. Researchers may also wish to combine items from several different surveys into one unified survey that more closely matches a particular research question. In these cases, researchers may be tempted to use only select items of interest. However, researchers must use caution when pulling individual items from larger surveys. As mentioned earlier, once survey items are altered, added, or omitted, one cannot assume the subset of items will yield data representative of previously published data. Even if a survey has been repeatedly evaluated and revised to maximize reliability, accuracy, and validity, one cannot assume individual items or groups of items will perform similarly when removed from the context of the survey in which they were developed. Removing items from a survey essentially creates a new survey that requires its own analysis for measurement properties. Prior to using individual items or groups of items from an existing survey, it is recommended that researchers pilot test such items for basic statistical properties and relevant analytics (e.g., internal consistency, factor analysis, etc.) with a subsample similar to the sample of interest. Doing so will help protect against erroneous results and improve confidence in the data. See Table 11-3 for additional resources.

SUMMARY

As an approach to examining important research questions related to the provision of special education to exceptional learners, survey research has both advantages and limitations. Most important is ensuring that survey methods are well-suited for answering the question(s) being asked. Once 'goodness of fit' has been confirmed, researchers must adhere to established guidelines for designing, conducting, and interpreting survey research. We hope that this chapter has provided readers with a useful introduction to and overview of survey research in special education.

TABLE 11-3. ADDITIONAL RESOURCES

RESOURCE	DESCRIPTION
Survey Monkey https://www.surveymonkey.com/ Redcap https://www.project-redcap.org/ Qualtrics https://www.qualtrics.com/	Common online survey platforms that enable users to customize questions, question types, and other user features. Surveys can be administered via email or web browser.
Center for Excellence in Survey Research at the University of Chicago. https://www.norc.org Fielding, N. G., Lee, R. M., & Blank, G. (Eds.). (2008). *The Sage handbook of online research methods.* Sage. Fowler, F. J. (2014). *Survey research methods* (5th ed.). Sage. Groves, R. M., Fowler Jr, F. J., Couper, M. P., Lepkowski, J. M., Singer, E., & Tourangeau, R. (2011). *Survey methodology* (Vol. 561). John Wiley & Sons. Marsden, P. V., & Wright, J. D. (Eds.). (2010). *Handbook of survey research.* Emerald Group Publishing. Rossi, P. H., Wright, J. D., & Anderson, A. B. (Eds.). (2013). *Handbook of survey research.* Academic Press. Survey Research Center, Institute for Social Research. University of Michigan. https://www.src.isr.umich.edu/about/	Select texts that address basic and advanced topics in the design, sampling, data collection, analysis, and application of survey research methods in education and related fields.

CHAPTER REVIEW

1. What types of research questions are suitable for survey research?
2. What factors must be considered when deciding between using an existing survey and creating a new survey?
3. How can researchers ensure data from a survey is valid and reliable?
4. How can children, youth, and adults with disabilities be included as respondents in survey research?

REFERENCES

Betts, J. E., Appleton, J. J., Reschly, A. L., Christenson, S. L., & Huebner, E. S. (2010). A study of the factorial invariance of the Student Engagement Instrument (SEI): Results from middle and high school students. *School Psychology Quarterly, 25*(2), 84-93. https://doi.org/10.1037/a0020259

Briesch, A. M., & Chafouleas, S. M. (2009). Exploring student buy-in: Initial development of an instrument to measure likelihood of children's intervention usage. *Journal of Educational and Psychological Consultation, 19*(4), 321-336.

Briesch, A. M., Chafouleas, S. M., Neugebauer, S. R., & Riley-Tillman, T. C. (2013). Assessing influences on intervention implementation: Revision of the Usage Rating Profile-Intervention. *Journal of School Psychology, 51*(1), 81-96.

Chafouleas, S. M., Briesch, A. M., Neugebauer, S. R., & Riley-Tillman, T. C. (2011). *Usage Rating Profile–Intervention (Revised).* University of Connecticut.

Cole, D. A. (1987). Utility of confirmatory factor analysis in test validation research. *Journal of Consulting and Clinical Psychology, 55*(4), 584.

Creswell, J. W. (2002). *Educational research: Planning, conducting, and evaluating quantitative, qualitative, and mixed methods approaches.* Prentice Hall.

Cronbach, L. J. (1951). Coefficient alpha and the internal structure of tests. *Psychometrika, 16*(3), 297-334.

Dillman, D., Smyth, J., & Christian, L. (2009). *Internet, mail, and mixed-mode surveys: The tailored design method.* John Wiley.

Dimitrov, D. M. (2013). *Quantitative research in education: Intermediate & advanced methods.* Whittier Publications.

Gagnon, J. C., Barber, B. R., & Soyturk, I. (2018). Positive behavior interventions and supports implementation in secure care juvenile justice schools: Results of a national survey of school administrators. *Behavioral Disorders, 44*(1), 3-19.

Green, V. A., Pituch, K. A., Itchon, J., Choi, A., O'Reilly, M., & Sigafoos, J. (2006). Internet survey of treatments used by parents of children with autism. *Research in Developmental Disabilities, 27*(1), 70-84. https://doi.org/10.1016/j.ridd.2004.12.002

Groves, R. M., Fowler Jr, F. J., Couper, M. P., Lepkowski, J. M., Singer, E., & Tourangeau, R. (2011). *Survey methodology.* John Wiley & Sons.

Harvey, M. W., Yssel, N., & Jones, R. E. (2015). Response to intervention preparation for preservice teachers. *Teacher Education and Special Education, 38*(2), 105-120. https://doi.org/10.1177/0888406414548598

Hess, K. L., Morrier, M. J., Heflin, L. J., & Ivey, M. L. (2008). Autism treatment survey: Services received by children with autism spectrum disorders in public school classrooms. *Journal of Autism and Developmental Disorders, 38*(5), 961-971.

Holland, P. W. (1986). Statistics and causal inference. *Journal of the American Statistical Association, 81*(396), 945-960.

Lane, K. L., Kalberg, J. R., Bruhn, A. L., Driscoll, S. A., Wehby, J. H., & Elliott, S. N. (2009). Assessing social validity of school-wide positive behavior support plans: Evidence for the reliability and structure of the Primary Intervention Rating Scale. *School Psychology Review, 38*(1).

National Research Council (2001). *Educating children with autism.* Committee on Educational Interventions for Children with Autism, Division of Behavioral and Social Sciences and Education. National Academy Press.

Osborne, J., & Waters, E. (2002). Four assumptions of multiple regression that researchers should always test. *Practical Assessment, Research, & Evaluation, 8*(2), 1-9.

Simpson, R. L., de Boer-Ott, S. R., Griswold, D. E., Myles, B. S., Byrd, S. E., Ganz, J. B., Tapscott Cook, K., Otten, K. L., Ben-Arieh, J., & Kline, S. A. (2005). *Autism spectrum disorders: Interventions and treatments for children and youth.* Corwin Press.

Siperstein, G. N., Parker, R. C., Bardon, J. N., & Widaman, K. F. (2007). A national study of youth attitudes toward the inclusion of students with intellectual disabilities. *Exceptional Children, 73*(4), 435-455.

Stevenson, N. A., Swain-Bradway, J., LeBeau, B. C. (2019) Examining high school student engagement and critical factors in dropout prevention. Assessment for Effective Intervention. https://doi.org/10.1177/1534508419859655

Taber, K.S. (2018) The use of Cronbach's alpha when developing and reporting \research instruments in science education. *Research in Science Education. 48*(6), 1273-1296. https://doi.org/10.1007/s11165-016-9602-2.

Travers, J. C., Tincani, M. J., & Lang, R. (2014). Facilitated communication denies people with disabilities their voice. *Research & Practice for Persons with Severe Disabilities, 39*(3), 195-202.

U.S. Department of Health and Human Services (2018). Subpart A of Part 46: Basic HHS Policy for Protection of Human Subjects. Retrieved https://www.hhs.gov/ohrp/sites/default/files/revised-common-rule-reg-text-unofficial-2018-requirements.pdf

Werts, C. E., & Linn, R. L. (1970). A general linear model for studying growth. *Psychological Bulletin, 73*(1), 17.

Woltman, H., Feldstain, A., MacKay, J. C., & Rocchi, M. (2012). An introduction to hierarchical linear modeling. *Tutorials in quantitative methods for psychology, 8*(1), 52-69.

Yazzie-Mintz, E. (2007). Voices of Students on Engagement: A Report on the 2006 High School Survey of Student Engagement. Center for Evaluation and Education Policy, Indiana University.

Qualitative Research

With contributions from Delia E. Racines, PhD

INTRODUCTION

This chapter serves as an iterative guide to support special education professionals in learning the key components of qualitative research design. Inductive in nature, qualitative research is a paradigm that is comprised of a variety of methodologies providing valuable insights—from what people think, do, know and can contribute to understanding people with disabilities and informing valuable policy and practice in special education (Bratlinger et al., 2005). Insights are gained by interviewing, observing, and analyzing documents—the three most commonly known methods in qualitative research (Patton, 2002). Qualitative methodologies, however, encompass more than data-gathering techniques; epistemology guides methodological decision-making including the collection and analysis of data; often iterative (Bryman, 1984; Koro-Ljungberg et al., 2009). Decisions on methodological preferences, including analysis for thesis and dissertation research, are often made without conceptual grounding in the philosophy behind chosen methods. Yet, our very presuppositions are what lead us to use different methods, ask different questions, and draw conclusions (Patton, 2002; Willis, 2007). This chapter begins with a researcher's choice of qualitative methods and evaluation in relation to their proposed use (Efinger et al., 2004). Key interconnected components are delineated, including research problem, conceptual framework, research question(s), method(s), validity, and results. This chapter is not prescriptive nor linear. However, as new developments occur (which they often do in a qualitative study), each component should be revisited; an iterative process is encouraged. An advanced genre of qualitative research called self-study research is also included, which has gained momentum in teacher education to improve practice, contribute to the knowledge base on teaching and learning, and acknowledges the role of the teacher in teachers' learning (Racines, 2016).

Hott, B. L., Brigham, F. J., & Peltier, C.
Research Methods in Special Education (pp. 217-238).
© 2021 SLACK Incorporated.

CHAPTER OBJECTIVES

→ Examine one's researcher identity in relationship to a chosen topic and method for qualitative research.

→ Describe the key components, processes, and purpose of qualitative research.

→ Distinguish the key components and purposes of qualitative research and the ways in which this approach differs from other research methods.

→ Critique design approaches to qualitative research and the implications of these for conducting and evaluating qualitative research in education.

→ Identify data collection and analysis techniques, including coding and thematic analysis, in relation to literature on qualitative research methods.

→ Distinguish self-study research methodology from traditional qualitative research methods and its five foci guideposts.

KEY TERMS

- **Axiology**: A philosophical assumption, in addition to epistemology and ontology, which acknowledges that biases are present and asks the researcher to share the role of values and how those values shape the narrative.

- **Bias**: Your subjectivities as a researcher, which may be innate or learned; unequal weight in favor of or against an idea.

- **Case Study**: An intensive study over time of an individual, group, or organization (a case) based on substantial data collection of real-life events; often employs a variety of data sources (direct observations, interviews, artifacts, documents).

- **Coding**: Representing a characteristic or theme in data set passages of text marked with codes and then studied to learn more about how an idea or theme is represented. Often referred to as indexing or categorizing.

- **Conceptual Framework** (also referred to as a theoretical framework): The theories, ideas, and definitions, often from multiple disciplines, that inform one's research (Glesne, 2016).

- **Critical Ethnography**: Criticizes the ethnographer's own production of an account.

- **Data Source**: Types of data collected for the study; typically from observations, focus groups, and interviews; all of which lend themselves to triangulation to enhance the validity of the study.

- **Emic**: Information provided by the participants from the study; the insider's point of view (the one being studied); essential in understanding how others see the world around them.

- **Epistemology**: The nature of knowledge; what it means to know and how we know it.

- **Ethnography**: Interpretative research that uses culture as the theoretical framework for studying and describing a group of people; methods include in-depth interviews, immersion in the field, and participant observation.

- **Etic**: The point of view of the observer (the one conducting the study); information represented by the researcher's interpretation of the participant's perspective.

- **Focus Group**: A collection of people who facilitate a discussion on a topic; selected by the researcher conducting the study.

- **Grounded Theory**: A process of developing a theory that is grounded in research through a reflexive process of gathering data (actions or events observed or recorded, or described in documents or interviews), coding, identifying themes, and then seeking out more data for comparison.

- **Historical Research**: The use of primary historical data to answer a research question; data sources include government records, birth and/or death certificates, and/or newspaper articles.
- **Inductive**: Reasoning that moves from the specific to the general or abstract and develops a theory that could explain patterns in the data collected from the study.
- **Iterative**: Involves a back-and-forth of processes and changes and evolves over time; leads to refinement of research.
- **Narrative Inquiry**: Inquiry procedures that focus on the lives of individuals as told through their own stories. Narrative research can take a variety of approaches: life history, oral history, biography, personal narrative, and narrative analysis. Data sources can include life histories, narrative interviews, journals, diaries, biographies, and memoirs.
- **Ontology**: The nature of being or reality; what makes up the world.
- **Phenomenology**: Interested in the experience of an individual and their lived experiences of a particular phenomenon or an event. Ravitch and Carl (2016) identify homeless parenting as an example. Portraying the comprehensive descriptions that provide the essence of the experience is the goal.
- **Qualitative Research**: Inquiry approach used to make sense of a phenomenon; collects views from participants through observations and/or interviews, analyzes data collected for themes; makes meaning of data, leads to interpretation and explicit statement of researcher bias.
- **Reliability**: Dependability, credibility, and transferability are often used in lieu of reliability in qualitative methods; idea of consistent results; two procedures can be used to check for reliability or dependability, triangulation, and member-checking.
- **Rhetorical Assumptions**: Asks what is the language of the research and encourages that writing in qualitative research be personal and literary in form to see reality from the eyes of the participants.
- **Self-Study**: A systematic research method in which the researcher inquires into problems situated in practice, engages in cycles of research, and systematically collects and analyzes data using the five foci to improve practice (Samaras & Freese, 2006).
- **Thematic Analysis**: A type of data analysis that involves searching for themes and patterns, separating data into categories, and analyzing the codes [coding].
- **Transcription**: Word-for-word written account of spoken words from interviews and/or focus groups that are further coded to identify themes.
- **Triangulation**: The process of using multiple methods or data sources to ensure validity and form themes in a study.
- **Trustworthiness**: Helps establish how a study's findings are credible, transferable, and dependable; how reliability and validity are conceptualized in qualitative research.
- **Validity**: Accuracy of the findings of the study; supported by the triangulation of various data sources.

CASE STUDY

Sonia E. is an instructional coach who supports teachers with students who are dually identified as English Learners (ELs) and with a disability who receive both EL services and special education services. Sonia works in a public school and is constantly surrounded with negative comments from teachers regarding ELs who are dually identified. Sonia's concern, however, is that there is a heavy emphasis on teachers and instruction for ELs, but not as much emphasis on exploring the experiences or opinions from ELs, particularly ELs with learning disabilities, or from teachers who work exclusively with ELs with learning disabilities. This is especially true for dually identified ELs in schools where the population is in stark contrast to the rest of the United States—a very low EL and Special Education population, as in Sonia's school. Sonia is concerned with where to begin in developing a qualitative research design to better understand the experiences directly from dually identified ELs and their teachers, and what types of questions to ask or not ask regarding their social-emotional experiences as well as student achievement. Sonia wants to provide teachers an opportunity to share their insights about the unique challenges they face and also identify specific recommendations from both dually identified ELs and teachers of dually identified ELs to ultimately improve both their academic and social experiences. Sonia, who grew up as an EL with a disability, also recognizes her own personal bias as a strong advocate and wonders how her values and expectations will influence her research and the conclusions of this study. How is personal bias addressed in qualitative research? Given the layers of questions and concerns, Sonia is not sure where to begin to develop a strong qualitative research design that will address school climate on the academic and social experiences of dually identified ELs and ultimately bring meaningful improvement in equitable opportunities and outcomes.

EPISTEMOLOGY AND THE CHOICE OF QUALITATIVE RESEARCH METHODS

Quantitative researchers use numbers as data, whereas qualitative researchers do not (Willis, 2007, p. 7). Quantitative is *objective*, and qualitative is *subjective*. Clearly, a T-chart can divide these two approaches to research, right? The terms *qualitative* and *quantitative* are popularly distinguished in the aforementioned manner; however, such definitions are oversimplified and untrue (Willis, 2007). The distinctions between qualitative and quantitative methods have often been discussed as if they belong to opposing alternatives; one referred to as soft and unscientific and the other as more mechanical, more mainstream (Valsiner, 2000). Instead of paradigm wars, Patton (2002), Valsiner (2000), and Willis (2007) invoke paradigm dialogues to distinguish the two, not necessarily by the type of data collected or preferred, but by their underlying foundational beliefs and assumptions. Ravitch and Carl (2016) similarly state that while some qualitative researchers apply qualitative criteria and standards to quantitative research and some quantitative researchers apply their standards and validity criteria to qualitative research in ways that generate defensiveness and misunderstanding, the truth is that many researchers work from the understanding that each paradigm has different goals and each research approach serves different purposes. Paradigms, philosophy, and research are interconnected, and researchers should have a conceptual grounding in the philosophy behind various methodologies.

Methods are the nuts and bolts of research. Understanding the paradigm of choices beyond conventional research methodologies develops scholarship in qualitative methods, strengthens credibility of qualitative research, and expands the future of qualitative tradition (Patton, 2002). "The search for method becomes one of the most important problems of the entire enterprise of understanding the uniquely human forms of psychological activity…method is simultaneously the prerequisite and product, the tool and the result of the study" (Vygotsky as cited in Luttrel, 2010, p. 171). As aforementioned, most research texts divide research methods into two main areas, quantitative and qualitative, and often quantitative methods are referred to as the "gold standard"; the more "scientific" approach to doing research (Klingner & Boardman, 2011, p. 208; Knox, 2004; Tewksbury, 2009). Indeed, quantitative methods have the ability to make predictions (its most outstanding characteristic) and can answer such questions regarding the efficacy of instructional methods, but do not provide the how and the why to support real-world applications (Tewksbury, 2009). Randomized samples in quantitative research also tend to poorly represent vulnerable populations, particularly detrimental to the work of special education professionals, questioning the assumption that simply because an intervention is evidence-based, that it is universally acceptable (Ferri et al., 2011). By focusing so intently on what works, we as a field are losing sight of what matters (Ferri et al.,

2011). Qualitative research is not done for purposes of generalization, but instead to produce evidence based on exploration of particular individuals that can inform policy (Bratlinger et al., 2005). Qualitative research gives voice to the people who have been historically silenced or marginalized, where studies by special education scholars often draw from the individual voices of recipients of special education services (Bratlinger et al., 2005). Yet, while qualitative methods provide insight to how and why, too many qualitative articles lack design and methodological details, simply stating use of "whichever methodology suits the study objectives and the research question" (Carter & Little, 2007, p. 1323). It has become too easy to select qualitative methods because they are more familiar or easier to implement without consideration of epistemology or the final products they will generate (Koro-Ljungberg et al., 2009). The result is weak research, which, without purpose, credibility, accuracy, relevance, and rigor, becomes questionable (Knox, 2004).

Given the controversial nature of methods decisions, both emerging and experienced researchers must be able to clarify the often inconsistently and interchangeably used terms of methods, design, and methodology in relation to their epistemological position (Patton, 1999). This provides researchers the know-how to not only properly embark on a research topic, but also to critique the value and appropriateness of qualitative design and method choices (Patton, 1999). Knox (2004) questions why engagement of such fundamental concepts practically go silent beyond the doctoral level, recognizing that the very misalignment between method and philosophical stances can create confusion throughout the entire research process for all researchers.

Carter and Little (2007) break this silence with an explicit definition of *methodology*, describing it as the plan of action, how the research process should proceed or essentially the design behind the use of particular methods; it is the explanation of methods, not the methods themselves. *Method* is the actual techniques used to gather and analyze data (Carter & Little, 2007; Nudzor, 2009). More often, the two aforementioned terms are left undefined or inconsistently defined so that their philosophical underpinnings are left unclear (Nudzor, 2009). Maxwell (as cited in Luttrel, 2010) further explains design as the "logic and coherence" of all the components of a research project, which in qualitative research is often recursive and much less restrictive than "conventional" or quantitative methods (Patton, 2002, p. 7). Willis (2007) defines *epistemology* as what it means to know and how we know it, while this knowledge is also influenced by the nature of truth, or *ontology*, which distinguishes what can be real and what cannot. Ontologically, in quantitative research, the assumption is that there is only one truth that is independent from the researcher and researchers should eliminate their biases from the study, whereas qualitative methods recognize subjectivity as an intimate part of the research (Twining et al., 2017; Willis, 2007). In addition to epistemology and ontology, two terms that describe philosophical assumptions include *axiology*, which acknowledges that biases are present and asks the researcher to share the role of values and how those values shape the narrative, and *rhetorical assumptions*, which ask what is the language of the research, and encourages that writing in qualitative research be personal and literary to see reality from the eyes of the participants (Creswell, 2013). An appropriate methodological approach is one that balances both purpose and the philosophical realm into which the issues under investigation fit (Nudzor, 2009). There is a need for all researchers to engage in more detailed explanations regarding these terms and approaches to justify their methodological choices.

Qualitative research provides valuable insights from finding out what people think, do, and know by interviewing, observing, and analyzing documents; the three most commonly known methods in qualitative research (Patton, 2002). Qualitative methodologies, however, encompass more than data-gathering techniques; epistemology guides methodological decision-making, including the formulation of research questions, selection of sampling criteria, data collection, data analysis, and reporting; whereas data collection and analysis are iterative (Bryman, 1984; Koro-Ljungberg et al., 2009). Qualitative research methods are not necessarily appropriate for every inquiry situation. The purpose of qualitative research is to describe and interpret issues or phenomena systematically from the point of view of the individual or population being studied, and to generate new concepts and theories. Qualitative studies explore attitudes and beliefs of several parties involved in special education and general education, and examine personal reactions to special education teaching strategies and contexts (Bratlinger et al., 2005). Qualitative research follows the paradigm based on the assumption that multiple realities exist, and such realities are constructed by research participants (Ryan et al., 2007). Qualitative designs can document and bring significant awareness from exploring how various practices effect individuals with disabilities and their families from their perspectives within various work or school settings (Bratlinger et al., 2005).

Although design and methods in qualitative research are continually refined, unlike in quantitative methods, without careful consideration of the purpose behind each method choice and the different philosophical underpinnings of each method, very different results can be produced from the same data collected (Carter & Little, 2007). There are many approaches to qualitative research, and while not all of them are described in depth here, Table 12-1 offers a summary of the primary research designs in qualitative methods along with resources for further reading. The primary designs include case study, ethnography, narrative, phenomenology, grounded theory, and historical research (Knox, 2004; Patton, 2002). By the time researchers are in charge of a research project, they tend to be fully socialized within a particular research tradition; the very choice of research injects subjectivity (Patton, 2002). Qualitative researchers are interested in people's interpretations of their experiences, events, and other inquiry domains (Ravitch & Carl, 2016). It is the role of the researcher that is the primary instrument in qualitative research and draws on the concept that a researcher's identity is central in qualitative research design. *Positionality*, or the researcher's role and identity, are central to understanding the researcher's role in every stage of the qualitative research process.

This dialogue regarding epistemology and a researcher's positionality is intended to increase awareness regarding the ultimate power researchers have in controlling the selection of methods and design, selection of participants, and ultimately reporting findings. Current and future researchers must have an understanding of how epistemological stances influence researchers' methodological choices and have implications on the research process, and more importantly on the final product. It is up to us to ethically ask, whose story are we telling (Holstein & Gubrium, 2008)? Scott and Alexander (2019) stress this very point regarding the need for further studies to investigate strategies for recruiting and retaining Black males in special education teacher preparation programs from Black male teachers (BMTs), particularly special education BMTs as multiple studies have been conducted; however, they are often a product of positing and not an actual investigation into specific experiences of BMTs. Researchers, whether they admit it or not, are also methodologists and epistemologists who make daily assumptions about epistemology, and methodological awareness carries substantial benefits. Although quantitative methods certainly do offer some information and understanding, all researchers must explain the relationship between philosophy and research to the value and appropriateness of methodological details. For a researcher to decide which method is best suited for a proposed study, the researcher must closely examine the research questions, which often stem from the research problem and research goal, and relate them to the philosophical and methodological differences between quantitative and qualitative methods of research (Carter & Little, 2007).

IDENTIFICATION OF RESEARCH PROBLEM AND GOAL IN QUALITATIVE RESEARCH

In order to identify solutions to a research problem, the problem itself must be explicitly identified. Three questions upon which to critically reflect in order to articulate the research problem include: (a) Why is this particular phenomenon important and to whom? (b) What problem or policy might this study solve or influence? and (c) So what? Yes, this is worded a bit harshly; however, it is necessary to describe why anyone should care about the results of the study. It is as important to further distinguish two additional terms along with the research problem, the research purpose and/or goal, and the research question(s). We will focus on the research problem and the purpose/goal,

TABLE 12-1. SUMMARY OF PRIMARY RESEARCH DESIGNS IN QUALITATIVE RESEARCH

DESIGN	METHOD
Case study	An intensive study over time of an individual, group, or organization (a case) based on substantial data collection of real-life events; often employs a variety of data sources (direct observations, interviews, artifacts, documents). Building theory from case study research involves an interactive process of which findings are extended from one case to the next. Yin, R. K. (2004). *The case study anthology*. Sage.
Ethnography	Interpretative research that uses culture as the theoretical framework for studying and describing a group of people; multiple data sources include in-depth interviews, immersion in the field (field notes), and participant observation; multiple forms of ethnography, including holistic, semiotic, and critical; critical ethnography criticizes the ethnographer's own production of an account; a focus on unacknowledged biases resulting from implicit values. Atkinson, P., Delamont, S., Coffee, A. J., Lofland, J., & Lofland, L. H. (Eds.). (2005). *Handbook of ethnography*. Sage.
Grounded theory	A process of developing a theory that is grounded in research through a reflexive process of gathering data (actions or events observed or recorded, or described in documents or interviews), coding, identifying themes, and then seeking out more data for comparison. Data analysis begins as soon as the first piece of data is collected. Glaser, B. G., & Strauss, A. L. (1967). *The discovery of grounded theory*. Aldine.
Historical research	The use of primary historical data (records, diaries, government records, birth and/or death certificates, oral histories, newspaper articles, photographs, and other artifacts) to describe, analyze, and explain past events. The artifacts and records used are driven by the particular study and its research question(s). Historical research relies significantly on inductive, logical reasoning. Brinkmann, S., Jacobsen, M. H., & Kristiansen, S. (2014). Historical overview of qualitative research in the social sciences. *The Oxford Handbook of Qualitative Research*, 17-42.
Narrative	Can refer to a phenomenon under study; describe stories of personal experience; gain deeper understanding of people's lived experiences and can be used as a starting point for understanding how people make sense of their lives; narratives can be useful in critical research as they offer an opportunity to include typically marginalized voices. Lyons, N., & LaBoskey, V. K. (Eds.). (2002). *Narrative inquiry in practice: Advancing the knowledge of teaching*. Teachers College Press.
Phenomenology	Interested in the experience of an individual and their lived experiences of a particular phenomenon or an event. Ravitch and Carl (2016) identify homeless parenting as an example. Portraying the comprehensive descriptions that provide the essence of the experience is the goal. Data sources can include participant observation interviews, documents, and poems. Moustakas, C. E. (1994). *Phenomenological research methods*. Sage.

which will both help develop the research questions that will be explained in a separate, yet interconnected, key component. A clear distinction between these terms will support a clear justification for the study.

The research problem itself is an educational issue or concern that leads to the need for your study to be researched (Creswell, 2008). To determine if your study is needed, it means it has not been conducted yet or it is filling a gap in the research (Creswell, 2013). Some studies perhaps have not examined a specific set of participants or might have a different experience based on a unique research site/setting, which can also lead to an unanswered, researchable question. The wording of the research purpose or goal often helps develop the wording of the research problem. One example of a research purpose is to raise awareness to an often overlooked or underserved population. The research question, on the other hand, narrows the purpose and identifies what the study can potentially answer (Maxwell, 2005). The following examples of a research purpose/goal, problem, and research questions are from a qualitative research study conducted in Fairfax County, Virginia.

Research Purpose/Goal

To gain an understanding of the personal experiences and descriptions of the school climate in a school with a low population of dually identified ELs with disabilities.

The purpose of this study is threefold: (a) to understand the experiences directly from a dually identified EL with a disability and English for Speakers of Other Languages (ESOL) teachers as well as special education teachers in a public high school with a low proportion of dually identified ELs with disabilities; (b) to understand how a dually identified EL and ESOL and special education teachers perceive the school climate's influence on academic achievement, and to (c) understand how dually identified ELs perceive themselves both academically and socially. The perspectives shared from both teachers and dually identified ELs will help policymakers, administrators, and teachers better understand the impact of school climate on the academic and social experiences of dually identified ELs, to ultimately identify specific recommendations to improve their academic and social experiences.

Research Problem

A major shift of the demographics in the United States, coupled with special attention to our nation's educational goals and standards, has stressed teacher preparation, particularly effective instructional approaches and differentiation of instruction for beginner to advanced proficiencies of ELs who are dually identified with a disability. However, while the focus has been on teachers and instruction for ELs, not as much emphasis has been about exploring the experiences or opinions from dually identified ELs or from ESOL or special education teachers who work exclusively with dually identified ELs. This is especially true for ELs in schools where the population is a very low dually identified EL population.

Research Questions

1. How do ELs and ESOL/special education teachers describe their experiences at a public high school with a low proportion of ELs?
2. How does school climate influence the academic achievement of dually identified ELs with disabilities?
3. What role does the ESOL department and special education department play in the dually identified ELs' school experience?
4. What type of pressure, if any, do ESOL and special education teachers and ELs experience at this school?
5. What recommendations do ELs and ESOL and special education teachers have for their school to enhance their academic or social experience?

A reflective exercise can help in the identification of the research problem and question as well as the why behind the initial ideas for the approach of the study. One helpful reflective inquiry process is used with doctoral students in an Advanced Qualitative Research Methods course at George Mason University in Fairfax, Virginia. It is referred to as a *Statement of Researcher Identity*; a strategy adapted from Maxwell's (2006) researcher identity memo used to encourage researchers to reflect on a specific set of questions to uncover personal experiences in relationship to the research (Samaras, 2011). See Figure 12-1 for an exemplar.

This problem helps identify what assumptions your researcher identity might create for the study. The purpose of this exercise is not to write a general account of your background and experiences, but instead to describe specific experiences, beliefs, emotions, and motives that emerged from them that have most directly influenced your planned research, and specifically discuss how these have informed and influenced your research (Samaras, 2011). Reflexive exercises assist you in understanding the ways in which your personal characteristics, values, and positions interact with others in the research situation to influence the methodological approach you choose, the methods you use, and the interpretations you make. Such thoughtfulness with the personal dimensions of research leads to more ethical work (Glesne, 2016).

Statement of Researcher Identity Guidelines

Jot down your thoughts to some or all of the following questions (do not analyze them):

- What questions do you want to answer by doing this study?
- What prior experiences have you had that are relevant to your topic?
- What beliefs and assumptions do you have about this topic or setting as a result of these experiences?
- What do you already believe or expect about the answers to your questions and why?
- How have these influenced the way you are approaching this study?
- What potential disadvantages do you think these may create for you and how might you deal with these?

Reflecting on these questions is not only helpful to identify your assumptions, but to identify how to raise your awareness to possible misassumptions that might undermine the validity of the study as you refine your research purpose (Maxwell, 2005; Racines & Samaras, 2015). Munby and Russel (1994) remind researchers that you do have permission to recognize the authority of your experience and it is important to not only recognize it, but to firmly stand in your truth. Our personal experiences influence our understanding of our research topics and the purpose of the study. Lastly, the development of the research problem, purpose, and question[s] is an iterative process and may be revisited before a clear approach is taken, and even then, may change. A visual map or a concept map to "see" all of the components of the study as it is developing might be helpful to better visualize how they are interconnected and used to further develop the conceptual framework.

CONCEPTUAL FRAMEWORK

A *conceptual framework*, or theoretical framework, is defined as the theories, ideas, and definitions, often from multiple disciplines, that inform one's research (Glesne, 2016). These concepts together can create a useful organizational schema for various inquiry questions, often expressed as a visual model to reflect interrelationships between concepts (Figure 12-2; Creswell, 2008). The intention of a conceptual framework is to focus on the major theories related to the concept or topic to help clarify how this research study will be an original contribution to research—answering the "So what?" The framework will ultimately support detailing in narrative form how and what you are studying.

Through this reflective process of my background, experiences, assumptions, feelings, and values with a filter to focus on the specific experiences, beliefs, and motives in relation to the topics, people, and setting for this study resources and concerns have emerged unique to my identity and experiences which may directly influence this planned research project. In an effort to help me really discuss *how* these have informed and influenced my research I have to write as if no one is reading this piece of writing.

I view my inquiry into the experiences of dually identified ELs and teachers of dually identified ELs, also referred to as ESOL teachers, through three distinct lenses that all seem to blend together based on my experiences.

A. What prior experiences have you had that are relevant to your topic or setting?
In terms of setting, I am curious about the experiences of dually identified ELs in a setting where the EL population with disabilities is low. Without previous reflection on this question, I had not realized that I, myself, was an EL student with a disability in a very diverse school, however, not one with a large EL population. Although it seems that most of my friends were African American or Hispanic, none of them spoke a different language at home, so I do remember feeling a bit out of place with my friends. I also remember translating for my parents for many school functions, and although my teachers were kind, I often felt out of place for speaking a language other than English.

With regard to the topic, I certainly do not feel as though any of my teachers had any idea that I felt isolated.

I was an EL student when it seemed as though it was not a negative thing, although I remember hearing people make comments about my family not speaking English or backhanded compliments. I think that is something that I strongly advocate against in my school now.

What beliefs and assumptions do you have about this topic or setting as a result of these experiences? How have these influenced the way you are approaching this project?

B. What questions do you want to answer by doing this study?
I want to know what it's like to be a dually identified EL and an ESOL and Special Education teacher at a public high school with a low proportion of dually identified ELs.

1. What is the perceived school climate of dually identified ELs at this school? How does school climate influence academic achievement of dually identified ELs?
2. How do dually identified ELs perceive themselves academically and socially in this school?
3. What recommendations do dually identified ELs have for their school, in general, and student services and/or instruction to enhance their experience?
4. What has been your interaction with your peers in this school?
5. How do you feel about reading and writing in another language? How do you feel about reading and writing in another language with a disability?
6. How do you feel about being able to speak and learn in two languages?

Figure 12-1. Exemplar researcher identity memo. *(continued)*

What do you already believe or expect about the answers to your questions, and why?

My beliefs about the answers to the aforementioned questions are truly divided between ELs having a neglected experience or one that is so positively supported that they are graciously accepted and transitioned into general education settings with no resistance. I lean more toward the latter only because of the school's location, which is a very affluent area. I feel that perhaps with an overabundance of resources and the lack of labels on this school because the number of minority students is low and the dually identified EL population is low that there is no unspoken stigma to this school climate. I state this because there is no labeling of students as "at-risk" students or treating some students as what is often referred to as triple threat students.

How have your experiences shaped these questions, beliefs, and expectations?

I think my experience as a teacher have been very negative at the school I am currently teaching in. Many of the reasons we do not make gains in our school becomes an endless blame game on dually identified ELs. I know that these experiences have only fueled my personal experience as once an EL with a disability. My personal experiences to persevere and my day-to-day experiences as a teacher have really influenced my questions, and I hope that this school will completely debunk my expectation that what I experience is going on everywhere, regardless of the numbers.

C. What potential advantages do you think the assumptions and experiences that you described create for your study? What potential disadvantages do you think these may create for you, and how might you deal with these?

I am very aware of the socio-historical forces that have constructed my knowledge and have shaped my values. I realize that both my personal experiences and work experience are unique to me. The only potential disadvantage is that I feel my experience has been tainted and will be looking for the negative remarks versus just allowing the data to speak for itself.

I know I have the ability to see things from DuBois' divided consciousness, which is the ability to see things both from the perspective of the dominant and from the perspective of the oppressed. I have only considered my own oppressed way of knowing and experiences and need to be aware of the unique perspectives from my research participants. I must listen intently and clear any agenda out of my head and allow the participants to speak. What a great experience to interview people I do not know and they do not know me. I am aware that I do not like to be judged and will not judge them, instead just listen and allow them to share their own stories.

Figure 12-1 (continued). Exemplar researcher identity memo.

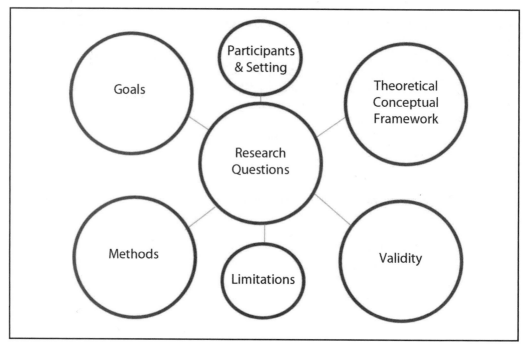

Figure 12-2. Sample organizational schema.

A conceptual framework is referred to as the general literature review of the research; however, it is a review of relevant literature that is also analyzed to further inform your research design and interview questions (Glesne, 2016; Maxwell, 2005). Ensure you are making connections between the concepts, not simply describing them, and that the connections you are making are new ones that cannot be found in previous studies. As you find journal articles and books that inform your study, make sure you review those reference pages to find other literature to review and look for what is missing from those studies—the gap in the research. Glesne (2016) suggests asking yourself further questions about the studies you read: Did the researcher ask surface-level questions? What were the limitations to that study? What recommendations for future research did they recommend? The conceptual framework frames the justification for the study and not only why it is important, but why all of the previous studies have not answered the specific research questions identified by this study. Becker (1986) reminds researchers to use the literature…don't let it use you! (p. 149).

Remember, once you complete your conceptual framework, even though it serves as a map or guide, you can come back to it and adjust it; it iterates throughout your research process and will simultaneously fine-tune your research (Glesne, 2016).

RESEARCH QUESTIONS

Research questions in qualitative research specify what it is you want to understand, and want the field to understand, by conducting your study. The research questions narrow the purpose of a study into specific, open-ended questions and guide how you will study this phenomenon. They do not have to be perfect the first time you develop them. It is helpful to share your drafted research questions with others and ask for feedback. Do they understand what you are asking and what you are trying to learn from this study? Reflect on them. Once you decide on a research question, it is helpful to write it down and keep it posted in front of you wherever you plan to write. This will help you to stay focused on what your study is attempting to answer. Remember that the development of the research question is also an iterative process, so the questions may change.

With epistemological knowledge, exploration of researcher identity and identification or purpose, questions, and problem, this information can help move into consideration of a method/design. As you continue through the process of qualitative research design, it is important to distinguish that the research question is what you want to understand, while interview questions are what you ask in order to gain such understanding (Maxwell, 2005).

METHOD

A qualitative research design intends to answer your research question and the *method* is a strategy that is used to implement that plan—how the study will be conducted. The methods of your design include the processes, procedures, and tools used to collect and analyze data. The primary research designs in qualitative methods include case study, ethnography, narrative, phenomenology, grounded theory, and historical research (Knox, 2004; Patton, 2002). Although this list is not exhaustive, these designs help to gain valuable insights from finding out what people think, do, and know by interviewing, observing, and analyzing documents of data collection, amongst various additional forms of data sources (Patton, 2002). Different research questions have different implications for data collection, and depending on the approach, determine the type of data that will be elicited to help gain an understanding of the phenomenon in question. You should be able to describe the type of data your method will produce, describe each data source used and why you chose it, and then what you will specifically do with that data as you collect it with a detailed timeline.

DATA COLLECTION

Participant and Site Selection

First things first. Where is this study going to take place? It is important to describe where this research will take place (and why) and describe the demographics, the population, and what surrounds the site. How was access gained to the site? A friend? A colleague? The previous example's site was selected due to the low population of ELs, socioeconomic status, and achievement scores and therefore was a unique setting that aligned with what the research question was trying to understand. This is referred to as *purposeful sampling* or extreme sampling (Creswell, 2008; Glesne, 2016).

Purposeful Sampling Strategies

Patton (2002) describes 16 different types of purposeful sampling strategies, some of which include extreme case sampling in which cases are selected based on something extreme or unusual, homogeneous sampling where the cases are all similar, and convenience sampling where the cases are selected based on convenience (Table 12-2). The most important thing to remember about the type of purposeful sampling you will use is that it depends on what you want to know. Each strategy allows you to learn different things about your topic, as does each site. Therefore, it is important to describe your rationale to justify your selections (Creswell, 2008; Glesne, 2016).

Written Informed Consent

Once the type of purposeful sampling is determined, written informed consent must be obtained from each of the participants prior to beginning the study. The consent form should include: (a) an explanation of the purpose of the study, (b) description of any foreseeable risks, (c) description of benefits to their school, education system, and/or district, (d) list of contacts for answers to

TABLE 12-2. SIXTEEN DIFFERENT TYPES OF PURPOSEFUL SAMPLING

TYPE OF PURPOSEFUL SAMPLING	PURPOSE
Extreme or deviant case sampling	Special or extremely unusual manifestations of the phenomenon of interest; can be outliers or extremes of a population
Intensity sampling	Rich examples of the phenomenon of interest; not extreme cases, instead they are cases that sufficiently reflect the phenomenon
Maximum variation (Heterogeneity) sampling	The aim is to sample heterogeneity; researchers use this type of sampling when they want to understand how a phenomenon is seen and understood among different people at different times in different settings
Homogeneous sampling	The aim is to achieve a homogeneous sample; all samples chosen because they have similar traits
Typical case sampling	The aim is to study a trend or phenomenon that is considered average or typical or "normal"
Stratified purposeful sampling	Overall population is separated into separate subgroups based on shared attributes, referred to as *strata*, then probability sample is drawn from those subgroups; facilitates comparisons
Critical case sampling	One case is chosen to study with the expectation that studying it will reveal insights that can be applied to similar cases
Snowball or chain sampling	Identifies people to identify critical cases or other people who have information about a certain phenomenon; the researcher follows this chain of contacts to identify critical cases
Criterion sampling	Selecting cases that meet some type of specific criterion
Theory-based sampling	Selecting cases based on representing a specific theory; this sampling approach aims to understand a concept across various conditions
Confirming and disconfirming cases	Researchers seek out confirming or disconfirming cases to develop a deeper understanding of a phenomenon; intention is to lend credibility to one's research
Opportunistic sampling	Commonly occurs in fieldwork; takes advantage of unexpected; sampling decisions are made during the process of collecting data; often used when little is known about a phenomenon
Random purposeful sampling	The aim is data saturation in qualitative research; the process of identifying a population of interest and developing a way to select cases not based on advanced knowledge of outcomes
Sampling politically important cases	The process of selecting or avoiding a politically sensitive site or unit for analysis
Convenience sampling	A process of selecting subjects based on saving time, money, and effort; lowest credibility; units are not purposefully or strategically selected
Combination or mixed purposeful sampling	Combination or mixed sampling to check credibility of findings; triangulation, flexibility, meets multiple sampling interests and needs

Adapted from Patton, M. Q. (2002). *Qualitative research and evaluation methods* (3rd ed.). Sage.

pertinent questions about this study, (e) a statement that participation is voluntary and that subjects (either student or parent) may refuse to participate without penalty, (f) a statement about the confidentiality of the results, and (g) the time required for the study (Gay et al., 2006). Information about each participant's identity may remain confidential.

Data Sources

One of the most common sources of data in qualitative research is interviews. Miranda (2003) teaches us that interviews are not solely conversations; they have empowerment potential whereby the researcher may assume control over the entire process and reporting of results, while informants also have the power to decide what to say and what to withhold, which both have potential for shifting the results of the study. Freeman (2000) and Enosh and Buchbinder (2005) point out that an interview is about human contact, true understanding of their reality, and respect. Maxwell (2005) also states that interviewing is an efficient and valid way to understand an individual's perspective. Interviews can be audio-recorded and participants should be reminded to speak freely. If devices are used to record audio, Twining et al. (2017) recommend that a full description of those devices be included. Reflective fieldnotes should be taken throughout the interview and should include notes regarding facial expressions, body movement, and nonverbal cues. It is critical to restate here that your research questions are what you want to understand, while interview questions are what you ask people in order to gain that understanding (Maxwell, 2005). The questions you ask must be open-ended and require insight so that participants can elaborate on what they think. Semi-structured interviews allow general questions to be asked and followed up by clarifying probes to further explain their thoughts. An example of interview questions that were asked of participants describing their experiences in a public high school with a low proportion of dually identified ELs with a disability included:

- What has been your experience as a student/teacher in this school?
- How would you describe the school climate?
- What has been your interaction with your peers in this school?
- What are your opinions on the school's student services and clubs/programs?
- What recommendations do you have for this school to enhance your experience?

Focus groups, also referred to as group interviews, provide an opportunity to collect data that may not arise in one-on-one interviews due to various interactions or simply dynamics like group-think within the group (Ravitch & Carl, 2016). Focus groups help examine how ideas develop within a certain cultural or group context and tend to generate the type of data related to content and/or process (Ravitch & Carl, 2016). Focus groups are advantageous to facilitating the expression of ideas and experiences that might be left unstated in a single interview. However, some participants may feel more reluctant to share their experiences or perspectives in front of a group of people. Participants should be encouraged to comment in relation to each other's comments, thoughts, and experiences. It also should be noted that the guidelines and considerations for transcripts that apply to interviews also apply to focus groups.

As aforementioned, qualitative research typically relies on more than one single method for obtaining data. This practice, referred to as *triangulation,* is used to further validate but also deepen interpretations of the data being collected (Glesne, 2016). Triangulation involves taking different lenses and examining a conclusion from them. *Member checking,* or informant feedback, is a technique used to triangulate data intended to further establish credibility as participants can verify the accuracy of transcripts as well as emergent findings. The goal of triangulation is to ensure enough data has been collected and the right kinds of data to provide information to answer each research question. Observations made at the research site can support you in drawing inferences that cannot necessarily be gained by only the interview data (Maxwell, 2005). A researcher can learn a lot about human behavior from direct observations that can help explain a specific action or event. Additionally, there are several documents that are collected including journals, court records, test scores, school records, and/or other sources of written documents. Triangulating observations, documents, and interviews can provide a more detailed account of what is really happening at a site and may provide more insight into the site's culture (Glesne, 2016).

DATA ANALYSIS

Data analysis is a recursive process throughout the entire data collection period and is iterative because a researcher should start to identify emerging patterns and themes for the coding process when the data collection process begins. An iterative process involves visiting and revisiting research questions numerous times and constantly scanning data for patterns and themes to be transformed into categories. This main categorizing strategy used, called *coding*, will organize the data into broader themes (Maxwell, 2005).

The initial step in qualitative analysis is to read the data or interview transcripts. The transcription of the interviews is a very demanding process, yet it is highly recommended to transcribe the notes yourself so you can truly listen to the words spoken by your participants. Transcription may also be conducted via various software options, such as Nvivo or Dragon NaturallySpeaking, or other voice recognition systems. It is important to note that software programs, while intended to save you time, often have punctuation issues, diction errors, and/or inaudible words that make phrases intelligible for transcription. With both types of transcription, each time you listen to the interview becomes an opportunity for analysis, as does the process of transcribing (Maxwell, 2005). A review of observational notes along with relistening to the interviews helps researchers develop an overall understanding of the phenomenon in question. A more systematic analysis begins after all data are collected and each interview is transcribed.

Coding consists of categorizing and organizing data into initial and broad themes to uncover patterns; thematic analysis (Glesne, 2016; Maxwell, 2005; Wolcott, 2009). The goal in qualitative research is not to count items, but to rearrange them into categories that help compare things in the same category in order to develop a theoretical concept or organize the data into general themes or topics (Maxwell, 2005). Such categories can provide insight into what is going on and can be generated from the exact words spoken by the participants, creating both emic and etic categories to analyze. *Emic* categories are provided by the insider's point of view (the one being studied), whereas *etic* is from the perspective of the observer and is essential in understanding how others see the world around them. Brantlinger et al. (2005) reiterate that qualitative studies typically include the emic to focus on participants' personal meanings and intend to give voice to historically marginalized people, including students with disabilities. This method of coding can begin with highlighting sentences in a specific color for each theme that emerges, where each code can be given an abbreviation under each category. See Table 12-3 for an example of initial emergent codes from a transcription excerpt.

This process can be extremely helpful in trying to create a sense of massive amounts of data in an organized manner. Strauss and Corbin (1998) remind researchers about this inductive process, an approach referred to as *grounded theory approach*, where the theory arises as you analyze your data and slowly begins to answer your research question. As you begin to identify codes to what is emerging, ask a colleague to confirm codes using a blank transcription. Also referred to as *member-checking*, researchers check with participants in their study to ascertain if participants' responses are being understood and data interpreted. Member-checking is also used to improve the accuracy, credibility, and validity of a study. Once the themes are identified and confirmed, go back to the observations, transcriptions, and documents once again, allow the data to start speaking for itself, and find confirmation, or triangulation, in the verbiage to validate each theme identified.

An example of five themes that emerged from the aforementioned study include: (a) dually identified EL cultural factors/experience, (b) school climate, (c) contradictions between policy and practice, (d) academic achievement, and (e) teacher quality/instruction.

TABLE 12-3. INITIAL EMERGENT CODES FOR TRANSCRIPTION AND INITIAL THEMES AND CATEGORIES EXCERPTS

SELECTIVE CODING

Cluster	Code	Description
ELL CULTURAL	CHALNGS	Challenges
FACTORS/EXPERIENCE		Faced/Acculturations
	ELLPRCS	ELL Self-Perception
SCHOOL CLIMATE	CHOICE	Different Choices Needed
	COTEACHING	Co-Teaching
	ESOLDPTS	ESOL Department Support
	ESOLNEEDS	ESOL Needs
	LANG	Languages
	PRESR	Pressure Faced
	RCMD	Recommendations
	SCLIMATE	School Climate
	SECLN	Seclusion
	TRADITION	High School Traditions
	UNQDEM	Unique School Demographics
CONTRADICTIONS	CNTRDCTIN	Contradictions
ACADEMIC ACHIEVEMENT	ELLCHAL	Barrier Faced by Els in Academics
	ESOLTACTBL	ESOL Teacher/Department Chair Accountability
	PEERTUT	Peer Tutoring for ELLs Resource
	STFNG	Staffing

It is your ethical responsibility as a researcher to be aware of the ultimate power that you have to control the selection of design and method, selection of participants, and ultimately report findings that will be outlined next. You must question yourself and be confident in whose story you have the responsibility of telling when your study is complete (Holstein & Gubrium, 2008). Qualitative research studies can find untold stories from unheard populations in the field of education who are often marginalized. It might be your story that is needed in the field to shift policy and improve practice to ultimately ensure equitable opportunities and outcomes for all students.

RESULTS (LIMITATIONS AND VALIDITY)

The results ask the researcher to return to their main research question for the study and use evidence from the data analysis process from stories shared, observations made, and documents collected. There are three topics that also must be included in the results section. These topics are *limitations*, *implications*, and *validity*. Let's begin with study limitations.

Researchers must take a hard look at the design of their study, which may be a limitation. To increase validity, you must ask yourself to go back and see if multiple other sources of data-collection methods could have been used (Maxwell, 2005). This might be the case when there is not a large number of participants and might limit the triangulation and validation of data. Maybe you had a small amount of data sources because you only interviewed a small amount of people and recognize that you could have used pictures, videos, or journaling to provide a more diverse range of information for a better assessment of the explanations developed (Maxwell, 2005). What about time? Did limited time play a factor in the decisions made in your study? Keep in mind that you can identify future studies from your limitations in site, participants, or data sources, so the implications could help you identify your next best researchable question.

In qualitative research, validity (or trustworthiness) and reliability (or consistency) are discussed in terms of the credibility and dependability of the instrumentation and results of the study. There must be credibility in order to have dependability; in qualitative research, credibility and trustworthiness is strengthened with a layer of transparency shared in the analysis and interpretation of data and how data interpretation is substantiated. Although being transparent and explicit about data is critical to enable credibility and trustworthiness, it is not sufficient (Twining et al., 2017). It is also the researcher's assumptions and decisions that must be made explicitly clear. A researcher's biases and assumptions must be included in the discussion that might influence the research.

Although researcher bias is another threat to validity, it can be addressed through critically reflecting before and continually throughout the data collection process through memos. Writing and reflecting, as in the Statement of Researcher Identity exercise, can be extremely helpful in raising your awareness before you begin conducting the study to help clarify how your values and expectations influenced your conduct and conclusions of the study (Maxwell, 2005). Indeed, reflecting helps you "experience the self through the eyes of the other" and can be powerful in ensuring your biases are brought to light (John-Steiner, 2000, p. 5).

SELF-STUDY OVERVIEW:
AN ADVANCED QUALITATIVE RESEARCH METHOD

This section is not left to the end as an afterthought. It is intended to provide a space to exclusively consider self-study research methods as a much-needed option in addition to more traditional qualitative research methods. Educators can begin to take control of their profession, especially in the field of special education, with greater emphasis on the knowledge and learning derived from researching their own practice. This overview will make clear the methodological imperatives associated with conducting a self-study, moving away from the deception that self-study is anything less than rigorous scholarship, and demonstrate how self-study research methodology transcends beyond the self across all disciplines (Racines, 2016; Racines & Samaras, 2015).

Can self-study incorporate other methods? Yes. Methods that have been included in self-study research include narrative inquiry, reflective portfolios, and/or arts-based methods (LaBoskey, 2004; Samaras & Freese, 2006). Feldman, Paugh, and Mills (2004) differentiate what sounds like action research from self-study and explain that action research provides the "methods for self-study, but what makes self-study is the methodological features" (p. 974). Self-study researchers use their experiences as a resource for their research and situate their 'self' in their practice with the goal of reframing their beliefs and improving their professional practice as well as themselves on a personal level (Feldman, 2003). Action research, in other words, is more about what the teacher does, and less about who the teacher is. Self-study also is not done in isolation and instead requires collaboration to build new understandings through dialogue, critical reflection, and validation of findings to ultimately improve student learning (Samaras, 2011). Self-study has shown to be useful to an array of educators coming from multiple disciplines and programs (Kosnik et al., 2006). Self-study, acknowledging the role of the teacher, has most recently been included in efforts to redesign courses in teacher preparation programs to again shift from talking to actionable steps toward inclusion in teaching and learning with the powerful use of personal narratives (Bertrand & Porcher, 2020). A brief outline of the following steps provides guidelines for educators who are new to self-study research (Samaras, 2011).

The five foci, or systematic methodological components of self-study, serve as guideposts or steps in applying self-study teacher research (Samaras, 2011). The first step begins with a question about your practice that begins from personal experiences or observations made in the classroom; personal situated inquiry . The second step is critical collaborative inquiry that is supported by a colleague or a peer, also referred to as a *critical friend* (CF) in self-study. The purpose of having a CF in self-study research is to move your practice beyond your own individual perspective, gained through critical and reflective questioning, in an effort to increase validity in your personal claims. The third foci is the overall purpose of self-study, which is to improve learning, and answers the question: What is the true value of this research study to the larger field and who will benefit? The fourth foci is transparency. The entire research process is to be clearly documented and as transparent as possible. The fifth foci is to make your study public so it is open to critique. The ultimate purpose is to share the new knowledge that is generated from the study and disseminate it with others. The result is the opportunity for growth in and out of the field of education, as well as the opportunity to influence policy and practice (Samaras, 2011). Table 12-4 includes a list of common misconceptions associated with the qualitative research, and Table 12-5 provides additional resources to consult.

SUMMARY

Qualitative research provides valuable insights from what people think, do, and know. It encompasses significantly more than data-gathering techniques; epistemology guides methodological decision-making as our very presuppositions are what lead us to our choices to use different qualitative methods, ask different questions, and draw conclusions (Bryman, 1984; Koro-Ljungberg et al., 2009; Patton, 2002; Willis, 2007). This chapter is not prescriptive nor linear. However, each key interconnected component presented—research problem, conceptual framework, research question(s), method(s), validity, and results—should be revisited, and an iterative process is encouraged throughout the research process. Research questions are key to clarifying what you want to understand, as well as what you want the field to understand, and should be kept at the forefront throughout the study. Qualitative research studies can tell powerful stories from our diverse field of education that need to be shared to improve practice and ultimately ensure equitable opportunities and outcomes for all students around the world.

CHAPTER REVIEW

1. In what ways does the researcher play a role in qualitative research methods?
2. How are the key components of qualitative research methods connected, and on which beliefs and assumptions are they based?
3. How can you ensure that your research questions are central to your research design and data collection?
4. How is qualitative data analysis iterative, and what does this mean for how you engage as a researcher in the data analysis process?
5. What are the five foci of self-study research methodology, and how does it differ from traditional qualitative research methods?

TABLE 12-4. COMMON MISCONCEPTIONS AND CLARIFICATIONS ABOUT QUALITATIVE RESEARCH

MISCONCEPTION	BETTER UNDERSTANDING
Selecting a method is the driving force toward choosing a study.	Methodology should not drive a study; research questions drive a study. Focusing on a specific methodology will inhibit the types of research questions addressed.
Self-study is an advanced qualitative method chosen to study the self and does not relate to special education.	Self-study is a growing genre of research methodology and is used by teacher educators to improve their practice, contribute to the knowledge base on teaching and learning, and acknowledge the role of the teacher educator in teachers' learning. It can bring awareness to often marginalized or underrepresented student and teacher populations.
Qualitative research is less scientific than quantitative research because findings cannot be generalizable as easily to the general population.	Qualitative research follows an iterative, yet structured process where each component must be included.

TABLE 12-5. ADDITIONAL RESOURCES

RESOURCE	DESCRIPTION
Glesne, C. (2016). *Becoming qualitative researchers: An introduction* (5th ed.). Pearson Education.	This text provides an introduction to qualitative methods of inquiry.
Maxwell, J. (2005). *Qualitative research design: An interactive approach* (2nd ed.). Sage.	This text provides an in-depth discussion of qualitative methods from a realist perspective.
Ravitch, S. M., & Carl, N. C. M. (2016). *Qualitative research: Bridging the conceptual, theoretical, and methodological.* Sage.	This text provides an introduction to qualitative research.
Samaras, A. P. (2011). *Self-study teacher research: Improving your practice through collaborative inquiry.* Sage.	This text provides an introduction to self-study.

REFERENCES

Becker, H.S. (1986). *Writing for social scientists: How to start and finish your thesis, book, or article*. University of Chicago Press.

Bertrand, S., & Porcher, K. (2020). Teacher educators as disruptors redesigning courses in teacher preparation programs to prepare white preservice teachers. *Journal of Culture and Values in Education, 3*(1), 72-88. https://doi.org/10.46303/jcve.03.01.5

Brandenburg, R. T. (2008). *Powerful pedagogy: Self-study of a teacher educator's practice*. Springer.

Brantlinger, E., Jimenez, R., Klingner, J., Pugach, M., & Richardson, V. (2005). Qualitative studies in special education. *Exceptional Children, 71*(2), 195–207. https://doi.org/10.1177/001440290507100205

Bryman, A. (1984). The debate about quantitative and qualitative research: A question of method or epistemology? *The British Journal of Sociology, 35*(1), 75-92.

Carter, S. M., & Little, M. (2007). Justifying knowledge, justifying method, taking action: Epistemologies, methodologies, and methods in qualitative research. *Qualitative Health Research, 17*(10), 1316-1328. https://doi.org/10.1177/1049732307306927

Creswell, J. W. (2008). *Educational research: Planning, conducting, and evaluating quantitative and qualitative research* (3rd ed). Pearson Education.

Creswell, J. W. (2013). *Qualitative inquiry and research design: Choosing among five approaches*. Sage.

Efinger, J., Maldonado, N., & McArdle, G. (2004). PhD student's perceptions of the relationship between philosophy and research: A qualitative investigation. *The Qualitative Report, 9*(4), 732-759.

Enosh, G., & Buchbinder, E. (2005). The interactive construction of narrative styles in sensitive interviews: The case of domestic violence research. *Qualitative Inquiry, 11*(4), 588-617. https://doi.org/10.1177/1077800405275054

Feldman, A. (2003). Validity and quality in self-study. *Educational Researcher, 32*(3):26-28.

Feldman, A., Paugh, P., & Mills, G. (2004). *Self-study through action research. International handbook of self-study of teaching and teacher education practices* (pp. 943–978). Kluwer Academic Publishers.

Ferri, B. A., Gallagher, D., & Connor, D. J. (2011). Pluralizing methodologies in the field of LD: From "what works" to what matters. *Learning Disability Quarterly, 34*(3), 222–223.

Freeman, M. (2000). Knocking on doors: On constructing culture. *Qualitative Inquiry, 6*(3), 359-269. https://doi.org/10.1177/107780040000600305

Gay, L. R., Mills, G., & Airasian, P. (2006). *Educational research: Competencies for analysis and applications* (8th ed.). Prentice Hall.

Glesne, C. (2016). *Becoming qualitative researchers: An introduction* (5th ed.). Pearson Education.

Holstein, J. A., & Gubrium, J. F. (Eds.). (2008). *Inside interviewing: New lenses, new concerns*. Sage.

John-Steiner, V. (2000). *Creative collaboration*. Oxford University Press.

Klingner, J. K., & Boardman, A. G. (2011). Addressing the "research gap" in special education through mixed methods. *Learning Disability Quarterly, 34*(3), 208-218. https://doi.org/10.1177/0731948711417559

Knox, K. (2004). A researcher's dilemma—Philosophical and methodological pluralism. *Electronic Journal of Business Research Methods, 2*(2), 119-127.

Koro-Ljungberg, M., Yendol-Hoppey, D., Smith, J. J., & Hayes, S. B. (2009). Epistemological awareness, instantiation of methods, and uninformed methodological ambiguity in qualitative research projects. *Educational Researcher, 38*(9), 687-699.

Kosnik, C., Beck, C., Freese, A. R., & Samaras, A. P. (Eds.). (2006). *Making a difference in teacher education through self-study: Studies of personal, professional, and program renewal*. Springer.

LaBoskey, V. K. (2004). The methodology of self-study and its theoretical underpinnings. In J. J. Loughran, M. L. Hamilton, V. L. LaBoskey, & T. Rusell (Eds.), *International handbook of self-study of teaching and teacher education practices* (pp. 817-870). Kluwer.

Luttrel, W. (Ed.). (2010). *Qualitative educational research: Readings in reflexive methodology and transformative practice*. Routledge.

Maxwell, J. (2005). *Qualitative research design: An interactive approach* (2nd ed.). Sage.

Maxwell, J. A. (2006). Literature reviews of, and for, educational research. *Educational Researcher, 35*(9), 28-31.

Miranda, M. "Keta." (2003). *Homegirls in the public sphere*. University of Texas Press.

Munby, H., & Russel, T. (1994). The authority of experience in learning to teach: Messages from a physics methods class. *Journal of Teacher Education, 45*(2), 86-95.

Nudzor, H. P. (2009). A critical commentary on combined methods approach to researching educational and social issues. *Issues in Educational Research, 19*(2), 114-127.

Patton, M. Q. (1999). Enhancing the quality and credibility of qualitative analysis. *Health Services Research, 34*(2), 1189-1208.

Patton, M. Q. (2002). *Qualitative research and evaluation methods* (3rd ed.). Sage.

Racines, D. (2016). Using self-study to advance research in TESOL teacher education: Examining my EL identity to improve my effectiveness as an instructional coach with teachers of ELs. *TESOL: The Newsletter of the Teacher Educator Interest Section*.

Racines, D. E., & Samaras, A. P. (2015). Duality in practice and mentorship of an English learner instructional coach. In K. Pithouse-Morgan & A. P. Samaras (Eds.), *Polyvocal professional learning through self-study research* (pp. 111-125). Sense Publishers.

Ravitch, S. M., & Carl, N. C. M. (2016). *Qualitative research: Bridging the conceptual, theoretical, and methodological*. Sage.

Ryan, F., Coughlan, M., & Cronin, P. (2007). Step-by-step guide to critiquing research. Part 2: qualitative research. *British Journal of Nursing (BJN), 16*(12), 738-744.

Samaras, A. P. (2011). *Self-study teacher research: Improving your practice through collaborative inquiry*. Sage.

Samaras, A. P., & Freese, A. R. (2006). *Self-study of teaching practices primer*. Peter Lang.

Scott, L. A., & Alexander, Q. (2019). Strategies for recruiting and retaining black male special education teachers. *Remedial and Special Education, 40*(4), 236-247. https://doi.org/10.1177/0741932517732636

Strauss, A., & Corbin, J. (1998). *Basics of qualitative research: Grounded theory procedures and techniques*. Sage.

Tewksbury, R. (2009). Qualitative versus quantitative methods: Understanding why qualitative methods are superior for criminology and criminal justice. *Journal of Theoretical and Philosophical Criminology, 1*(1), 38-58.

Twining, P., Heller, R., Nussbaum, M., & Tsai, C. (2017). Some guidance on conducting and reporting qualitative studies. *Computers & Education, 106*, A1–A9. https://doi.org/10.1016/j.compedu.2016.12.002

Valsiner, J. (2000). Data as representations: Contextualizing qualitative and quantitative research strategies. *Social Science Information, 39*(1), 99-113.

Willis, J. W. (2007). *Foundations of qualitative research: Interpretive and critical approaches*. Sage.

Wolcott, H. F. (2009). *Writing up qualitative research* (3rd ed.). Sage.

Mixed-Methods Research

With contributions from Melissa C. Jenkins, PhD

INTRODUCTION

This chapter introduces mixed-methods research in education with an emphasis on its potential role in special education. An overview of the characteristics of mixed-methods research is provided, along with comparisons to quantitative research, qualitative research, and multi-method research. The value of integrating quantitative and qualitative data to provide contextualized understanding of what works in special education is discussed. The three core mixed-methods research models (convergent mixed methods, explanatory sequential mixed methods, and exploratory sequential mixed methods) are described. Examples from published special education research are used as illustrations of those models. A systematic framework for formulating, planning, conducting, and reporting a mixed-methods study is provided, with a detailed explanation of the steps within each stage. A case study is used to further elaborate the steps within the framework and facilitate discussion and application. Finally, features of quality mixed-methods research are shared to guide readers and researchers in evaluating this emerging methodology.

Hott, B. L., Brigham, F. J., & Peltier, C.
Research Methods in Special Education (pp. 239-255).
© 2021 SLACK Incorporated.

CHAPTER OBJECTIVES

→ Identify the characteristics of mixed-methods research.

→ Distinguish mixed-methods research from mono-method research and multi-method research.

→ Explain the rationale for using mixed methods for special education research.

→ Relate the basic models of mixed-methods research to specific research questions.

→ Identify quality indicators for mixed-methods research.

KEY TERMS

- **Convergent Mixed Methods**: A mixed-methods research design in which quantitative and qualitative data are collected at approximately the same time, analyzed separately, then merged for interpretation.

- **Explanatory Sequential Mixed Methods**: A mixed-methods design in which qualitative data are collected after quantitative data for the purpose of elaborating or explaining findings from the quantitative phase.

- **Exploratory Sequential Mixed Methods**: A mixed-methods design in which qualitative data are used to develop an intervention or measure that is subsequently administered and quantitatively analyzed.

- **Integration**: Systematic and intentional blending of quantitative and qualitative research elements.

- **Legitimation**: Documenting evidence of design quality and interpretive rigor across all phases of a mixed-methods design.

- **Mixed-Methods Research**: A research design that systematically integrates elements of quantitative and qualitative research in order to expand the breadth of understanding of a given research topic.

- **Mono-Method Research**: Research involving a single methodology—either quantitative or qualitative.

- **Multi-Method Research**: Research designs that incorporate quantitative and qualitative elements that are studied, analyzed, and interpreted separately.

CASE STUDY

Rhonda F. is a special educator at a large urban high school. Her school failed to meet state accreditation standards, partially due to low pass rates of students with disabilities on the end-of-course assessment for Algebra 1. Beyond the school impact, the students' difficulties with Algebra 1 have long-term implications for their on-time graduation. Rhonda would like to address this problem through her dissertation research. She recognizes that her research topic presents many layers of complexity that will need to be addressed. First, although her potential participants are all students with disabilities, they are a diverse group in terms of number of learning characteristics. They receive special education services under a variety of eligibility categories (e.g., Specific Learning Disability, Autism, Other Health Impairment), many of them are English Language Learners, and some of them are repeating Algebra 1. Rhonda's second concern relates to outcome measures. She knows there are a number of assessments that she could use as quantitative measures of algebraic reasoning, but she also wants to have a deeper understanding of the students' problem-solving processes as they work through the intervention stages. Rhonda is not sure how to develop a strong research design that will address these complexities.

Mixed-Methods Research

Mixed-methods research has been described by some as the third wave or third paradigm in research, following quantitative and qualitative methods (Collins et al., 2012; Klinger & Boardman, 2011). Mixed-methods research emerged as a distinct methodology over a period of approximately four decades and was formalized as a community of research in 2000, after the Handbook of Mixed-Methods Research (Onwuegbuzie & Corrigan, 2018) was developed. Mixed-methods research experienced a rapid expansion of use in many social sciences fields in 2006 and subsequent years (Timans et al., 2019). Although it is still evolving, mixed-methods researchers have developed their own vocabulary, procedures, and philosophical perspectives that are distinct from quantitative and qualitative methods (Lavelle et al., 2013). Mixed-methods research is also distinct from quantitative and qualitative research designs in that its roots are grounded in applied disciplines such as nursing and education (Timans et al., 2019).

Mixed-methods research, as the name suggests, combines elements of quantitative and qualitative research approaches. Quantitative methods are characterized by collection and analysis of numeric data to answer focused questions, whereas qualitative research seeks to develop understanding of a phenomenon by collecting information from participants in the form of words or imagery (Creswell & Guetterman, 2019). Please see Chapter 2 for more information about each of these mono-method research designs. Elements from each of the mono-method forms, which may include perspectives, data collection, data analysis, and inferencing techniques, are systematically blended for the purpose of expanding the depth of understanding of the research topic (Office of Behavioral and Social Sciences Research [OBSSR], 2011; Plano Clark, 2019; Timans et al., 2019). This intentional blending of quantitative and qualitative elements is called *integration*. Integration is key to distinguishing mixed-methods research from other multi-method research designs, which include quantitative and qualitative elements that are studied, analyzed, and interpreted separately (OBSSR, 2011; Plano Clark, 2019). Figures 13-1 and 13-2 provide a visual comparison of multi-method research and mixed-methods research.

Value of Mixed-Methods Research

Proponents of mixed-methods research value the differing perspectives of quantitative and qualitative methods in contributing to the understanding of a research problem (Timans et al., 2019). Quantitative methods are valued for direct observation and measurement of events that allow researchers to identify relationships, while qualitative methods are valued for providing contextual information that contributes to understanding the mechanisms behind those relationships (Collins et al., 2006; Plano Clark, 2019). In some mixed-methods designs, integration of quantitative and qualitative methods allows researchers to understand what happened and why or how it happened. In other designs, integration guides the development of tools, measures, or interventions that reflect the needs and experiences of those who will use them (McCrudden et al., 2019). Mixed-methods research is valued for addressing complex research questions in ways that facilitate practical application (Klinger & Boardman, 2011; Plano Clark, 2019).

Mixed-Methods Research in Special Education

Educational researchers and practitioners agree that understanding how individuals learn is a complex problem (Klinger & Boardman, 2011; Plano Clark, 2019). Rhonda's potential research topic in the case study demonstrates some of the complexities that must be addressed. These complexities were elaborated by Schoonenboom, Hitchcock, and Burke Johnson when they wrote, "It is difficult to overstate the degree of diversity across students, the settings in which they are educated, and how these interact with contexts outside of school" (2018, p. 34).

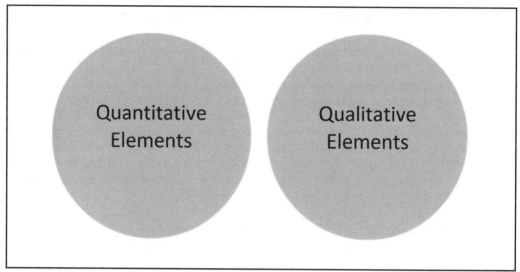

Figure 13-1. Diagram showing the separate quantitative and qualitative elements in multi-method designs.

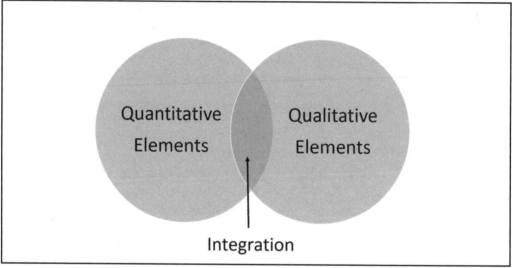

Figure 13-2. Diagram showing the integration of quantitative and qualitative data in mixed methods designs.

Education is a complex endeavor for researchers and practitioners and special education adds an additional layer of complexity. Special education, as an applied practice, is focused on identifying the unique learning characteristics of the individual student and matching those characteristics to interventions that are grounded in research (Ghesquiere & Van der Aalsvoort, 2004). Historically, quantitative methods have dominated education research, and randomized controlled trials have been described as ideal for identifying functional relations between students and outcomes (National Research Council, 2002). Yet, these purely quantitative methods may overlook meaningful contextual information about participant learning characteristics, the learning environment, treatment acceptability, feasibility, and instructional delivery that advance our understanding of teaching and learning (Ghesquiere & Van der Aalsvoort, 2004; Lavelle et al., 2013; Schoonenboom et al., 2018). These types of contextual factors are of particular relevance in special education (Seethaler & Fuchs, 2005).

It is proposed that thoughtfully integrating quantitative and qualitative elements into a mixed-methods design allows researchers to draw on the strengths of the mono-method forms while off-setting the weaknesses (Lavelle et al., 2013). In the field of special education research, this means that combined quantitative data and detailed contextual information from qualitative sources can potentially guide the development of interventions that are well aligned with real-world classroom environments (Klinger & Boardman, 2011; Plano Clark, 2019). This, in turn, may be a factor in addressing the research-to-practice gap in special education (Plano Clark, 2019).

Although the potential for mixed-methods research to address the complexities of special education is well documented, special education researchers have been slow to adopt the methodology. A recent study of publication prevalence rates found that mixed methods were used in 11.15% of special education research published between 2000 and 2005, and 14.53% of special education research studies published in *Exceptional Children* from 2000 to 2015 (Onwuegbuzie & Corrigan, 2018). In contrast, mixed-methods research made up over 30% of publications in the fields of nursing, program evaluation, and mathematics education (Onwuegbuzie & Corrigan, 2018). The slow adoption by special education researchers may be linked to incomplete understanding of the types of mixed-methods research and limited guidance related to use of mixed methods for special education (Houchins, 2015).

CHARACTERISTICS AND MODELS OF MIXED-METHODS RESEARCH

As many as 35 different variations of mixed-methods research designs have been identified in published research (Leech & Onwuegbuzie, 2009). The variations reflect differences in the sequence of and weight given to the quantitative and qualitative strands, the degree of integration, and the role of a philosophical or theoretical framework in guiding the research (Creswell & Guetterman, 2019; McCrudden et al., 2019; Timans et al., 2019). Three basic models of mixed-methods research designs lie at the core of these variations: convergent designs, explanatory sequential designs, and exploratory sequential designs (Creswell & Guetterman, 2019). Table 13-1 presents an overview of these three designs, which are described in detail in this chapter.

Convergent Designs

Convergent designs may also be called concurrent or parallel designs. Researchers using convergent mixed-methods research collect quantitative and qualitative data at approximately the same time. The data from each strand are analyzed separately, then merged for interpretation (Creswell & Guetterman, 2019; McCrudden et al., 2019). Integration during convergent design data collection entails using overlapping quantitative and qualitative measures of a construct. Integration during the analysis and interpretation phases is intended to expand depth of understanding, provide corroboration, or identify divergence in findings (McCrudden et al., 2019).

Bostrom and Broberg (2017) used a convergent design when they studied the construct of well-being in youth with intellectual disabilities using a quantitative measure, the Wellbeing in Special Education Questionnaire (Bostrom et al., 2016), and a qualitative measure, semi-structured interviews. In the interpretation phase, they compared the findings from the questionnaire and interviews and found that the interviews corroborated the findings of the questionnaire. The convergent design used by Bostrom and Broberg is diagrammed in Figure 13-3.

Explanatory Sequential Designs

Explanatory sequential mixed-methods designs use qualitative data collection and analysis to elaborate or explain findings from the quantitative phase of a study (McCrudden et al., 2019). Quantitative data are collected and analyzed first. Quantitative findings guide the selection of

TABLE 13-1. COMPARISON OF THE BASIC MIXED-METHODS RESEARCH DESIGNS

DESIGN	DATA COLLECTION SEQUENCE	DATA ANALYSIS SEQUENCE	PURPOSE
Convergent	Quantitative and qualitative data are collected simultaneously.	Quantitative and qualitative data are analyzed separately at approximately the same time, then merged to compare results.	Merged data are used to identify points of convergence or divergence.
Explanatory	Quantitative data are collected and analyzed first. Qualitative data are collected in a second phase.	Quantitative data are analyzed first and guide qualitative data collection.	Qualitative data are used to explain or elaborate quantitative findings.
Exploratory	Qualitative data are collected and analyzed first. Quantitative data are collected in a second phase.	Qualitative data are analyzed first to guide quantitative data collection methods.	Qualitative data guide the development of quantitative variables or measures.

participants for the subsequent qualitative phase. The participants for the qualitative phase may be selected as representatives of a specific quantitative outcome. For example, researchers may wish to obtain contextual (i.e., qualitative) data related to high-performers or low-performers on a specific quantitative measure.

Damianidou and Phtiaka (2018) used an explanatory sequential design in their study of teacher attitudes and inclusive instructional practices for students with disabilities. They surveyed 536 teachers to evaluate general trends and attitudes related to inclusive instruction. Descriptive and inferential statistics revealed contradictions between the teachers' reported values related to inclusive practices and their implementation of inclusive practices. The researchers then utilized purposeful sampling to select and interview 21 teachers who represented specific response patterns found in the survey data. The intent of the interviews was to elicit additional information related to the contradictory findings from the quantitative phase. The qualitative data were analyzed to identify themes and make connections to social, historical, and ideological values related to disabilities and inclusion. Data from both phases were then integrated to describe teacher attitudes related to inclusive instruction and contextual factors that contribute to those attitudes. The explanatory sequential design used by Damianidou and Phtiaka is diagrammed in Figure 13-4.

Exploratory Sequential Designs

Exploratory sequential mixed-methods designs include qualitative data that is collected and analyzed before quantitative data. The qualitative data are often used to develop a measure or intervention, which is subsequently administered and quantitatively analyzed (McCrudden et al., 2019). The final integrated analysis and interpretation supports the generalization or application of the findings from the initial qualitative phase (Creswell & Guetterman, 2019).

Boveda and Aronson (2019) utilized an exploratory sequential design in a large, multiphase research project designed to develop and establish validity for the Intersectional Competence Measure

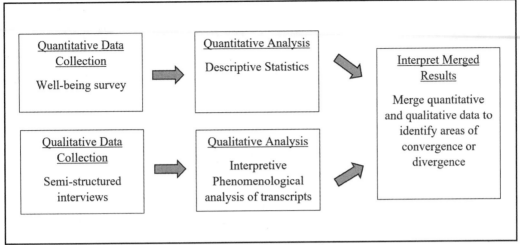

Figure 13-3. Diagram of the convergent mixed-methods design used by Bostrom and Broberg (2018).

(ICM) as a tool to assess the readiness of preservice educators to work with diverse students and families. The researchers utilized qualitative focus groups to identify contextually situated indicators of intersectional competence among general and special educators. (Intersectional competence refers to an understanding of the relationship of biological, social, and cultural characteristics with an individual's life experiences.) The analysis of the data from the focus groups resulted in the development of draft items for the ICM. The researchers then returned to the focus groups seeking clarity of the drafted items, which ultimately became questions on the published version of the ICM. Figure 13-5 provides a diagram of the exploratory sequential design used by Boveda and Aronson.

PLANNING AND CONDUCTING A MIXED-METHODS RESEARCH STUDY

In broad terms, the sequence of planning and conducting a mixed-methods study is not markedly different from that of a mono-method study. However, there is added complexity in formulating a design that can logically and efficiently integrate quantitative and qualitative methods in a manner that leads to meaningful and defensible results (Plano Clark, 2019). Special attention must be given to the feasibility of conducting a study that incorporates both quantitative and qualitative methods (Collins et al., 2006; OBSSR, 2011). Furthermore, because integration is such a defining feature of rigorous mixed-methods research, researchers are advised to consider integration options for each stage of the study. Planning for integration is a fundamental methodological challenge for novice and experienced mixed-methods researchers alike (Plano Clark, 2019).

Collins, Onwuegbuzie, and Sutton (2006) proposed a four-stage process for conducting mixed-methods research: (1) formulation, (2) planning, (3) implementation, and (4) interpretation. Here, we incorporate the work of Collins et al. (2006) and other mixed-methods research experts to further explain the steps within each stage and propose integration considerations. Although the stages occur in sequential order, the suggested sequence of steps within each stage vary across mixed-methods research experts. We will use ideas and information related to Rhonda's research in the Case Study to explore the concepts in each stage and demonstrate planning for a mixed-methods research study in special education.

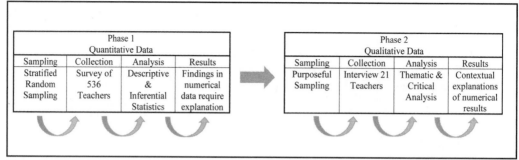

Figure 13-4. Diagram of the explanatory sequential design. (Adapted from Damianidou, E., & Phtiaka, H. [2018]. Implementing inclusion in disabling settings: The role of teachers' attitudes and practices. *International Journal of Inclusive Education, 22*[10], 1078-1092.)

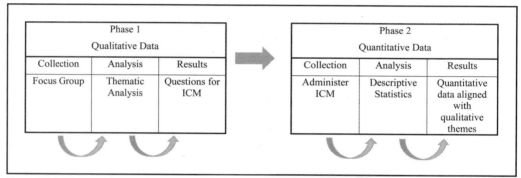

Figure 13-5. Diagram of the exploratory sequential design. (Adapted from Boveda, M., & Aronson, B. A. [2019]. Special education preservice teachers, intersectional diversity, and the privileging of emerging professional identities. *Remedial and Special Education, 40*[4], 248-260.)

Formulation Stage

The formulation stage is the point at which the researchers determine the value and purpose of conducting the study. Researchers determine if mixed methods are feasible and aligned with the research purpose. There are four steps in the formulation stage.

Identify the Problem and Purpose for Conducting the Research

Problems identified for educational research are often grounded in concerns or controversies that are present in the field (Creswell & Guetterman, 2019). The purpose of research is to add information to the existing body of knowledge to better illustrate or address the problem. Problems that are well-suited to mixed-methods research are often layered with complexities from personal, social, situational, historical, and/or ecological domains (Lavelle et al., 2013).

It is important to note that quantitative and qualitative research methodologists traditionally have different processes for identifying research problems and purposes. Quantitative methodologists will often conduct an extensive literature review to document the problem and provide evidence of the need for additional study. Qualitative research methodologists use existing literature to organize their research but are cautious about developing preconceptions that limit their ability to identify new perspectives (Maxwell, 2013). Given these two divergent perspectives, mixed-methods researchers may choose to conduct the literature review in phases aligned with quantitative and qualitative methods of their study.

Rhonda's research seeks to address the problem of math difficulties for students with disabilities, specifically as they impact performance on algebraic reasoning. She knows that there is a large body of research documenting the problem of mathematics difficulties for students with disabilities.

Her literature review revealed that the studies of mathematics intervention at the secondary level do not always account for within-group differences for students with disabilities, an issue that is of particular concern in her setting. Her purpose is to better understand the development of algebraic reasoning in the diverse representation of students with disabilities.

Provide a Rationale for Conducting Mixed-Methods Research

As with all research, it is important to justify the methodology that will be used. Research questions drive the selection of methodology. In the case of mixed-methods research, the researchers consider the information that they hope to obtain from quantitative, qualitative, and integrated elements of the study and explain how the integrated design will provide a more thorough response to the research problem than a mono-method research design (Collins et al., 2006; Lieber, 2016). In special education research, the rationale may be linked to the researchers' intent to address the multilayered complexities of learner characteristics, educator characteristics, instructional presentation, and environmental factors.

In Rhonda's case, the diverse needs of the students and her desire to evaluate algebraic reasoning through both process-oriented measures and outcome-oriented measures create the multi-layered complexity that mixed-methods were designed to address. Rhonda recognizes that a combination of qualitative and quantitative methods can provide more in-depth understanding of her research problem than a mono-method design.

Evaluate the Feasibility of Conducting Mixed-Methods Research

Beyond considering the rationale for using mixed methods to address a particular research problem, researchers must consider if the method is feasible. This entails ensuring that they have sufficient knowledge, time, and funding to conduct both quantitative and qualitative methodologies (Collins et al., 2006; OBSSR, 2011). Further, the researchers must determine if their intended audience will be receptive to a mixed-methods study.

Rhonda knows that her dissertation committee will be open to the use of mixed-methods research if she can formulate a strong and logical design. She also recognizes that she has a significant amount of work to do to develop the needed skills in both quantitative and qualitative methods. Additionally, a mixed-methods study will take much more time than a mono-method study. Rhonda determines that she is willing to give the time in order to get answers to her complicated research questions.

Identify Philosophical and Theoretical Views

The philosophical and theoretical beliefs of a researcher are often closely linked to why research is conducted in a specific way (Morgan, 2018). When researchers identify and disclose their philosophical and theoretical views, they add a degree of transparency to the study that allows future readers to contextualize the findings in light of their own views. Additionally, identifying philosophical and theoretical views can assist researchers in selecting and justifying design decisions (Maxwell, 2013).

Because quantitative and qualitative research traditionally emerge from divergent theories of knowledge, it is important for researchers to specifically identify the stance that guides the integration of the two methodologies (Chen, 2006). Researchers employing mixed methods often find pragmatism, dialectical pluralism, or transformativism to be meaningful frameworks for this purpose.

Rhonda's emerging interest in mixed-methods research prompted her to explore some of the worldviews and theories associated with the methodology. She connects with the concepts of pragmatism, which are focused on practical utility in real-world contexts. As a practicing teacher, she recognizes the need to access a variety of resources to meet the needs of her students. She also finds herself interested in learning more about the transformative framework because her research is guided by an advocacy stance to ensure positive outcomes for diverse students with disabilities.

Planning Stage

The planning stage encompasses three steps in which the researchers formulate and describe their research methods. The researchers identify data sources aligned with key research constructs, form research questions, and develop a mixed-methods design. Thoughtful consideration of integration options in this stage creates opportunity for insightful conclusions drawn from well-aligned quantitative and qualitative data sources.

Identify Quantitative and Qualitative Data Sources

Many data sources are specifically aligned with quantitative or qualitative methods. When conducting mixed-methods research, the researchers may use distinct and separate sources to address some constructs. However, the identification of quantitative and qualitative sources that measure the same construct can facilitate integration (Plano Clark, 2019). A table outlining data sources by construct is a useful tool for planning and can also be meaningful to readers when research is published. See Table 13-2 for an example.

Through the process of developing a data source table (see Table 13-2), Rhonda determines that the construct of algebraic reasoning can be measured through quantitative measures, such as scores on a math test, or through qualitative measures, including interviews or student language and strategy use during problem-solving activities. These varied measures of math reasoning can inform one another and facilitate integration at the data analysis and interpretation stages.

Develop Research Questions

Mixed-methods studies will have mixed-methods questions that clearly demonstrate the need for integration (Plano Clark, 2019). They may also have separate quantitative and qualitative questions (Creswell & Guetterman, 2019). Quantitative and qualitative questions will follow the standard formats of their respective methodologies and data sources. Mixed-methods questions often clearly delineate the mixed-method design that will be required.

Plano Clark (2019) described ways that questions associated with each of the three basic designs are formulated. Questions associated with convergent mixed-methods designs indicate a need to compare and/or contrast quantitative and qualitative findings. A generic example might be, "In what ways do the findings of the quantitative and qualitative phases converge?" Questions associated with sequential designs indicate that the second phase of the study will emerge from or expand upon findings from the first phase. An example of a question that would lead to an explanatory sequential design might be, "How do the observed word attack strategies of students performing in the low-average range of the phonics assessment compare to those of students performing in the borderline or low range?" Conversely, a question that would lead to an exploratory sequential design might be, "What themes emerged from student interviews to guide the subsequent reading intervention?"

As Rhonda develops potential research questions, the alignment between questions and research designs becomes increasingly apparent. Questions that she is considering include: (a) Does the intervention impact the algebraic reasoning performance of students with disabilities? and (b) In what ways are differing levels of student performance on the algebraic reasoning pretest associated with student problem-solving language and strategy use during functional algebraic reasoning tasks?

Choose and Diagram the Mixed-Methods Research Design

The research purpose, data sources, and questions guide the selection of the mixed-methods research design (OBSSR, 2011). Researchers choose a convergent, explanatory sequential, or exploratory sequential model as the base for their research design. These basic designs may be expanded upon by including multiple stages or by placing the basic design within a larger framework such as an experiment, intervention, or theory (Fetters et al., 2013). Once the design is selected, it is useful to create a procedural diagram that maps out the sequence and priority, as previously demonstrated in

TABLE 13-2. RHONDA'S TABLE OF QUANTITATIVE AND QUALITATIVE MEASURES OF ALGEBRAIC REASONING

QUANTITATIVE MEASURES	QUALITATIVE MEASURES
Algebra Curriculum Based Measure	Student think-aloud
Teacher-made quizzes	Student-written explanations of how they solved a problem
Textbook unit test forms A and B	Student interviews
Division-Wide Common Formative Assessment	Student language during group work

Figures 13-1 through 13-3. Documenting points of integration on the diagram can be useful to the researchers during planning and to future readers upon publication (Plano Clark, 2019).

The first question that Rhonda is considering can be measured by quantitative and qualitative measures, which could be administered at approximately the same time. This question suggests a convergent mixed-methods design. The second question that Rhonda is considering clearly indicates a sequential design in which a quantitative measure is administered first, and subsequent qualitative data are used to provide additional clarification or expansion. This question suggests a sequential explanatory design.

Implementation Stage

The mixed-methods design selected during the planning phase provides structure to implementation. The researchers collect and analyze data separately, concurrently, or both. Additionally, during the implementation phase, researchers may follow an iterative process of data collection and data analysis. In these cases, findings from one phase of the study may impact data collection in sequential designs or create new research questions that transition basic convergent designs to advanced multistage designs (Collins et al., 2006).

Collect Data

Data collection for mixed-methods design requires researchers to employ rigorous methods that are aligned with each phase. Proactive planning and thoughtful selection of data sources in the planning phase increases the likelihood that data collected during implementation can be integrated in meaningful ways. The inclusion of both quantitative and qualitative data dictates that mixed-method data collection will require more time than mono-method data collection.

The sequence of data collection varies by the mixed-methods research design. In convergent mixed-methods designs, quantitative and qualitative data occur at approximately the same time. In explanatory sequential designs, the quantitative data are collected first. Qualitative data collection will follow and may involve a subset of the original participants to obtain additional information related to the quantitative findings. Conversely, qualitative data are collected first in exploratory sequential designs. When used for the purpose of developing a measure or intervention, the participant group for the qualitative phase of an exploratory sequential study may be smaller than the group in the quantitative phase. In some cases, the phases of an exploratory sequential design may have completely different participant groups. For example, when used to develop and validate an assessment, qualitative data may be gathered from subject matter experts to establish construct validity. Subsequently, quantitative data might be gathered from students to establish concurrent or predictive validity.

Analyze the Data

Data analysis is a critical and challenging component of mixed-methods research (Onwuegbuzie & Corrigan, 2018). Data drawn from the individual phases are often analyzed in isolation before integrated analysis occurs. Researchers employ rigorous data analysis techniques on the individual data sets, then explore interrelationships.

As with the data collection, the sequence of data analysis is directly linked to the mixed-methods research design. In convergent designs, the quantitative and qualitative data are analyzed separately, but not in any designated order, before being integrated for interpretation. The integrated analysis seeks to identify points of convergence or divergence in the findings of the two data sets and deepen the understanding of the construct as a whole. In the explanatory sequential design, quantitative data are analyzed first. The findings directly impact the selection of participants for the qualitative phase. Once both quantitative and qualitative data are collected and analyzed, integrated analysis occurs with a focus on using the qualitative data to explain or expand upon the quantitative findings. In exploratory sequential designs, qualitative data are collected and analyzed before the quantitative data. Integrated analysis of the two data sources is used to support application or generalization of the findings.

Validate Findings

Mixed-methods research proponents suggest that the multidisciplinary perspective created by systematic integration inherently increases quality and supports validity (Lavelle et al., 2013). There are challenges in defining and describing validity in mixed methods due to divergent philosophical stances of quantitative and qualitative researchers. The concept of *validity* is relatively straightforward in quantitative research. It describes the degree to which the data derived from a measure represent the intended construct. The concept has been more controversial in qualitative research based on the theoretical assumption that knowledge of a construct is contextually situated. Maxwell attempted to address the concerns of validity in qualitative research by proposing what he identified as a commonsense description. He wrote that the concept of validity in qualitative research references the "credibility of a description, conclusion, interpretation, or other sort of account" (Maxwell, 2013, p. 122).

Given the differing stances of quantitative and qualitative methodologists, the concept of validity in mixed-methods research is often described as *legitimation*. Legitimation refers to evidence of design quality and interpretive rigor across all phases of a mixed-methods study (Collins et al., 2012; Onwuegbuzie & Burke Johnson, 2006). This evidence supports the premise that the researchers have used method-specific techniques to account for potential threats in each phase of the research. In quantitative phases, this may include sampling techniques, control groups, and statistical controls, while qualitative techniques may include identification of possible researcher bias, respondent validation, and rich data (Maxwell, 2013).

Interpretation and Reporting Stage

In the final stage of the mixed-methods research project, the researchers fully integrate findings to identify connections across the phases of the study and to the broader body of research for a given research topic. Finally, the researchers identify potential outlets for publication and prepare a scholarly report of the project (Creswell & Guetterman, 2019).

Form Integrated Interpretations

The defining purpose of mixed-methods research is to address a complex research problem in a way that is superior to what would have been achieved through mono-method research (Creswell & Guetterman, 2019). Arriving at deeply meaningful integrated interpretations may involve interactive and cyclical review of the data analysis from each phase in order to identify relationships (Collins et al., 2006). These relationships are then placed in the context of the larger body of published knowledge related to the research topic.

Three primary methods have been identified for integrated interpretation: merging, connecting, and embedding data sets (OBSSR, 2011). *Merging* occurs when the results of quantitative and qualitative data collection are reported together, demonstrating ways in which the two forms converge or diverge in explaining measured constructs. When merging qualitative data with quantitative data for integrated interpretation, the qualitative data are sometimes quantified by determining the frequency at which certain themes or codes were identified (McCrudden et al., 2019). Data interpretation is described as *connected* when the analysis of the first data set informed the collection of the second data set (i.e., sequential designs). In these cases, the integrated interpretation involves using the second data set to explain or explore the first data set (OBSSR, 2011). *Embedding* occurs when the second (or lower priority) data set supplements or adds information to the primary data set. An example would be using qualitative data regarding student experiences of an intervention to supplement the quantitative data describing how they performed (OBSSR, 2011).

Report Findings

Once data from all phases have been collected, analyzed, and interpreted in an integrated fashion, researchers choose how to present the findings (Collins et al., 2006). In some cases, reporting may take the form of multiple publications, each focused on a different element of the study (Collins et al., 2006; Creswell & Guetterman, 2019). Note that breaking one study into multiple publications may result in different interpretations of the data. The entire mixed-methods research project could also be reported in a single publication. However, page limitations may impact publication options (Houchins, 2015).

EVALUATING QUALITY OF MIXED-METHODS RESEARCH

As mixed-methods research develops, so do the criteria for evaluating quality. There are several publications addressing various elements of quality in mixed-methods research (e.g., Collins et al., 2006, 2012; Levitt et al., 2018; OBSSR, 2011; Plano Clark, 2019), though no single set of standards has been developed at this time. Here, we summarize key features of quality in conducting and reporting mixed-methods research. Quality mixed-methods research, regardless of the specific design, will include the following:

- The research purpose provides evidence of the need for integrated quantitative and qualitative data (Levitt et al., 2018; Plano Clark, 2019).
- The mixed-methods design is aligned with the research purpose and question (Collins et al., 2012; Plano Clark, 2019).
- The design employs rigorous data collection and analysis with fidelity across both the quantitative and qualitative strands (Collins et al., 2012; OBSSR, 2011).
- Integration procedures are evident throughout the study (OBSSR, 2011; Plano Clark, 2019).
- The design is logical and efficient (Plano Clark, 2019).

The following features provide evidence of quality in the publication of mixed-methods research:
- The study is clearly identified as mixed-methods research in the title or statement of purpose (Collins et al., 2012; Levitt et al., 2018; OBSSR, 2011).
- The mixed-methods design is clearly identified (Collins et al., 2012; Plano Clark, 2019).
- Separate descriptions of the participant samples for the quantitative and qualitative phases are provided, particularly when the samples differ (Levitt et al., 2018).

- Quantitative, qualitative, and mixed-analysis procedures are distinctly described (Levitt et al., 2018).
- The findings and discussion sections of the written report reflect the sequence of the mixed-methods design (Levitt et al., 2018).
- Integration procedures are explained for each stage of the study (OBSSR, 2011; Plano Clark, 2019).
- The researchers document their philosophical stances as they apply to the components of the study (Collins et al., 2012).

SUMMARY

Special education researchers may consider mixed-methods research designs to address complex questions related to instruction and assessment of diverse learners under varied learning conditions. Mixed-methods designs are valued in special education for contextualizing quantitative data with qualitative information such as learner characteristics, educator characteristics, features of instructional presentation, and environmental factors. Mixed-methods research designs can take many forms; however, three core designs provide the foundation for all other mixed-methods research. These core designs are the convergent design, the explanatory sequential design, and the exploratory sequential design. The designs have differing intents, and thus different sequences for the collection and analysis of the quantitative and qualitative data. Selection of a mixed-methods design is driven by the research purpose and questions.

Although the overall sequence of planning and conducting mixed-methods research is similar to mono-method research, additional consideration must be given to developing a logical and efficient design that truly integrates the quantitative and qualitative elements. Strategies that support integration should be included in each phase of a mixed-methods study. Quality mixed-methods research with thorough and thoughtful integration procedures may result in findings that are well-aligned with the real-world experiences of special education teachers and students, and therefore contribute to reducing the research-to-practice gap. Table 13-3 includes a list of common misconceptions associated with mixed-methods research, and Table 13-4 provides additional resources to consult.

CHAPTER REVIEW

1. What are the critical differences between mixed-methods research, mono-method research, and multi-method research?
2. In what ways does mixed-methods research have the potential to benefit special education researchers and practitioners?
3. What additional research questions might Rhonda F (see Case Study) propose to address her research problem and purpose?
4. What strands (quantitative, qualitative, or integrated) or mixed-methods designs (convergent, sequential explanatory, or sequential exploratory) are best aligned with each of the questions you developed?
5. In what ways do the quality indicators for mixed-methods research most differ from quantitative research?
6. In what ways do the quality indicators for mixed-methods research most differ from qualitative research?

TABLE 13-3. COMMON MISCONCEPTIONS AND CLARIFICATIONS ABOUT MIXED-METHODS RESEARCH

MISCONCEPTION	BETTER UNDERSTANDING
Studies are described as mixed-methods research when they include both quantitative and qualitative elements.	Mixed-methods research systematically integrates quantitative and qualitative information to provide a deeper understanding of the research topic than could be derived from separate analysis of the two types of data.
Mixed-methods research is a new practice.	Mixed-methods research was formalized as a distinct methodology in 2000 with the publication of the *Handbook of Mixed Methods Research*. However, there is evidence of thoughtful integration of quantitative and qualitative methods in research designs dating back at least 40 years.
Quantitative research, specifically randomized controlled trials, provide the best evidence of a practice's value to the field of special education.	Quantitative research is valuable for identifying practices that work. By integrating quantitative and qualitative research into mixed-methods designs, researchers can develop an understanding of what works, with whom, and under what conditions. The added layer of contextual information may facilitate implementation in special education classrooms and assist in bridging the research-to-practice gap.

TABLE 13-4. ADDITIONAL RESOURCES

RESOURCE	DESCRIPTION
Creswell, J. W. (2013, February 19). What is mixed methods research? Video file. https://www.youtube.com/watch?v=1OaNiTlpyX8	Dr. John Creswell provides an overview of the elements of mixed-methods research with exemplars.
Creswell, J. W. (2013, March 1). Developing mixed methods research. Video file. Retrieved from https://www.youtube.com/watch?v=PSVsD9fAx38	Dr. John Creswell provides a description of key steps in developing mixed methods research.

Additional Readings

Creswell, J. W. (2014). *A concise introduction to mixed methods research*. Sage.

Creswell, J. W., & Plano Clark, V. L. (2018). *Designing and conducting mixed methods research* (3rd ed.). Sage.

Tashakkori, A., & Teddlie, C. (Eds.). (2011). *Handbook of mixed methods in social and behavioral research* (2nd ed.). Sage.

REFERENCES

Bostrom, P., & Broberg, M. (2017). Protection and restriction: A mixed-methods study of self-reported well-being among youth with intellectual disabilities. *Journal of Applied Research in Intellectual Disabilities, 31*, 164-176. https://doi.org/10.1111/jar.12364

Bostrom, P., Johnels, J. A., Thorson, M., & Broberg, M. (2016). Subjective mental health, peer relations, family, and school environment in adolescents with intellectual developmental disorder: A first report of a new questionnaire administered on tablet PCs. *Journal of Mental Health Research in Intellectual Disabilities, 9*(4), 207-231.

Boveda, M., & Aronson, B. A. (2019). Special education preservice teachers, intersectional diversity, and the privileging of emerging professional identities. *Remedial and Special Education, 40*(4), 248-260. https://doi.org/10.1177%2F0741932519838621

Chen, H. T. (2006). A theory-driven evaluation perspective on mixed methods research. *Research in the Schools, 13*(1), 75-83.

Collins, K. M. T., Onwuegbuzie, A. J., & Burke Johnson, R. (2012). Securing a place at the table: A review and extension of legitimation criteria for the conduct of mixed research. *American Behavioral Scientist, 56*(6), 849-865. https://doi.org/10.1177%2F0002764211433799

Collins, K. M. T., Onwuegbuzie, A. J., & Sutton, I.L. (2006). A model incorporating the rationale and purpose for conducting mixed-methods research in special education and beyond. *Learning Disabilities: A Contemporary Journal, 4*(1), 67-100.

Creswell, J. W., & Guetterman, T. C. (2019). *Educational research: Planning, conducting, and evaluating quantitative and qualitative research.* Pearson.

Damianidou, E., & Phtiaka, H. (2018). Implementing inclusion in disabling settings: The role of teachers' attitudes and practices. *International Journal of Inclusive Education, 22*(10), 1078-1092. https://doi.org/10.1080/13603116.2017.1415381

Fetters, M. D., Curry, L. A., & Creswell, J. W. (2013). Achieving integration in mixed methods designs: Principles and practices. *Health Services Research, 48*(2), 2134-2156. https://doi.org/10.1111/1475-6773.12117

Ghesquiere, P., & Van der Aalsvoort, G. M. (2004). Special needs education as a social system: Responding to the challenge of methodology. *International Journal of Disability, Development, and Education, 51*(2), 217-222. https://doi.org/10.1080/10349120410001687418

Houchins, D. E. (2015). President's message July 2015. http://higherlogicdownload.s3.amazonaws.com/SPED/b7acd4b4-bc4d-4c1f-a7d4-efab3d52da44/UploadedImages/DR%20Pres%20Msgs/President%27s%20Message%20July%202015.pdf

Klinger, J. K., & Boardman, A. G. (2011). Addressing the "research gap" in special education through mixed methods. *Learning Disability Quarterly, 34*(3), 208-218. https://doi.org/10.1177%2F0731948711417559

Lavelle, E., Vuk, J., & Barber, C. (2013). Twelve tips for getting started using mixed methods in medical education research. *Medical Teacher, 35*, 272-276. https://doi.org/10.3109/0142159X.2013.759645

Leech, N. L., & Onwuegbuzie, A. J. (2009). A typology of mixed methods designs. *Quality & Quantity, 43*(2), 265-275.

Levitt, H. M., Bamberg, M., Creswell, J. W., Frost, D. M. Josselson, R., & Suarez-Orozco, C. (2018). Journal article reporting standards for qualitative primary, qualitative meta-analytic, and mixed methods research in psychology: The APA publications and communications board task force report. *American Psychologist, 73*(1), 26-46. http://dx.doi.org/10.1037/amp0000151

Lieber, E. (2016). Harnessing Discovery: Writing a Strong Mixed-Methods Proposal. https://wtgrantfoundation.org/library/uploads/2016/06/Harnessing-Discovery.pdf

Maxwell, J. A. (2013). *Qualitative research design.* Sage.

McCrudden, M. T., Marchand, G., & Schutz, P. (2019). Mixed methods in educational psychology inquiry. *Contemporary Educational Psychology, 57*, 1-8. https://psycnet.apa.org/doi/10.1016/j.cedpsych.2019.01.008

Morgan, D. L. (2018). Pragmatism as a paradigm for social research. *Qualitative Inquiry*, 1-9. https://doi.org/10.1177%2F1077800413513733

National Research Council. (2002). *Scientific research in education.* Committee on Scientific Principles for Educational Research. R. J. Shavelson & L. Towne, Editors. Center for Education. Division of Behavioral and Social Sciences and Education. National Academy Press.

Office of Behavioral and Social Sciences Research, National Institutes of Health. (2011). Best practices for mixed methods research in health sciences. Retrieved from https://obssr.od.nih.gov/training/online-training-resources/mixed-methods-research/

Onwuegbuzie, A. J., & Corrigan, J. A. (2018). What is happening now? An overview of mixed methods applications in special education. *Research in the Schools, 25*(2), 1-22.

Onwuegbuzie, A. J., & Burke Johnson, R. (2006). The validity issue in mixed research. *Research in Schools, 13*(1), 48-63.

Plano Clark, V. L. (2019). Meaningful integration within mixed methods studies: Identifying why, what, when, and how. *Contemporary Educational Psychology, 57,* 106-111. https://doi.org/10.1016/j.cedpsych.2019.01.007

Schoonenboom, J., Hitchcock, J. H., & Burke Johnson, R. (2018). How to interact with differences in special education intervention research: Six guidelines. *Research in the Schools, 25*(2), 34-43.

Seethaler, P. M., & Fuchs, L. S. (2005). A drop in the bucket: Randomized controlled trials testing reading and math interventions. *Learning Disabilities Research & Practice, 20*(2), 98-102.

Timans, P., Wouters, P., & Heilbron, J. (2019). Mixed methods research: What it is and what it could be. *Theory and Society, 48,* 193-216. https://doi.org/10.1007/s11186-019-09348-2

Program Evaluation

With contributions from Maeghan N. Hennessey, PhD; Jason P. Herron, PhD; and Reginald B. Snoddy, MS

INTRODUCTION

This chapter introduces program evaluation as an alternative to traditional research paradigms. Though the methods used can be the same, program evaluation is uniquely suited for situations when an evaluator's interest is about effectiveness of a specific program. An emphasis on the importance of communication with and the involvement of stakeholders also distinguishes program evaluation from other educational research endeavors. An overview of the components and processes of setting up a logic model to operationalize the theory of action undergirding the program is provided. This is followed by descriptions of differing phases of program evaluation (i.e., needs assessment, formative evaluation, process evaluation, and summative evaluation). Information regarding communicating evaluation results to stakeholders is given, followed by ethical considerations unique to the program evaluation process. Examples from a case study are provided throughout the chapter.

Hott, B. L., Brigham, F. J., & Peltier, C.
Research Methods in Special Education (pp. 257-276).
© 2021 SLACK Incorporated.

CHAPTER OBJECTIVES

→ Distinguish program evaluation from other research paradigms.
→ Identify characteristics of stakeholders and their importance in evaluation processes.
→ Explain the structure and components of a logic model.
→ Classify evaluation goals into the appropriate phases of program evaluation.
→ Recommend methods for communicating evaluation results to different stakeholder groups.
→ Detect ethical challenges unique to program evaluation.

KEY TERMS

- **External Evaluator**: Expert evaluator, independent from the program, hired to conduct an evaluation.
- **Formative Evaluation**: Evaluation methods used to determine the extent to which new programs are being implemented as designed.
- **Internal Evaluator**: Program staff member or other employee conducting an evaluation of the program with which they are associated.
- **Logic Model**: Visual representation of a theory of action including the major inputs/resources, activities, outputs, and outcomes of the program.
- **Member-Checking**: Process of allowing stakeholders to view and comment on program data and reports to ensure accuracy and trustworthiness of findings and interpretations.
- **Needs Assessment**: Systematic process for determining gaps or deficiencies in services.
- **Outcome Evaluation**: Evaluation methods used to determine the extent to which program implementation results in meeting intended goals.
- **Process Evaluation**: Evaluation methods used to assess the quality and purposes of program activities.
- **Stakeholders**: Individuals who either have a particular interest in a program or are in some way served by the program.
- **Theory of Action**: Operationalization of a theory of change in a specific context designed to achieve a desired outcome.

CASE STUDY

The Greendale Garden Project (GGP) is a program for high school students served under the exceptionality category of Emotional Disturbance. We will refer to this category as Emotional Behavioral Disorder (EBD) to remain consistent with practices in the field. GGP operates in a moderately sized city within the United States to implement behavioral interventions for students with EBD. The program provides access to therapeutic, creative, and productive outlets outside of the confines of schools. Upon referral to the program, students receive access to the garden daily (after school), and they are responsible for the general operation of the garden (e.g., planting, watering, or planning of garden activities). Currently, GGP has 20 high school students and five staff members who are local high school teachers who receive funding to work with the program. The program encourages responsibility, empathy, compassion, and critical thinking skills.

The GGP received initial funding through a state grant supporting pilot programs for students with exceptionalities. The award had an initial allocation of $30,000, with a state option to renew the funding every 3 years based on evidence of program effectiveness. GGP must provide evidence through program evaluation, produced in the final quarter of the third year of activities. The evidence is based on five broadly stated questions: (1) How effective is the program at improving academic outcomes for students receiving special education services? (2) How effective is the program at improving nonacademic outcomes for students who receive special education services? (3) To what extent is the program meeting its internal standards or goals? (4) To what extent do stakeholders and the local community value the program? and (5) How efficiently is the program utilizing grant funding?

PROGRAM EVALUATION

Within schools, community-based organizations, nonprofits, or businesses, questions are often asked about the value and impact of the work being done. Program evaluation is a paradigm uniquely suited to answering these questions. Though it borrows methods from quantitative, qualitative, mixed-method, and single case research paradigms to collect the data necessary to answer questions about the efficacy of programs, program evaluation is distinct. The main goal of program evaluation is to use a systematic method for collecting and analyzing information to assess a specific program or organization, with a particular eye toward the implementation or effectiveness of that program (Centers for Disease Control and Prevention, 2012). Often, an accountability component is embedded in the design.

Because evaluation of a program or organization within a specific context, or proposing the need for a new intervention, is of paramount importance, generalization to a new context is typically not the goal of evaluation research. Rather, program evaluations often are conducted to show evidence either for or against the quality of a particular program. Because the method is context specific, a number of different questions can be asked and answered (such as the necessity, efficacy, or improvement of services or interventions within a context) that would not normally be asked in research, making program evaluation an attractive method for answering day-to-day, practical questions that stakeholders may have about the programs in which they are involved.

Distinction Between Program Evaluation and Research

Though we will focus here on distinguishing the two, educational research and program evaluation share much in common. Both require systematic processes and methods (Mathison, 2007) to disseminate information to communities, synthesize knowledge, and share common data collection techniques. Contrasts between program evaluation and research can be viewed in relation to their purpose. The purpose of research is often related to the examination of phenomena, to test complex hypotheses, or to explain (or describe) behavior. In contrast, the purpose of program evaluation is to examine the effectiveness, efficiency, or progress toward goal/s of an organization, initiative, or program. Both research and program evaluation utilize similar methods, but the goal-directed nature of evaluation mandates that all methods are used for the sake of examination rather than exploration. For example, an evaluator examining the GGP may create an instrument to measure the perceptions staff members have of the program's ability to meet its goals. This is different from the purpose researchers may have if they were interested in creating an instrument to investigate high school teachers' perceptions of the abilities of students with EBD to work independently in a garden setting. In the first example, the evaluative nature of the question seeks to understand the effectiveness of the program within its natural context (Chen & Rossi, 1983), whereas in the second scenario, the researcher is interested in investigating the theoretical assumption underlying the research questions (Figure 14-1).

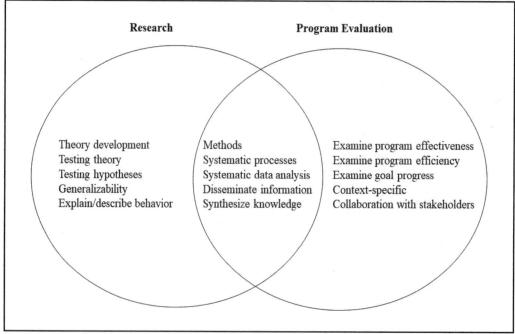

Figure 14-1. Comparison of program evaluation and research.

Generalizability

Although research is often concerned with questions of generalizability, program evaluation is mostly focused on the effectiveness of a specific program, in a specific context. This is to say, the focus of program evaluation is narrower and goal-driven, thus evaluators are normally not concerned with generalizability. Moreover, the goal-driven nature of program evaluation necessitates an iterative methodological process, which is not always conducive to the goals of generalizability or replicability found in research. This does not mean that aspects of a program's success cannot inform similar programs. For example, the success (or failures) related to GGP may be examined by similar (special education or garden) programs to facilitate their own growth. In this sense, a program evaluation report would be valuable to entities outside of the program itself.

Importance of Stakeholders

Another stark contrast between program evaluation and other research methods is the reliance on information gathered from and interpreted with stakeholders. Before embarking on a discussion of the methods used to evaluate the efficacy of programs in which stakeholders are involved, it is important to nail down the definition of *stakeholders*. Unlike other research paradigms, identifying stakeholders is important in program evaluation research because the evaluator will work closely with the stakeholders to determine the goals of the evaluation as well as the feasibility of specific methods to address evaluation goals.

Stakeholders are those individuals who have a particular interest in a program (Royse et al., 2016) or who are somehow served by the program in question (Bryson & Patton, 2010; Yarbrough et al., 2010). Examples may include those who have decision-making authority over a program, program users, beneficiaries of services, or those with valued perspectives on the program. Stakeholders' involvement in the evaluation process is necessary because they can provide an indication of the feasibility and accuracy of an evaluation (Yarbrough et al., 2010). It is difficult for an evaluator to learn about certain aspects of the program under question without having meaningful interaction with stakeholders both inside and outside that program. Moreover, one cannot expect stakeholders to "buy into" evaluation recommendations if they have not in some way been engaged in the process (Morris, 2002; Patton, 2008). To increase buy-in and use of evaluation findings, it is important to identify and collect data from all relevant stakeholder groups (Ayers, 1987; Centers for Disease Control and Prevention, 2012).

The reliance on collaboration between stakeholders and evaluators is one of the things that distinguishes program evaluation from more traditional research paradigms. It is generally expected that the client for whom you are conducting the evaluation (who is a stakeholder) and the evaluator will collaborate to some extent throughout the design (Bryson & Patton, 2010). This collaboration often begins with the determination of evaluation questions. Programs are evaluated for a variety of different reasons, including requirements from funding sources, competition for new funding, determining the extent to which interventions are benefitting those they serve, or accountability reasons (Royse et al., 2016). Gathering perspectives from stakeholders about the evaluation's goals "may be invaluable in confirming, revising, or even renegotiating the purposes and boundaries of the evaluation" (Yarbrough et al., 2010, Standard U2).

However, care must be taken when involving the opinions of diverse stakeholders in evaluations. Stakeholders perceive evaluations of programs through their own lens, rendering their judgements subjective (Verschuren & Zsolnai, 1998). Subjective judgment is not necessarily bad, but we must consider that most stakeholders do not have the benefit of interacting with others with different perspectives about the program under question. For example, in the case of the GGP, the evaluator would collect information from stakeholders such as the staff members involved, parents of the students enrolled in the program, personnel at the schools the students attend, or other community members or organizations who may interact with the GGP or the enrolled students. All involved stakeholder groups will perceive the program goals differently depending on their interaction with the program. Thus, the evaluator must take care to balance input from all stakeholders regarding the boundaries, goals, and actions completed during the evaluation (Gilliam et al., 2002).

THEORY OF CHANGE, THEORY OF ACTION, AND LOGIC MODELS

Programs exist because the developers of a specific program adhere to (or develop) a certain theory of change. According to the Center for Theory of Change (2019), a theory of change refers to:

a comprehensive description and illustration of how and why a desired change is expected to happen in a particular context...by first identifying the desired long-term goals and then work[ing] back from these to identify all the conditions (outcomes) that must be in place (and how these relate to one another causally) for the goals to occur. (para. 1)

Theories of change generally refer to large, societal changes, and are put into effect through theories of action. A *theory of action* operationalizes a theory of change in a specific context to achieve a desired outcome. Specifically, theories of action describe how programs are set up and the specific inputs or resources available to accomplish the activities planned in the program. Often, theories of action, referred to as "program theories" by McLaughlin and Jordan (2010), are implicitly defined by organizations. Making explicit the implicit logic between a program's resources and actions and how those translate to outcomes is a necessary step before embarking on an evaluation to determine the efficacy of a particular program. Thus, an evaluator should create a logic model representing the implicit theory of action.

Logic models depict a theory of action, often using a visual representation, and include the inputs invested in the program, the actions undertaken, the outputs produced, and the short- and long-term outcomes assumed to be attained as a result of program implementation. In other words, a logic model is a pictorial representation (analogous to a roadmap) of outcomes we should see resulting from the program, given the resources the program has and the actions constituting the program (Royse et al., 2016) within the given context. Before discussing steps necessary to build logic models, it is necessary to discuss the four major parts of the models (i.e., inputs/resources, activities, outputs, and outcomes) to ensure they are built properly.

Inputs/Resources

Before embarking on an evaluation of a program, evaluators must take stock of the resources available to that program. These inputs in the program evaluation process can consist of human and financial resources, as well as other resources such as partnerships required to support the program. Moreover, information about the needs the program attempts to serve and the specific objectives set prior to program implementation can be essential resources.

Activities

The activities of the program are what we think of as "the program itself." Specifically, these are the action steps necessary to produce the desired outcomes by implementing the program (McLaughlin & Jordan, 2010). Activities consist of things done or created by program staff (Royse et al., 2016) to meet identified client needs.

Outputs

Outputs in a program consist of the bridge between the activities and the desired outcomes. Essentially, outputs consist of the resources, documents, or other services produced by the program that serve as a monitor of program activities, as well as document that the activities defined within the program have taken place. They are the "products, goods, and services provided to the program's direct customers or program participants" (McLaughlin & Jordan, 2010, p. 57), and are part of the intended results of the program. Often, outputs consist of numerical counts of the products or services produced during program activities.

Outcomes

Outcomes of a program evaluation refer to the desired changes in clients' or participants' behavior after their involvement in the program (W. K. Kellogg Foundation, 2006). They are the benefits to people or organizations that are expected to result should the program function the way it was intended. Outcomes may be either short- or long-term, but should result from program activities. Relatively immediate impacts resulting from program activities, or short-term outcomes, should be directly related to, or caused by, the program's outputs (McLaughlin & Jordan, 2010). Long-term outcomes are related to the goals the program has in meeting the future needs of participants.

Building Logic Models

McLaughlin and Jordan (1999, 2010) provide guidance regarding strategies needed to build a logic model to represent the theory of action behind the implementation of a program, with the first step being to collect information relevant to the theory of action to determine how best to depict it in the form of a logic model. Evaluators will need to work jointly with key stakeholders both inside and outside the program to: (a) gain an accurate representation of program components and intended outcomes; (b) collect program documentation, strategic plans, goals, previous program evaluations (if they exist), and relevant legislation; and (c) a variety of other information, to uncover the shared vision the stakeholders have about the program. In cases where programs are not clearly defined, facilitating this discussion between stakeholders with differing perspectives becomes even more important.

Because "the program should be grounded in an understanding of the problem that drives the need for the program" (McLaughlin & Jordan, 1999, p. 68), clearly defining that problem is of key importance for the definition of the logic model and all subsequent evaluation components. When working with stakeholders, then, it is necessary to come to a shared understanding of the bounds of the program, or the demarcation line between the goals of the particular program and other worthwhile goals that fall outside the program's confines, as well as the specific goals to be attained after program implementation. This step is likely done at the same time as collecting relevant information but is critical for determining the specific goals of the evaluation to be conducted.

After collecting relevant information and determining the boundaries of the evaluation, the key elements of the logic model can be defined with stakeholder input. Because programs are generally large, not all program details need be included in the logic model. The evaluator must be sure to continually check the accuracy of the definitions used with a working group of key stakeholders. To determine where the logic model needs either clarity or pruning, McLaughlin and Jordan (1999) recommend looking at each component and asking questions like, "how did we get here," and "why are we aiming for that outcome?" (p. 69).

Once the key elements for inclusion in the logic model are determined, a one-page visual representation can be drawn to show the interaction and flow between model components. Often, logic models show inputs/resources, followed by activities, outputs, and outcomes from left to right, connected with arrows to show links between components. Rows can be included in the model, particularly if a sequential flow is present in the logic model where some outcomes lead to other activities. Again, arrows between components on different rows are drawn in the model. Both Peyton and Scicchitano (2017) and the W. K. Kellogg Foundation (2006) provide resources to help with drawing logic models. Figure 14-2 provides a general example of a logic model, and Figure 14-3 gives the logic model for the GGP.

It is important to remember that logic models are simplified visual representations of the network of connections between only major elements of a program and expected outcomes (McLaughlin & Jordan, 1999). When verifying the logic model with stakeholders,

> the work group responsible for producing the Model should continuously evaluate the Model with respect to its goal of representing the program logic—how the program works under what conditions to achieve its short-, intermediate- and long-term aims. (McLaughlin & Jordan, 1999, p. 69)

Although it is a simplification of the larger program, the work group must ensure the level of detail provided in the logic model is sufficient for understanding the relations between program components, as well as ensuring that the logic behind those modeled relations is sound.

PHASES OF PROGRAM EVALUATION

Program evaluation methods can be used to answer several questions regarding the efficacy of a particular program depending on the stage of development of that program (Pancer & Westhues, 1989). In this section, we will highlight four phases of program evaluation that can be used by the evaluator depending on the developmental needs of the program.

Needs Assessment

Our goal when doing program evaluation often is to determine the extent to which the program has met goals and is successful. However, the first step should be an assessment of the needs of the community, or a way to systematically evaluate whether there exist deficiencies in services provided to the community (Royse et al., 2016). This systematic determination, called a *needs assessment*, can

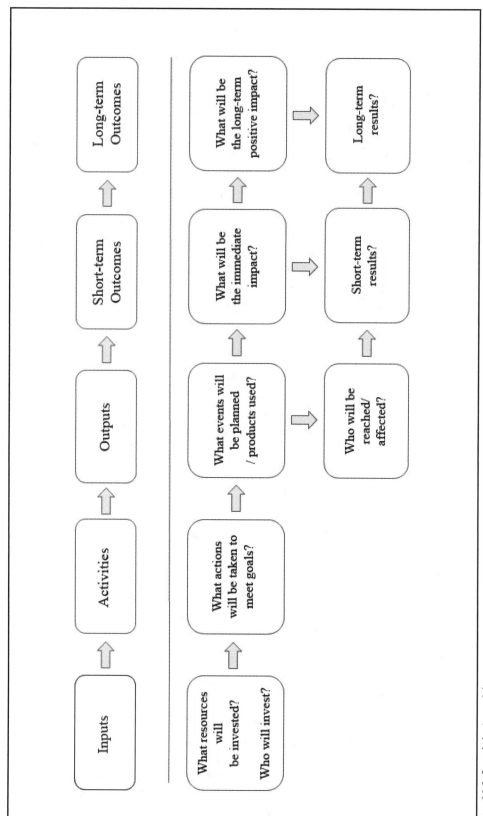

Figure 14-2. Sample logic model.

Purpose: to examine the effectiveness, efficiency, or progress towards goal/s of an organization, initiative, or program

Goal: to determine the efficacy of GGP and to ensure proper implementation of behavioral interventions for students with Emotional Behavior Disorder (EBD)

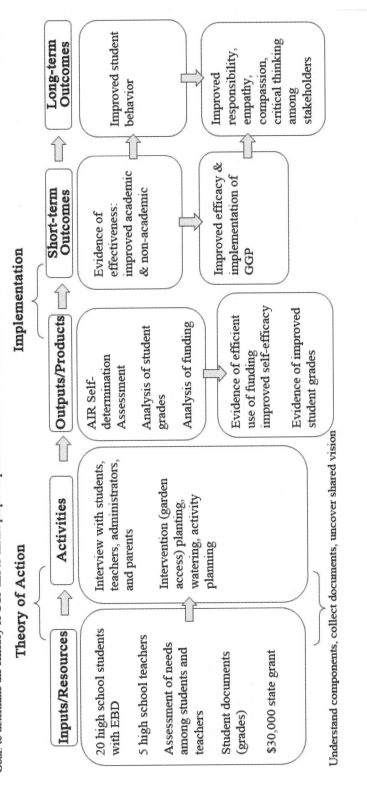

Figure 14-3. Logic model for program evaluation of the Greendale Garden Project.

be used to ascertain whether new programs are needed, whether a suspected gap in services is actually present, reasons for a gap in services, or even the extent to which existing programs can be modified to meet the needs of the community. When we do a needs assessment, we are asking whether we need something new in order to address an existing problem.

The process of conducting a needs assessment is similar to that of the overall program evaluation process. First, parameters are defined, such as the purpose and breadth of the needs assessment, the stakeholders to be involved, and the budget and time allowed to conduct the needs assessment. It is important to note that stakeholders have different perspectives on needs, and some will express "wants" as "needs." Moreover, the evaluator may uncover competing needs amongst stakeholders (Yarbrough et al., 2010). The evaluator must be judicious in balancing varying information to determine the boundaries of the needs assessment.

Because needs assessment is a diagnostic process to determine deficiencies in programs or services, a number of questions can be asked, such as the specific needs that are not being met, the individuals who are not being served by an existing program, or those who would be likely to use a new service. After determining the parameters surrounding the needs assessment, evaluators must identify the specific sources of information to be included in the evaluation, which often include existing information not collected directly from stakeholders (e.g., government data, prior records, mission statements or strategic plans, or other program information).

The evaluator must create any new assessments, surveys, or questionnaires needed to collect information necessary that is not already available, as well as design the plan for how information will be collected from relevant stakeholders. Any combination of quantitative, qualitative, mixed-methods, or single case designs could be used depending on the needs being investigated and the specific purpose of the needs assessment. Feedback from key stakeholders at all stages of the needs assessment is important, particularly when developing preliminary findings before disseminating the final report.

Several types of approaches to needs assessments can be used independently or in combination. Some of the common approaches to needs assessment are:

- Secondary data analyses: using existing data to paint a picture of existing problems or needs.
- Impressionistic approaches: collecting data from key informants to gain an overall impression of the gaps in services when the desire is to focus on a human perspective.
- Varying sampling methods: using diverse small-group sampling methods to collect data from different perspectives. An example of this would be the Delphi method (Gross, 1981) in which experts are asked to answer anonymous questionnaires. The evaluator summarizes the information gathered and distributes it back to experts, who subsequently revise their previous answers in light of this new information. This cycle is repeated until consensus is achieved. Another example would be the use of focus groups in which informants with different perspectives are brought together to discuss issues interactively.
- Survey approaches: creating surveys to efficiently collect data from larger, diverse numbers of people.

Formative Evaluation

When a new program designed to meet identified needs is implemented, formative evaluation can occur. *Formative evaluation* methods are used to determine the extent to which programs are being implemented in their early stages as they were designed (Royse et al., 2016). Formative evaluations are concerned with providing constructive feedback to refine, adjust, or enhance the interventions within a program, with a focus on acquiring information useful for program improvement. An examination of the original plan and goals for the program should occur, followed by seeking information from stakeholders or clients regarding program operation. In the case of the Greendale Garden Project, the grant proposal funded by the state, notes from meetings taken during program development, and written goals and objectives can be examined to determine if departures from program design have occurred, or if things such as communication difficulties or training needs exist. Moreover, observations of actual program implementation will provide the evaluator with information necessary to determine the extent to which the program is meeting its stated objectives.

To ascertain the answers to these types of formative questions, an evaluator can take several approaches. One common approach is to compare the new program to established programs that are successful in their areas to determine best practices. Best practices also can be found in sets of standards that clearly describe programs meeting the same needs. In some cases, though, standards or comparable programs do not exist. In these cases, the evaluator may choose to consult with experts who work with programs meeting similar needs. To avoid the expenses involved with hiring outside consultants, evaluators can establish an ad hoc evaluation committee of stakeholders with different perspectives about the program under question. Committee members can visit similar programs or review proven policies or procedures from those groups to compare with the newly established program.

Process Evaluation

Whereas formative evaluations are done to ensure new programs are being implemented properly, process evaluation is used for well-established programs. *Process evaluations* assess the quality and purposes of program activities and the extent to which they relate to the desired outcome or produce desired results (Royse et al., 2016). The purpose of process evaluation is to look at the process of planning, implementing, and modifying an existing program to determine if the outcomes seen are related to the procedures employed or if unexpected outcomes are related to difficulties with program implementation.

Documentation of program activities is key in process evaluation, with a focus on three areas. First, a thorough program description is warranted. These descriptions should include details about the operations of a program (Royse et al., 2016). Most agencies collect many details regarding program operations, such as client demographics, program usage reports, information about the characteristics and training of staff, meeting minutes, correspondence, satisfaction surveys, program costs and expenditures, and the like. This information can answer questions about why the program was implemented, program components, changes made to the program, the extent to which the program is serving the intended people, the roles played by staff members, and changes in funding that may have affected program processes.

Evaluators also should collect information regarding program monitoring to understand what has happened previously in a program and who was affected (Royse et al., 2016). Ongoing program monitoring is essential for all programs, not just in the process of an evaluation. A program mission statement, along with overarching goals and the specific, measurable objectives arising from those goals should be examined by the evaluator and compared with the data collected by the program. This information will prove valuable to determine if the program maintains its original focus or if the purpose and intended audience has changed over time (often due to shifts in funding or personnel).

As part of their standard procedures, organizations will generally collect data regarding the quality of the interventions and services they provide, which will be important for the evaluator to use in a process evaluation. This type of quality assurance data will help the evaluator (and program staff) determine whether program interventions comply with accepted standards and remain dependable and constant, which should account for positive outcomes. Because an advantage of collecting quality assurance data is program accountability (Royse et al., 2016), organizations collect and complete documentation to ensure clients are ethically treated with appropriate interventions, and this documentation can also be used for process evaluation.

Outcome Evaluation

When one conceptualizes program evaluation, thoughts immediately move to what is known as outcome evaluation. An *outcome evaluation* addresses questions related to execution of the program (Mohajeri-Nelson & Negley, 2020), the extent to which the program "works," the outcomes observed, or how the outcomes differed from intended program goals. Here are some example questions evaluators can ask when evaluating program outcomes:

- Did the program reach its intended outcome/s or goals?
- What effects did the program intend and what was achieved?
- What was the magnitude of the outcome or change?
- Did the program yield a similar outcome for a majority of participants?
- Why was the program more successful for certain participants?
- Were there any unforeseen consequences (negative or positive) related to the program?
- Were there any external forces that influenced (negative or positive) outcomes related to the program?

An investigation of program goals and objectives is key in an outcome evaluation. The goals the program purports to achieve, coupled with the specific, measurable objectives stated in program documentation, give the evaluator a criterion on which to measure program success. Program objectives are analogous to research questions for an empirical study and should drive the underlying methodological choices.

Outcome evaluation questions stemming from program objectives may be contextualized in terms of time (i.e., short-, intermediate-, and long-term effects; Jaegers et al., 2014). In the case of many educational evaluations, it may be appropriate to measure only intermediate- or long-term effects. For example, the Greendale Garden Project may show a positive influence on students' abilities to regulate their emotions, but this change would not happen immediately (e.g., Thoder et al., 2010).

Moreover, the quality of an outcome evaluation is reliant on the choices made in other aspects of the evaluation process. Though it is widely recognized that experimental designs more easily allow an evaluator to attribute changes in outcomes to the effects of the program, in educational evaluation it is often implausible or unethical to assign participants into control conditions (e.g., Salabarría-Peña & Walsh, 2007) because this means the evaluator will deny some individuals access to an intervention (McCoy & Castner, 2020). Care must be taken in the design of an evaluation's activities to ensure program clients are treated ethically while also maintaining the quality of evaluation activities.

COMMUNICATING FINDINGS TO STAKEHOLDERS

One of the main differences between program evaluation and more research-based paradigms is the potential of immediacy of impact to stakeholders. As mentioned earlier in this chapter, the focus of program evaluation is to analyze the effectiveness of an organization or program run by that organization. Of course, the ultimate goal of the evaluation process is to improve the program. However, the data collection process may bring to light information that could be in favor of or against the program's current structures, procedures, and outcomes. With this in mind, a key component in program evaluation is the communication of collected data from the evaluation team to stakeholders.

Once data are collected and analyzed, the evaluation team should be cognizant of the possibility that stakeholders might be disappointed with the findings. It is important to get to know the audience that will eventually consume the data. For program evaluation, that audience includes the stakeholders themselves. Evaluators should remember, as mentioned earlier in this chapter, that stakeholders might bring a biased, "rose-colored" outlook to interviews or other parts of the data collection process (Verschuren & Zsolnai, 1998). Indeed, political struggles could arise if disgruntled stakeholders present less than favorable information. On the other hand, evaluators might feel pressured to ignore unfavorable findings due to political substructures (Royse et al., 2016). Ethical dilemmas like this must be considered when presenting results of program evaluation.

Data presentation can become even more complex when considering the perspective of the evaluator. The position of the evaluator in relation to the program itself must be considered when presenting results. Internal evaluators are typically viewed as being more trustworthy, available, and generally in-tune with the organization in question. By the same token, they are viewed as having a limited, sometimes biased perspective in the evaluation process. External evaluators are typically viewed as having a more unbiased perspective, but hold a limited level of trust with the stakeholders (Royse et al., 2016).

A way to bridge the stakeholder-evaluator gap is to try to engage stakeholders in the data presentation process. Evaluators can venture outside of conventional unilateral formats for data presentation often found in traditional research. Monologue delivery of information from evaluator to stakeholder can be replaced with interactive discussions or poster-board sessions that are open to feedback. Lewis and colleagues (2019) recommend facilitating a data party for stakeholders. They recommend setting up data placemats, poster boards, and gallery walks to increase participation among stakeholders.

The need to engage in more collaborative research within special education has been well documented (Bell et al., 2009; Robertson et al., 2012; Zetlin et al., 2011). Salerno and Kibler (2016) conducted an ethnographic study at a university in a South Atlantic state concerning teachers' discourse about students perceived to have special needs or exceptionalities. The results of the study revealed that preservice teachers (PSTs) often referred to particular minorities and students with exceptionalities with monolithic titles, displaying perhaps the most negative aspect of teaching, which can be described as labeling students as "low" or "abnormal." The authors concluded that such labeling can inadvertently occur through poor instruction or simply a lack of awareness of the needs of students with exceptionalities. Potentially, the same could happen in special education program evaluation. A participatory approach could be particularly useful in building trust among minority and marginalized groups (Royse et al., 2016), as well as with special needs groups. Depending on the backgrounds of the stakeholders, it also may be wise to have an ethnically, culturally, or professionally diverse evaluation team, if possible. Doing so may reduce fear of mistreatment, especially among groups who may distrust researchers due to past unethical research (Royse et al., 2016).

After collecting and interpreting the data, and before presenting the final report, we need to address the question of presenting our interpretations and subsequent conclusions to the stakeholders. Before the final report is completed and submitted for publication, it is generally good practice to allow all stakeholders to read through the report (Brandon, 1999). In qualitative research, this process is commonly referred to as *member-checking*. Member-checking is one of the last steps in qualitative research before presenting the final report, and it can involve allowing participants, or stakeholders in program evaluation, to read through interview transcriptions and questionnaires, as well as a triangulation of notes from focus group memos and observations recorded by the evaluation team. This type of member-checking with stakeholders can add to the trustworthiness of the evaluation findings and interpretations (Johnson & Christensen, 2017).

For program evaluation, the member-checking process is necessary to prepare stakeholders for findings that could potentially have adverse effects, including misrepresentation of information by the evaluation team, resentment between colleagues in an organization and, in some cases, loss of employment. By allowing stakeholders to first review the findings, interpretations, and conclusions, the evaluation team can edit the report before presentation or publication and avoid shock among stakeholders. By maintaining ongoing communication between evaluators and stakeholders, it is more likely stakeholders will be prepared to hear and enact the recommendations in the final report.

Yarbrough et al. (2010) recommend that evaluation approaches, activities, and results be communicated in an ongoing fashion in order to respond to changes in evaluation needs and timelines. They also suggest that detailing the ongoing evaluation process might enhance the feasibility and accuracy of the evaluation, as well as the evaluator's credibility in the eyes of stakeholders. More specifically, Yarbrough et al. (2010) recommend the following six steps to ensure timely and appropriate reporting:

1. Consider when and how to best share information
2. Communicate information at intervals and phases of the evaluation process (but not in overwhelming detail)
3. Use both formal and informal communication to relay information (as opposed to only a written final report of findings and interpretations)
4. Be sensitive to broader social implications when planning how to communicate with stakeholders
5. Plan on helping stakeholders and consumers of the evaluation report understand and apply technical language
6. Provide an executive summary that directly responds to stakeholders' needs

Inherent in program evaluation is the potential for immediate impact, for better or worse, to an organization. For this reason, these recommendations become particularly important. This is especially true when communicating findings with specific cultures, including minority groups, marginalized cultures, and special needs populations.

When preparing to present interpretations and conclusions to stakeholders, traditional research dissemination by itself may not be the best option. Of course, the evaluation team should prepare a formal written report, fit for publication. The language of the report should be accessible to stakeholders and grantees. For presentation and dissemination, we can also think outside the box by looking beyond traditional formats. For example, evaluators might consider sharing findings through various channels, including website presentations, social media, infographics, town hall meetings, radio interviews, or podcasts. Evaluators might also opt to use the data party format (Lewis et al., 2019) with data place mats, poster boards, and gallery walks, as mentioned previously. In this sense, the evaluator can make the presentation of data and interpretation of conclusions a collaborative process between evaluator and stakeholder. For program evaluation, the most appropriate format will depend on the stakeholders—a more static, unilateral presentation or one that is more interactive and inclusive.

When the appropriate format is chosen, it is a good idea to develop a dissemination plan. Table 14-1 is an example communication matrix for how information about the program evaluation findings might be communicated to different stakeholders of the GGP.

In this planning matrix, we have potential for varying levels of expertise and reading levels to promote accessibility. The authors of the matrix have considered these varying levels by preparing a more formal presentation/handout for teachers and a less formal, more interactive, platform for students. In this way, evaluators can define who their stakeholders or audiences are, what bottom-line information is most important, how and when to best disseminate the information, and with whom to communicate first. This type of chart can also help evaluators avoid becoming unorganized if they choose a nontraditional format for communication.

It bears repeating that these outside of the box ideas for alternative formats are not recommended as replacements for formal written reports and presentations. They are simply additions that might aid in the information communication process.

COSTS AND OTHER IMPORTANT ISSUES

Several cost factors should be considered when conducting a program evaluation. The W.K. Kellogg Foundation recommends considering labor costs for external versus internal evaluators, compensation for participants, translation and interpretation fees, cost of supplies, and Institutional

TABLE 14-1. MATRIX FOR COMMUNICATION OF FINDINGS FROM PROGRAM EVALUATION

STAKEHOLDERS	INFORMATION NEEDS	MODE OF COMMUNICATION	TIMING OF COMMUNICATION	PRIORITY
Students	Results: AIR Self-Determination Assessment and analysis of student grades and behavior	Digital interactive poster session	Beginning of first quarter (August) and third quarter (January) for U.S. academic calendar	High
Parents	Results: Analysis of student grades and behavior	Evening town hall meeting/Q&A session/ student testimonials	Winter break and post-end of instruction	Medium
Administrators	All data, including funding efficacy report	Interactive videoconference/ executive reports	Earliest availability	High
Teachers	All student-/teacher-related data	Grade-level group conferences	Quarterly in-service meetings	High
Surrounding community	Short- and long-term outcome results	Town hall meeting/ Q&A session	End of academic school year (May)	Low

Review Board (IRB) fees, where applicable. Additionally, method of payment might vary according to whether evaluators are internal or external members of the program. If evaluators are external, travel costs might become a prohibitive factor, and if they are program employees, consideration must be made about whether evaluating the program will be part of job responsibilities or require extra work time and compensation.

Software and hardware should also have their place in the budget. Although some hardware may only require a one-time purchase, many software packages and a growing list of digital applications offer limited subscriptions that can become expensive, depending on evaluator and program needs. Data analysis software, such as SPSS for quantitative purposes, can range from the hundreds to the thousands. Qualitative data analysis software (e.g., NVivo, MAXQDA, or ATLAS.ti) can also vary in price, depending on the scope of the project.

Of course, all these factors are linked with the timeline of the program evaluation. Longer evaluation projects can be more expensive in terms of compensation and data analysis. When evaluating education programs, the budget might need to cover several semesters or years, which can easily double or triple an initial estimate for costs. Additionally, these costs may need to be considered for multiple phases of an evaluation. By looking at costs for prior evaluations, we can see total costs can easily exceed the $30,000 awarded to the GGP program. Some examples include K-12 efforts like the New York City Teacher Incentive Program at approximately $50,0000 and the community-wide intervention program, Triple P (Positive Parenting Program) at approximately $300,000 (Coalition for Evidence-Based Policy, 2012). Thus, evaluators must carefully balance evaluation goals with the costs to conduct a thorough evaluation when planning their methods.

A Word About Ethics in Program Evaluation

Because program evaluation is a subtype of research, the same basic rules of ethics apply as would elsewhere (see Chapter 3). Specifically, the Department of Health and Human Services has codified regulations related to the use of human subjects in research (Protection of Human Subjects, 2009), and evaluators must adhere to these regulations, particularly as they relate to guidelines for those from protected populations. However, program evaluations, particularly when the intent of the evaluation is to improve the delivery of services, are often exempted from IRB review.

In this section, we will highlight the ethical considerations that are unique to program evaluation. First and foremost, evaluators must be familiar with the ethical guidelines in the field in which they will work. In special education, look to the Council for Exceptional Children (2015) for ethical guidelines. Others that may be important in work with special populations are published by the American Evaluation Association (2018), the American Educational Research Association (2011), the American Psychological Association (2017), and the National Association of Social Workers (2017).

Remember, the implications of evaluation research can have consequences. Because funding decisions are often made based on evaluation results, individuals may lose services and people may lose their jobs if funding is cut. This is not said to scare evaluators into reporting only positive program results, disregarding data contrary to that which shows program success, or even falsifying data. Rather, it is a call for the necessity of staying in communication with stakeholders throughout the duration of the evaluation. Evaluators will want to communicate findings incrementally rather than blindsiding stakeholders at the end with negative results. If there is bad news to deliver, stakeholders can be a vital source in helping you determine how to best craft the message.

However, your stakeholders should not determine the message. Not only do stakeholders perceive the evaluation through their own lens or perspective (meaning they do not have all relevant information at their disposal), but their perception is often clouded by funding decisions. They will be keenly aware that negative results may mean program funding will be cut, resulting in consequences for the program. As the evaluator, you must avoid letting your evaluation recommendations be influenced too greatly by stakeholders' perspectives, but rather use their experience with program participants and staff to help you craft the message in the way it will be best received.

TABLE 14-2. COMMON MISCONCEPTIONS AND CLARIFICATIONS ABOUT PROGRAM EVALUATION	
MISCONCEPTION	**BETTER UNDERSTANDING**
Program evaluation is simply a watered-down version of research.	Research and program evaluation utilize similar methods of inquiry; however, the goal-driven nature of program evaluation mandates that the evaluation be focused on describing the extent to which the program is effective rather than describing or explaining a larger phenomenon as a whole.
Program evaluation is only necessary when external funding is at stake.	It is true that program evaluation is often done in order to determine program efficacy, and to ensure that programs are meeting grant-mandated strides, in order to receive additional funding. These are only two of the important reasons to conduct program evaluation. Academic programs often conduct self-studies to ensure effectiveness, and improve or diagnose problems.
Effective evaluations can only be done by an individual external to the organization.	Evaluation success is often determined by evaluator skill, evaluator support, and a desire to paint a realistic picture of the program. These are all goals that can be accomplished with an internal evaluator. In fact, an evaluator native to a program will likely receive more support from the organization. The internal evaluator also knows enough about internal politics and policies to ensure the evaluation is effective.

Because general research guidelines apply to program evaluation, confidentiality of data is of utmost importance (see Chapter 4). Often, respondents/participants will know each other. Maintaining the confidentiality of responses is important so that those responses do not create divisions or problems within the organization, particularly between employees and their supervisors. Moreover, because evaluators are often paid by the program or funding agency, the client will require access to all collected data. This means you may not be able to collect the data you wish because you may not be able to maintain confidentiality. Table 14-2 includes a list of common misconceptions associated with program evaluation, and Table 14-3 provides additional resources to consult.

SUMMARY

Program evaluation is uniquely designed to examine the implementation and effectiveness of programs intended to impact outcomes for clients and participants. The close connection with people and programs required in evaluation research, coupled with the immediate impacts an evaluator can make on individuals, make program evaluation an attractive paradigm for conducting novel investigations. In the course of the development of evaluation goals and logic models with stakeholders and continuing throughout the evaluation processes, concluding with the presentation of findings, special educators who employ program evaluation methods have a unique ability to inform best practices and affect change in the lives of others.

TABLE 14-3. ADDITIONAL RESOURCES

RESOURCE	DESCRIPTION
Centers for Disease Control and Prevention. (2012, May 11). Introduction to program evaluation for public health programs: A self-study guide. https://www.cdc.gov/eval/guide/cover/index.htm	This website by the Centers for Disease Control and Prevention consists of a concise and easy-to-understand "how-to" guide to aid novice evaluators in the evaluation process.
Council for Exceptional Children. (2015). Ethical principles and professional practices for special educators. https://www.cec.sped.org/Standards/Ethical-Principles-and-Practice-Standards	This website details the ethical principles and practices adopted by the Council for Exceptional Children. All special education professionals should adhere to these ethical guidelines.
W. K. Kellogg Foundation. (2006, February 2). Logic model development guide. https://www.wkkf.org/resource-directory/resources/2004/01/logic-model-development-guide	The W. K. Kellogg Foundation has provided a downloadable document to aid evaluators in the development of a logic model for their own evaluation projects.
W. K. Kellogg Foundation. (2017, November 29). The step-by-step guide to evaluation: How to become savvy evaluation consumers. https://www.wkkf.org/resource-directory/resource/2017/11/wk-kellogg-foundation-step-by-step-guide-to-evaluation	Designed to be accessible to individuals having little experience with program evaluation, the W. K. Kellogg Foundation published a step-by-step guide to the evaluation process.

Additional Readings

Royse, D., Thyer, B. A., & Padget, D. K. (2016). *Program evaluation: An introduction to an evidence-based approach* (6th ed.). Cengage Learning.

Wholey, J. S., Hatry, H. P., & Newcomer, K. E. (Eds.). (2010). *Handbook of practical program evaluation.* Jossey-Bass.

Yarbrough, D. B., Shula, L. M., Hopson, R. K., & Caruthers, F. A. (2010). *The program evaluation standards: A guide for evaluators and evaluation users* (3rd ed.). Corwin Press.

CHAPTER REVIEW

1. Thinking about what you have learned about research and program evaluation, how would you contrast the fundamental differences between the two processes? How are they similar?
2. Why is it important to have obtain perspective from various stakeholders?
3. What is the conceptual purpose of a logic model?
4. What are the major components of the logic model?
5. Contrast the stages of program evaluation. In which stage do you believe it is the easiest to conceptualize? Explain your answer.
6. What are the approaches that an evaluator may take in order to provide evidence that a program has been implemented as designed? Which approach do you believe would be the most effective? Explain your answer.
7. As an evaluator, how would you account for ethical challenges you might encounter?

REFERENCES

American Educational Research Association. (2011). Code of ethics. http://www.aera.net/Portals/38/docs/About_AERA/CodeOfEthics(1).pdf

American Evaluation Association. (2018). American Evaluation Association guiding principles for evaluators. https://www.eval.org/p/cm/ld/fid=51

American Psychological Association. (2017). Ethical principles of psychologists and code of conduct (2002, amended effective June 1, 2010, and January 1, 2017). https://www.apa.org/ethics/code/index.aspx

Ayers, T. D. (1987). Stakeholders as partners in evaluation: A stakeholder-collaborative approach. *Evaluation and Program Planning, 10*(3), 263-271. https://doi.org/10.1016/0149-7189(87)90038-3

Bell, S. M., McCallum, R. S., Kirk, E. R., Brown, K. S., Fuller, E. J., & Scott, K. W. (2009). Psychometric properties of the foreign language attitudes and perceptions survey for college students. *Assessment for Effective Intervention, 35*(1), 54-60. https://doi.org/10.1177/1534508408326206

Brandon, P. R. (1999). Involving program stakeholders in reviews of evaluators' recommendations for program revisions. *Evaluation and Program Planning, 22*(3), 363-372. https://doi.org/10.1016/S0149-7189(99)00030-0

Bryson, J. M., & Patton, M. Q. (2010). Analyzing and engaging stakeholders. In J. S. Wholey, H. P. Hatry, & K. E. Newcomer (Eds.), *Handbook of practical program evaluation* (3rd ed., pp. 30-54). Jossey-Bass.

Centers for Disease Control and Prevention. (2012, May 11). Introduction to program evaluation for public health programs: A self-study guide. https://www.cdc.gov/eval/guide/cover/index.htm

Center for Theory of Change. (2019). What is theory of change? Retrieved March 15, 2020, from https://www.theoryofchange.org/what-is-theory-of-change/

Chen, H.-T., & Rossi, P. H. (1983). Evaluating with sense: The theory-driven approach. *Evaluation Review, 7*(3), 283–302. https://doi.org/10.1177/0193841X8300700301

Coalition for Evidence-Based Policy. (2012). Rigorous program evaluations on a budget: How low-cost randomized controlled trials are possible in many areas of social policy. (ED541837). ERIC. https://files.eric.ed.gov/fulltext/ED541837.pdf

Council for Exceptional Children. (2015). Ethical principles and professional practice standards for special educators. https://www.cec.sped.org/Standards/Ethical-Principles-and-Practice-Standards

Gilliam, A., Davis, D., Barrington, T., Lacson, R., Uhl, G., & Phoenix, U. (2002). The value of engaging stakeholders in planning and implementing evaluations. *AIDS Education and Prevention, 14* (Suppl. A), 5-17.

Gross, J. G. (1981). Delphi: A program planning technique. *Journal of Extension, 19*(May/June), 23-28.

Jaegers, L., Dale, A. M., Weaver, N., Buchholz, B., Welch, L., & Evanoff, B. (2014). Development of a program logic model and evaluation plan for a participatory ergonomics intervention in construction. *American Journal of Industrial Medicine, 57*(3), 351-361.

Johnson, R. B., & Christensen, L. (2017). *Educational research: Quantitative, qualitative, and mixed approaches.* (6th ed.). Sage.

Lewis, K. M., Ewers, T., Bird, M., & Wilkins, T. (2019). Engage stakeholders in program evaluation: Throw them a party! *Journal of Extension, 57*(4).

Mathison, S. (2007). What is the difference between evaluation and research? And, why do we care. In N. L. Smith & P. Brandon (Eds.). *Fundamental issues in evaluation*. Guilford Publishers.

McCoy, C. A., & Castner, J. (2020). Logic models for program evaluation in emergency nursing. *Journal of Emergency Nursing, 46*(1), 12–15. https://doi.org/10.1016/j.jen.2019.11.005

McLaughlin, J. A., & Jordan, G. B. (1999). Logic models: Tools for telling your program's performance story. *Evaluation and Program Planning, 22*(1), 65-72. https://doi.org/10.1016/S0149-7189(98)00042-1

McLaughlin, J. A., & Jordan, G. B. (2010). Using logic models. In J. S. Wholey, H. P. Hatry, & K. E. Newcomer (Eds.), *Handbook of practical program evaluation* (3rd ed., pp. 55-80). Jossey-Bass.

Mohajeri-Nelson, N., & Negley, T. (2020, March 25). Best practices in program evaluation. Colorado Department of Education. https://www.cde.state.co.us/fedprograms/dper/evalrpts

Morris, D. B. (2002). The inclusion of stakeholders in evaluation: Benefits and drawbacks. *The Canadian Journal of Program Evaluation, 17*(2), 49-58.

National Association of Social Workers. (2017, August 4). Code of ethics (1996, amended effective August 4, 2017). https://www.socialworkers.org/About/Ethics/Code-of-Ethics/Code-of-Ethics-English

Pancer, S. M., & Westhues, A. (1989). A developmental stage approach to program evaluation. *Evaluation Review, 13*(1), 56-77. https://doi.org/10.1177/0193841X8901300105

Patton, M. Q. (2008). *Utilization-focused evaluation* (4th ed.). Sage.

Peyton, D. J., & Scicchitano, M. (2017). Devil is in the details: Using logic models to investigate program process. *Evaluation and Program Planning, 65*, 156-162. http://dx.doi.org/10.1016/j.evalprogplan.2017.08.012

Protection of Human Subjects, 45 C.F.R. 46 (2009). https://www.hhs.gov/ohrp/sites/default/files/ohrp/policy/ohrpregulations.pdf

Robertson, P. M., García, S. B., McFarland, L. A., & Rieth, H. J. (2012). Preparing culturally and linguistically responsive special educators: It "does" take a village. *Interdisciplinary Journal of Teaching and Learning, 2*(3), 115-130.

Royse, D., Thyer, B. A., & Padgett, D. K. (2016). *Program evaluation: An introduction to an evidence-based approach* (6th ed.). Cengage Learning.

Salabarría-Peña, Y., & Walsh, C. M. (2007, January). Practical use of program evaluation among sexually transmitted disease (STD) programs. Centers for Disease Control and Prevention. https://www.cdc.gov/std/program/pupestd.htm

Salerno, A. S., & Kibler, A. K. (2016). "This group of difficult kids": The discourse preservice English teachers use to label students. *Journal of Education for Students Placed at Risk, 21*(4), 261-278. https://doi.org/10.1080/10824669.2016.1205496

Thoder, V. J., Hesky, J. G., & Cautilli, J. D. (2010). Using reliable change to calculate clinically significant progress in children with EBD: A BHRS program evaluation. *International Journal of Behavioral Consultation and Therapy, 6*(1), 45-66. https://doi.org/10.1037/h0100897

Verschuren, P. J. M., & Zsolnai, L. (1998). Norms, goals, and stakeholders in program evaluation. *Human Systems Management, 17*(2), 155-160.

W. K. Kellogg Foundation. (2006, February 2). Logic model development guide. https://www.wkkf.org/resource-directory/resource/2006/02/wk-kellogg-foundation-logic-model-development-guide

Yarbrough, D. B., Shula, L. M., Hopson, R. K., & Caruthers, F. A. (2010). *The program evaluation standards: A guide for evaluators and evaluation users* (3rd ed.). Corwin Press.

Zetlin, A., Beltran, D., Salcido, P., Gonzalez, T., & Reyes, T. (2011). Building a pathway of optimal support for English language learners in special education. *Teacher Education and Special Education, 34*(1), 59-70. https://doi.org/10.1177/0888406410380423

Translating Special Education Research to Practice

With contributions from Maria B. Peterson-Ahmad, PhD; Randa Keeley, PhD;
and Kimberly Floyd, PhD

INTRODUCTION

Special educators have access to a variety of evidence-aligned strategies. Modalities such as open educational resources and social media can afford easier access to such materials; however, it is important to understand how to justify the validity of content in such platforms and the way in which they fit into the overall scope of the school and/or district continuous improvement plan. This chapter discusses how to translate research to practice through the lens of multiple variables related to special education research, such as: implementation science, effective and sustainable research dissemination practices, how social media and open source materials impact research, and how to communicate research to the general public. Each section of this chapter presents critical considerations for researchers and suggestions for best practices related to the collection of data as well as dissemination. Additionally, the primary topics of the chapter are presented in a hypothetical scenario to facilitate discussion on variables related to translating facets of research as presented in this chapter.

Hott, B. L., Brigham, F. J., & Peltier, C.
Research Methods in Special Education (pp. 277-291).
© 2021 SLACK Incorporated.

CHAPTER OBJECTIVES

→ Identify characteristics of implementation science.

→ Distinguish methods to ensure that special education research is disseminated in an effective and sustainable manner.

→ Explain how social media and open source materials can afford additional opportunities for special education research and dissemination of research.

→ Identify ways to communicate special education research to the general public.

KEY TERMS

- **Community-Based Participatory Research**: A research process that is intentionally conducted among specific groups that have a vested interest in the outcome of the research.

- **Continuous Improvement**: A cyclical process intended to improve processes within a system.

- **Implementation Science**: A method of improvement that focuses on how proposed changes related to the specific educational setting/context are carried out to ensure that specific variables and contextual factors are taken into consideration throughout the process to ensure data-driven decision making.

- **Open Educational Resources**: Freely accessible, openly licensed text, media, and other digital assets that are useful for teaching, learning, and assessing as well as for research purposes.

- **Open Source Materials**: Any software or other intellectual property that is distributed and made available to the public without cost.

- **Research-to-Practice Gap**: Differences in observed practices within school settings and what empirical research suggests to improve student outcomes.

- **Social Media**: Forms of electronic communication through which users create online communities to share information, ideas, messages, or other content.

CASE STUDY

Hannah J. is a full-time special education teacher and graduate student working on her master's degree in special education at her university. She is completing her final research project and has learned about how to conduct research and analyze research data. She wants to make her research findings available and assist in continued change in her elementary school, which is undergoing a data review and strategic planning process. She is not interested in publishing her work but would like to share her findings with other district personnel as well as parents. Further, Hannah would like to continue collecting data for this project and have a sustainable data-driven process for her school. She would like to use this self-study to make necessary changes in her elementary school. Hannah is trying to decide how to evaluate the data that she has collected to make long-term changes at her elementary school as well as how to continuously share her findings with other district leaders, teachers at the elementary school, and parents.

RESEARCH DISSEMINATION

The gap between research and practice is not a new concept and continues to be a recurring theme in education, despite considerable efforts to bridge this gap and disseminate information to practitioners (e.g., Cook et al., 2009; Odom et al., 2005). Students receiving special education services have greater outcomes when credible strategies, interventions, practices (e.g., evidence-based practices), and programs are developed with rigorous standards through formal research design and implementation (Cook et al., 2012). Evidence-based practices (EBPs) are supported by the rigor of science and mathematical evidence to influence guidance and decision-making specific to the effectiveness of the practice. Unfortunately, practitioners often rely on traditional practices not backed by evidence because it is the way that the intervention or practice has always been done or they simply believe it is more effective. Implementation and dissemination of valid and reliable intervention practices, such as EBPs, is the critical link between research and practice. However, special education practitioners have reported using ineffective instructional practices that have been debunked by research (e.g., learning styles, ability to multitask during learning process, testing is harmful to learning) with the same or greater frequency than effective, research-based practices (Cook & Odom, 2013). In this scenario, Hannah is basing her decisions and findings on data collected from a well-designed pilot study.

The way in which EBPs or other education research is disseminated must be considered. New researchers may not readily understand the vast array of not only types of articles, but also levels of journals (e.g., tier, impact factor, readership, paid versus free access) in which those articles may be printed. Additionally, there are different types of articles (e.g., practitioner, literature review, meta-analysis, research) that all have value. Although practitioner articles may be more accessible to educators in the field, research articles can contribute to identifying additional EBPs, depending on the rigor of the data collection process. Both types of publications have merit, but researchers should consider where their research might be published prior to data collection. Effective dissemination can be understood as: (a) embedding new initiatives in local structures and procedures that caused changes to occur to them (Stringfield & Datnow, 1998); and (b) scaling and translating the initiative into other areas such as other departments, faculties, or institutions (Coburn, 2003). Special education practitioners need information that is easy to understand with practical strategies and a feasible way to implement them. In fact, less can be more when reporting information on EBPs (Zikmund-Fisher et al., 2010). When readers are overloaded with too much information, shortcuts may be taken or they may focus on only one facet of information. Further, practitioners may even fail to make a choice at all and default back to the status quo (Hibbard & Peters, 2003). The SUCCESs (simple, unexpected, concrete, credible, emotional, stories) method can assist with disseminating research (Cook et al., 2013). Table 15-1 illustrates the incorporation of effective dissemination practices with this method.

IMPLEMENTATION SCIENCE

Implementation science is defined as "the scientific study of methods to promote the systematic uptake of research findings and other evidence-based practices into routine practice" (Eccles & Mittman, 2006, p. 1). Implementation science involves the study of how proposed changes related to a specific educational setting or context are carried out to ensure that specific variables are considered to ensure data-driven decision making. Implementation science assists educational organizations with understanding how processes, procedures, and/or conditions promote or prohibit the transfer, adoption, and use of specific educational practices in school settings (McKay, 2017). It applies voices from multiple stakeholders, including K-12 teachers, students, administration, related service providers, institutions of higher education, researchers, and/or community-based organizations. These voices provide overarching guidance through all phases of the implementation process,

TABLE 15-1. SUCCESS: PRINCIPLES FOR EFFECTIVE DISSEMINATION PRACTICES	
S (Simple)	• Provide core messages that can be easily recalled that provide generalized guidance. • Understand specific needs of districts and teachers and present the most critical information.
U (Unexpected)	• Utilize creative manners to present key information (e.g., audio, visual, various styles) and raise curiosity to learn more.
C (Concrete)	• Give examples and nonexamples of how a practice works and is implemented. • Use visual depictions to support numerical representations of data.
C (Credible)	• Collaborate with districts and their leaders to disseminate information.
E (Emotional)	• Use heuristics.
S (Stories)	• Use real-life, relevant experiences that correlate to the information being presented.
Adapted from Cook, B. G., Cook, L., & Landrum, T. J. (2013). Moving research into practice: Can we make dissemination stick? *Exceptional Children, 79*(2), 163-180.	

with each stakeholder playing a specific role in the variety of contexts that contribute to adapting chosen interventions accordingly to support the continuous improvement goals of the school/district (McKay, 2017). This is evidenced in the case study as Hannah is seeking an outlet to provide her findings to a larger audience within the K-12 stakeholder arena. Providing data to such key stakeholders will provide for decision-based recommendations for school and learning change.

The Implementation Science Process

The implementation science process occurs across four different stages with each having a unique function (Fixsen et al., 2009). The first step of the implementation science process begins with consideration of adopting a new program and/or practice. Implementing and sustaining new practices involves a host of complex and interrelated challenges, including issues related to the practice being promoted (e.g., relevance and fit target environment, efficiency, practicality), users (e.g., available time, mistrust of research, knowledge of EBPs, skills), and the institutional context (e.g., available resources, organizational structures and culture, staffing, coaching, training, administrative support; Fixsen et al., 2005; Tseng, 2012).

First, partnerships should conduct preimplementation assessments, make well-informed decisions about adapting interventions to the context, and plan strategies to build necessary capacity at the local level (McKay, 2017). The second step of the process is to move forward with a specific plan of action. After investigation of variables has occurred, school personnel form local implementation teams and participate in training to determine onset of implementation and establish communication protocols. Identification of current strengths and collection of resources and materials needed to launch the work and development of an implementation action plan is conducted (McKay, 2017). The third step is when initial implementation occurs and team members start using the specific practices in their schools, with assistance from team members. During this stage, the timelines and strategies for collecting and using data to make decisions and modify the strategy (if necessary) are vital. Sustaining structure during implementation requires support to assist teachers and address feedback to ensure that implementation runs smoothly and effectively. Feedback should be combined from all stakeholders to determine what did and did not work and what can be improved for the future in an

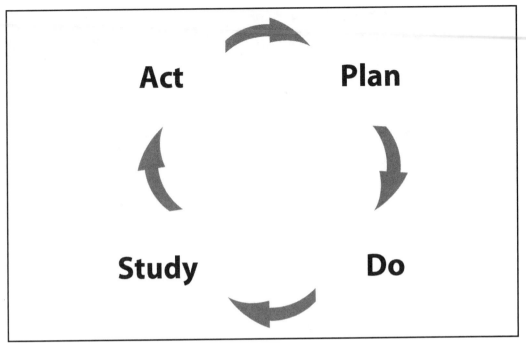

Figure 15-1. Plan-Do-Study-Act cycle.

effort to scale and sustain implementation (McKay, 2017). Lastly, full implementation occurs when the practices become a part of the standard operating procedure for schools and may be utilized with minimal or no assistance from external coaches or other technical assistance providers (Saldana et al., 2011). This strength can be seen in the mechanisms and processes for gathering feedback from stakeholders and identifying and facilitating the necessary adaptations to implement continuous improvement (McKay, 2017).

Plan-Do-Study-Act Cycle

A common inquiry cycle that can be used in conjunction with the implementation science process is the Plan-Do-Study-Act cycle (Figure 15-1). The Plan-Do-Study-Act cycle identifies clear goals and measures that connect specific strategies, over an established timeline, to accomplish the identified goals. The cycle is designed to assist project managers in thinking systematically by connecting observed outcomes and comparing predictions while noting discrepancies between predictions and observed outcomes (Blase et al., 2011; Carnegie Foundation for Advancement of Teaching, n.d.). Research plays a vital role in this process because the findings of a Plan-Do-Study-Act cycle for continuous improvement allow for informed decisions based on data gathered from testing a change identified by the educational entities specific goal(s) (Indiana Department of Education, 2018; Shakman et al., 2017). Table 15-2 illustrates how each step of the implementation science process and the Plan-Do-Study-Act cycle can work in tandem (Fixsen et al., 2005; Shakman et al., 2017, p. 5).

Fidelity of interventions and programs used in education settings must be implemented and monitored for accuracy and consistency of delivery to ensure that components are provided in a reliable manner across settings and individuals. In other words, fidelity of implementation ensures that an intervention or program is presented and implemented as originally intended (Davidson et al., 2003). Measurement of newly implemented practices or programs should rely on multiple data points that have been collected to assess improvements made, starting from baseline until after the specific strategies and processes used during the Plan-Do-Study-Act cycle of inquiry were

TABLE 15-2. IMPLEMENTATION SCIENCE PROCESS AS RELATED TO THE PLAN-DO-STUDY-ACT CYCLE

	IMPLEMENTATION SCIENCE PROCESS		PLAN-DO-STUDY-ACT CYCLE
Step 1	• Explore potential new program/practice • Relevancy to school/district • Efficiency/practicality • Who will use it? • What is the institutional context? • Collect baseline data to inform choice in target goal(s)/objectives • Formation of local implementation teams • Establish communication protocols	Plan	• Clarifies the problem • Identifies overall aim • Identifies the tool, process, or change that will be implemented • Targets objectives of the continuous improvement process
Step 2	• Implementation of chosen strategies • Provide support to teachers and other staff who are implementing strategies • Provide ongoing feedback	Do	• Implementation of the tool, process, or changes • Collection of data of the process to determine outcomes
Step 3	• Look at collected data in combination with feedback from stakeholders to determine adaptations needed	Study	• Analysis of data to determine extent of aim/goal(s) met from the Plan phase
Step 4	• Implement adaptations for continued improvement	Act	• Stakeholders make adjustments specific to aim/goal(s) based on data • Formulation of new theories/predictions • Changes made to overarching aim • Modification of tools or processes • Begin cycle again with new modifications

implemented (Shakman et al., 2017, p. 8). These data points drive decisions made throughout the entire implementation science cycle of continuous improvement. Understanding how these processes intertwine and the role that research and data collection play is vital for the success of an improvement science process within an educational context. Essentially, the overarching goal of implementation science is to research and understand how innovations are adopted and maintained (Greenhalgh et al., 2004). In our scenario, Hannah is interested in collecting data in order to have a sustainable data-driven process for her school. It will be imperative that there is implementation fidelity oversight so that ongoing data collection efforts are evaluating the same variables with the same integrity as the original study. By doing so, her data can be analyzed across time to inform the efficacy of practice.

ENSURING SUSTAINABILITY

Designing a sustainable line of research can be daunting and overwhelming for a new researcher. Careful planning and consideration of factors such as research method and design (i.e., quantitative, qualitative), research team, cost, and timeframe for data collection contribute to developing a research line that can be sustainable across an academic career. Additionally, novice researchers might consider the idea of shared research assets by developing research partnerships to extend their overall capacity for research (Steiner et al., 2014). The National Science Foundation (NSF) explains that while quantitative research tends to have more credibility in the research community, the value of the richness of qualitative research is likewise undeniable.

Ensuring the sustainability of research begins in the early stages of planning. There are two types of research: quantitative and qualitative. Seasoned researchers understand that the decision to conduct one or the other is not sustainable; rather, the research question guides the method of data collection that is implemented. The Corporation for National and Community Service (2020) suggests that four main components exist related to the design of a research agenda: (a) planning, (b) implementation, (c) analysis and reporting, and (d) using evaluation results for action and improvement. Each part of the cycle is interconnected and feeds off of the previous stage (Figure 15-2).

When planning a research agenda in totality or for a singular project, researchers should consider the following potential issues related to data collection: (a) potential credibility of the findings, (b) skill level of research partners, (c) potential cost of the research, and (d) time constraints (NSF, 2020). Regardless of the method selected for data collection, rigor in the data collection process tends to have the most weight when dissemination of research comes into play. Therefore, when planning for a sustainable line of research, researchers should ensure that the research is rigorous and that data collection, whether quantitative or qualitative, is free from flaws (Steiner et al., 2014). Additionally, collecting trustworthy data is critical in sustaining a long-term research agenda, and a noteworthy component of valid data is the research partners that assist researchers in the data collection process (Steiner et al., 2014). NSF suggests that quantitative studies require less consideration in the training of data collection due to the characteristics of numerical type data, but that qualitative data collection partners should be well trained and include high levels of supervision in an effort to garner trustworthy data.

The overall cost of a research project is often associated with the overall number of participants. Research with a higher number of participants can garner results that are more generalizable, but this type of research is costlier, whereas smaller studies may be less expensive, but the results may not be as generalizable. As a result, planning for a sustainable research agenda should include the benefits and drawbacks of the size of a proposed study, as well as potential funding opportunities for future, large-scale studies. Researchers may begin with smaller pilot studies and gradually build to larger studies after the research design has been perfected and the intervention has demonstrated promise.

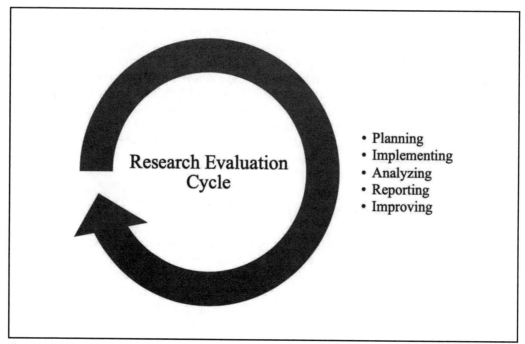

Figure 15-2. Research evaluation cycle.

Time constraints are a consideration in designing a research study. For example, research in the field of education is often beholden to the 9-month academic calendar, as well as any state-level testing or other school-related events. Therefore, planning to conduct a study in a PK-12 educational setting should take into consideration the time constraints placed on the research process by the school site or district. Additionally, the appropriate amount of time should be allocated regardless of the data collection method. As discussed in Chapter 13, a survey study may seem to take very little time to design and complete. This is not always the case when rigor of the study is considered. For example, for a rigorous survey study, researchers would have created survey questions after careful consideration of the literature, tested and validated those questions, and then allowed enough time for a high response rate from participants. Similarly, as presented in Chapter 10, qualitative research takes a significant amount of time in that data collection and analysis tend to overlap. As a result, researchers should plan to allow for ample time to collect data regardless of the study design.

Holve (2013) presents four pillars that are directly related to establishing a sustainable research agenda: (a) trust and value, (b) governance, (c) management, and (d) financial and administrative support. Trust and value are related to the relationship that researchers build with stakeholders. Researchers should ensure that commitments are held to all participants, including funders, participants, community partners, and collaborators, and that the research is of some value to the community and participants. Governance relates to the systems and personnel in place to ensure that the research project is run smoothly, and the privacy of participants is well protected. Management requires that the partners involved with the project have had time clearly allocated to fulfill responsibilities related to the research project. Finally, financial and administrative support can be a great benefit for the potential success of sustainable research. Researchers adhering to the first three pillars can expect to be competitive for future funding opportunities (Figure 15-3).

Steiner and colleagues (2014) suggest that when developing a research agenda, researchers should consider potential partnerships that could be developed across related research topics. The group refers to this as developing "shared research assets" to "facilitate a sequence of research studies in a specific content area or multiple areas" (p. 4). Sharing assets across researchers can increase

Figure 15-3. A graphic description of the Four Pillars for Sustainable Research. (Reproduced with permission from Holve, E. [2013]. Ensuring support for research and quality improvement [QI] networks: Four pillars of sustainability-an emerging framework. *The Journal of Electronic Health Data Methods, 1*[1], 1005. https://doi.org/10.13063/2327-9214.1005)

the volume of studies that a researcher can complete, and in turn the dissemination of that research, as well as development of future studies. Further, they promote developing a valid and trustworthy research process that can be used in multiple ways across a multitude of settings so that researchers are not continuously reinventing their research design for each study conducted.

Consideration of each of the factors related to developing a sustainable research agenda can be overwhelming for a new researcher. Understanding the interconnectedness of each component described above is critical to comprehending the research process.

OPEN SOURCE RESOURCES

Most educational research requires a rigorous peer-review process, long before the information is published and disseminated. Unfortunately, much of this peer-reviewed research is housed on systems where only institutions of higher education (IHEs) and other researchers have access. Consequently, this makes it difficult for practitioners to easily access the materials they need—to learn about new developments in their fields, or to read, replicate, and verify others' findings (OpenSource.com, 2019). Tying this to our case study, it is important to Hannah that all stakeholders have access to the implications and findings gleaned from her current and future studies. Although many of those stakeholders would not have access to publications from a peer-review outlet, an option is work published in open sources. *Open educational resources* (OERs) are learning materials including items such as presentation slides, podcasts, syllabi, images, lesson plans, lecture videos, maps, worksheets, and textbooks that can be accessed free of charge (OpenSource.com, 2019).

TABLE 15-3. OPEN EDUCATIONAL RESOURCE SITES FOR SPECIAL EDUCATION

RESOURCE	WEBSITE
Creative Commons	https://creativecommons.org/
Open Educational Research Commons	https://www.oercommons.org/
Collaboration for Effective Educator Development and Reform (CEEDAR) Center	https://ceedar.education.ufl.edu/innovation-configurations/
IRIS Center	https://iris.peabody.vanderbilt.edu/resources/iris-resource-locator/
do2Learn Teacher Toolbox	https://do2learn.com/disabilities/FASDtoolbox/index.htm
Center for Effective Collaboration & Practice	https://www.air.org/project/center-effective-collaboration-and-practice-cecp
Open Textbook Library	https://open.umn.edu/opentextbooks/subjects/5
The National Academies Press	https://www.nap.edu/topic/282/education
Merlot	https://www.merlot.org/
Internet Archive	https://archive.org/
Teaching Commons	https://teachingcommons.us/

Applying open licenses to educational materials can allow researchers further opportunities to collaborate with practitioners, particularly when sharing valid and reliable information on EBPs or building materials specifically differentiated for students. Practitioners can download materials for use in their classrooms that are timely, relevant, and become increasingly useful when distributing with others. There are multiple platforms on which both researchers and practitioners can access OERs (Table 15-3).

ROLE OF SOCIAL MEDIA

Social media has become commonplace in daily living and has afforded new opportunities for researchers to access information in a multitude of ways compared to traditional methods of research and data collection. Like OERs, social media platforms can serve as a powerful tool by allowing for research in which respondents can participate at a time best suited to them. Data sets that may include a broader scope of information from a more diverse population, efficiency of time in gathering and analyzing data, and increased authenticity of responses, data collection, and analysis can be achieved in many online social platforms. To date, conducting research on social media involves common platforms such as Facebook, Twitter, LinkedIn, and Reddit.

Characteristics of social media platforms align with the connectivism approach to learning. *Connectivism* acknowledges the role of information technology in the processes of accessing information from multiple sources and takes into account how certain information technologies can limit or expand the types of information available to learners and how the ability to draw distinctions between important and unimportant information is vital (Dunaway, 2011; Hertel & Wessman-Enzinger, 2017). Social media platforms foster spaces rich in discussion and knowledge of topics where people can affiliate around shared interests and encourage those with varying levels of knowledge to contribute ideas and mentor each other (Gee, 2004; Figure 15-4).

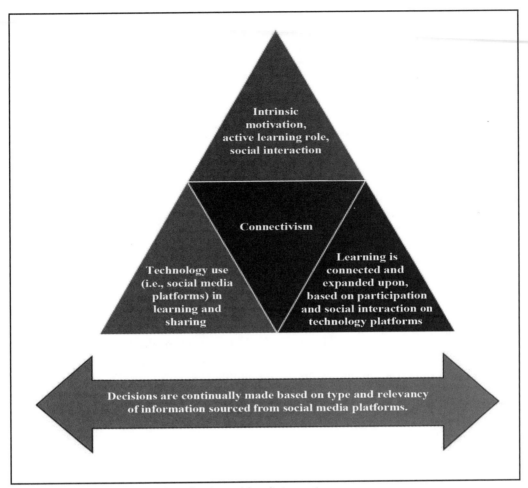

Figure 15-4. Connectivism approach as related to social media integration.

RESEARCH THROUGH PROFESSIONAL LEARNING NETWORKS

The rise of social media platforms has increased the utility of professional learning networks (PLNs) that support continuous learning and professional growth by creating relevant and meaningful connections and establishing a broader base of ideas on which to draw (Trust et al., 2017). PLNs can support research efforts with a wide variety of people, spaces, and tools that might not otherwise be readily available for traditional research methods and can allow for increased exposure to unexpected ideas that can improve practice and positively influence students' learning (Darling-Hammond et al., 2009). Participants involved in PLNs, including researchers, can share and gain knowledge on a variety of topics and gather insights and experiences from the varied network of participants.

Validity and Reliability of Social Media

The ability to discern quality resources is of the utmost necessity when using a social media platform for research purposes. However, it is important to note weaknesses of social media platforms in collecting data, including: only individuals with access to social media can participate, compositions of social profiles may be limited, and technical issues (Trust et al., 2017). Overall, it is imperative that researchers investigate the validity and reliability of any tool used for research on a social media platform and consider implications of both strengths and weaknesses within the research design. Social media can break down traditional barriers separating academic research from teaching, work-based learning, and informal learning (Kukulska-Hulme, 2012) and are no longer limited by their local networks or contexts. Researchers can connect and learn with a broader set of participants and discover new and relevant information.

Communicating Research to the General Public

Academics Chen, Diaz, Lucas, and Rosenthal (2010) explain that dissemination of research is often narrowly defined to include published articles or peer-reviewed presentations, while providing research project results to the participants or larger community is often not considered. Ironically, the participant group used in research projects is often where researchers would like to see change happen and yet sharing findings with this group is many times an afterthought or not done at all. Further, Holt and Chambers (2017) noted that in health-related research, only a fraction of research findings ever make an impact on the field or the participants.

Communicating research findings to the general public is an ethical responsibility (Chen et al., 2010). However, researchers should make certain considerations prior to sharing findings. Brettell (1994) describes potential complications that can arise when an author shares findings with participants. After reading findings from a researcher, a participant may feel as though some ideas, concepts, or phrases were interpreted incorrectly by the researcher and that the identities of the participants were too easily discovered (Brettell, 1994). This can lead to a distrust between researchers and participants and negatively impact the sustainability of the research.

The general public will often access research-related information online, but academics retrieve research from library systems or journal repositories (Thelwall & Harries, 2004). The general public does not have access to university library systems or journal repositories because these resources require a fee. However, academics need to be cognizant of ensuring that the general public have access to valid research. Although this problem is becoming less of an issue as online research services have developed over time with systems like Google Scholar, ResearchGate, and open source materials, the general public is less knowledgeable about the existence of these systems because they are all so interconnected with academia. A major issue with finding research in other areas online is that quality control continues to be a problem (Thelwall & Harries, 2004). Although it may be difficult to reach a wide, general audience when disseminating research, it is the ethical responsibility of researchers to ensure participants of the project are informed about outcomes. As mentioned previously, social media is a good option for Hannah to share her research. Social media will provide an outlet for greater viewership and, potentially, participation.

Chen, Diaz, Lucas, and Rosenthal (2010) describe community-based participatory research (CBPR), which is a research design often used in health-related fields to collect data on a specific population that would directly benefit from the knowledge of the research findings. Essentially, the population used in the study would have unique circumstances and would be personally invested in the outcomes of the project. When a CBPR project is implemented, dissemination of findings is a critical component in maintaining a strong relationship between researchers and community partners. When researchers abide by the ethical responsibility to disseminate all findings to research partners, the partnership remains healthy and the sustainability of the research becomes stronger. Although publication of research is tied to academic employment, dissemination of research findings to community partners is connected to the possibility of future research projects, as well as potential funding options. As a result, while developing strong partnerships through sharing information may seem unrelated to publication, cultivating those research partnerships has an impact on future research projects, funding, and publications (Chen et al., 2010). Table 15-4 includes a list of common misconceptions associated with translating research to practice, and Table 15-5 provides additional resources to consult.

TABLE 15-4. COMMON MISCONCEPTIONS AND CLARIFICATIONS ABOUT TRANSLATING SPECIAL EDUCATION INTO PRACTICE

MISCONCEPTION	BETTER UNDERSTANDING
Research in best education practices is easily accessible to everyone.	While some excellent free resources exist to access high level educational research (e.g., What Works Clearinghouse, Google Scholar, ResearchGate), there is much more research out there that can be found in academic journals that require a subscription. Many people outside of academia do not pay to have these subscriptions, and school districts do not often provide educators access to this type of research.
Open educational resources are not useful for researchers.	Applying open licenses to educational materials can allow researchers further opportunities to collaborate with practitioners, particularly when sharing valid and reliable information on evidence-based practices or building materials specifically differentiated for students.
A sustainable line of research should be derived from dissertation research.	While a sustainable research line could be derived from dissertation research, sustainable research is a result of careful planning and consideration of factors such as research method and design (i.e., quantitative, qualitative), research team, cost, and timeframe for data collection.

SUMMARY

It is important that special education practitioners have access to evidence-based research and classroom strategies found through open educational resources and social media. Having access to these types of platforms allows easier access in finding materials that support the school and/or district in its continuous improvement plan through the implementation science process and the Plan-Do-Study-Act cycle. Upholding the Four Pillars of Sustainable Research supports sustainability and (community) partnerships. The SUCCESs strategy can serve to effectively disseminate findings, allowing for greater access to a broader scope of professionals to foster educational discussions and decision making. Additionally, considerations must be taken when communicating special education research to the general public through transparency of findings/results and defined in a way that is understandable, so that all stakeholders continue to maintain a strong relationship.

CHAPTER REVIEW

1. What role can implementation science have in the research process, specific to special education?
2. What factors must be considered when using social media platforms to collect research data?
3. List steps that a new researcher might take when developing a sustainable research agenda.
4. What are some elements that researchers should consider prior to publishing research in open source repositories?
5. How does sharing research findings with the general public impact a researcher's overall line of research?

TABLE 15-5. ADDITIONAL RESOURCES	
RESOURCE	**DESCRIPTION**
https://ies.ed.gov/ncee/wwc/PracticeGuides	What Works Clearinghouse Practice Guides: provides recommendations for educators to address challenges in classrooms and schools based on research, practitioner experience, and expert opinions.
https://intensiveintervention.org/	National Center on Intensive Intervention: information and resources for administrators and practitioners to support the implementation of intensive intervention.
https://buildingrti.utexas.org/links-websites/center-response-to-intervention-american-institutes-for-research	Center on Response to Intervention: information and resources to support successful implementation and scale up of the components within Multi-Tiered Systems of Support and Response to Intervention.
https://iris.peabody.vanderbilt.edu/	IRIS Center: resources for evidence-based practices and interventions for individuals with disabilities ages birth to 21.
https://ceedar.education.ufl.edu/innovation-configurations/	CEEDAR Center Innovation Configurations: resources and modules to promote the implementation of evidence-based teacher preparation and professional development.

Additional Reading

Bryk., A. S., Gomez, L. M., Grunow, A., & LeMahieu, P. G. (2017). *Learning to improve: How America's schools get better at getting better.* Harvard Education Press.

REFERENCES

Blase, K. A., Fixsen, D. L., & Duda, M. (2011, February 8). Implementation science: Building the bridge between science and practice [PowerPoint slides]. https://fpg.unc.edu/sites/fpg.unc.edu/files/resources/presentations-and-webinars/FPG-Blase-Fixen-Duda-Implementation-Science-02-08-2011.pdf

Brettell, C. B. (Ed.). (1994). *When they read what we write: The politics of ethnography.* Bergin & Garvey.

Carnegie Foundation for Advancement of Teaching (n.d.). PDSA (Plan-Do-Study-Act). Retrieved March 17, 2020, from https://carnegienetworks.zendesk.com/hc/en-us/articles/115001233928-PDSA-Plan-Do-Study-Act-

Chen, P. G., Diaz, N., Lucas, G., & Rosenthal, M. S. (2010). Dissemination of results in community-based participatory research. *American Journal of Preventative Medicine, 39*(4), 372-378. https://doi.org/10.1016/j.amepre.2010.05.021

Coburn, C. E. (2003). Rethinking scale: Moving beyond numbers to deep and lasting change. *Educational Researcher, 32*(6), 3-12.

Cook, B. G., Cook, L., & Landrum, T. J. (2013). Moving research into practice: Can we make dissemination stick? *Exceptional Children, 79*(2), 163-180.

Cook, B. G., & Odom, S. L. (2013). Evidence-based practices and implementation science in special education. *Exceptional Children, 79*(2), 135-144.

Cook, B. G., Smith, G. J., & Tankersley, M. (2012). Evidence-based practices in education. In K. R. Harris, S. Graham, T. Urdan, C. B. McCormick, G. M. Sinatra, & J. Sweller (Eds.), *APA handbooks in psychology. APA educational psychology handbook, Vol. 1. Theories, constructs, and critical issues* (pp. 495-527). American Psychological Association. https://doi.org/10.1037/13273-017

Cook, B. G., Tankersley, M., & Landrum, T. J. (2009). Determining evidence-based practices in special education *Exceptional Children, 75*(3), 365-383.

Corporation for National and Community Service. (2020). Evaluation resources. https://www.nationalservice.gov/resources/evaluation/evaluation-resources

Darling-Hammond, L., Wei, R. C., Andree, A., Richardson, N., & Orphanos, S. (2009). *Professional learning in the learning profession.* National Staff Development Council.

Davidson, K. W., Goldstein, M., Kaplan, R. M., Kaufmann, P. G., Knatterud, G. L., Orleans, C. T., Spring, B., Trudeau, K. J., & Whitlock, E. P. (2003). A conceptual framework for implementation fidelity. *Implementation Science, 2*(40). https://doi.org/10.1186/1748-5908-2-40.

Dunaway, M. K. (2011). Connectivism: Learning theory and pedagogical practice for networked information landscapes. *Reference Services Review, 39*(4), 675–685.

Eccles, M. P., & Mittman, B. S. (2006). Welcome to implementation science. *Implementation Science, 1*(1). https://doi.org/10.1186/1748-5908-1-1

Fixsen, D. L., Blase, K., Horner, R., & Sugai G. (2009). Concept paper: Developing the capacity for scaling up the effective use of evidence-based programs in state departments of education. http://ea.niusileadscape.org/docs/FINAL_PRODUCTS/LearningCarousel/DevelopingCapacity.pdf

Fixsen, D. L., Naoom, S. E, Blase, K. A., Friedman, R. M., & Wallace, F. (2005). Implementation research: A synthesis of the literature. The National Implementation Research Network (FMHI Publication #231). https://fpg.unc.edu/node/4445

Gee, J. P., (2004). *Situated language and learning: a critique of traditional schooling.* Routledge.

Greenhalgh, T., Robert, G., MacFarlane, F, Bate, P., & Kyriakidou, O. (2004). Diffusion of innovations in service organizations: Systematic review and recommendations. *The Milbank Quarterly, 82,* 581-629.

Hertel, J. T., & Wessman-Enzinger, N. M. (2017). Examining Pinterest as a curriculum resource for negative integers: An initial investigation. *Education Sciences, 7*(2), 1-11.

Hibbard, J. H., & Peters, E. (2003). Supporting informed consumer health care decisions: Data presentation approaches that facilitate the use of information in choice. *Annual Review of Public Health, 24,* 413-433.

Holt, C. L., & Chambers, D. A. (2017). Opportunities and challenges in conducting community-engaged dissemination/implementation research. *Translational Behavioral Medicine, 7*(3), 389-392. https://doi.org/10.1007/s13142-017-0520-2

Holve, E. (2013). Ensuring support for research and quality improvement (QI) networks: Four pillars of sustainability-an emerging framework. *The Journal of Electronic Health Data Methods, 1*(1), 1005. https://doi.org/10.13063/2327-9214.1005

Indiana Department of Education (2018, September 13). Plan, Do, Study, Act/Adjust Template for School Improvement Initiatives. Retrieved March 18, 2020 from https://www.doe.in.gov/school-improvement/siresourcehub/plan-do-study-actadjust-template-school-improvement-initiatives

Kukulska-Hulme, A. (2012). Language learning defined by time and place: A framework for next generation designs. (In J.E. Díaz-Vera, Ed.). *Left to My Own Devices: Learner Autonomy and Mobile Assisted Language Learning. Innovation and Leadership in English Language Teaching.* Emerald Group Publishing Limited.

McKay, S. (2017, March 15). Quality improvement Approaches: Implementation science. Carnegie Commons Blog. Retrieved March 12, 2020 from https://www.carnegiefoundation.org/blog/quality-improvement-approaches-implementation-science/

Odom, S. L., Brandinger, E., Gersten, R., Horner, R. H., Thompson, B., & Harris, K. R. (2005). Research in special education: Scientific methods and evidence-based practices. *Exceptional Children, 71,* 137-148.

Opensource.com. (2019). What is open education? Retrieved March 18, 2020 from https://opensource.com/resources/what-open-education

National Science Foundation. (Retrieved March 2020). Data collection methods: Some tips and comparisons. Retrieved March 19, 2020 from https://www.nsf.gov/pubs/2002/nsf02057/nsf02057_4.pdf

Saldana, J. (2011). *Fundamentals of qualitative research.* Oxford University Press.

Saldana, L., & Chamberlain, P. (2012). Supporting implementation: The role of community development teams to build infrastructure. *American Journal of Community Psychology, 50,* 334–346. https://doi.org/10.1007/s10464-012-9503-0

Shakman, K., Bailey, N., & Breslow, J. (2017). A primer for continuous improvement in schools and districts [White Paper]. Carnegie Foundation for the Advancement of Teaching. https://www.edc.org/sites/default/files/uploads/primer_for_continuous_improvement.pdf

Steiner, J. F., Paolino, A. R., Thompson, E. E., & Larson, E. B. (2014). Sustaining research networks: The twenty-year experience of HMO research network. GEMs (Generating Evidence and Methods to improve patient outcomes), 2(2), 1-10.http://dx.doi.org/10.13063/2327-9214.1067

Stringfield, S., & Datnow, A. (1998). Scaling up school restructuring designs in urban schools. *Education and Urban Society, 30*(3), 269–276.

Thelwall, M., & Harries, G. (2004). Can personal web pages that link to universities yield information about the wider dissemination of research? *Journal of Information Science, 30*(3), 240-253. https://doi.org/10.1177/0165551504044669

Trust, T., Carpenter, J. P., & Krutka, D. G. (2017). Moving beyond silos: Professional learning networks in higher education. *The Internet and Higher Education, 35,* 1-11.

Tseng, V. (2012). The uses of research in policy and practice. http://www.srcd.org/index.php?option=com_content&task=view&ici=232ôiltemid=658

Zikmund-Fisher, B. J., Fagerlin, A., & Ubel, P. A. (2010). A demonstration of "less can be more" in risk graphics. *Medical Decision Making, 30,* 661-671.

FINANCIAL DISCLOSURES

Dr. Reesha Adamson has no financial or proprietary interest in the materials presented herein.

Dr. Frederick J. Brigham has no financial or proprietary interest in the materials presented herein.

Dr. R. Nicolle Carr has no financial or proprietary interest in the materials presented herein.

Dr. Jason C. Chow has no financial or proprietary interest in the materials presented herein.

Dr. Art Dowdy has no financial or proprietary interest in the materials presented herein.

Dr. Kimberly Floyd has no financial or proprietary interest in the materials presented herein.

Rachel N. Freedman has no financial or proprietary interest in the materials presented herein.

Lynn E. Gates has no financial or proprietary interest in the materials presented herein.

Dr. Maeghan N. Hennessey has no financial or proprietary interest in the materials presented herein.

Dr. Jason P. Herron has no financial or proprietary interest in the materials presented herein.

Dr. Aleksandra Hollingshead has no financial or proprietary interest in the materials presented herein.

Dr. Brittany L. Hott has no financial or proprietary interest in the materials presented herein.

Dr. Melissa C. Jenkins has no financial or proprietary interest in the materials presented herein.

Dr. Joshua Jessel has no financial or proprietary interest in the materials presented herein.

Dr. Beth A. Jones has no financial or proprietary interest in the materials presented herein.

Dr. Randa Keeley has no financial or proprietary interest in the materials presented herein.

Dr. John William McKenna has no financial or proprietary interest in the materials presented herein.

Dr. Jessica Nelson has no financial or proprietary interest in the materials presented herein.

Dr. Corey Peltier has no financial or proprietary interest in the materials presented herein.

Dr. Maria B. Peterson-Ahmad has no financial or proprietary interest in the materials presented herein.

Dr. Felicity Post has no financial or proprietary interest in the materials presented herein.

Dr. Delia E. Racines has no financial or proprietary interest in the materials presented herein.

Dr. Kathleen M. Randolph has no financial or proprietary interest in the materials presented herein.

Dr. Andrew R. Scheef has no financial or proprietary interest in the materials presented herein.

Dr. Tracy E. Sinclair has no financial or proprietary interest in the materials presented herein.

Reginald B. Snoddy has no financial or proprietary interest in the materials presented herein.

Dr. Nathan A. Stevenson has no financial or proprietary interest in the materials presented herein.

Dr. Sharon Sullivan has no financial or proprietary interest in the materials presented herein.

Dr. Wilhelmina van Dijk has no financial or proprietary interest in the materials presented herein.

Dr. Andrew L. Wiley has no financial or proprietary interest in the materials presented herein.

INDEX